HOW TO GET A JOB IN THE PACIFIC RIM

ROBERT SANBORN, ED.D.
ANDERSON BRANDAO

THE INSIDER'S GUIDE SERIES

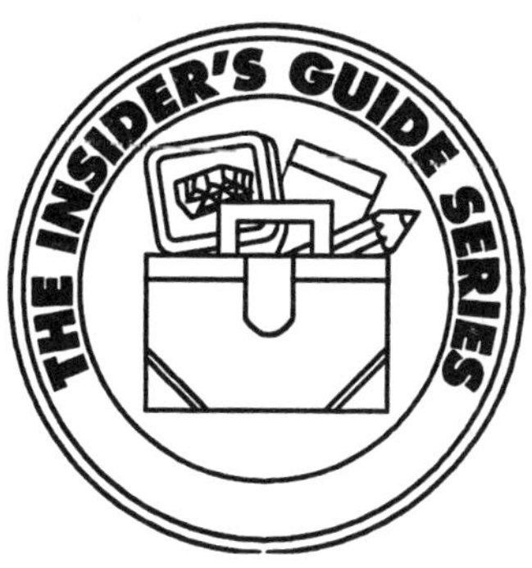

SURREY BOOKS
230 East Ohio Street
Suite 120
Chicago, Illinois 60611

HOW TO GET A JOB IN THE PACIFIC RIM

Published by Surrey Books, Inc., 230 E. Ohio St., Suite 120, Chicago, IL 60611. Telephone: (312) 751-7330.

This book is manufactured in the United States of America.

1st Edition. 1 2 3 4 5

Library of Congress Cataloging-in-Publication data:

Sanborn, Robert, 1959-

How to get a job in the Pacific Rim / by Robert Sanborn and Anderson Brandao.—1st ed.

432p. cm.

Includes bibliographical references and index.

ISBN 0-940625-42-3 (pbk): $17.95

1. Americans—Employment—Pacific Area—Handbooks, manuals, etc. I. Brandao, Anderson. II. Title.

HF5549.5.E45S265 1992 91-36376

650.14'099—dc20 CIP

AVAILABLE TITLES IN THIS SERIES — $15.95 (*Pacific Rim* $17.95)

How To Get a Job in Atlanta by Diane C. Thomas, Bill Osher, Ph.D., and Thomas M. Camden.

How To Get a Job in Greater Boston by Paul S. Tanklefsky and Thomas M. Camden.

How To Get a Job in Chicago by Thomas M. Camden and Susan Schwartz.

How To Get a Job in Dallas/Fort Worth by Richard Citrin and Thomas M. Camden.

How To Get a Job in Europe by Robert Sanborn, Ed.D.

How To Get a Job in Houston by Thomas M. Camden and Robert Sanborn.

How To Get a Job in The New York Metropolitan Area by Thomas M. Camden and Susan Fleming-Holland.

How To Get a Job in the Pacific Rim by Robert Sanborn, Ed.D., and Anderson Brandao.

How To Get a Job in The San Francisco Bay Area by Thomas M. Camden and Evelyn Jean Pine.

How To Get a Job in Seattle/Portland by Thomas M. Camden and Sara Steinberg.

How To Get a Job in Southern California by Thomas M. Camden and Jonathan Palmer.

How To Get a Job in Washington, DC, by Thomas M. Camden and Karen Tracy Polk.

Single copies may be ordered directly from the publisher. Send check or money order plus $2.50 per book for postage and handling to Surrey Books at the above address. For quantity discounts, please contact the publisher.

Editorial production by Bookcrafters, Inc., Chicago.

Cover design by Hughes Design, Chicago.

Typesetting by On Track Graphics, Inc., Chicago.

"How To Get a Job Series" is distributed to the trade by Publishers Group West.

ACKNOWLEDGMENTS

We would like to thank Don Kindred, Alex Dominguez, and Linda Breed for their many hours of work and research on this volume. Also worthy of gratitude is the staff of the Career Center at Rice University, who certainly contributed to our work and morale. We would also like to dedicate this book to the most special people in our lives: Ellen, Virginia, Claudette, and Dave.

CONTENTS

PART I
GETTING A JOB IN THE PACIFIC RIM

PART I
GETTING A JOB IN THE PACIFIC RIM

So You Want to Get a Job in the Pacific Rim

The "Pacific Century" is the term used by many to describe the next 100 years. The rising economic power of Japan, the miraculous growth of other East Asian nations, the potential that is China—all of these are part of the Pacific Rim saga. How does one best experience life in the Pacific and history in the making? Get a job there! An international experience has always allowed one to grow and learn. A career in the Pacific can, probably more than in any other area in the world, lead to growth and an appreciation of cultural diversity, as well as be a learning experience.

A job in the Pacific can be anything from a corporate professional position in Hong Kong to teaching English in Kyoto to bartending in a Sydney pub. All of these and many more jobs are available or can become available to quench one's desire for an international work experience. This book offers a wide variety of options and resources for the American seeking a job in the Pacific Rim.

Using This Book

The book will be of most value when read in its entirety, but it also offers the option of skipping around among chapters to find the areas most relevant to your particular search. Areas covered include what you should do before you go on the job hunt, some of the myths about international work, and advice on which locations offer the best employment opportunities. The regions to be discussed will be the Far East: Japan, the People's Republic of China, Taiwan, Hong Kong, Macau, Vietnam, Cambodia, Laos, Thailand, Singapore, Malaysia, Indonesia, the Philippines, and Brunei; Australasia: Australia and New Zealand; the Pacific Islands: Hawaii, Samoa, Papua New Guinea, the Solomon Islands, Fiji, Nauru, Kiribati, Tonga, Tuvalu, Vanuatu, and French Polynesia; and the Americas.

Chapter 2 focuses on the Pacific Rim economy and the changes that have occurred there and will occur over the next few years. Political and economic changes have also created a number of additional options that may not have previously existed for Americans in the Pacific. The less developed nations of East Asia are becoming increasingly industrialized, democratized, and open to the West. People within many of these nations are increasingly interested in Western culture and, more specifically, in learning English. China may present some options, as past political turmoil fades and it becomes ready to absorb Hong Kong. These changes in the East hold many benefits for Americans but also create some limitations. All of this will be examined.

Before You Go

Preparation is the key in any type of job search, and it is especially true when embarking upon a search internationally. Before dreaming about that exotic Pacific career, it is best to prepare yourself for changes that may occur in your lifestyle and to options that may or may not be available to you. Chapter 3 focuses on the qualifications needed for work internationally and gives some insights into educational opportunities in the Pacific and those in the United States that best prepare you for work abroad.

One of the major steps to take before going to the Pacific for the job search, is to decide what you want to do. A number of options exist, from professional positions in banking, publishing and the media, and education to temporary positions in teaching and hospitality. The countries you wish to target and what you want to do should be decided early on. Chapter 4 should facilitate this decision process.

Additional preparation by way of reading about the Pacific Rim economy and political events is also recommended. A number of publications are available in the United States and in the Pacific countries that can help the prospective job seeker examine the possibilities and difficulties that he/she may have to overcome. *The Economist* is a multi-faceted weekly that examines business and current events internationally, with each issue containing a section focused on Asia. This is probably the one best accessible source of information on changes occurring politically and economically.

The Economist
P.O. Box 14
Harold Hill, Romford
Essex RM3 8EQ, U.K.

Or contact the American office:

The Economist
10 Rockefeller Plaza
New York, NY 10020, U.S.A.
Tel.: (212) 541-5730

Daily newspapers can also provide insight into current business in the Pacific and ongoing employment trends:

The Wall Street Journal
Dow Jones
420 Lexington Ave.
New York, NY 10170

Asian Wall Street Journal Weekly
GPO Box 9825
1 Stubbs Rd.
A1A Building
Hong Kong, Hong Kong

Hong Kong Guide for the Business Visitor
(Text in Chinese, English, French, German, Italian, Japanese, and Spanish)
Hong Kong Trade Development Council
Great Eagle Centre, 31st Floor
23 Harbour Rd.
Hong Kong, Hong Kong
Tel.: 5 833 4333

Japan Economic Daily
Kyodo News International, Inc.
50 Rockefeller Plaza, Suite 832
New York, NY 10020
Tel.: (212) 586-0152

Japan Letter
Asia Letter Ltd.
P.O. Box 33477
Sheungwan Post Office
Hong Kong, Hong Kong
U.S. address: P.O. Box 54149
Los Angeles, California 90054

Japan Times
Japan Times Ltd.
5-4 Shibaura 4-Chome
Minato-Ku, Tokyo 108
Japan

Australasian Post
Southdown Press
32 Walsh St.
Melbourne, Victoria 3003
Australia

Bulletin
Australian Consolidated Press
P.O. Box 4088
Sydney, New South Wales 2001
Australia
(Incorporates The Australian Financial Times)

National Times
John Fairfax & Sons Ltd.
GPO Box 506
Sydney, New South Wales 2001
Australia

Honolulu Advertiser
P.O. Box 3350
Honolulu, Hawaii 96801
Tel.: (808) 538-6397

Los Angeles Times
145 Spring St.
Los Angeles, CA 90053
Tel.: (213) 237-5000

San Franscisco Chronicle
925 Mission St.
San Franscisco, CA 94103
Tel.: (415) 777-7000

A number of business and business-related weeklies are published in both the United States and the Pacific that provide coverage of Asian business and economic activity:

Asian Finance
Asian Finance Publication Ltd.
Suite D, 9th Floor
Hyde Centre, 223 Gloucester Rd.
Hong Kong, Hong Kong

Asia's 7500 Largest Companies
E.L.C. International
30 Eastbourne Terrace
London, England W2 6LG
Tel.: 01 706 0919
Fax: 01 723 6854
(General activities and financial data for Southeast Asia's top 7,500 companies)

Asiaweek
Toppan Building
22 Westlands Rd.
Quarry Bay, Hong Kong
Tel.: 5 630232

American Subscriptions
Medialink International
191 Atlantic Ave.
Brooklyn, NY 11201

Far Eastern Economic Review
Review Publishing Co. Ltd.
GPO Box 160
Hong Kong, Hong Kong

A number of American business weeklies are also published in both the United States and the Pacific Rim and provide some coverage of Asian business and economic activity:

Business Week
McGraw-Hill
1221 Ave. of the Americas
New York, NY 10020

Forbes
American Heritage
A Division of Forbes, Inc.
60 5th Ave.
New York, NY 10011

Fortune
Time, Inc.
1271 Ave. of the Americas, Rockefeller Center
New York, NY 10020

A number of publications exist that are directed toward specific audiences but can also provide valuable information about economics and employment possibilities in the Pacific Rim:

Asia-Pacific Currency Report
700 Walnut St., Suite 202
Cincinnati, OH 45202
Tel.: (513) 421-5447

Asiabanking
Asiamedia Co. Ltd.
2 Wellington St.

16-F
Hong Kong, Hong Kong

Asian Economic and Social Review
Asian Studies Press
23-354 Azadnagar
Jaiprakash Rd.
Andheri, Bombay 400058
India

Southeast Asia Report
U.S. Joint Publications Research Service
1000 N. Glebe Rd.
Arlington, Virginia 22201
Tel.: (703) 487-4630
Orders to: NTIS
Springfield, Virginia 22161

A great many other newspapers and periodicals exist in the Pacific published in English and Asian languages. These are primarily devoted to events within particular countries. These resources should not be passed up if you intend to do a job search and live in one particular country or region of the Pacific. Lists of these papers and periodicals can be found in Chapters 8 through 17 under specific country listings.

Another resource available to the international job seeker and especially those that are students is *Transitions Abroad.* This monthly magazine lists a great deal of helpful information on jobs, study, and travel abroad. Students looking for a temporary international job should check it out:

Transitions Abroad
Transitions Publishing
18 Hulst Rd., Box 344
Amherst, MA 01004

BOOKS ON WORKING ABROAD

The Directory of Overseas Summer Jobs
Writer's Digest Books
9933 Alliance Road
Cincinnati, OH 45242

Educators' Passport to International Jobs
Peterson's Guides
Jacob Way
Princeton, NJ 08543
(609) 243-9111

International Jobs
by Eric Kocher
Addison-Wesley Publishing Company
202 Carnegie Center
Reading, MA 01867
(617) 944-3700

Taking Off
A Fireside Book
Simon and Schuster Building
1230 Ave. of the Americas
New York, NY 10020

Work, Study, Travel Abroad
Council for International
Educational Exchange
St. Martin's Press
175 5th Ave.
New York, NY 10010

The Pacific Job Search

Chapter 4 outlines the steps to take when looking for and getting a job in the Pacific Rim. From networking to the interview, all steps in the process are important. Chapter 5 gives details and samples of resumes and cover letters that work internationally; they can be excellent guides to your own success. Chapter 6 details how placement organizations can and can't help you in your search. The summer or temporary job search is discussed in Chapter 7, with a country-by-country outlook for short-term work. Part II of the book focuses on the Pacific countries themselves and what they have to offer in terms of employment.

Many prospective job seekers have exotic notions of what a job search in the Pacific Rim is like. Those of you who think that an international job search is easy should abandon that thought immediately. The international world and the Pacific specifically is a tough place to find employment. Getting a good, permanent job involves a great deal of work. For those who work at it, follow advice from the experts, network, and have a lot of gumption, the rewards of international work can be well worth it.

When you do land a job abroad, your lifestyle will probably change radically from your old one in the United States. People abroad have a different way of life, different business customs, a different social life, and they learn to live with less purchasing power than we have in the United States. You should be aware of the many differences you will encounter; it is a good idea to read as much as you can on life overseas:

BOOKS AND ARTICLES ON LIVING ABROAD

Kohls, L. Robert, *Survival Kit for Overseas Living* (2nd ed.), Intercultural Press, 1984.

Mendenhall, M. E., and Oddou, Gary, "The Overseas Assignment: A Practical Book," *Business Horizons* 31: 78-84, Sept.-Oct., 1988.

Axtell, Robert E., *Dos and Taboos* (2nd ed.), compiled by the Parker Pen Company.

American Citizens Abroad, *USA Today's Handbook for Citizens Living Abroad*, Doubleday, 1990.

Before you decide to pursue international employment, it is important to examine your current situation against what your international situation might be. An international job is not always one in which you travel constantly, and you will often be expected to work for less money than in the United States. You will more likely than not have to speak a foreign language, and your two years of high-school French leave you with language ability comparable to a French second grader, which is not much help in getting you a job in French Polynesia, and no help in Japan. Your living conditions will probably be more cramped than you are used to (even if you are moving from Manhattan). But these can be experiences you look forward to. You may find that you relish the variety, newness, and diversity of a different culture—not to mention the great stories you will have to tell.

Myths About International Work

1. Foreign languages get you a job

There seems to be some misconception among Americans that if you learn a foreign language, you are entitled to an international job. I have met a countless number of students and graduates who would like to work internationally and think it shouldn't be a problem to locate international work because they have majored in a foreign language. This borders on the ridiculous. It would be equivalent to saying, "If you speak English, you can get any job in the United States." We know this is not true. Foreign languages can and certainly do help. Fluency in the language of the country you wish to work in is a must, but it is not the sole factor in your eligibility for a position. Skills and experience are what employers will look for. Knowledge of a foreign language is taken for granted.

2. Classes on Asian culture and similar topics help you get a job

Most college students often have the opportunity to take courses on Asian culture, current events in the Far East, and many other international relations courses. As a student, the perception often develops that the more of these courses you have taken the better chance you have of getting an international job. That is false. An understanding of current history and political events is needed, but as with foreign language experience, this will be taken for granted. You should take these courses and have this knowledge, but do not expect to sell employability based on the knowledge acquired through your international relations course work.

3. American subsidiaries hire lots of Americans

Americans very often believe that at the very least they can be hired by the many American companies with offices and branches abroad. Americans are hired by American firms in the Pacific, but these are most likely to be Americans who have skills that are needed abroad and people who have worked with that company for some time, proving their abilities. Most American firms in the Pacific Rim are run and staffed by nationals of the country in which the office is located, and that is often the preference of American multinational corporations. Employment opportunities do exist with these companies, but you must prove you have the skill to be needed in the Pacific, know people in the company, or be in the right place at the right time.

4. If you go to the Pacific country of your choice, you are bound to find something

Americans, especially American college students, often go abroad with the idea that once they arrive, some type of job opportunity will arise. That is probably one of the biggest mistakes you can make in the job search. Preparation before you go is essential. Without preparation your chances of locating employment are slim and your chances of being very depressed are great. Going to Asia or other Pacific Rim countries to find a job can be done, but it is not as simple as getting on the next plane and looking for employment after you arrive. Figure out all the angles first and know what is in store for you. Chapter 4 will outline the steps needed for preparation.

5. Culture shock is easily overcome

Everyone who prepares to travel or work abroad hears about culture shock. With all the things to worry about, this usually has a low priority. It is easy to pass over this concern and convince oneself that culture shock can not be that bad. Wrong. Culture shock is real and very much worth thinking about, especially when traveling to Pacific countries. Australia can present problems you never thought about, and Japan will be even more different. The Pacific has been known to give Americans a real sense of homesickness. This is something to be aware of and prepare for.

Addresses of Chambers of Commerce

Chambers of Commerce, whether located in the United States or in the Pacific Rim, can offer information on businesses and organizations in the country of your choice. Information on economic trends and living conditions is also often available. Write to specific chambers for information.

ASIAN PACIFIC RIM

Japan

Japan Business Association of Southern California
345 Figueroa St., #206
Los Angeles, CA 90071
Tel.: (213) 485-0160

Japanese Chamber of Commerce of Southern California
244 S. San Pedro St., Rm. 504
Los Angeles, CA 90012
Tel.: (213) 626-3067

Japanese Chamber of Commerce of Northern California
World Affairs Center, 312 Sutter St., Rm. #408
San Francisco, CA 94108
Tel.: (415) 986-6140

Honolulu-Japanese Chamber of Commerce
2454 S. Beretania St.
Honolulu, HI 96826
Tel.: (808) 949-5531

Japanese Chamber of
Commerce of Chicago
401 N. Michigan Ave., Rm. 602
Chicago, IL 60611
Tel.: (312) 332-6199

Japanese Chamber of
Commerce of New York
145 W. 57th St.
New York, NY 10019
Tel.: (212) 246-9774

China

Chinese Chamber of Commerce of San Francisco
730 Sacramento St.
San Francisco, CA 94108
Tel.: (415) 982-3000

Chinese Chamber of Commerce of New York
Confucius Plaza, 33 Bowery, Rm. C203
New York, NY 10002
Tel.: (212) 226-2795

Korea

Korean Chamber of Commerce
981 S. Western Ave., Rm. 201
Los Angeles, CA 90006
Tel.: (213) 733-4410

U.S.-Korea Society
725 Park Ave.
New York, NY 10021
Tel.: (212) 517-7730

Indonesia

American-Indonesian Chamber of Commerce
12 E. 41st St., Suite 701
New York, NY 10017
Tel.: (212) 637-4505

Philippines

Philippine-American Chamber of Commerce
c/o Philippine Consulate
447 Sutter St.
San Francisco, CA 94108
Tel.: (415) 433-6666

Philippine-American Chamber of Commerce
711 3rd Ave., 17th Floor
New York, NY 10017

LATIN AMERICAN PACIFIC RIM

Mexico

American-Mexican Chamber of Commerce
P.O. Box 626
Phoenix, AZ 85001
Tel.: (602) 252-6448

U.S.-Mexico Chamber of Commerce
1900 L St. N.W., #612
Washington, DC 20036
Tel.: (202) 296-5198

Mexican Chamber of Commerce of the U.S.
655 Madison Ave., The Woolworth Bldg., 16th Floor
New York, NY 10021
Tel.: (212) 759-9505

Mexican Institute for Foreign Trade
9 E. 53rd St., 25th Floor
New York, NY 10022
Tel.: (212) 759-9505

U.S.-Mexico Quadripartite Commission
Center for Inter-American Relations
680 Park Ave.
New York, NY 10021
Tel.: (212) 249-8950

Ecuador

Ecuadorean-American Association
115 Broadway, Rm. 1408
New York, NY
Tel.: (212) 233-7776

Colombia

Colombian-American Association
111 Broadway, Rm. 1408
New York, NY 10006
Tel.: (212) 233-7776

Peru

Peruvian-American Association
50 W. 34th St., 6th Floor, #C2
New York, NY 10001
Tel.: (212) 564-3855

Chile

Chile-North American Chamber of Commerce
220 E. 81st St.
New York, NY 10028
Tel.: (212) 288-5691

Getting to the Pacific from the U.S.: The Best Way to Go

Once you get to the stage where you are ready to start planning your voyage, there are a number of inexpensive options available. Most travel agents can help with many of the essentials. However, if you are interested in locating non-advertised, bottom-barrel rates, "bucket shops" or consolidators are your best bet. These ticket handlers, often found in large cities such as New York, San Francisco, and Los Angeles, get tremendous discounts on bulk ticket buying. Savings are passed on to the customer. Restrictions on the tickets almost always apply. Students can also get discounts through agents who specialize in student discount travel. Corporate travelers have a number of options that can still mean comfortable travel, providing they work with the right people.

The best option for all of the above is to find an organization that handles all areas of international travel: corporate, student, and discount. One agency outside of New York City does all three and has developed a very positive reputation for responsibility, friendliness, and discount rates. Call the agency, Anderson Travel, with information on where you are headed and any specifics that you need; flexibility in your schedule is always helpful. *Bon voyage*!

Anderson Travel
31 Anderson Avenue
Fairview, NJ 07722
Contact: Sylvia Roy
1-800-733-9430

Key Employment Sectors and Trends in the Pacific Rim

The Pacific Rim is a relatively new concept in business and even political circles. It represents not any one compact geographical region, but rather the interaction among the countries of Asia, Oceania, and the Americas, which are coincidentally connected by the Pacific Ocean. Today, the Pacific Rim is rapidly capturing global attention. The increasing interchange among the nations bordering all sides of the Pacific is redefining world economic interests.

As the Pacific Rim emerges as an economic entity, traditional notions of East and West are blurring and merging. The countries in Asia that comprise the Western Pacific Rim are customarily referred to as Eastern, with terms in use such as the Far East, East Asia, the Orient, and Southeast or Northeast

Asia. Similarly, the west coast of North America, which forms the Eastern Pacific Rim, is normally considered a part of the Western World.

Countries of the Pacific Rim

In the process of building economic interdependence, new powers are emerging in the western Pacific. While Japan has already established its international economic position, the most vibrant economies in East Asia are the group referred to as the "tigers" or "dragons": South Korea, Taiwan, Singapore, and Hong Kong. Additionally, the developing economies now attracting new investment and growing most rapidly are Thailand, Malaysia, and Indonesia. Despite recent economic problems, the Philippines still ranks among the region's largest economies.

The long-closed socialist economies of the region are also in a period of transition. The People's Republic of China has pursued significant economic reforms and presents the world's largest consumer market. After the Tiananmen Massacre in 1989, foreign investment in China and development loans decreased. Presently, however, China is again receiving large amounts of foreign funds. While foreigners may now be more realistic about the possibilities for dramatic political and economic liberalization in China, they are certainly willing to reap profits from its economy.

In addition, Vietnam is examining economic liberalization and has already loosened some sectors of its economy. Laos has maintained economic ties to Thailand. The entrepreneurial Thais are also eager to invest in Cambodia and "turn battlefields into marketplaces." The Japanese have pledged to offer massive development aid to Indochina if the region stabilizes. North Korea, the only Stalinist holdout in Asia, is nonetheless attempting to improve relations with both South Korea and Japan.

Besides the East Asian economies, Australia and New Zealand also form a part of the Pacific Rim. Colonized by the British, both countries historically have maintained close trade relations with Britain and the U.S., but they are now diversifying their economies and pursuing greater investment and trade with Japan and other East Asian countries. Australia and New Zealand are major trading partners of the smaller Pacific islands as well.

Investment Among Asian Countries

The economies of Pacific Asia are presently integrating the region into a powerful economic bloc. Massive Japanese investment in South Korea, Taiwan, and Southeast Asia has long fueled those economies. Today, new investment is pouring into the less developed economies. As labor costs rise in Korea, Taiwan, and Hong Kong as a result of increased industrialization and higher living standards, the lower labor and production costs of economies such as Malaysia, Indonesia, and Thailand become comparatively advantageous. Detailed information on Japanese investment patterns will be found in Chapter 8 of Part II of this book.

Japan is leading the investment drive in Southeast Asia, but South Korea, Hong Kong, and Taiwan are also building new facilities in the region. In fact, Hong Kong and South Korea are now investing more than the U.S. in Indonesia, Thailand, and China. The result is an investment spiral in which Japan's seemingly limitless capital inflows stimulate growth in South Korea, Taiwan, Hong Kong, and Singapore. These countries in turn invest in China, Malaysia, Indonesia, Thailand, and the Philippines. Thailand has also reached the point where its investors are active in the slowly opening economies of Indochina.

Although Southeast Asia presents attractive investment opportunities due to lower production costs, investors also realize that the domestic markets in these countries are growing rapidly. Much of the new Japanese investment, for example, is for production to serve regional domestic markets. This represents a change in investment strategy from the past, when companies established facilities in these countries in order to export their products to the U.S. and Europe. Investors are beginning to fully appreciate the potential of massive East Asian markets. Indonesia, for instance, has over 150 million consumers.

Trade Among Asian Economies

Similarly, trade among the Asian countries of the Pacific Rim is increasing. In 1990, trade among the East Asian countries reached over $200 billion, while trade among the same countries and the U.S. was slightly over $280 billion. By the turn of the century, the total value of inter-Asian trade is expected to exceed that of Asian-U.S. trade. Raw materials, consumer goods, industrial production equipment, and business-support services are all flowing across borders in the western Pacific.

This is occurring, in part, because newly industrializing economies, such as those of Southeast Asia, are now providing living standards sufficiently high to create significant demand for finished consumer export goods from the more advanced economies, such as Japan and South Korea. At the same time, the developing economies also require more sophisticated technology, especially industrial machinery and information systems, which Japan and South Korea can provide. They also need the financial and banking services available from firms based in Japan, Singapore, and Hong Kong.

In return, the developing countries still provide much of the raw materials necessary for the more advanced industrial nations. Indonesia, Malaysia, and Brunei all export oil to Japan and elsewhere. By helping these economies to develop, the Japanese and others are safeguarding a nearby oil supply which they hope will prove more stable than Middle Eastern oil shipments. Southeast Asia also provides most of the rubber and lumber utilized in the advanced countries.

The Rise of Trading Blocs

Economic analysts and government trade officials in the developed economies of Japan, South Korea, Taiwan, and Hong Kong are focusing on Asian investment for political reasons as well. They are aware of the economic integration efforts now underway in the West and are apprehensive about the potential for trade protectionism, especially in Europe and North America. As new, large trading blocs emerge in Europe and the Americas, Asians fear that they will be excluded from the new markets.

The European Community will formally inaugurate its single market in 1992, which will essentially eliminate all trade and investment barriers among member countries. This should become the first step to European economic union, ultimately resulting in a single currency and financial system. International financial analysts believe that European economic integration will focus around the German economy and may lead to protectionist barriers to allow European companies time to adjust to the single market. The French prime minister, Edith Cresson, was known to be avidly anti-Japanese when she served as minister of trade.

The Japanese and others also fear the protectionist potential arising from North American economic integration. The U.S. and Canada already approximate free trade, but the upcoming North American Free Trade Agreement, to include Mexico, will create a new market that may turn protectionist. Many U.S. political and business leaders are demanding trade retaliation against perceived Japanese and South Korean trading practices. The North American bloc may facilitate the erection of barriers against Asia by providing new markets in the Americas.

The U.S. government has declared that a free trade zone in North America will extend from "Yukon to Yucatan," but a panamerican trade bloc may very well extend even farther southward. As Latin American economies pursue economic and trade integration, particularly Brazil and Argentina, these regional agreements may soon join with the North American free trade zone to create an economic bloc encompassing all the Americas. Japanese companies are attempting to safeguard their positions by adding new investments in Mexico and elsewhere in Latin America to those already existing in the U.S. and Canada.

The U.S. in the Pacific Rim

The U.S. has historically focused on its Atlantic neighbors, particularly Western Europe. Nonetheless, the significance of the Pacific Rim to the U.S. economy has been steadily increasing. Trade relations are the most familiar form of Pacific Rim interaction. In the late 1980s, the trade relationship became more balanced, as Asian demand for American products grew at a faster rate than American demand for Asian goods and services.

The U.S. trade deficit with East Asia will probably remain for the foreseeable future, but the gap should narrow. As the Asian Pacific economies develop, their labor and production costs should increase, ultimately making the final costs for their products higher than at present. Moreover, countries are discovering that trade imbalance leads to political tension and demands for protectionism. To protect their long-term interests, the Japanese and others are encouraging their consumers to purchase American products and are attempting, at least formally, to open their markets.

More importantly, local Asian economies are stimulating their domestic consumer markets. In case protectionism arises in the European Community or North America, Asian firms will require strong domestic markets to offset the loss of foreign markets. The end result will be greater demand for consumer products. The U.S. will likely benefit from this trend, as governments continue to open their markets to foreign competition and encourage consumer spending.

Although trade relations provide the most obvious signs of Pacific interdependency, American business investment in East Asia has been prominent in most of the region's economies. American investment in the Asian Pacific has fueled economic growth, allowed for critical technology transfers, and enabled these economies to access U.S. markets. In exchange, American firms have benefitted from lower production costs. As a result of increasing inter-Asian investment, the relative significance of American capital will decrease in the region. Nonetheless, most of the economic reasons that brought American companies to Asia still remain, and local economies will still encourage investment.

Because mistrust of Japanese intentions lingers in many parts of East Asia, the U.S. also has political reasons for maintaining its involvement there. The developing economies in the region definitely need the foreign investment and aid programs that the Japanese provide and want to integrate into a larger economic sphere, which they realize will naturally be dominated by Japan. The result is great apprehension about complete Japanese hegemony. These fears have been aggravated by the potential of a lower American presence in the western Pacific, especially militarily. Consequently, many East Asian political and business leaders would like to see a strong, continued U.S. presence to counterbalance Japanese influence.

The U.S. participates in the Asian-Pacific Economic Cooperation (APEC) process aimed at fostering better Pacific Rim relations and solving regional problems. APEC includes the U.S., Canada, Japan, South Korea, Australia, Singapore, Indonesia, New Zealand, Thailand, Malaysia, and the Philippines. The APEC effort is expected to facilitate a multilateral approach to problem-solving, rather than relying exclusively on U.S.-Japanese initiatives. Involving the smaller countries should diffuse political tensions and lead to more appropriate solutions. APEC may also serve as a mechanism to avoid destructive trade disputes among the emerging East Asian and North American trading blocs.

Growing economic ties are also promoting greater interchange of people and ideas throughout the Pacific Rim. In the past, the U.S. has faced eastward, toward Europe, from New York and other major cities of the U.S. Northeast. Recently, demographic growth has accelerated in the western parts of our country, especially California and the Northwest. Los Angeles, San Francisco, San Diego, and Seattle will assume the important roles in our relations with the Pacific that New York, Philadelphia, Boston, and Baltimore played in our relations with the Atlantic countries.

TOP 25 INTERNATIONAL COMPANIES AND U.S. OFFICES (Ranked by Market Value 1990):

1. **Nippon Telegraph & Telephone (Japan)**
Pan Am Building, Rm. 2905
200 Park Ave.
New York, NY 10166
Tel.: (212) 867-1511

2. **I.B.M. (U.S.)**
Old Orchard Rd.
Armonk, NY 10504
Tel.: (914) 765-1900

3. **Industrial Bank of Japan (Japan)**
245 Park Ave.
New York, NY 10167
Tel.: (212) 557-3500

4. **Royal Dutch-Shell Group (Netherlands)**
P.O. Box 148, Strand
London, Wc2r Od
U.K.- England
Tel.: 01-257-3000

5. **General Electric (U.S.)**
3135 Easton Tpk.
Fairfield, CT 06432
Tel.: (203) 373-2431

6. **Exxon Corp. (U.S.)**
1251 Ave. of the Americas
New York, NY 10020-1198
Tel.: (212) 333-1000

7. **Sumitomo Bank (Japan)**
320 California St.
San Fransisco, CA 94104
Tel.: (415) 445-8000

8. **Fuji Bank (Japan)**
1 World Trade Center
New York, NY 10048
Tel.: (212) 839-6800

9. **Toyota Motor (Japan)**
Solow Building, 45th Floor
9 W. 57th St.
New York, NY 10019
Tel.: (212) 223-0303

10. **Mitsui Taiyo Kobe Bank (Japan)**
350 Park Ave.
New York, NY 10022
Tel.: (212) 750-1050

11. **Dai-Ichi Kangyo Bank (Japan)**
1 World Trade Center, Suite 5047
New York, NY 10048
Tel.: (212) 432-8464

12. **Mitsubishi Bank (Japan)**
800 Wilshire Blvd.
Los Angeles, CA 90017
Tel.: (213) 621-1200

13. **A.T.&T. (U.S.)**
550 Madison Ave.
New York, NY 46220
Tel.: (212) 605-5500

14. **Sanwa Bank (Japan)**
444 Market St.
San Fransisco, CA 94111
Tel.: (415) 765-9500

15. **Tokyo Electric Power (Japan)**
1-3 Uchisaiwai-Cho, 1-Chome
Chiyoda ku, Tokyo 100
Japan

16. **Phillip Morris (U.S.)**
120 Park Avenue
New York, NY, 10017
Tel.: (212) 880-5000

17. **Hitachi (Japan)**
50 Prospect Ave.
Tarrytown, NY 10591-4698
Tel.: (914) 332-5800

18. **Merck (U.S.)**
P.O. Box 2000
Rahway, NJ 07065
Tel.: (908) 594-4000

19. **Nomura Securities (Japan)**
180 Maiden Ln.
New York, NY 10038
Tel.: (212) 208-9300

20. **Long Term Credit Bank of Japan (Japan)**
Greenwich Capital Markets
600 Steamboat Rd.
Greenwich, CT 06830
Tel.: (203) 629-2570

21. **Bristol-Myers Squibb (U.S.)**
345 Park Ave.
New York, NY 10154
Tel.: (212) 546-4000

22. **Wal-Mart Stores (U.S.)**
702 SW 8th St.
Dentonville, AR 72712
Tel.: (501) 273-4000

23. **Coca-Cola (U.S.)**
1 Coca-Cola Plaza NW
Atlanta, GA 30313
Tel.: (404) 676-2121

24. **Matsushita Electrical Industrial (Japan)**
1 Panasonic Way
Secaucus, NJ 07094
Tel.: (201) 348-7000

25. **British Petroleum (England)**
200 Public Square
Cleveland, OH 44114
Tel.: (216) 586-4141

Employment Sectors in the Pacific Rim

Various fields will be affected in different ways by Pacific Rim economic integration. The individual country chapters in Part II of this book explain in detail how particular economies are likely to be affected by greater regional trade and investment. You will also find the most significant employers in each country and a listing of principal trading partners and products. But for now, here are the sectors that promise the most potential for Americans seeking jobs. Lists of employers in each of these areas are contained in most of the individual country chapters.

TRADE AND MANUFACTURING

Manufacturing and trade of consumer durables and industrial equipment will accelerate in the Pacific Rim. As the developing countries continue to grow, their consumers demand increasingly sophisticated consumer goods and services. Literally hundreds of millions of people, especially in Southeast Asia, are achieving consumer buying power sufficient to stimulate massive new investment in manufactured consumer products. This will subsequently promote investment in new technology and processes in the manufacturing sector.

Factories all over the Pacific Rim, both those producing for the domestic market and for export, will require expansion and upgrading with new industrial equipment and machinery. Most of this technology is produced in the advanced countries, such as Japan and South Korea, which will generate economic growth there as well. American companies will need to invest in the developing economies and integrate themselves into the local distribution and supply systems. In some economies, such as China, joint ventures with the state or other foreign and domestic companies will be necessary.

Business Guides in International Trade

American Register of Exporters and Importers. New York: American Register of Exporters and Importers Corp. Updated each May. Covers 30,000 U.S. manufacturers and distributors in the import/export trade and service firms assisting foreign private and public customers. Lists company name, address, and product.

Bureau of International Commerce, Trade Lists. Washington, DC: U.S. Department of Commerce. Updated annually. Lists American firms, subsidiaries, and affiliates in each country, with brief descriptions and addresses.

Directory of Directories, 1st edition. Ethridge ed. Detroit, MI: Gale Research Corp., 1980. Annotated guide to business and industrial directories, professional and scientific rosters, and other lists and guides.

Dun & Bradstreet Exporter's Encyclopedia, World Marketing Guide. New York: Dun & Bradstreet International. Updated annually. Guide to exporting, organized by country.

Everybody's Business: The Irreverent Guide to Corporate America. Moskowitz, Katz & Levaring, eds. San Francisco: Harper & Row, 1983. Almanac providing candid profiles of most of the influential corporations in the U.S.

Everybody's Business Scoreboard: Corporate America's Winners, Losers, and Also-Rans. Moskowitz & Katz, eds. San Fransisco: Harper & Row, 1983. Companion volume to guide listed above.

Foreign Commerce Handbook, 17th edition. A. Maffry. Washington, DC: International Division of the Chamber of Commerce of the U.S., 1981. Review of organizations and institutions worldwide that offer international business and foreign trade services.

Fortune 500: Top 50 Exporters. Fortune Magazine, Time & Life Building, Rockefeller Center, New York, NY 10020-1393. Annual list and information on top U.S. exporters.

Multinational Marketing and Employment Directory, 8th edition. J. Angel, compiler. New York: World Trade Academy Press Inc., 1981. Listing of more than 7,500 corporations operating in the U.S. and abroad, with address and phone number of the U.S. headquarters and, when available, names of president, foreign operations officers, and/or personnel director, the firm's principal product or service, and the countries where branches, subsidiaries, or affiliates are located. Also contains a section on the preparation of a resume.

National Trade and Professional Associations of the United States and Canada and Labor Unions. C. Colgate, ed. Washington, DC: Columbia Books. Updated annually. Listing of 5,800 organizations arranged alphabetically, geographically, by name of executives, by amount of budget, and by type of product or field with which the organization is concerned.

Standard & Poor's Register of Corporations, Directors and Executives. New York: Standard & Poor's Corp. Updated annually (11 volumes). Includes listing of manufacturers by special product and leading trade and brand names as well as an alphabetical listing with addresses, branch offices, subsidiaries, products, and estimated capitalization.

Using the U.S. Department of Commerce

U.S. Department of Commerce
Foreign Trade Reference Room- Rm. 2233
14th St. & Constitution Ave., NW
Washington, DC

The U.S. Department of Commerce maintains a wide range of programs to stimulate business abroad. A few of their services that may be of interest to job seekers include:

World Traders' Data Reports: describe companies' financial references, activities, reputation, area of operation, date established, number of employees, and general profiles by U.S. Commerce Service Attaches abroad.

Country Desk Offices: specific country files on U.S. and foreign businesses.

Foreign Commercial Service: assists U.S. corporations through export promotions, market research, counseling, and liaison with foreign businesses and government officials.

Trade Operations Program: specifies products, countries of interest, and opportunities desired through Foreign Service field post telex updates.

Export Counseling Service: coordinates information and consults with new export businesses through nationwide district offices, helping direct representation and sales to foreign government lenders.

BANKING AND FINANCE

American firms are aggressively expanding in the banking and finance sectors of Pacific Rim economies. Japan and Hong Kong are already major world financial centers, with some of the world's largest banks. Singapore is rapidly approaching the same level. Additionally, the banking houses and stock exchanges in Taipei and Sydney are growing as the region's economies create new demand for financial services.

American banks have been eclipsed long ago by the Japanese in terms of assets, but a few still invest heavily in the Pacific Rim and are actively involved with financing East Asian economic expansion. American brokerage firms, on the other hand, are considerably more advanced than their counterparts in Tokyo. Several large brokerage houses now operate in the Pacific Rim but often find that local investors and regulators are skeptical about American financial methods. Nonetheless, former Wall Street brokers are finding jobs with Asian firms eager to learn their skills.

TOP 25 BANKS WORLDWIDE, 1990
(with U.S. offices when available)

1. **Dai-Ichi Kygo Bank (Japan)**
1 World Trade Center,
Suite 5047
New York, NY 10048
Tel.: (212) 432-8464

2. **Sumitomo Bank (Japan)**
320 California Ave.
San Fransisco, CA 94104
Tel.: (415) 445-8000

3. **Fuji Bank (Japan)**
1 World Trade Center
New York, NY 10048
Tel.: (212) 839-6800

4. **Mitsubishi Bank (Japan)**
800 Wilshire Blvd.
Los Angeles, CA 90017
Tel.: (213) 621-1200

5. **Sanwa Bank (Japan)**
444 Market St.
San Fransisco, CA 94111
Tel.: (415) 765-9500

6. **Industrial Bank of Japan (Japan)**
245 Park Ave.
New York, NY 10167
Tel.: (212) 557-3500

7. **Norinchukin Bank (Japan)**
8-3, Otemachi 1-Chome,
Chiyoda ku,
Tokyo, Japan 100

8. **Credit Agricole (France)**
520 Madison Ave., 42nd Floor
New York, NY 10022
Tel.: (212) 418-2200

9. **Tokai Bank (Japan)**
534 W. 6th St.
Los Angeles, CA 90014
Tel.: (213) 972-0200

10. **Banque National de Paris (France)**
BNP International Financial Services
499 Park Ave.
New York, NY 10022
Tel.: (212) 418-8200

11. **Citicorp (U.S.)**
399 Park Ave.
New York, NY 10043
Tel.: (212) 559-1000

12. **Bank of Tokyo (Japan)**
100 Broadway
New York, NY 10005
Tel.: (212) 766-3400

13. **Mitsubishi Trust and Banking (Japan)**
520 Madison Ave., 42nd Floor
New York, NY 10022
Tel.: (212) 715-9888

14. **Mitsui Bank (Japan)**
277 Park Ave., 45th Floor
New York, NY 10172-0121
Tel.: (212) 644-3679

15. **Credit Lyonnais (France)**
CL Global Partners
95 Wall St., 17th Floor
New York, NY 10005
Tel.: (212) 428-6100

16. **Sumitomo Trust and Banking (Japan)**
320 California St.
San Fransisco, CA 94104
Tel.: (415) 445-8000

17. **Barclays (Britain)**
75 Wall St.
New York, NY 10265
Tel.: (212) 412-4000

18. **Deutsche Bank (Germany)**
40 Wall St.
New York, NY 10005
Tel.: (212) 612-0600

19. **Long-Term Credit Bank of Japan (Japan)**
Greenwich Capital Markets
600 Steamboat Rd.
Greenwich, CT 06830
Tel.: (203) 629-2570

20. **Mitsui Trust and Banking (Japan)**
1 World Financial Center, 200 Liberty St.
New York, NY 10281
Tel.: (212) 341-0200

21. **National Westminster Bank (Britain)**
175 Water St.
New York, NY 10038
Tel.: (212) 602-1000

22. **Taiyo Kobe Bank (Japan)**
350 Park Ave.
New York, NY 10022
Tel.: (212) 750-1050

23. **Bank of China (China)**
410 Madison Ave.
New York, NY 10017
Tel.: (212) 935-3101

24. **Societe Generale (France)**
520 Madison Ave.
New York, NY 10022
Tel.: (212) 832-0022

25. **Daiwa Bank (Japan)**
75 Rockefeller Plaza
New York, NY 10019
Tel.: (212) 399-2710

ENGINEERING AND CONSTRUCTION

Engineering and construction is currently booming in Asia. The rapid expansion of the Pacific Rim economies, particularly those of Southeast Asia, is generating new construction projects. Buildings, roads, bridges, and housing are under construction to accommodate growth. Infrastructure projects provide employment for engineers and individuals experienced with the construction industry. In Taiwan, for example, construction projects accounted for 5 percent of the country's gross national product in 1990. Taiwan has a $300 billion infrastructure program underway.

American engineering and construction firms are at a significant disadvantage. Construction projects funded by Japanese foreign aid usually have strings attached, stipulating that the contracting must go to Japanese firms. In this way, the Japanese build the business relationships with suppliers and subcontractors, which will enable them to legitimately win low bids against other foreign companies.

EDUCATION

Americans have been very successful in finding employment in education in the Pacific Rim. Teaching positions, generally in English, are readily available for Americans throughout the region. English has traditionally been the language learned by business people and others who frequently deal with foreigners. Because most of these economies must trade in order to survive, speaking some English is a basic business necessity.

Schools that teach English as a second language can be found almost everywhere in the Pacific Rim. Japan is the most lucrative English teaching center, with over a hundred schools in Tokyo alone. Americans can teach English as a job in the language schools or informally through individual tutoring. International schools, which teach an American curriculum in English, are also plentiful and can offer positions to Americans with some teaching experience.

To teach at the elementary and secondary school level, most overseas schools require a bachelor's degree and teacher certification, in addition to at least two years of teaching experience. Appointments for positions at most schools are made months before the school year begins, so you should apply well ahead of time.

The biggest employers of American teachers at the pre-university level in the Pacific are American-sponsored and international schools, as well as Department of Defense Dependent Schools. American-sponsored schools are private schools that consist of American and multinational students and are founded by American citizens but not controlled by the U.S. government. International schools are independent but feature a largely American curriculum. Department of Defense Dependent Schools are for the dependents of military and civilian government employees working on overseas bases.

For information about **American-sponsored schools,** write:

Office of Overseas Schools
U.S. Dept. of State
Washington, DC 20520
Tel.: (703) 235-9600

For information on **international schools,** your best bet is to consult *The ISS Directory Of Overseas Schools,* compiled by International Schools Services, Inc. This is a directory of international schools all over the world. While the directory is aimed primarily at the prospective student, an address is included for each school, so you can write for more information. ISS also assists teachers in placement overseas. If you use ISS facilities, you must pay an initial fee as well as a second fee if you are placed in a job.

To contact ISS, write:

International Schools Services
P.O. Box 5910
Princeton, NJ 08540
Tel.: (609) 452-0990

For more information about independent international schools, here are some more directories:

Peterson's Annual Guide to Independent Secondary Schools, published by Peterson's Guides, Inc., P.O. Box 2123, Princeton, NJ 08540.

Schools Abroad of Interest to Americans, published by Porter Sargent Publications, Inc., 11 Beacon Street, Boston, MA 02108.

If you would like to work for the **Department of Defense,** you should be aware of a few things. While your preferences are taken into account, you must prepare to be assigned anywhere worldwide. Also, in addition to teaching certification and work experience, you must pass physical examinations. For more information, write:

Department of Defense Dependents Schools
Teacher Recruitment Section
Hoffman Building I
2461 Eisenhower Ave.
Alexandria, Virginia 22331

Another option for those interested in elementary or secondary teaching overseas is to look into a program sponsored by the U.S. Department of Education. They offer programs such as teacher exchanges in which you would exchange positions with a teacher abroad. Summer seminars are another alternative to consider. For information on both of these programs, write:

Teacher Education Branch
Division of International Services and Improvement
International Education Programs
U.S. Department of Education
Washington, DC 20202

Getting a Job in the Pacific Rim

If you are interested in a teaching position in **higher education** abroad, there are several options you should investigate. The University of Maryland, in conjunction with the U.S. Department of Defense, offers various programs in undergraduate study for armed services personnel and members of federal agencies stationed abroad. For information about a teaching opportunity with this program, write:

Office of Overseas Program
University of Maryland
University College
University Blvd. at Adephi Rd.
College Park, Maryland 20742
Tel.: (301) 985-7070

You do not have to search for specific programs in order to teach in a university abroad. Foreign universities routinely recruit in the United States to fill teaching positions. Placement offices and various publications will prove helpful in finding these jobs. Two helpful publications are the *Chronicle of Higher Education* and the *New York Times.*

You may also consider teaching in **international organizations** such as the United Nations, the Peace Corps, or the YMCA Overseas Service Corps. The United Nations has an agency in charge of education, United Nations Educational, Scientific, and Cultural Organization (UNESCO), which recruits teachers with doctoral degrees and at least five years of experience. For information, write:

UNESCO Recruitment
Division of International Education
U.S. Department of Education
Washington, DC 20202-6103

For information about educational assignments abroad with the Peace Corps, write:

ACTION
806 Connecticut Ave., N.W.
Washington, DC 20525

General resource books for those interested in teaching abroad include:

Inter-Ed. Gainesville, Florida: Association for the Advancement of International Education.

International Handbook of Education Systems. New York: John Wiley & Sons.

International Handbook of Universities. London: Macmillan Press.

The Overseas List. Minneapolis: Augsburg Publishing House.

World Guide to Universities. New York: R.R. Bowker Co.

The World of Learning. London: Europa Publications.

OTHER SOURCES OF INFORMATION ON TEACHING OVERSEAS:

East Asia Regional Council of Overseas Schools
c/o Singapore American School
60 King's Road
Singapore 1026, Singapore
Tel.: 65 4670022

International Schools Association
CIC Case 20, Ch-1211
Geneva 20, Switzerland
Tel.: 609 4520990

Friends of World Teaching
P.O. Box 1049
San Diego, CA 92112-1049
Tel.: (619) 275-4066

TESOL Placement Service
1118 22nd St. N.W., #205
Washington, DC 20037
Tel.: (202) 872-1271

WorldTeach
Phillips Brooks House
Harvard University
Cambridge, MA 02138
Tel.: (617) 495-5527

Institute of International Education
809 U.N. Plaza
New York, NY 10017
Tel.: (212) 984-5413

Experiment in International Living
Kipling Road
Brattleboro, VT 05301
Tel.: (800) 257-7751 ext. 258

Fulbright Teacher Exchange Program
E/ASX, USIA
301 4th St. S.W.
Washington, DC 20547
Tel.: (202) 485-2555

International Educator's Institute
P.O. Box 103
West Bridgewater, MA 02379
Tel.: (508) 580-1880

Overseas Academic Opportunities
949 E. 29th St., 2nd Floor
Brooklyn, NY 11210

TOURISM AND HOSPITALITY

The hotel and tourism industry is another high-growth area that offers employment opportunities for Americans in the Pacific Rim. English language tour guides are frequently in demand throughout the region's tourist areas. Hotels and resorts in Hong Kong, Taiwan, Thailand, the Philippines, and elsewhere present Americans with a wide variety of jobs. Australia and New Zealand have well-developed tourist industries and present no language barrier. The South Pacific countries are also heavily involved with tourism.

TOP TOUR OPERATERS IN THE PACIFIC RIM

Abercombie & Kent Travel
Sloane Square House, Holbein Place
London SW1W 8NS, Great Britain
Tel.: 01 730 9600

Adventure Agency
The Square 9, Ramsbury, Marlborough
Wiltshire SN8 2PE, Great Britain
Tel.: 0672 20569

Alfred Gregory Phototreks
Woodcock Travel, 25-31 Wicker
Sheffield S3 8HW, Great Britain
Tel.: 0742 729428

Amesz Adventure Charters
223 Collier Road
Bayswater, Western Australia
6053
Tel.: 619 271 2696

Arrow Tours
626 Wilshire Blvd., Suite 300
Los Angeles, CA 90017
Tel.: (213) 626-2362

Bufo Ventures, Ltd.
3 Elim Grove, Bownes-on-Windermere
Cumbria LA23 2JN, Great Britain
Tel.: 09662 5445

Caravan Tours
401 N. Michigan Ave.
Chicago, IL 60611
Tel.: (312) 321-9800

China Educational Tours
272 Centre Street
Newton, MA 02158
Tel.: (617) 969-5250

Club Med
40 W. 57th St.
New York, NY 10019
Tel.: (212) 977-2100

Contiki
Wells House, 15 Elmfield Road
Bromley
Kent BR1 1LS, Great Britain
Tel.: 01 290 6777

Thomas Cook Travel
380 Madison Ave.
New York, NY 10017
Tel.: (212) 916-0395

Deckers Travel Centre
15/25 Hogarth Road
London SW 9AW, Great Britain
Tel.: 01 373 3024

Dragoman, Ltd.
10 Riverside, Framlington
Suffolk IP13 9AG, Great Britain
Tel.: 0728 724184

Earthwatch
680 Mount Auburn Street
P.O. Box 403N
Watertown, MA 02172
Tel.: (617) 926-8200

Encounter Overland
267 Old Brompton Road
London SW5 9JA, Great Britain
Tel.: 01 370 6845

Exodus Expeditions
All Saints Passage
100 Wandersworth High Street
London SW18 4LE, Great Britain
Tel.: 01 870 0151

Explorasia
13 Chapter Street
London SW1P 4NY, Great Britain
Tel.: 01 630 7102

Explore Worldwide, Ltd.
7 High Street, Aldershot
Hampshire GU11 1BH, Great Britain
Tel.: 0252 319448/9

Express International, Inc.
Main Street
Saltillo, PA 17253
Tel.: (814) 448-3941

Five Valley Treks
Lowertown Farm Cottage, Landrake
Cornwall PL12 5EA, Great Britain
Tel.: 075 538725

Fresco
36 Great Russell Street
London WC1, Great Britain
Tel.: 01 323 4690

Four Winds Travel
175 5th Ave.
New York, NY 10010
Tel.: (212) 777-0260

General Tours
711 3rd. Ave.
New York, NY 10017
Tel.: (212) 687-7400

Globepost Travel
324 Kennington Park Road
London SE11 4PD, Great Britain
Tel.: 01 587 0303

Globus-Gateway
105-14 Gerard Place
Forest Hills, NY 11375
Tel.: (212) 268-4711

Hemphill/Harris Travel
16000 Ventura Blvd., Suite 200
Encino, CA 91436
Tel.: (213) 906-8086

Himalayan Travel, Inc.
P.O. Box 481
Greenwich, CT 06830
Tel.: (203) 622-0055

Ibex Expeditions, Ltd.
G66 East of Kailash
New Delhi 110 065, India
Tel.: 91 11 634738

International Weekends
1168-1170 Commonwealth Ave.
Boston, MA 02134
Tel.: (617) 731-9600

Inter-Pacific Tours International
485 Fifth Ave.
New York, NY 10017
Tel.: (212) 953-6010

Long Haul Expeditions
Tamar Travel Agents, Ltd.
56 Bohun Grove East Barnet
Herts EN4 8UB, Great Britain
Tel.: 01 440 1582

Lindblad Travel
8 Wright Street
P.O. Box 912
Westport, CT 06881
Tel.: (203) 226-8531

Maupintour
1515 St. Andrews Drive
Lawrence, KS 66044
Tel.: (913) 843-1211

Mountain Travel
1398 Solano Ave.
Albany, CA 94706
Tel.: (415) 527-8100

National Registration Center for Study Abroad
823 N. 2nd Street
Milwaukee, WI 53202
Tel.: (414) 278-0631

Nature Expeditions International
474 Willamette Street
P.O. Box 11496
Eugene, OR 97440
Tel.: (800) 634-0634

Northwest Sea Ventures
P.O. Box 522
Annacortes, WA 98221
Tel.: (206) 293-3692

Ocean Voyages, Inc.
1709 Bridgeway
Sausalito, CA 94965
Tel.: (415) 332-4681

Olson-Travelworld
5855 Green Valley Circle
Culver City, CA 90230
Tel.: (213) 670-7100

Overseas Adventure Travel
10-D Mt. Auburn Street
Harvard Square
Cambridge, MA 02138
Tel.: (617) 876-0533

Regent Holidays
13 Small Street
Bristol BS1 1DE, Great Britain
Tel.: 0272 211711

Sacu Tours
(Society for Anglo-Chinese Understanding)
152 Camden High Street
London NW1 ONE, Great Britain
Tel.: 01 482 4292

Simone Travel Bureau
2112 Broadway, Suite 500
New York, NY 10023
Tel.: (212) 496-1900

Sobek Expeditions, Inc.
1 Sobek Tower
Angles Camp, CA 95222
Tel.: (209) 736-4524

Society Expeditions
723 Broadway, East
Seattle, WA 98102
Tel.: (206) 324-9400

Students Abroad
179 N. Fulton Ave.
Mount Vernon, NY 10550
Tel.: (914) 699-8335

Tours of Distinction
141 E. 5th Ave.
New York, NY 10017
Tel.: (212) 661-4680

Top Deck Travel
133 Earls Court Road
London SW5 9RH, Great Britain
Tel.: 01 373 8406

Travcoa
Hancock Center
875 N. Michigan Ave.
Chicago, IL 60611
Tel.: (312) 951-2900

Trailfinders
42-48 Earls Court Road
London W8 6EJ, Great Britain
Tel.: 01 938 3366

Transcontinental Safaris
"The Ravine" Wildlife Park,
PMB 251, Kingscote
Kangaroo Island, South Australia
5223
Tel.: 61 848 93256

University Research
Expeditions Program (U.R.E.P.)
University of California, Desk L-10
Berkeley, CA 94720
Tel.: (415) 642-6586

Venture Treks
P.O. Box 3761
Auckland, New Zealand
Tel.: 799 855

World Travel Consultants
Executive Guild Bldg.
22974 El Toro Road
El Toro, CA 92630
Tel.: (800) 854-6733

Wright Way Tours International
16000 Ventura Blvd., Suite 201
Encino, CA 91436
Tel.: (818) 906-1141

INTERNATIONAL MEDIA

The work of foreign correspondents has always held an interest for those who wish to travel and live the adventurous life. Many would argue that this life is not as adventurous as it might seem but is certainly interesting and, most importantly, it appeals to many. These jobs are in great demand, so finding them requires a considerable amount of patience and determination. Even those who follow everything suggested here will need much talent and luck to land a good media job.

Many editors consider a journalism degree too narrow. They claim to prefer candidates who have a broad liberal arts background and a knowledge of politics, history, and international affairs. Fluency in more than one language is helpful in the communications field as well. Reporters are sent mainly to Pacific capitals and financial centers like Hong Kong and Tokyo.

News organizations want, first and foremost, good writing, editing, and reporting skills. These can best be developed through work experience and internships, although taking courses at a journalism school, especially a "writing and report" course, is also helpful. It is essential to have a file of "clips," published articles with your byline. A good work experience or internship will allow you to accumulate them. Generally, successful applicants for reporting jobs already have several internships under their belts. Internships can also lead directly to jobs through an improved network of contacts or simply by being hired by the organization where you interned.

The largest employers of foreign correspondents are the wire services. The Associated Press, for example, has 200 reporters stationed around the world. *The New York Times* has the largest overseas staff of any newspaper by far, with more than 100 correspondents. *The Los Angeles Times, The Wall Street Journal, The Washington Post, Time* magazine, and *Newsweek* also have large overseas staffs. Other large metropolitan papers keep overseas staffs of from 10-50 people. Internationally oriented publications, such as *The International Herald Tribune,* owned by *The Washington Post* and *The New York Times,* and *The Christian Science Monitor,* employ many Americans abroad.

Getting on staff is best accomplished through demonstrated ability, luck, contacts, or simple, physical courage. The willingness to jump into the thick of the fighting in Saudi Arabia or Vietnam has often been the ticket to employment as a foreign correspondent, as has being next to the editor's desk when something big happens on an empty beat.

But if you are hired by a wire service, they'll probably assign you first to a smaller office in the U.S. If you are good and make your interest in foreign reporting known, you may eventually be transferred to the foreign desk in New York, from whence you can be sent overseas. Experienced, senior personnel are likely to occupy the desirable European capital bureaus. Another approach is to work for an English-language paper overseas. They often need native English speakers as writers and editors.

Newspapers and magazines are less systematic than the large wire services, but one still must work up to the foreign jobs from within the organization. Getting a job on a newspaper, large or small, is no mean feat. Blanket the market with resumes and clips addressed to the managing editor in most cases. Newspapers are not as efficiently managed as other corporations so you will probably have to follow up more assiduously than usual to arrange an interview.

Once you get a job, do not let your contacts in other news organizations dwindle. Journalism is a nomadic profession, and most people change positions every 2-3 years, at least in the beginning. Keep up your "special" skills after you have been hired, even if you do not use them in your current position. If the paper needs to fill its Tokyo bureau, your knowledge of Japanese might make all the difference.

RESOURCES IN INTERNATIONAL MEDIA

Broadcasting/Cablecasting Yearbook.

Editor and Publisher International Yearbook. New York: Editor and Publisher. Contains information on the international newspaper industry and publishing associations in the United States and Canada.

International Literary Marketplace. Found, Peter, ed. Published by R.R. Bowker. Lists information on the book market in 160 countries, including information on 7,327 publishers.

Mass Media Internship Guide. Information on internships with newspapers, magazines, public relations firms, publishers, TV and radio stations. Listing by subject and location. (See also *The Student Guide to Mass Media Internships.*)

New England Media Directory. State by state listings of newspapers, media associations, TV and radio stations.

Newspapers International. Lists newspapers and newsweeklies in over 90 countries. National Register Publishing Company. Updated annually.

O'Dwyer's Directory of Corporate Communications. Lists public relations and communications departments of America's largest companies and trade associations.

Publisher's International Directory. R.R. Bowker. Contains names and addresses of 20,000 publishers in 144 countries.

Standard Periodicals Directory. Oxbridge Communications Inc. Lists over 35,000 U.S. and Canadian periodicals.

Ulrich's International Periodicals Directory. R.R. Bowker. Lists 66,000 periodicals from all over the world in 557 subject areas.

SELECTED INTERNATIONAL COMMUNICATIONS ORGANIZATIONS

BROADCASTING

ABC News
7 W. 66th St.
New York, NY 10023

Cable News Network
1050 Techwood Dr., N.W.
Atlanta, GA 30318

CBS
51 W. 52nd Ave.
New York, NY 10019

National Broadcasting Company (NBC)
30 Rockefeller Plaza
New York, NY 10020

Turner Broadcasting System
1 CNN Center, Box 105366
Atlanta, GA 30305

MAGAZINES

Business International
1 Dag Hammarskjold Plaza
New York, NY 10017

Business Week
1221 Ave. of the Americas
New York, NY 10020

Diplomatic World Bulletin
99 Wall St.
New York, NY 10005

The Economist
10 Rockefeller Plaza
New York, NY 10020

Foreign Affairs Journal
58 E. 68th St.
New York, NY 10021

Investment Dealers' Digest
150 Broadway
New York, NY 10038

The Nation
72 5th Ave.
New York, NY 10011

National Geographic Society
17th and M Sts., N.W.
Washington, DC 20036

Newsweek, Inc.
444 Madison Ave.
New York, NY 10022

Time, Inc.
Time and Life Building
New York, NY 10020

U.N.I.C.E.F. News
United Nations
New York, NY 10017

World Press Review
P.O. Box 915
Farmingdale, NY 11737

NEWSPAPERS

Christian Science Monitor
P.O. Box 125, Astor Station
Boston, MA 02123

Financial Times
14 E. 60th St.
New York, NY 10022

Gannett
P.O. Box 7858
Washington, DC 20044

Hearst Corp.
959 8th Ave.
New York, NY 10019

Knight-Ridder Newspapers
1 Herald Plaza
Miami, FL 33101

Los Angeles Times
Times Mirror Square
Los Angeles, CA 90053

New York Times
229 W. 43rd St.
New York, NY 10036

Wall Street Journal
Dow Jones and Co.
206 Liberty St.
New York, NY 10281

Washington Post
1150 15th St., N.W.
Washington, DC 20071

NEWS SERVICES

Associated Press
50 Rockefeller Plaza
New York, NY 10020

Foreign Press Center, USIA
18 E. 50th St., 11th Floor
New York, NY 10020

Interlink Press Service
777 U.N. Plaza
New York, NY 10017

Internews, Ltd.
1 Lincoln Plaza
New York, NY 10023

Reuters Information Services
85 Fleet St.
London, England EC4P4AJ

United Press International
1400 I St., N.W.
Washington, DC 20005

INTERNATIONAL NON-PROFITS

Non-profit organizations offer a wide array of opportunities for the international affairs professional both in the United States and in the Pacific. These range from analyst positions in think tanks to managerial positions in issue-specific non-profits. It is one of the largest industries in the U.S., employing an estimated one-eighth of all professionals. Its appeal lies in the opportunity to make you feel you are involved in socially relevant work.

Non-profit organizations have fostered great social change, from civil rights to elderly care. This sector's wages, however, are lower than the for-profit sector, and since a large amount of their funding depends on grant money, fund-raising becomes a very important task.

If you decide that you want to work in the non-profit field, your first task will be to clarify your interests. Which issues do you want to deal with: Pacific Rim economic cooperation, health, the environment, human rights, development, international security, etc. What kind of work do you want to do: fund-raising, research, program planning, etc.

Your second challenge will be to ferret out job openings. That is not easy in the non-profit sector because most organizations are small, have little turnover, and can not afford to spend resources on extensive recruitment. Therefore, it takes persistence on your part to make contacts and learn about openings. In the long run, it will pay off in the amount of satisfaction you will feel, knowing that you are making a valuable contribution to society.

SELECTED INTERNATIONAL NON-PROFIT ORGANIZATIONS IN THE U.S.

American Association for the International Commission of Journalists
777 U.N. Plaza
New York, NY 10017

American Committee on U.S.-Soviet Relations
109 11th St. S.E.
Washington, DC 20003

American Enterprise Institute
International Programs
1150 17th St. N.W.
Washington, DC 20003

American Society of International Law
2223 Massachusetts Ave.
Washington, DC 20008

Amnesty International, U.S.A.
304 W. 58th St.
New York, NY 50019

Arms Control Association
11 DuPont Circle N.W.
Washington, DC 20036

Asia Foundation
P.O. Box 3223
San Francisco, CA 94119

Brookings Institution
Foreign Policy Studies Program
1775 Massachusetts Ave. N.W.
Washington, DC 20036

Pearl S. Buck Foundation
Green Hills Farm
Perkasie, PA 18944-0181

Business Council for International Understanding
420 Lexington
New York, NY 10017

Center for Defense Information
303 Capitol Gallery West
600 Maryland Ave. S.W.
Washington, DC 20024

Center for Population Communication International
777 U.N. Plaza, Suite 4D
New York, NY 10017-3521

Center for Social Development and Humanitarian Affairs
Rm. DC2-2350, U.N.
New York, NY 10017

Center for Strategic and International Studies
1800 K St. N.W.
Washington, DC 20006

Coalition for a New Foreign and Military Policy
712 G St. S.E.
Washington, DC 20003

Committee for Economic Development
477 Madison Ave.
New York, NY 10022

Committee to Protect Journalists
36 W. 44th St.
New York, NY 10036

Coordinating Committee for International Voluntary Services
c/o UNESCO
1 rue Miollis
Paris 75015, France

Council for a Livable World
100 Maryland Ave. N.E.
Washington, DC 20002

Economic and Social Research Institute
4 Burlington Rd.
Dublin, Ireland

Fellowship of Reconciliation
P.O. Box 271
Nyack, NJ 10960

Foreign Policy Association
729 7th Ave., 8th Floor
New York, NY 10019

Foundation for the Peoples of South Pacific
158 W. 57th St.
New York, NY 10019

Global Opportunities
1594 N. Allen, No. 7
Pasadena, CA 91104

Hudson Institute
620 Union Dr., P.O. Box 648
Indianapolis, IN 46206

Institute for Policy Studies
1901 Q St. N.W.
Washington, DC 20009

International Institute for Environment and Development
1717 Massachusetts Ave. N.W., Suite 302
Washington, DC 20036

International Labor Organization
CH-1211 Geneva 22,
Switzerland 99 61 11
Tel.: 22 7996111

Helen Keller International
15 W. 16th St.
New York, NY 10011

National Democratic Institute for International Affairs
2000 M St. N.W.
Washington, DC 20036

National Republican Institute for International Affairs
601 Indiana Ave. N.W.
Washington, DC 20004

Nature Conservancy International
1785 Massachusetts Ave. N.W.
Washington, DC 20036

Union of Concerned Scientists
1616 P St. N.W.
Washington, DC 20036

Volunteers in Overseas Cooperative Assistance
1800 Massachusetts Ave. N.W.
Washington, DC 20036

Women's International League for Peace and Freedom
1213 Race St.
Philadelphia, PA 19107

INTERNATIONAL WORK WITH THE U.S. GOVERNMENT

This section pertains to international affairs positions in the federal government, one of the greatest potential employers for individuals interested in working internationally. You need to find a federal agency with internationally oriented concerns. The challenge is finding the agency and understanding its hiring procedures. The U.S. government presence in the Pacific Rim includes the Foreign Service, Commerce Department, trade missions, and security and defense personnel. Finding a position in a federal agency in Washington can be a very good route to eventually transferring abroad. You should realize that most federal employers with an international affairs office are not necessarily focused exclusively upon the Pacific Rim, and you may not receive a Pacific or Asian assignment.

Executive Branch

Most Executive Branch divisions of the federal government deal with domestic issues, but many also deal with Pacific Rim issues. The following list contains Executive Branch employers that hire individuals with international experience or educational backgrounds.

Office of Management and Budget
Old Executive Building
Washington, DC 20500
Staff of 600. International Affairs Division includes Trade, Monetary, Investment Policy, Summer Internships.

Office of U.S. Trade Representative
600 17th St. N.W.
Washington, DC 20506
Staff of 140. One-year Internship Program. No pay; 18% acceptance rate.

Department of Agriculture
14th St. and Independence Ave. S.W.
Washington, DC 20250
The department has a management development program; most foreign service assignments are made through the ranks on a merit basis. Employs Global/Regional Trade Analysts, Managers, Agricultural Policy Analysts, Statisticians. The following divisions are concerned with international issues:

World Agricultural Outlook Board
International Economics Division
Foreign Agricultural Service
Office of International Cooperation and Development
PL 480 Surplus Commodity and Export Credit Programs

Department of Commerce
Main Commerce Building
14th St. and Constitution Ave. N.W.
Washington, DC 20230
The International Trade Administration uses the Cooperative Education Program extensively to recruit and train mid-level management. Employs: Systems Analysts, Statisticians, Economists, Trade Analysts, Writer/Editors, Consulate Posts, Regional/Program Managers, Policy Analysts. The following divisions are concerned with international issues:

International Trade Administration
Bureau of Economic Analysis
U.S. Travel and Tourism Administration
Center for International Research
Foreign Trade Program

Department of Defense
Office of the Assistant Secretary for Security Affairs
The Pentagon
Washington, DC 20301

Department of Education
Office of Inter-Government and Inter-Agency Affairs
400 Maryland Ave. S.W.
Washington, DC 20202

Department of Energy
Office of the Assistant Secretary for International Affairs and Energy Emergencies
1000 Independence Ave. S.W.
Washington, DC 20585

Department of Health and Human Services
Office of International Health
200 Independence Ave. S.W.
Washington, DC 20201

Department of Housing and Urban Development
Office of International Affairs
H.U.D. Building
451 7th St. S.W.
Washington, DC 20401

Department of the Interior
Office of Territorial and International Affairs
Main Interior Building, 18th St. N.W.
Washington, DC 20240

Department of Labor
Bureau of International Labor Affairs
200 Constitution Ave. N.W.
Washington, DC 20210

Department of State
Main State Building
2201 C St. N.W.
Washington, DC 20520

Department of Transportation
Office of Policy and International Affairs
400 7th St. S.W.
Washington, DC 20590

Department of the Treasury
Office of the Assistant Secretary for International Affairs
Main Treasury Building
15th St. and Pennsylvania Ave. N.W.
Washington, DC 20220

The Foreign Service

The Department of State's Foreign Service has its own separate entrance procedure, consisting of a formal written examination and a more wide-ranging series of tests called the Oral Assessment, given directly to the applicant by an examiner.

The written test, given once a year, lasts 3 1/2 hours. The average applicant takes the test three times before passing. The passing grade is 70% for English expression, general educational background, and one of six functional fields: four from the State Department (administrative, consular, economic, political), one from the U.S. Information Agency (information-cultural), and one from the Commerce Department (commercial).

The Oral Assessment consists of an oral examination lasting 45 minutes, a 45-minute essay, a written "in-basket" test, and 1 hour and 45 minutes of group exercises designed to measure oral presentation and negotiating skills. Certain specialist positions, summer employment, and internships do not require this examination.

Appointees are trained and oriented in Washington for a period of 2-12 months, which is usually followed by a 4-year probationary period. Initial assignments are entirely at the discretion of the department. Pay for master's graduates runs from FS-9 ($22,907 - $29,783) to FS-11 ($27,716 - $36,032). Advancement is highly competitive, dependent upon periodic review and evaluation.

RESOURCES FOR GOVERNMENT CAREERS

1990-91 Congressional Yellow Book. Washington, DC: Monitor Publishing Co., annual.

1990-91 Federal Yellow Book. Washington, DC: Monitor Publishing Co., annual.

Capital Jobs: An Insider's Guide to Finding a Job in Congress. Dumbough, Kerry, and Serota, Gary. Washington DC: Tilden Press, 1986.

Congressional Quarterly. Washington, DC.

Federal Agencies, 1990. Published annually.

Federal Career Opportunities and *Federal Jobs Newsletter.* P.O. Box 1438, Leesburg, VA 22075.

Federal Personnel Guide. Federal Personnel Publications, Washington, DC, 1985.

U.S. Employment Opportunities 1990. Published annually.

U.S. Government Manual. Published annually.

Washington IV: A Comprehensive Directory of the Nation's Capital, Its People and Institutions. Washington, DC: Potomac Books, 1976. Check for revised editions.

Washington Information Directory. Published annually.

SELECTED U.S. GOVERNMENT AGENCIES WITH INTERNATIONAL AFFAIRS DIVISIONS

Agency for International Development
Main State Building
2201 C St. N.W.
Washington, DC 20523

Arms Control and Disarmament Agency
Main State Building
2201 C St. N.W.
Washington, DC 20451

Central Intelligence Agency
Dept. A
P.O. Box 1925
Washington, DC 20505

Congressional Budget Office
H.O.B. Annex 2
2nd & D Sts. S.W.
Washington, DC 20515

Congressional Research Service
101 Independence Ave. S.E.
Washington, DC 20540

Customs Service
1301 Constitution Ave. N.W.
Washington, DC 20229

Defense Intelligence Agency
The Pentagon
Washington, DC 20340

Drug Enforcement Administration
1405 I St. N.W.
Washington, DC 20537

Environmental Protection Agency
401 M St. S.W.
Washington, DC 20460

Export-Import Bank
811 Vermont Ave. N.W.
Washington, DC 20571

Federal Communications Commission
1919 M St. N.W.
Washington, DC 20554

Federal Maritime Commission
1100 L St. N.W.
Washington, DC 20573

Federal Reserve System
20th & C Sts. N.W.
Washington, DC 20551

Federal Trade Commission
6th St. & Pennsylvania Ave. N.W.
Washington, DC 20580

General Accounting Office
441 G St. N.W.
Washington, DC 20548

House Foreign Affairs Committee
2170 Rayburn House Office Building
Washington, DC 20515

Immigration and Naturalization Service
425 I St. N.W.
Washington, DC 20536

International Trade Commission
500 E St. S.W.
Washington, DC 20436

National Aeronautics and Space Administration
400 Maryland Ave. S.W.
Washington, DC 20546

National Security Council
Executive Office Building
Washington, DC 20506

Overseas Private Investment Corporation
1615 M St. N.W.
Washington, DC 20527

Securities and Exchange Commission
450 5th St. N.W.
Washington, DC 20549

Senate Foreign Relations Committee
Dirksen Senate Office Building, #423
Washington, DC 20510

Smithsonian Institution
Office of Personnel Administration
900 Jefferson Dr. S.W.
Washington, DC 20560

Trade and Development Program
State Annex 16
Washington, DC 20523

What the Pacific Rim Means to Americans Seeking Jobs

The integration of Pacific Rim economies means that trade and investment will increasingly flow throughout the countries involved in APEC. Greater interdependence will allow for the exchange of skilled workers as well. Because many of the countries in the Pacific Rim are still developing, a wide variety of opportunities are becoming available. The developing economies simply lack sufficient people skilled in certain sectors of the economy. Consequently, these countries are eager to find individuals with the appropriate experience and training to meet their needs.

While Americans may not find heavy competition among nationals in the developing countries, job seekers from other parts of the Pacific Rim are also available to fill positions. Skilled workers from Japan, South Korea, Taiwan, Hong Kong, and Singapore are in a much better position than Americans to find employment throughout the Pacific Rim. These more developed economies are already large investors in the less developed nations. Moreover, their companies are outpacing the U.S. in new investment.

Most of the jobs available now and in the near future in the Pacific Rim will be with East Asian, not American firms. Companies investing in another country generally prefer to hire local staff for their foreign subsidiaries. If locals are unavailable to fill particular positions, then the job is likely to go to a worker from the parent company's country instead of someone from a third country. This places American workers at an overall disadvantage because U.S. firms are not in as good a position as their Asian competitors.

There are, of course, many openings that Americans can fill after familiarizing themselves with the regulations and possibilities. Americans can overcome employment problems by emphasizing their unique skills and intelligently marketing themselves to potential employers. Many American firms are already in the Asian Pacific, Australia, and the South Pacific.

Your best opportunity to find a job in the Pacific Rim is probably with an American company engaged in operations there. The most practical route is to land a position in the U.S. first and transfer abroad later. Working for a foreign company in the U.S. and then transfering abroad is quite feasible, too. Employment abroad may sometimes be found with foreign firms, but they are more likely to hire their own nationals before Americans. Summer work and internships in the Pacific Rim also serve to introduce a potential employer to an applicant's talents. The rest of Part I of this book presents detailed information on how you can maximize your employment opportunities in the Pacific Rim.

3 Do You Qualify for an International Job?

As you begin your quest for the international job, it would certainly be wise to evaluate yourself to see if you're qualified for employment in the Pacific Rim. Many factors figure in to whether you can get an international job. First of all you must have interest (since you are reading this book, that is a given). You must also have the will to travel and go to the Pacific, and only you can decide that. Other factors are a bit more concrete. Are you flexible enough to adapt to the exigencies of another culture? Do you speak any foreign languages? How will that affect you? Education can also play a major part in your qualifications. All of these factors should be examined.

Adapting to International Living

Americans working abroad need to possess certain character and educational traits in order to benefit from the experience.

Mere knowledge of a foreign language will not automatically insure an international job. Rather than concentrate upon the differences between American and foreign cultures, you should attempt to appreciate the other country's civilization and traditions. Living and working overseas requires an emotional and mental effort.

Efforts need to be made to communicate with others. In another country, Americans should attempt to learn the language and communicate effectively on a daily basis. Remaining ignorant of the language will lead one to become introverted or self-conscious. Likewise, try to understand why people conduct themselves as they do. Understanding why cultural traits and traditions exist will enable you to communicate effectively with people.

Americans working abroad must also realize that stereotypes and other cultural attitudes will influence how they are perceived in a particular country. Although people in the Pacific Rim, for example, stereotype each other and not just Americans, coping with these perceptions will likely challenge your ability to adjust abroad. Try to ascertain what specific attitudes and stereotypes exist about Americans in a particular country and avoid behavior confirming such views. In many countries, for instance, inability or unwillingness to learn even basic phrases in the native language creates resentment.

Several factors consistently trouble Americans living overseas. The language barrier clearly poses adjustment difficulties but can be overcome with persistent effort. Accustomed to directness in conversation and negotiations, Americans are often surprised by the vague and indirect nature of communication, especially negotiations, in some countries. Similarly, conversations with strangers, and even acquaintances, in many cultures mandates formality and structure, occasionally leading to a perception of aloofness.

Americans are also likely to find the pace of life and work habits abroad different from typical American lifestyles. You should expect a general lack of conveniences and personal mobility in most societies (e.g., most Asians, unlike Americans, do not own automobiles). Patience and experience will facilitate adaptation to these cultural patterns. But living and working abroad will trouble individuals who can not adapt to new situations or adjust to unaccustomed practices and attitudes.

Pacific Rim Employment Regulations

Regulations for working in the Pacific Rim are different in each country. One fact is true of all countries: it is very difficult to get permission to work. Many countries mandate that you must have employment before you can apply for a work visa, while employers mandate that you must have work visas before they hire you. Chapters 8 through 17 outline specific work visa regulations for each country. If you want to work within a large multinational company, you should know that the company can often obtain any documentation necessary for international work. Be aware, however, that companies do not necessarily like obtaining your paperwork and would prefer that this be done by you.

Within certain countries, temporary work permits can be obtained through work-permit organizations such as CIEE (see Chapters 6 and 7). Many Americans seeking work in the Pacific do not bother with regulations and search for employment that ranges from English teaching to working in a tourism-oriented business. These areas can be less restrictive though often illegal. Early planning is the best bet. Do whatever is possible to have some sort of work permit, temporary or otherwise. That will make your search much easier and certainly less worrisome.

Foreign Language Requirements

Clearly, knowledge of a foreign language will only improve your employment opportunities abroad. Although many Americans have taken foreign language courses in high school and college, such experience usually fails to provide the appropriate level of fluency. Additionally Asian languages are traditionally not taught in American schools. Employers may be impressed by your ability to understand the symbolism of an Akira Kurasowa film or the outback slang in Crocodile Dundee, but they will primarily be concerned with your ability to communicate effectively on a daily basis.

Your language skills should include the ability to engage in small-talk and casual conversation as well as a knowledge of basic business phrases. If a potential employer contacts you by telephone in a foreign language, you should be able to respond and engage in conversation until you can gracefully shift into English at an appropriate time. Only send a cover letter in the host language if you are as fluent in the spoken language as you seem to be in writing.

Speaking a foreign language fluently is generally not necessary, although tremendously helpful, when applying for an international job, but you must demonstrate a willingness to improve your language skills by enrolling in intensive language courses and accepting language training if offered by the company. Such courses should emphasize practical skills, especially business terminology, rather than a tourist-oriented vocabulary. You will eventually need to learn how to order lunch in another country, but understanding common business terms when dealing with customers and co-workers deserves a higher priority. Intensive conversational foreign language courses with qualified instructors are available at most community colleges and continuing education programs at universities. Commercial courses are more expensive but often emphasize business language skills.

Within Asian countries, it may be impossible for you to learn the language in a short period of time. This is taken into consideration as you search for employment. You should be ready, however, to take a position that uses your strengths in English rather than your business abilities and skills. In some instances, it is more important to know the native language than in others. But one should not count on this in finding a rewarding position. For instance, it would be practically impossible to learn Chinese or Japanese in a short period of time and no one is expected to.

Areas Where Jobs for Americans Are Scarce

The person who works diligently to find employment in the Pacific Rim is going to locate something. There are, however, places that will not prove very fruitful to most job seekers. Small Asian companies engaged in non-tourism or non-trade-related business, for instance, have little use for American workers. This type of company will only hire you if you offer some special skill that it directly needs and local workers can not supply. Computer programming, for instance, is one such skill in demand.

The chances of finding quick employment with a United Nations organization or an international agency are bleak. These organizations have very bureaucratic hiring processes. If you ardently desire to work for this type of organization, you should apply two years in advance and wait. There is a small chance that they may look at your application.

It is unrealistic to expect to find high-paying work in the Pacific without a great deal of experience and much advance preparation. The high-paying professional positions are usually occupied by Americans who have worked for their international company for many years and have proven themselves on a job in the United States.

Higher Education and the International Career

Your education can have a great deal to do with the type of position that you can find in the international sector. A number of different types of schools can prepare you for your career. Some are more obvious than others. Thus, if you want to do computer programming in the Pacific, a degree in computer science is appropriate; if you want to do accounting, you should have an accounting degree, and so on. Those interested in the various fields of international affairs should consider the top schools in the United States and acquire specific hard-core coursework that enables the development of specific skills. Once again, simple political science and history courses are not going to get you a job. The top international affairs schools and other relevant university programs are listed below.

TOP GRADUATE AND PROFESSIONAL SCHOOLS OF INTERNATIONAL AFFAIRS

Columbia University
School of International and Public Affairs (SIPA)
420 W. 118th St., Rm. 1427
New York, NY 10027
Tel.: (212) 854-8690

Georgetown University
Edmund A. Walsh School of Foreign Service
301 ICC
Washington, DC 20057
Tel.: (202) 687-5696

Johns Hopkins University
School of Advanced International Studies (SAIS)
1740 Massachusetts Ave. N.W.
Washington, DC 20036
Tel.: (202) 663-5700

Princeton University
Woodrow Wilson School of Public and International Affairs
Princeton, NJ 08544
Tel.: (609) 258-4831

Tufts University
Fletcher School of Law and Diplomacy
Medford, MA 02155
Tel.: (617) 381-3040

A Master of Business Administration (MBA) degree from a school that offers a specialization in international business will facilitate your search for international employment. Many MBA programs offer this type of degree, so it is important to look at the international placement rates of their placement offices. The following are a few of the top programs.

TOP INTERNATIONAL MBA PROGRAMS

University of Pennsylvania
School of Arts and Sciences and Wharton School
Joseph H. Lauder Institute of Management and International Affairs
3620 Locust Walk
Philadelphia, PA 19104-6368
Tel.: (215) 898-1215

Columbia University
Graduate School of Business
101 Uris Hall
New York, NY 10027
Tel.: (212) 854-3401

New York University
Stern School of Business Administration
Department of International Business
100 Trinity Place

New York, NY 10006
Tel.: (212) 285-6200

University of Chicago
Graduate School of Business
1101 E. 58th St.
Chicago, IL 60637
Tel.: (312) 702-7121

University of South Carolina
Graduate School, College of Business Administration
Program in International Business Studies
Columbia, SC 29208
Tel.: (803) 777-3176
This program is listed not because it is a top MBA school but because it offers the specialized degree of Master of International Business.

OTHER NOTEWORTHY GRADUATE PROGRAMS WITH INTERNATIONAL OR ASIAN/PACIFIC EMPHASIS

American Graduate School of International Management (Thunderbird)
International Studies
15249 N. 59th Ave.
Glendale, AZ 85306

Brandeis University
Lemberg Program in International Economics and Finance
Sachar International Center
Waltham, MA 02254-9110
Tel.: (617) 736-2263

Chaminade University of Honolulu
Japanese Business Studies
Honolulu, HI 96816
Tel.: (808) 735-4740

Dominican College of San Rafael
Graduate Programs in Pacific Basin Studies
50 Acacia Avenue
San Rafael, CA 94901
Tel.: (415) 457-4440

Stanford University
School of Humanities and Sciences
Stanford CA 94305
Tel.: (415) 723-4291

Washington University
Graduate School of Arts and Sciences
(Program in Asian Studies)
St. Louis, MO 63130
Tel.: (314) 889-5156

University of California at Berkeley
Walter A. Haas School of Business and Group in Asian Studies
Berkeley, CA 94720
Tel.: (415) 642-0333

University of California at San Diego
Graduate School of International Relations and Pacific Studies
La Jolla, CA 92093
Tel.: (619) 534-4661

University of Chicago
Graduate School of Business
1101 E. 58th St.
Chicago, IL 60637
Tel.: (312) 702-7121

University of Pittsburgh
Graduate School of Public and International Affairs
Pittsburgh, PA 15260
Tel.: (412) 648-7640

University of Southern California
Graduate School of Business Administration
(International Business and International Finance)
Los Angeles, CA 90089
Tel.: (213) 743-5175

University of Washington
Henry M. Jackson School of International Studies
DR-05 Thomson Hall
Seattle, WA 98195
Tel.: (206) 543-6001

Internships

If you are a college student, you are eligible for many international internship programs. These are usually in areas such as political organizations, businesses, and non-profit organizations. You should contact the student career office at your university for information on these programs. Many programs are available for academic credit and offer no pay. These do, however, provide invaluable experience that will help you in any future international job search. Many organizations that organize and provide international internship opportunities are listed in Chapters 6 and 7. One program run by the federal government is the Intern Program of the U.S. State Department. This program, though very competitive, is worth looking into.

Managing Director, Intern Program
U.S. and Foreign Commercial Service
11000 Wilshire Blvd., Rm. 9200
Los Angeles, CA 90024

This program offers university students an internship with the U.S. Foreign Service. There are U.S. and Foreign Commercial Service branches all over the world (67 in the U.S. and 125 abroad). The goal of the U.S.F.C.S. is to help U.S. trade growth worldwide through promotion and marketing services. The program provides experience in international trade, and university credit is available. To be eligible, you must be a U.S. citizen with an applicable major area of study such as economics, business administration, international relations, law, public administration, political science, international business, or marketing. Send resumes to the above address.

Temporary Jobs and the "Black Market"

Jobs such as tourist work, work camps, agriculture work, and menial labor that do not require a formal education are easier to obtain. Employment in these areas comes about through hard work, persistence, luck, and timing.

Work camps for volunteers and agricultural work are plentiful in Australia and New Zealand during specific seasons. Fruit-picking season produces an extreme demand for labor. Working in resorts, like agriculture, is also seasonal. Chapter 7 presents a rundown of all the possibilities for these and other temporary positions.

Work permits will not always be available in the country where you wish to work. As these situations arise, many Americans resort to working in the country illegally or "on the black market." This sounds more sinister than it really is. A number of options are available for those interested in working without a permit. These include: farm work, which is often locally advertised, work in bars or restaurants, and menial labor jobs. These are all types of work that sometimes involve informal agreements and are not always reported. Unfortunately, because you generally must locate this kind of work on the local level, you already have to be in the country to look for it, and there are no guarantees of finding employment.

You should be aware that if you arrive with a tourist visa and no work permit, many countries will require proof of a return ticket and/or money to support yourself during your stay, without which you will not be allowed to leave the airport. This means that the romantic notion of flying into a country with a tourist visa but no money and no return ticket in hopes of "working your way back home" is not a very good idea.

The Pacific Rim Job Search and Interviewing Techniques

The Pacific Rim job search for Americans in most cases should not begin abroad. The possibilities of international employment vary widely and need research and preparation. Before any job search, preparation is the key; this becomes especially true when conducting a search for a job far from home. Many would argue that one of the best ways to achieve an international position is by first securing a job in an international company and later asking for a transfer to another country. In that manner, learning the business and proving your skills occurs in the United States. Understanding the industry and the company before entering a foreign country should facilitate cultural adjustment. Likewise, firms may be more likely to offer an international position to an experienced and trained employee. But for most people, the possibilities for an immediate international job are much too exciting to wait for a possible transfer. We will continue on the assumption that a job does not exist within an international corporation in the United States and that you are seeking the job of a lifetime in the Pacific.

12 Steps to Getting a Job in the Pacific Rim

Step 1. Decide what you want out of an international job.

What do you want to get out of working in the Pacific Rim? Deciding what you want to do and what you are capable of doing will further sharpen your career focus. Concentrate on those activities that have brought you the most enjoyment in your life and what it was about those activities that made them so rewarding. Focus on interests, values, and cultural objectives, and try not to connect these to occupational titles at this stage. Here are a few practical matters to consider:

A. You should consider how much you wish to **travel** when you are working. You may desire the flexibility to tour and see other countries, or to truly explore the one you are in. Also, you may want to consider a job that in itself requires a lot of traveling.

B. The **experience** you will gain is also an important consideration. You may be seeking a job that will provide you with practical work experience (e.g., working with an international bank because you intend to go into international banking). Or you may simply wish exposure to another culture. In the latter case, you would need to consider the location of the workplace to see whether it is near cultural centers and whether you would have the opportunity to meet other people.

C. You also need to consider how much **money** you intend to make. Are you simply trying to break even, or do you intend to make a good deal of money? The cost of living is much higher in many Asian countries than in the U.S., so you need to evaluate what kind of lifestyle you intend to lead and what kind of salary will maintain it.

Step 2. Decide what type of job or career would suit you best.

This decision is based primarily on your values, interests, personality, and work style. To a large extent, your happiness with your work coincides with how closely it meets your needs and motivates you. As you embark on the Pacific Rim job search, decide what it is that motivates or interests you about a career in general.

There are other factors to be considered after you determine what your motivations are. Think about the characteristics of your ideal work environment. This is not as simple a decision as you might think. You want to choose an organization or work area that meshes as closely as possible with your own values and personality.

Consider these factors:

Product or Service Provided: Generally, employers fall into two main categories: manufacturing and services. Manufacturing organizations produce and sell tangible products while service organizations provide services to clients. Beyond this simple distinction there is, of course, the question of which products or services you wish to be involved with.

Organizational Style: This has less to do with the public face of the organization (as you may have seen it in advertisements, promotional material, etc.) than with the private face of the organization—the pervading atmosphere of the facility, the use of authority, the type of supervision you are liable to come under or execute. Some job seekers are more comfortable and productive in an atmosphere of informality in terms of dress, interaction between junior and senior managers, supervision, and work-hours flexibility. Other job seekers prefer a more formal or structured environment, while still others want a combination of styles.

Organization Size: The trend toward corporate mergers has created some huge conglomerates. Generally speaking, larger organizations offer more long-term job security and a more developed training program than do new businesses. Since one of your best chances of working at the professional level overseas is with U.S. companies that have international branches, large firms will provide most of your opportunities. On the other hand, smaller organizations provide more involvement in decision making.

Rate of Growth: How fast or slowly an organization is growing has a significant effect on all positions in that organization. Faster growing companies can be exciting and provide many more opportunities for speedy advancement. To some, such an environment may seem dynamic; to others it seems chaotic.

Location and Physical Environment: It is important that you consider which part of the world or country you would like to work in. One of the most frequent causes of indecision in a job search is the question of where one is or is not willing to relocate. A related factor is the physical environment of the workplace. Would you like to work in an urban, suburban, or rural setting? Would you like to work indoors or outdoors? Would you like to work in traditional office surroundings or in a more innovatively designed workplace? Give it some thought.

Step 3. Explore and decide where the market is best for your skills and desires.

First of all, evaluate what you have to offer an employer. This includes your abilities, skills, areas of special knowledge, and your interests, as developed through your education and experience. After knowing what you have to offer and what you can and can't do, you must research the Pacific Rim market to decide where these skills and interests can be applied. By looking through chapters 2 and 8-17, you can check the economic outlook for each Pacific Rim country and determine which areas might best use the skills you have. In addition, you may want to consult international company directories, a few of which are listed in this chapter, world trade centers, which are listed in this chapter, chambers of commerce, which are listed in Chapter 1, and the consulates and embassies for the countries that you are researching, which can be found in the chapters on individual countries.

Step 4. Research your country.

After you have determined the type(s) of work you would like to pursue, you must research where you want to work. The chapters in this book on individual countries provide information on their respective job markets and conditions. Collect as much information as possible about your selected country from some of the outside sources listed in Step 3, above. Knowing your chosen country well will facilitate your search as well as your transition once you have found your job.

Step 5. Network.

Using contacts, or networking, is generally the best job-search strategy. Make up a list of all your contacts, let them know you are job hunting, and ask for their assistance. Contacts include friends, professionals you meet through professional organizations, relatives, alumni, speakers at on-campus events, professors, former employers, and many others. Be creative in expanding your contacts, and don't delay building your network. Networking for a Pacific Rim job may be more difficult for someone a continent away, but not impossible. World trade centers provide a good starting point; international alumni from schools attended can also be helpful. Any international companies located near you should also be utilized to meet international personnel or Americans with experience in your desired field. People with international experience are almost always willing to discuss their experiences and offer help to those interested in going abroad.

Step 6. Set up information interviews.

As you begin networking, you will need to become familiar with the information interview. Information interviews are not the same as job interviews. They are interviews in which you ask people not for jobs but for information on their company or field. Their purpose is to teach you more about a particular career field and to acquaint you with professionals in that field.

These are some questions you may want to ask when you meet with, or talk over the phone with, a contact. It is your responsibility to know something about the purpose of your visit and about the organization, and to take responsibility for the progress of the interview. Your questions can be broken down into four main groups, as follows.

JOB DESCRIPTION

1. In the position you now hold, what are your major duties and responsibilities?
2. What might a typical day be like?
3. What aspects of your job do you find most interesting?
4. What aspects do you enjoy least?
5. With what people in your organization (superiors, subordinates, peers) do you find you have the most contact?
6. How does your position fit into the organization structure?
7. What changes do you see occurring in this field? Will the type and number of jobs in the field change significantly over the next 10 years? Is there a rapidly changing technology in this field?

CAREER PATH

8. What were the positions you had that led up to this one?
9. What are the typical entry-level jobs in this field?
10. What positions could someone in this field pursue for career advancement?
11. How long does it usually take to move from one step to the next in this field?
12. Are there any specifically defined prerequisites for advancement (examinations, years in service, higher degrees, board interviews, etc.)?
13. Are there other areas in this field to which people may be transferred? What are they?

PREPARATION

14. What are the academic and experience prerequisites for entry-level jobs in this field?
15. Are there any specific courses I might take that would be particularly useful?
16. Are there any extracurricular or other experiences (work, volunteering, internships, etc.) that would enhance my chances of employment?
17. What special advice would you give to a person entering this field?

18. What types of training do companies give persons entering this field?

GENERAL

19. Is there currently a demand for people in this field?
20. What are the salary ranges for various levels?
21. How many hours a week does someone typically work?
22. May I read the job descriptions and specifications for some of the positions?
23. Could you look over and critique my resume?
24. Are there other people in this field with whom you would suggest I talk?
25. Is the degree you received recognized in your field?

One of the most important aspects of the information interview is to ask for names of people within the field that you can contact. These names will not only be valuable to you as you learn about the field but they, in turn, can give you other names to write to about possible job openings. It's all part of networking—the job-search technique that holds the greatest potential for success.

Step 7. Use business directories and World Trade Centers.

Business directories can provide a great many contacts to the job seeker and networker. Here are some directories you may want to use if you wish to contact firms directly:

America's Corporate Families and International Affiliates 1991, Vol. II
Dun's Marketing Services
3 Sylvan Way
Parsippany, NJ 07054

Directory of American Firms Operating in Foreign Countries
World Trade Academy Press
50 E. 42nd St.
New York, NY 10017
Covers around 3,200 American firms with international branches.

Encyclopedia of Business Information Sources
Gale Research Co.
Book Tower
Detroit, MI 48226

The International Corporate 1000
Monitor Publishing Co.
104 5th Ave.
New York, NY 10011

International Directory of Corporate Affiliations 1991, Vol.1
National Register Publishers Co.
3004 Glenview Rd.
Wilmette, IL 60091

International Directory of Importers
Blytmann International
195 Dry Creek Road
Healdsburg, CA 95448

Major Companies of the Far East and Australasia Vol. 1, South East Asia—1990-91
Graham and Trotman Ltd.,
66 Wilton Rd.
London, SW1V 1DE
England

Principal International Businesses: The World Marketing Directory
Dun & Bradstreet International Ltd.
99 Church St.
New York, NY 10007
Covers around 50,000 employers outside the Soviet sphere.

Ward's Business Directory of 15,000 Major International Corporations
Information Access Company
11 Davis Drive
Belmont, CA 94002
Covers 15,000 of the larger international corporations.

World Trade Centers can provide you with information regarding international business markets, job markets within individual companies, and influential people in the international business world. Here is a list of World Trade Centers within the United States:

Atlanta
World Trade Club of Atlanta
240 Peachtree St., Suite 2200
Atlanta, GA 30303
Tel.: (404) 525-4144

Baltimore
The World Trade Center, Baltimore
Baltimore, MD 21202
Tel.: (301) 659-4544

Boston
International Business Center of New England
22 Batterymarch St.
Boston, MA 02210
Tel.: (617) 542-0426

Colorado Springs
Rocky Mountain World Trade Center
Red Rock Canyon Project
3221 W. Colorado Ave.
Colorado Springs, CO 80904
Tel.: (303) 633-9041

Columbus
World Trade and Technology Center of Columbus
10793 State Route 37 West
Sunbury, OH 43074
Tel.: (614) 965-2974

Des Moines
Iowa World Trade Center, Des Moines
3200 Ruan Center
666 Grand Ave.
Des Moines, IA 50390
Tel.: (515) 245-2555

Ft. Lauderdale
World Trade Center Fort Lauderdale, Florida
P.O. Box 13066
1800 Eller Drive
Port Everglades, FL 33316
Tel.: (305) 523-5307

Greensboro
World Trade Center, North Carolina
P.O. Box 19290
Greensboro, NC 27419
Tel.: (929) 854-0078

Houston
Houston World Trade Association
1100 Milam, 25th Floor
Houston, TX 77002
Tel.: (713) 658-2401

Jacksonville
Jacksonville International Trade Association
Jacksonville Chamber of Commerce
3 Independent Drive
P.O. Box 329
Jacksonville, FL 32201
Tel.: (904) 353-0300

Long Beach
The Port of Long Beach
925 Harbor Plaza
P.O. Box 570
Long Beach, CA 92801
Tel.: (213) 437-0041

Miami
Execucentre International
444 Brickell Ave., Suite 650
Miami, FL 33131
Tel.: (305) 374-8300

New Orleans
International House - WTC
611 Gravier St.
New Orleans, LA 70230
Tel.: (504) 522-3591

New York
World Trade Center, New York
The Port Authority of New York and New Jersey
1 World Trade Center, Suite 63 West
New York, NY 10048
Tel.: (212) 466-8380

Norfolk
World Trade Center, Norfolk
600 World Trade Center
Norfolk, VA 23510
Tel.: (804) 623-8000

Orlando
World Trade Center, Orlando
P.O. Box 1234
Orlando, FL 32801
Tel.: (305) 425-1234

Pomona
Inland Pacific World Trade Institute
422 W. 7th St., Suite 302
Los Angeles, CA 90014
Tel.: (213) 627-6738

Portland
Columbia World Trade Center
121 S.W. Salmon
Portland, OR 97204
Tel.: (503) 220-3067

San Francisco
World Trade Center of San Francisco
1170 Sacramento St., Penthouse B
San Francisco, CA 92108
Tel.: (415) 928-3438

Santa Anna
World Trade Center Association of Orange County
200 E. Sandpointe Ave.
Santa Anna, CA 92707
Tel.: (714) 549-8151

Sarasota
World Trade Council of Southwest Florida
P.O. Box 911
Sarasota, FL 33578
Tel.: (813) 366-4060

Seattle
Seattle World Trade Center
500 Union St., Suite 840
Seattle, WA 96101
Tel.: (206) 622-4121

St. Paul
Minnesota World Trade Center
444 Cedar St., 1300 Conwed Tower
St. Paul, MN 55101
Tel.: (612) 297-1580

Tacoma
World Trade Center, Tacoma
P.O. Box 1837
Tacoma, WA 96401
Tel.: (206) 383-5841

Tampa
Tampa Bay International Trade Council
P.O. Box 420
Tampa, FL 33601
Tel.: (813) 228-7777, Ext. 234

Toledo
Toledo World Trade Center
136 N. Summit St.
P.O. Box 2087
Toledo, OH 43603
Tel.: (419) 255-7226

Washington, D.C.
World Trade Center, Washington
1000 Connecticut Ave. N.W., Suite 707
Washington, DC 20036
Tel.: (202) 955-6164

Alumni associations

One option you may want to try is your alumni association. Many alumni associations have a contact service that can put you in touch with alumni overseas who are willing to help graduates of their *alma mater.* While this by no means assures you of a job, since the alumni abroad may have nothing to do with hiring, it can provide a contact within various overseas companies. The individual alumnus may be able to help you get an interview, help you find accommodations in an area you would visit for an interview, or perhaps even provide a place for you to stay during your visit.■

Step 8. Write a resume and cover letter.

Writing an international resume and a cover letter to accompany it is an important and major task in marketing yourself and in securing interviews for an international position. Chapter 5 focuses on the international resume and cover letter. It is important to remember that this step can be crucial to your other steps. Do not accept just anyone's advice on the resume, and almost everyone has some to give. Try to develop a resume that portrays you as a hardworking, enthusiastic, bright person with a lot to offer an organization.

Step 9. Organize your job search—mail letters.

The task of finding a job is demanding and challenging. A job search in a foreign country is even more trying and requires patience and persistence. Whether you are looking for a full-time, summer, or temporary job, the process is the same. Approach your task methodically, with a detailed plan. Keeping records, a daily planner, and scheduling a day's activities will improve the efficiency of the job search.

Here are some tips to make your job search more productive:

- Decide how to spend your time each day. Schedule two or three hours a week for job-search tasks if it's a part-time endeavor, two or three hours a day if it's full-time.
- Keep a personal calendar with your appointments.
- Keep all your job-search information organized in a notebook or index-card file so you'll have complete records and know what to follow through on.
- Don't expect quick success. Job searches often take six months to a year.
- Develop a support system. Job searching can be frustrating. Make sure you have friends and family to bolster you.
- Get an interim or temporary job if necessary to pay your rent.
- Allow free time to do fun things and give yourself breaks.

The information on *each* employer you keep track of should include:

- Name, address, and phone number of the employer
- Brief description of the employer
- Where you found out about the job (professor, friend, etc.)
- Specific or possible openings
- Date you sent initial resume
- Follow-up by you or prospective employer (if the employer doesn't call within two weeks of your mailing, you can call them)
- Date of interview and other interview information
- Date you sent thank you letter
- Resolution—what happened with this employer?

Job search strategies. Generally, the more diversified you are in your approach, the better. Job-search strategies fall into three categories: contacts, specific openings, and targeted mailings. You should use all three approaches. Depending on your interests, some of these approaches may be more effective than others. For example, non-profit organizations often don't advertise job openings, so you need to find out about their openings through contacts and targeted mailings. On the other hand, the federal government has very specific hiring procedures. Networking, or contacts, should always be your first option, though all routes should be examined.

Targeted Mailings. Targeted mailings can be effective if done properly. Researchers have found that only well-researched mailing lists will produce enough response to merit their time and effort. A 10 percent response rate is considered good. Your criteria for setting up a targeted mailing might include: 1) Type of employer; 2) Geographic location; 3) Size of employer; 4) Hiring history, e.g., have they hired Americans with your background?

You may want to start with a targeted mailing to 20 employers. Try to get your package to a specific person who manages a department in which you would like to work (you could also send the same package to personnel). Each package will require an individualized cover letter (see the section on cover letters in Chapter 5) and follow-up. You need to be persistent but polite when you do follow-up. To get an idea of which organizations and people to target, talk to your contacts, use library resources, directories, and chambers of commerce.

Step 10. Follow job listing leads.

Job openings are advertised in a variety of locations, and you should take advantage of all of them. They include local newspapers, employment agencies, professional organization newsletters, and the job bulletins. International positions are frequently advertised in the *Economist,* the *International Herald Tribune,* and other publications serving the international business community.

Step 11. Follow up on all calls and letters; keep talking with people.

Maintain your communication with anyone who can assist you in your job search. Also, be sure and keep up your contacts within any company to which you apply. Employers are more likely to treat you seriously if you promise to follow up on your initial calls or letters. They are less likely to shove your resume under a stack of personnel files if you make it clear that you will be calling back soon. Also, the more contact you can establish without seeming pushy, the more likely you are to be remembered. Follow-up phone calls to Asia from the United States, however, are difficult and expensive.

The international phone call

The international phone call is not much more difficult than a normal long distance call. There are two ways to make one: dialing direct or with operator assistance. The former requires that you have a long distance carrier. In that case, merely dial: **011 + Country Code + City Code + local number.** To make an operator-assisted call, dial: **01 + Country Code + City Code + local number.** Not all phone numbers listed in this book include the country codes. The following is a list of country codes and major city codes.

	Country Code	City Code
America Samoa	684	
Australia	61	
Brisbane		7
Melbourne		3
Sydney		2
Chile	56	
Fiji	679	
French Polynesia	689	
Hong Kong	852	
Hong Kong		5
Kowloon		3
Indonesia	62	
Japan	81	
Kobe		78
Kyoto		75
Tokyo		3
Korea, South	82	
Seoul		2
Malaysia	60	
Kuala Lampoor		3
Pusan		51
Mexico	52	
Mexico City		5
Monterrey		83
New Zealand	64	
Auckland		9
Wellington		4
Nicaragua	505	
Panama	507	
Papua New Guinea	675	
Philippines	63	
Singapore	65	
Taiwan	86	
Taipei		2
Thailand	66	
Bangkok		2
U.S.S.R.	7	■

Step 12. Go to the Pacific and pound the pavement

There is no substitute for interviews in person. No matter how professional your resume is, it can only help your chances of securing a job if you establish personal contact. By visiting the companies in person, you will impress them with the seriousness of your interest in working with them. Also, if you have the opportunity to visit the organizations you are interested in, you will have a better idea of where you would or would not feel comfortable working. Going to the Pacific Rim without a job, however, should be a last resort move. Being in a far-away country without a job and getting rejections can be very depressing.

The International Interview

After going through all of these steps you should come to the point where you are invited to interview. But getting a job in the Pacific Rim will many times not necessitate interviewing at all. You may live across the ocean, but many will trust that your written credentials represent you well. If you are looking for work with a corporation with offices in the United States, a representative from their American office may interview you. Finally, a lucky few may be flown in for an interview, though this does not happen often. No matter how you are interviewed, you must be prepared to represent yourself in the best way possible. If you reach the interview stage, the job is yours—providing the interview goes well.

Because of travel constraints in the international job search, the phone interview can play a very crucial role in your chances of securing employment. It is to your advantage to practice well ahead of time what you intend to say so that you will sound smooth and articulate over the phone, for the prospective employer's impression of you will rest almost solely on your verbal communication skills. You should have a quiet place to speak from, with no noises, distractions, or potential interruptions to break the flow of your interview. It is a good idea to write down what you want to say so you don't forget anything. Also write down points to bring up in case the employer poses any questions. Questions asked during the phone interview will probably be the same as during a regular interview.

The purpose of an interview is to give you and an employer the opportunity to evaluate each other. The interview should be an active two-way exchange of information. The interviewer wants to evaluate your personality in terms of the position and the organization. You, the one being interviewed, can use the interview to find out if the position interests you, to "sell" yourself by highlighting your positive points, and to gain a job offer. Remember that the employer wants to hire you if you can convince him/her that you are right for the job.

QUALITIES ON WHICH YOU ARE EVALUATED

These are some qualities on which a typical interviewer might evaluate you:

1. Personal appearance—A neat, attractive appearance makes a good impression and demonstrates professionalism.

2. Work experience—If you have had work experience, be able to articulate its value and how it might relate to the job you are applying for. Even if the work experience is unrelated to your field, employers look upon knowledge of the work environment as an asset.

3. Education—The importance of degrees and grades varies from organization to organization. Be prepared, however, to answer questions about your academic background and explain deficiencies.

4. Verbal communication skills—The ability to express yourself articulately is very important to most interviewers. This includes the ability to listen effectively, verbalize thoughts clearly, and express yourself confidently.

5. General personality qualities—Poise, sincerity, enthusiasm, self-confidence, maturity, and motivation are valued by most employers. Of course, depending on the personality of the organization and the available position, some of these qualities may be stressed more than others.

6. Skills—The interviewer will evaluate your skills for the job, such as organization, analysis, and research. It is important to emphasize the skills that you feel the employer is seeking and to give specific examples of how you developed them. This is the main reason why it is important to engage in self-assessment prior to the interview.

7. Goals/Motivation—Employers will assess your ability to articulate your short-term and long-term goals. You should seem ambitious, yet realistic about the training and qualifications needed to advance. You should demonstrate interest in the functional area or industry and a desire to succeed and work hard.

BEFORE THE INTERVIEW

- Identify your strengths, skills, goals, and personal qualities. This self-assessment is crucial to knowing what you have to offer an employer and being able to convey that to him/her.
- Research the organization by reading annual reports and other literature. This will demonstrate that you are sincerely interested in the position and will enable you to ask intelligent questions. An interview is supposed to be a dialogue; you want to learn about them just as they want to learn about you.
- Rehearse what you plan to say during the interview. Practice answers to commonly asked questions and determine how you will emphasize your strengths and skills.
- Dress professionally and conservatively. If you make a negative first impression you may not be fairly considered for the job. Women should wear a tailored suit or dress. Limit jewelry and cosmetics and keep hair neat. Men should wear a suit and tie, with hair, beard/mustache trimmed.

- Also, keep in mind that if you are applying for work in the Pacific Rim, your employer may ask you some questions about the country in which you might be working. It is a good idea to do some research about the region, its customs, people, political situations, etc. You might want to pick up an English copy of a recent newspaper from the area so you will have a bit of small talk to draw from. Anything that will make you sound informed about the area will make you appear as a serious job candidate and give you an advantage.

DURING THE INTERVIEW

- Make sure that you arrive for your interview on time or a few minutes early. That will ensure you the amount of time planned.
- Greet the interviewer by his or her last name, offer a firm handshake and a warm smile.
- Be aware of your non-verbal behavior. Wait to sit until you are offered a chair. Sit straight, look alert, speak clearly and forcefully but stay relaxed, make good eye contact, avoid nervous mannerisms, and try to be a good listener as well as a good talker. Smile.
- Follow the interviewer's lead, but try to get the interviewer to describe the position and duties to you fairly early in the interview so that you can later relate your background and skills in context.
- Be specific, concrete, and detailed in your answers. The more information you volunteer, the better the employer gets to know you and thereby is able to make a wise hiring decision.
- Do not mention salary in a first interview unless the employer does. If asked, give a realistic range and add that the opportunity is the most important factor for you.
- Offer examples of your work and references that will document your best qualities.
- Answer questions as truthfully and as frankly as you can. Do not appear to be "glossing over" anything. On the other hand, stick to the point and do not over-answer questions. The interviewer may steer the interview into ticklish political or social questions. Answer honestly, trying not to say more than is necessary.
- Do not ever make derogatory remarks about present or former employers or companies.

CLOSING THE INTERVIEW

- Don't be discouraged if no definite offer is made or specific salary discussed.
- If you get the impression that the interview is not going well and that you have already been rejected, do not let your discouragement show. Once in a while, an interviewer who is

genuinely interested in you may seem to discourage you to test your reaction.

- A typical interviewer comment toward the close of an interview is to ask if you have any questions. Do not just say "no." Keep a question in mind to ask. If that question has been answered in the course of the interview, refer to it, saying that it has now been answered to your satisfaction.
- At the conclusion of the interview, ask when a hiring decision will be made. Also, thank your interviewer for his or her time and express your interest in the position.

After the interview, make notes on what you feel you could improve upon for your next interview. If you are offered the position on the spot, it is not unreasonable to ask for a few days or a week's time to make your decision if you are undecided.

QUESTIONS YOU MAY BE ASKED DURING AN INTERVIEW

Bear in mind that all questions you are asked during an interview serve a specific purpose. Try to put yourself in the interviewer's shoes—imagine why he or she is asking the questions, and try to provide the answers that are most desirable. Direct your responses toward the particular position for which you are applying. Here follow some questions that employers often ask those being interviewed. It is advisable to rehearse answers to these questions prior to your interview so you can appear relaxed and confident.

1. Ice breakers—These are designed to put you at ease and to see how well you engage in informal conversation. Be yourself, act natural, and be friendly.

a. Did you have any trouble finding your way here?
b. How was your plane flight?
c. I see you come from Omaha. Why do you want to work in New Zealand?
d. Can you believe this weather?

2. Education and work history—These are to assess if your background and skills are appropriate for the position. Talk about your skills coherently and relate them to the job to be filled. Give specific examples of how you used skills in the past. Also, remember that questions you are asked concerning your past will help the employer determine how you might react and make decisions in the future.

a. Tell me about yourself.
b. Why did you choose to get a history degree?
c. How will your degree help you in an overseas position?
d. How has your education reflected your desire to work overseas?

e. Tell me about your grades, overall and in your concentration.
f. In what activities have you participated outside of class?
g. Tell me what you know about the customs and culture of this country.
h. Tell me about any experiences you have had living or working overseas.
i. Tell me about the most satisfying job/internship you ever held.
j. What have you learned from some of the jobs you've held?
k. What are you looking for in an employer?
l. What are you seeking in a position?

3. Ambitions and plans—These are questions to evaluate the degree of your ambition, how clearly you have thought about your future goals, their feasibility, and how actively you seek to meet them.

a. Are you a joiner or a loner? A leader or a follower? A committee member or chairperson?
b. What job in our company would you choose if you were free to do so?
c. How much money do you hope to earn in five years? Ten years?
d. What does success mean to you? How do you judge it?
e. Assuming you are hired for this job, what do you see as your future?
f. What personal characteristics are necessary for success in this field?
g. Will you fight to get ahead?
h. Are you willing to prove yourself as a staff member of our firm? How do you envision your role?
i. Are you willing to work overtime?
j. Where do you see yourself five years from now? Ten years?

4. Company or organization—These questions are to determine if you have conscientiously researched the company and if you would be a "match" for them. They also indicate your interest in the company.

a. Do you prefer working for a small or large organization?
b. What kind of work are you interested in doing for us?
c. What do you know about our organization?
d. Do you prefer a private or non-private organization? Why?
e. Why did you choose to interview with us?
f. What do you feel our organization has to offer you? What do you feel you have to offer us?

5. Values and self-assessment—These help the interviewer get to know you better and to determine how well you understand yourself. They also help to inform the interviewer of what motivates you.

a. What kinds of personal satisfactions do you hope to gain through work?
b. If you had unlimited funds, what would you do? Where would you live?
c. What motivates you?
d. What are your strengths and weaknesses?
e. How would you describe yourself?
f. What do you enjoy doing in your free time?
g. What kind of people do you like to work with?
h. How do you adapt to other cultures?

Thank-you letters

This type of letter should be written following each interview. The letter may be brief, but it should express your appreciation for the interview, mention some key points that were discussed, reiterate your continued interest in the possibility of employment, and indicate your desire that your candidacy receive favorable consideration. Try to state one or two additional reasons, not covered in the interview, why you would be an asset if hired. A thank-you letter should be written within two days of the initial interview. Make sure you know the name, title, and correct address of the person who interviewed you.

Dear Mr. Calvin Dundee:

Thank you for the time spent and the information given in our interview yesterday. Talking with you further supported my interest in__________ Company. I am even more certain that__________is the field in which I can make a sustained contribution and that____________ is the company that offers the best opportunities for me.

I look forward to hearing from you soon. Thank you again for your insights.

Sincerely,■

AFTER THE INTERVIEW

The interview is over and now the waiting begins. Try not to be too impatient, and remember that, for the time being, no answer is better than a rejection. There could be many reasons why you have not heard from the company. It could be that the interview process has not concluded or that other commitments have kept the company from making a decision.

The most important point to remember during this time is that all your hopes should not be placed on one or two interviews. The job search is continuous and should not stop until you have accepted a job offer. Keeping all your options open is the best plan possible.

However, if much time has passed and you have not heard anything from a company in which you are particularly interested, a telephone call or letter asking about the status of your application is appropriate. This inquiry should be stated in a manner that is not pushy but shows your continued interest in the company. Remember that waiting is natural, yet a demonstration of your continued interest is appropriate.

The rejection. When you receive a rejection letter or phone call, as everyone does at one time or another in the job-hunt process, evaluate the reasons why you may have received it. Did you not receive an offer because you were really not suited for the position? Perhaps your job search should be more specifically designed and targeted. Were you rejected because your personal and professional goals were different from those of the company? Make sure, as you prepare for each interview, that you have realistic expectations regarding initial positions and career paths. Could it be that you simply did not interview well? Perhaps you were not well enough prepared or you were a bit preoccupied that day. In that case, you could benefit from feedback regarding your interviewing skills. Try a mock interview with a career counselor or a friend. Do not let a rejection get you down; if you learn from one job interview, the next may be more successful.

The Offer. When you receive a job offer, consider the following in making your decision: make sure the details of the offer are clear, preferably, put in writing. Details should include starting date, salary, responsibilities, location, and the date by which you must respond.

Evaluating job offers. Evaluating a job offer can be both exciting and difficult. It can be exciting in the sense that the long job search may be coming to an end, and difficult because you must decide if the position offered is really what you have been looking for. In deciding whether to accept an offer, reflect on your original reasons for being interested in this company. Carefully evaluate what your job requirements will be. Think also how this position will affect your future and whether it is consistent with your long-term goals. Finally, review the criteria that are most significant to you and evaluate if the company can satisfy them. These include salary, geographic location, work culture, co-workers, working conditions, educational opportunities, and opportunities for advancement.

In deciding whether a company can satisfy your needs, refer back to your interviews and the things that were discussed. Research all the available literature about the company that you can find. Finally, if at all possible, talk with people in the company about working there. After studying the opportunities, evaluate whether your personality matches the company personality. That can sometimes be the most important factor in making your decision.

Response date. Make sure the response date gives you time to complete negotiations with other potential employers if possible. Up to two weeks is generally considered a reasonable response time. Once you are made an offer, you can call other employers with whom you are still dealing and explain the situation and ask them how quickly they can let you know of their decisions. You may have to make a decision before you have complete information on all possible job offers. However, you should only accept an offer if you really intend to stick with it. Remember, if the company to which you are applying is based in the Pacific Rim, it will take longer for your acceptance letter to reach the organization within the acceptable time, so you may have to send it a bit earlier. Faxing communications, of course, can save significant time at both ends.

Starting date. Companies with formal training programs have set starting dates. However, with many other employers you can negotiate a start date that is acceptable to both of you. If you want to take a vacation before starting, try to arrange it before accepting the offer.

Negotiating for time. The time may come when you receive a job offer for which you are just not ready. It could be that you need more time to decide, or that you are interested in hearing from another company before you accept this offer. When that happens, you are ready to negotiate for more time. There are a few cautionary notes in asking for extra time. Never ask for an extension if you are not interested in the organization; not only is this unethical but it keeps the organization from hiring another person. Also, remember that asking for too much time puts the organization in a vulnerable position and disrupts its hiring process, again keeping other people from being hired.

If your reason for asking for an extension is to consider other organizations that hold your interest, immediately contact those organizations, informing them of your job offer and mentioning that you are still interested in their organization. After hearing from you, they may choose to speed up their interviewing process. You must remember, however, that this will only happen if they have flexibility and a very strong interest in you.

A job search requires persistence, organization, and aggressiveness. It is one of the most challenging, frustrating, and ultimately rewarding tasks we all face. No one can conduct your job search but *you*—there are resources to help, but you need to take the ultimate responsibility. And once you obtain a job, you will feel tremendous satisfaction knowing that you made it happen!

The International Resume

The Basics of the International Resume

The international resume is no different from any other resume in its main objective: a selling tool that attempts to get you a job or an interview. Most of the components of the international resume are the same as any resume that you would use in the United States. The difference is that you must stress those points that make you unique in an international market. Internationally, many people are accustomed to resumes that are long and tell a life story. However, the short one or two-page version, with selected highlighted information areas, is becoming increasingly popular. This type of resume should focus on the information you wish to put across to the prospective employer. Within the resume, try to stress every aspect of your experience and education that might make you valuable to the employer.

The purpose of a resume is to concisely tell an employer:

- Who you are
- What you have done
- What you do
- What you can do

Your resume is designed to advertise your skills, experiences, and accomplishments to an employer. It plays an important role in your job search and therefore should be carefully prepared. The amount of attention given to your resume will alert an employer to the kind of care you will demonstrate on the job. Remember, the ultimate objective of your resume is to get you an interview. Often, in the international search it can lead to a job without the interview. If it does, it has been successful.

Resume Format

Even though there are some important rules for resume writing, there is no one "right" style or format. You can choose a format that works well for you and that you find appealing. Employers will not read your resume; they will skim it. Therefore, make sure it is presented in a clear and concise manner.

Some general format "tips" for all resumes:

- Use one-inch margins on all sides
- Place material in order of importance
- Use a reverse chronological sequence
- Underline or capitalize important points
- Fit the resume on one page unless you have a long work history

Here are some additional "helpful hints" for your resume:

- Use the jargon of your profession
- Stress your assets; downplay your liabilities
- Use the present tense for current experiences and the past tense for previous experiences
- Write in telegraphic style; avoid using personal pronouns
- Avoid abbreviations; write everything out in full
- Have clear copies made on good quality bond paper
- Proofread carefully for grammatical, spelling, or typographical errors
- Have the draft of your resume reviewed by a friend or someone in the field before making a final copy

There are a number of different methods for composing a quality resume. Every career counselor and resume compiler has his or her own favorite method and style. As the person being represented by the resume, *you* must choose the style and format that best suits and sells you. Many resume books will use different terms for the various styles. We will highlight the three most popular types.

1. **The chronological resume** is the traditional style most often used in the workplace and job search; that does not mean it is the most effective. Positive aspects of the chronological resume include the traditionalist approach that employers may expect. It also can highlight past positions that you may wish your potential employer to notice. This resume is also very adaptable, with only the reverse chronological order of items as the essential ingredient.

2. **The functional resume** is most common among career changers, people reentering the job market after a lengthy absence, and those wishing to highlight aspects of their experience not related directly to employment. This resume ideally focuses on the many skills one has used at his or her employment and the accomplishments one has achieved. It shows a potential employer that you can do and have done a good job. What it doesn't highlight is where you have done it.

3. **The combination resume** combines the best features of a functional resume and a chronological resume. This allows job seekers to highlight skills and accomplishments while maintaining the somewhat traditional format of reverse chronological order of positions held and organizations worked for.

Contents of an International Resume

Organize and present your resume material as briefly and clearly as possible. Evaluate and emphasize your assets. Following are the general content areas that should be included. They need not be in this order but should be in an order that shows your strengths.

Name, Address, Phone: This information should be at the top of the page. If you list two addresses or phone numbers, label them appropriately. Include the area codes with your phone numbers. Make sure that you include a phone number where employers can reach you or leave a message for you during their work day. It would be a good idea to find out what the individual employer's time zone is so you know just when their work day starts and ends in relation to your time zone.

Professional Objective: This is optional, especially if you are including a cover letter in which you specifically tailor your career objective to the job for which you are applying. You may want to use a few different resumes, highlighting different objectives. If you do choose to include an objective, write one that is concise and specific.

Education: Degrees expected or received should appear in reverse chronological order with their dates, names and locations of the institutions, and concentrations or major field of studies. Grade point averages should be included if they enhance your presentation and are recent. If appropriate, you may also include academic honors, awards, and extracurricular activities in this section; these will indicate to your employer that you are a self-initiator who excels in whatever you undertake.

Experience: This is probably the most important section of your resume. Use action words and avoid phrases like "my duties included" or "my responsibilities were." In addition to describing duties, mention special skills or accomplishments. Your work experience should be listed in reverse chronological order and should include job titles, dates of employment, names and locations of employers. Include volunteer work here if it is career related.

International Experience: State anything that will show your exposure to and experience in international work or culture.

Languages: Here you want to stress your knowledge of languages. If you are fluent in, have a working knowledge of, or simply have studied a foreign language, you want to mention it. Any exposure at all is a plus. Do not, however, exaggerate. For instance, if you claim to be fluent in a language but are not, you will be sorely embarrassed the first time your prospective employer calls on the phone and attempts to carry on a conversation with you. Most international employers, unless the job specifically requires complete fluency in another tongue, will be concerned mainly that you have had some experience in a language and/or are trying to acquire conversational skills (e.g., taking courses at a language school).

Research Activities: This is optional. However, if it is an asset for the job you are applying for, include it. Be specific and include the project title, employer, and activities.

Additional Information: This can include hobbies, foreign languages, volunteer work, memberships, awards, travel. Remember that your resume is only one page, so only include information that will enhance your presentation. For example, include foreign travel since you are applying for international jobs.

References: Do not list references by name, but you can include a statement that "references will be available upon request." Remember that employers usually value references from your past employers the most. Make sure you receive permission before using anyone as a reference.

Active Verbs: Here is a partial list of active verbs useful in resume writing:

Administering: a department of people; programs; a specific activity, such as a test

Analyzing: quantitative data, statistical data, human/social situations

Appraising: evaluating programs or services, judging the value of property, evaluating performance of individuals

Budgeting: outlining costs of a project, assuring that money will not be spent in excess of funds, using money efficiently and economically

Compiling: gathering numerical, statistical data; accumulating facts in a given topic area

Controlling: exercising financial control, crowd behavior, children, environmental control

Coordinating: numerous events involving groups of people, quantities of information, activities in several locations, events in a time sequence

Creating: artistically (visual arts, etc.); new ideas for an organization; new ways to solve mechanical problems; inventing new apparatus, equipment

Dealing with pressure: risks toward self, physical and otherwise; risks toward others; time pressure, deadlines for getting work done

Delegating: distributing tasks to others, giving responsibility to others on a work team

Distributing: products to people personally; marketing products, making them available to customers

Editing: newspaper, magazine pieces, book manuscripts, etc.

Estimating: judging likely costs of an operation, projecting possibilities of future income, judging physical space accurately

Evaluating: assessing a program to determine its success, judging the performance of an individual

Imagining: new ways of dealing with old problems, theoretical relationships, artistic ideas or perspectives

Initiating: personal contacts with strangers; new ideas, ways of doing things; new approaches

Interpreting: other languages, obscure phrases or passages in English, meaning of statistical data, relative import of situations

Interviewing: evaluating applicants for organizations, obtaining information from others

Investigating: seeking information that may be hard to obtain, seeking the underlying causes of a problem

Listening: to conversations between others, to extended conversation from one person to recording devices, to instructions

Managing: being responsible for the work of others, having responsibility for the processing of information, guiding activities of a team, having responsibility for meeting objectives of an organization or department

Monitoring: following progress of another person, observing progress of equipment or apparatus

Negotiating: financial contracts, between individuals or groups

Planning: anticipating future needs of a company or organization, scheduling a sequence of events, arranging an itinerary for a trip

Processing: the orderly flow of data and/or information, introducing an individual to the routines and procedures of an organization, identifying human interactions taking place in a group, channeling information through a system

Programming: for computers, developing and arranging a sequence of events

Promoting: through written media; on a personal level, one-to-one; arranging financial backing

Recruiting: attempting to acquire the services of people

Researching: extracting information from library, archives, etc.; obtaining information for other people (surveys); obtaining information from physical data

Reviewing: observing, inspecting, summarizing a collection of documents, information, etc.; assessing effects of a program; assessing performance of an individual

Selling: convincing an individual or organization to purchase or accept a product, service, idea, policy

Speaking: addressing an audience, individual, or group in person or through electronic media

Supervising: holding direct responsibility over the work of others, final responsibility; overseeing the maintenance of a physical plant, building, etc.

Teaching: instructing students in an academic setting; training individuals to perform certain tasks; familiarizing or orienting people in the context of a given system

Translating: expressing words of one language in another language; reducing sophisticated language to simpler terms

Troubleshooting: finding sources of difficulty in human relations, systems, or physical apparatus

Writing: copywriting for sales; creative writing; reports or memos

Sample international resumes follow.

Sample Resume #1—Chronological

Matthew J. Roberts
5411 Grand Street
Washington, DC 20052
(202) 555-0909

EDUCATION

Georgetown University, Washington, DC
M.B.A., May 1991
Concentration in Marketing
Extensive Coursework in International Business
Chair of International Society

Northern Illinois University, DeKalb, Illinois
B.A. Economics, May 1987
Presidential Scholar, cum laude
Coursework in International Relations

EXPERIENCE

PROFESSIONAL ASSISTANT, **Price Waterhouse,** Houston, Texas.
Participated in a summer internship aimed at M.B.A. students entering their second year. Assisted management in auditing and accounting affairs.
May 1990-August 1990.

MARKETING ASSISTANT, **Health and Fitness Magazine,** Chicago, Illinois.
Initiated a new marketing strategy to increase circulation of the magazine in the Chicago restaurant community.
August 1989-April 1990.

COMPUTER CONSULTANT, **Northern Illinois University,** DeKalb, Illinois.
Advised students in the usage of Microsoft Word and other software programs on the Macintosh SE.
January 1988-July 1989.

INTERNATIONAL ACTIVITIES

Speak Indonesian and Dutch; elementary knowledge of Malay and Swedish
Have traveled throughout Southeast Asia and Indonesia

LEADERSHIP ACTIVITIES

Youth City Representative in the P.W. Williams Campaign for Governor
President of Student Government
Tutor for Student Volunteer Program

Sample Resume # 2—Functional

Virginia Elisabet Baker
111 Kent Street
Yakima, Washington 00030
(823) 555-1313

CAREER OBJECTIVE

Seeking a position as an English teacher.

AREAS OF EXPERTISE

Interpersonal/Communication Skills

- Conducted 20-30 parent-teacher conferences per month
- Counseled individual students as needed
- Supervised and advised one student teacher per semester for three years
- Interviewed applicants for employment; provided supervision and training
- Successfully sold and marketed merchandise to customers
- Served in leadership capacity with educational association

International

- Speak French and elementary Japanese
- Volunteered for 2 months in Micronesia
- Lived in Auckland for one year during high school

Planning

- Initiated and executed seminars and meetings
- Developed lesson plans for all subjects taught
- Assisted with leadership goals of the school and district
- Planned and developed educational programs for in-service teacher groups

EXPERIENCE

Teacher, fourth grade, Yakima School District, Yakima, Wahington, 1987-present.
Assistant Manager, The Limited, Seattle, Washington, 1985-87 (summers).
Administrative Aide, Shearson Brothers, Portland, Oregon, 1983-85 (summers).

EDUCATION

University of Washington, Seattle, Washington
B.S., Elementary Education, 1987
G.P.A. 3.7/4.0
Honors/Activities—Dean's List, 3 semesters; Drab Hall Vice-President

Sample Resume # 3—Combination

Ellen C. Tzatziki
100 Charles Street
Houston, TX 77306
(713) 555-1000

OBJECTIVE: A computer programming related position, preferably utilizing software engineering skills.

EDUCATION: **University of South Florida,** Tampa, Florida
GPA 3.5/4.0
B.S., Computer Science, 5/83

QUALIFICATIONS: **Career-related projects:**

- Designed and implemented multi-tasking operating system for the IBM-PC.
- Implemented compiler for Pascal-like language.
- Designed electronic mail system using PSL/PSA specification language.
- Designed menu-based interface for beginning UNIX users.

Computer languages and operating systems:

- Proficient in **Ada, Modula-2, Pascal, COBOL.**
- Familiar with C, Fortran, Lisp, Prolog, dBaseIII, SQL, QBE.
- Working knowledge of IBM-PC hardware and 8088 assembly language.
- Experienced in **UNIX, MS-DOS, XENIX, CP/M** operating systems.

Hardware:

- IBM-PC (MS-DOS,Xenix), Pyramid 90x (UNIX), Cyber 990 (NOS),
- Data General MV/10000 (UNIX,AOS/VS)

International:

- Speak Japanese and Spanish
- Have traveled throughout Japan and South America
- Lived in Lima, Peru, for one year

WORK EXPERIENCE:

Gonzalez Programming Services, Houston, TX, 10/86-Present

- **UNIX Programmer**—Responsible for porting MS-DOS database applications to IBM-PC/AT; running Xenix System V; system administration.

Wortham Arts Center, Houston, TX, 11/83-9/86

- **Computer Programmer**—Performed daily disk backup on Burroughs B-1955 machine. Executed database update programs and checks. User assistance.
- From 8/81 to 11/83, held full-time positions as **Box Manager and Accountant** for arts organization in Tampa.

REFERENCES: Furnished upon request.

Sample Resume #4—Chronological

Hunter E. Stone
8423 Hearth,
White Plains, New York 00090
(714) 555-5309

CAREER OBJECTIVE

Position in economic analysis and management with a multinational firm.

EDUCATION

Columbia University, School of International and Public Affairs. Master's degree in International Econometrics, May 1991.
Specialization: East Asia.

Emory University, Atlanta, Georgia.
Bachelor's degree in Econometrics, May 1987.

RELEVANT COURSE WORK

Financial Management and Statistical Analysis.
International Trade Analysis.

EXPERIENCE

Hong Kong and Shanghai Bank, Hong Kong, Summer 1990.
Assisted in Central Office, International Division, North America.
Responsible for learning Asian and U.S. banking rules, Euromarket instruments and activities, and aiding team members on correspondence and investment banking projects dealing with U.S. banks and corporations.

Emory University, Atlanta, Georgia, 1986-87.
Teaching Assistant. Taught first semester micro- and macroeconomics courses.

ADDITIONAL INFORMATION

Knowledge of Lotus 1-2-3, SPSSPC+, and Wordprocessing packages.

LANGUAGES

Fair knowledge of Mandarin.

References Available Upon Request

Sample Resume #5—Chronological

Catherine J. Seymore
6807 Biffkin Boulevard
Narberth, Pennsylvania 87675
(713) 555-4055

Objective Position in International Banking

Experience

CHASE MANHATTAN, Asia Pacific Group, New York, York
Banking Associate: 1990-present
Developed marketing strategy for Japanese institutional and corporate clients.
Formatted department's cost structure and expenses on budget on Lotus 1-2-3.
Assessed investment implications of recent changes in Chinese tax law.
Researched bank's competitive position vis-a-vis Japanese banks in U.S. markets.

BUDGET HOTELS, Ltd., Auckland, New Zealand
Consultant: March 1985-July 1989
Analyzed cost and pricing structure of unprofitable hotel restaurant.
Conducted profit feasibility study of private sector hospital.
Designed and executed audio/visual sales presentations to corporate clients.

MELBOURNE TOOLS, Sydney, Australia
Marketing Intern: July 1984-February 1985
Designed two-year strategy for welding machine sales to U.S. market.
Promoted products at trade shows in U.S. and Australia.

AIESEC-OHIO, International Exchange Program
President: 1983; **Director of Corporate Fundraising:** 1982
Launched sales campaign resulting in 15 internships for foreign and American students.
Raised $5,000 in corporate contributions.

Education	**Harvard University, Graduate School of Business Administration,** Cambridge, Massachusetts Master of International Affairs: May 1990 MBA in International Finance and Banking, 1990
	Rice University, Houston, Texas **Bachelor of Arts** in English: May, 1984 National Merit Scholarship, four years Semester abroad: University of East Anglia, England and American literature
Languages	Spanish, beginning Japanese.

The Cover Letter

The cover letter is a valuable—often crucial—part of your job-hunting campaign. This letter, along with your resume, serves to introduce you to a potential employer and to develop sufficient interest in you to warrant a personal interview.

While every letter should be a creative effort and individually written, there are generally accepted standard features of a cover letter. It should be addressed to a particular person. It should be short (one page at most) and concise, designed to be read by a person with limited time. Cover letters should always be (or at least look) individually prepared.

The letters should be specifically tailored to the organization. Specific knowledge of the job requirements is a great help in writing the cover letter. With this knowledge, you can demonstrate exactly how your previous background, experience, or skills can be of value in meeting the requirements of the particular job. Of course, some "requirements" are universal: intelligence, aggressiveness, imagination, good interpersonal skills. These can be demonstrated either experientially (work) or inferentially (academic or community service achievements, interests, hobbies).

Contact the American affiliate of a particular company, if possible, by telephone to find out exactly where resumes should be sent. Also, if you do not want your resume put immediately into the inactive file, include in your cover letter words to the effect: "I will be contacting you within three weeks regarding...." In this way, you prompt a timely response; and if they do not respond, they should expect your follow-up.

Another method that often prompts a quick response is to "cc" a copy to the Department Head or Manager within the division you are interested in. This puts more responsibility on the recipient of your letter, letting them know that they will not be the only person in that organization to read it. In this way, your resume has a better chance of being acted upon.

Basics of the Cover Letter

First Paragraph: This is a quick introduction: who you are; why you are writing; how you heard of the opening; what position you seek; who suggested you write; or what it is about the organization that is motivating you to write.

Second Paragraph: Referring to your work and/or academic background, demonstrate why you are both interested and qualified for the position, the organization, or the field. Try not simply to repeat the resume but to amplify on the achievement aspects of your background—briefly! It is better to highlight how well you did something than just what you did. This may be your opportunity to "update" the resume with a new bit of activity (honors, projects, etc.)

Third Paragraph: The concluding paragraph is the action you wish to see taken. Specifically, you would like to meet with the person you have written to in order to discuss your background in a personal interview. You have several options on how to manage this. You can await a written or phoned reply or you can follow up with a phone call yourself. The cover letter/resume, followed by a phone call is most aggressive and direct and is more likely to lead to an interview. The phone call is particularly appropriate to local offices of organizations, where travel will not be a problem. If you are writing a distant company and are planning to be in the area, let them know this. However, organizations usually will not pick up your expenses merely on the basis of a letter and a resume.

Sample Cover Letter # 1

69 Mountain View
Portland, Oregon 50444
July 18, 1991

Mr. Lee Chien
Manager, International Division
Asian Investments International
77 Gong Yuan Road
Taipei, Taiwan

Dear Mr. Chien:

I am currently Assistant Finance Manager for the Bank of the Northwest in Portland Oregon. In reading the *Asian Wall Street Journal* of March 16, 1991, I learned about the expansion of your international division, in which I would like to work.

As part of my responsibilities I have worked in a number of relevant areas including marketing, accounting, and finance. After graduating from the MBA program at Stanford University, I held positions at Citicorp and AT&T. Both of these positions and my current one have strengthened my understanding of international markets and finance. I have also lived abroad in Australia, studied Japanese business, and speak elementary Chinese.

I am enthusiastic and hardworking and would welcome the opportunity to apply my skills at your corporation, in your international division. I will call you in a few weeks to discuss my application further. In the interim, feel free to call me at (545) 555-5454.

Thank you for your consideration.

Sincerely,

Donald X. Anderson

Enclosure

Sample Cover Letter #2

April 9,1991
912 East 37th Street
Chicago, Illinois 60664
(312) 555-5454

Ms. Claudia Roy
Recruiting Coordinator
International Bank of Australia
CBA Center, 29 Level
60 Margaret St.
Sydney, New South Wales 2000
Australia

Dear Ms. Roy:

I am currently a senior at Northwestern University and am specializing in international business and finance. I am writing to express interest in a banking position with IBA.

At Northwestern I have focused on preparing myself for the world of international finance. My coursework includes the basic tools of business, accounting and financial analysis. Other coursework includes the international aspects of trade, economics, and foreign policy analysis.

As can be seen in my resume, I also have strong experience in working in a research environment and have successfully managed numerous projects involving the supervision of personnel.

Again, I would like to express my interest in a position with IBA and assure you of my ability to perform well. I look forward to hearing from you soon and giving you a chance to assess for yourself my qualifications. I will be calling you within the next two weeks regarding the position. Thank you for your consideration.

Sincerely,

Joshua B. Cyr

6 International Placement Organizations

The thought that an international placement agency can find you a job overseas without going through all the hassle of finding the job yourself may sound enticing. But exercise caution when using this route. Many placement agencies are legitimate and can offer you much needed help in locating an international job as well as help maneuvering through the necessary paperwork. However, not all of these organizations should be trusted. This is especially true of those that are private and make their money solely from people wishing to work overseas.

International placement organizations run the gamut from executive search firms, which specialize in high-level business people with experience and special skills, to non-profit organizations, which specialize in placing students in summer jobs abroad. Whatever your own situation might be, check into these organizations for what they can offer you before you sign up.

Most agencies will charge a fee to cover the cost of locating employment or obtaining required papers and related materials. Some of this help is well worth the minor cost. Paying $75 to receive working papers is money very well spent. But when asked to pay $500 to $5,000, you should start looking elsewhere. Before using any placement agency, always find out what you are getting in return for your money and always ask for a placement list of where they have previously placed people. Non-profit organizations such as the CIEE are very trustworthy and helpful, but private organizations should be examined more closely to determine fees and success ratios.

The ideal placement agency would be one that does not charge any fee for services and obtains a number of possibilities for you in the Pacific Rim. Unfortunately, these do not exist. Placement agencies can do some of the job-search work, but almost always at a price. There are basically two types of for-profit placement organizations: executive search firms and private placement agencies.

Executive Search Firms

Executive search firms cater to the business professional or engineer with specific skills and a good deal of experience. The placement fee is usually paid by the firm doing the hiring. Executive search firms can give you an idea of your value in the Pacific Rim and whether placement is possible. Because they are paid by the hiring organization, they will not usually waste their time with someone they can not place. It is probably an excellent idea not to use a search firm if they ask you for a fee; you will get further on your own and at much less cost.

EXECUTIVE SEARCH FIRMS

Boyden International
260 Madison Ave.
New York, NY 10016
Tel.: (212) 685-3400
Contact main office for branch addresses. Must apply through branch office for placement.

Korn/Ferry International
1800 Century Park E., Suite 900
Los Angeles, CA 90067
Tel.: (213) 879-1834
Offices in Australia, Hong Kong, Japan, Malaysia, and Singapore.

Heidrick and Struggles International
125 S. Wacker
Chicago, IL 60606
Tel.: (312) 372-8811

Ward Howell International
99 Park Ave.
New York, NY 10016
Tel.: (212) 697-3730

A. T. Kearney, Inc.
222 S. Riverside Plaza
Chicago, IL 60606
Tel.: (312) 648-0111

Lamalie Associates
13920 N. Dale Mabry
Tampa, FL 33618
Tel.: (813) 961-7494

Paul R. Ray & Co.
301 Commerce, Suite 2300
Fort Worth, TX 76102
Tel.: (817) 334-0500

Russell Reynolds
200 Park Ave.
New York, NY 10166
Tel.: (212) 351-2000

Spencer Stuart & Associates
401 N. Michigan, Suite 2525
Chicago, IL 60611
Tel.: (312) 822-0088

Private Placement Agencies

The agencies listed here operate like regular employment agencies, with the exception that they locate jobs internationally. Agencies that place people in summer and temporary positions are listed in Chapter 7. These positions include agricultural work, office and clerical positions, teaching English, and positions in resorts and tourism. Volunteer and other non-profit agencies are also listed in the same chapter as well as with the individual countries listings in Part II of this book. Opportunities for volunteers are available in areas such as conservation, development, and children's camps.

PLACEMENT AGENCIES IN THE U.S.

Dunhill Search International
59 Elm St.
New Haven, CT 06510
Tel.: (203) 562-0511

ESOL Placement Service
Center for Applied Linguistics
3520 Prospect St. N.W.
Washington DC 20007
Tel.: (202) 298-9292
For teaching professionals only.

Robert Half Employment Agency
3600 Wilshire Blvd.
Los Angeles, CA 90010
Tel.: (213) 386-6805

International Schools Services
P.O. Box 5910
Princeton, NJ 08543
Tel.: (609) 452-0990
International placement for certified teachers.

Pacific Rim Human Resources Services
690 Market St., Suite 625
San Francisco, CA
Tel.: (415) 956-6250

PLACEMENT ORGANIZATIONS IN THE PACIFIC RIM

Akamsa International
2nd Floor, Annex Bldg., Sen. Gil J. Puyat Ave.
Makati, Metropolitan Manila, Philippines
Tel.: 63 2 8185796

Alga Moher International Placement Services
1273 Batangas, Makati
Metropolitan Manila, Philippines
Tel.: 63 2 851398

Asia Central Employment Services
Goodwill Bldg., Makati
Metropolitan Manila, Philippines
Tel.: 63 2 8189006

Asia-World Recruitments
1807 San Marcelino
Metropolitan Manila, Philippines
Tel.: 63 2 595612

Bureau Group
Level 4, 8-12 Bridge St.
Sydney, New South Wales, Australia
Tel.: 61 2 2522722

FLB Enterprises
664 Quirino Hiway
Bagbag, Novaliches, Q.C., Philippines
Tel.: 63 905041
Fax: 63 63554

Gibsons Search International
69 Campbell St.
Sydney, New South Wales, Australia
Tel.: 61 2 2122777

International Nanny Network
2nd Floor, 97 William St.
Perth, Western Australia, Australia
Tel.: 61 9 3213343

La Cura Elsie T
Rm. 203-204 Aurora Plaza
Ermita, Metropolitan Manila, Philippines
Tel.: 63 2 500560

Persona/Japan Downunder
143 Brougham St.
Potts Point 2011, New South Wales, Australia
Tel.: 61 3562055
Recruits Japanese- and English-speaking people for positions with Japanese companies.

Prudential Employment Agency
8953 Aranga, Makati
Metropolitan Manila, Philippines
Tel.: 63 2 876808

Recruit Co. Ltd.
7-3-5 Ginza 8-chome
Chuo-ku, Tokyo 104, Japan
Tel.: 81 3 5751111

Southeast Asian Placement Center
1623 J. Bocobo
Metropolitan Manila, Philippines
Tel.: 63 2 500001

Staffbuilders International
Philcox Bldg., Makati
Metropolitan Manila, Philippines
Tel.: 63 2 850631

G Tongol Placement Services
Midland Plaza
Metropolitan Manila, Philippines
Tel.: 63 2 5212958

Unison International Management & Personnel Consultants
376 George
Brisbane, Queensland, Australia
Tel.: 61 7 2363066

Sources Listing International Job Openings

Many major newspapers and periodicals carry Pacific Rim job listings. These include the *Asian Wall Street Journal,* the *National Business Employment Weekly,* and *The Economist.* Journals within specific fields often carry international job listings as well. The international newsletter is another area that is worth exploring. Here are a just a few newsletters that list jobs overseas. You may want to write them, asking for their subscription rates, when the periodical is issued, and perhaps a sample copy.

ACCESS: Networking in the Public Interest
50 Beacon St.
Boston, MA 02108
Tel.: (617) 720-JOBS
Carries listings of international positions with non-profit organizations.

International Employment Hotline
Will Cantrell, Editor
P.O. Box 6170
McLean, VA 22106
Tel.: (703) 620-1972

International Jobs Bulletin
Frank Dlein, University Placement Center
Southern Illinois University at Carbondale
Carbondale, IL 62901
Tel.: (618) 453-2391

Job Opportunities Bulletin
Trancentury Recruitment Center
1724 Kalorama Rd. N.W.
Washington, DC 20009
Tel.: (202) 328-4486

Overseas Employment Newsletter
P.O. Box 460
Town of Mount Royal
Quebec H3P 3C7, Canada

Temporary and Summer Jobs in the Pacific Rim

Summer and temporary jobs are not all that easy to find in the Pacific Rim. Due to language barriers and unemployment in these countries, the prospects of finding something for only a short time are limited. However, with persistence and forethought, jobs can be found. In almost each of the Pacific Rim countries, employment must be obtained before a working visa or permit is issued to allow you to enter the country for employment purposes. Otherwise, you may be required to show proof of either return or onward transportation and possession of enough currency for the duration of your stay. The regulations of individual countries regarding employment and visas for Americans can be found in the country-by-country listings in Part II of this book.

Unofficial temporary work is always an option for the summer traveler who can find it. Such opportunities allow you to bypass the cumbersome bureaucratic restrictions for gaining employment and sometimes avoid local taxes and deductions. But be warned: if you accept unofficial work, you also forfeit any rights to governmental protection and may be prey to exploitative practices from employers. If such a situation occurs, for example, your employer fails to pay you, your options for recompense are very limited.

Temporary Jobs in the Pacific Rim by Occupation

AGRICULTURAL WORK

Although agricultural work is demanding and laborious, it is usually easily obtained through local farmers in countries such as Australia and New Zealand. This type of work requires few skills except physical strength and endurance, and tasks include picking, planting, shearing, and heavy lifting. Obtaining this sort of job is usually simply a case of being at the right place at the right time, but listings at local hostels or notice boards are also places to find farmers looking for help. Another option is to approach a farmer directly to ask for work. Occasionally an arrangement may be agreed upon where a farm hand works in exchange for room and board. Check the individual countries section of this book for crop picking dates in the different countries.

OFFICE/CLERICAL WORK

Secretaries and clerks with good typing skills can sometimes find office jobs in Pacific Rim countries. Often, a national can be found to do the work at a lower wage than you would, so your advantage should lie in the accuracy and speed of your skills and your language capabilities. If you don't mind the insecurity of temporary work, you can usually apply with American temporary placement companies that operate offices in the Asian country you wish to visit. Some of the larger temporary agencies will allow you to take their aptitude tests here in America and then will forward the results to their branch in the foreign country. You must be fluent in the language of the country, however, and be committed to the job.

RECREATIONAL RESORT CENTERS

Due to the growing popularity of vacation centers such as Club Med, there has been an increase in the demand for sports instructors and teachers at these places. Other tourist resort work includes drivers, security personnel, food servers, and various forms of low-skill labor. Employers will generally require language proficiency and previous experience of some kind. These jobs also require a written application, and the employers often request letters of reference. Specific employment information for some countries is found in the individual country chapters in Part II of this book. Club Med operates facilities in Japan, Indonesia, Malaysia, Thailand, and Australia. Write to the address below for application and employment requirements.

Club Mediterranee (Club Med)
106/110 Brompton Rd.
London SW3 1JJ, England
Tel.: 44 071 5811161

TEACHING ENGLISH

For the person seeking summer or temporary work in Pacific Rim countries, opportunities abound in the field of teaching English. With Pacific Rim countries such as Japan, Hong Kong, and Taiwan becoming increasingly more important in world economics, Asian professionals are seeking to become fluent in English and other languages for business purposes. Asian students also desire to learn English with hopes of one day attending American schools.

For the most part, people in these countries enjoy a high standard of living and can afford to take language lessons either at a language school or privately. This, fortunately, has made getting a job in these countries relatively easy for the native English speaker. One may teach English either at organized English schools, or a person may opt to market himself or herself and give private lessons. Requirements vary from language school to language school; some require teaching certification or experience, whereas others will hire anyone who can speak the local language. AFS International recruits teachers for positions (mainly ESL) in China, Thailand, the U.S.S.R., and other countries.

AFS International/Intercultural Programs
313 E. 43rd St.
New York, NY 10017
Tel.: (800) AFS-INFO

TOURISM, HOTELS, RESTAURANTS

As the Pacific Rim countries become more and more attractive as tourist sites, the tourist industry is also becoming more attractive for its employment possibilities. Hotels and restaurants throughout Asia and the Far East hire young people to work in varied positions in their growing establishments. Often this work is rather hectic, and if things get busier than usual, you may be expected to work overtime or perform other duties without compensation. The pay is not great, but with the growth in the industry the opportunities in this field should only increase over time. For more information regarding employment and a list of major hotels in specific countries, consult the individual countries section in Part II of this book or contact the tourism department of the country you wish to visit.

Expectations Achieved Ltd.
Trafalgar House, Grenville Place
London NW7 3SA, England
Expectations Achieved recruits for various positions with tour operators all over the world. Positions include sports instructors, cooks, resort representatives, and nannies. Language knowledge is beneficial but not required.

VOLUNTEER WORK

In countries where employment possibilities are limited due to either cultural or governmental restrictions, volunteering is often the best alternative for seeing the country. Volunteers are needed, especially in the lesser developed nations, to work on such projects as conservation, agriculture, construction, and renovation. Sometimes you must pay for your own accommodations, but other organizations will often provide for your room and board and maybe even a small allowance. See the individual countries section in Part II of this book for volunteer, or workcamp, organizations in specific countries. Below are some volunteer organizations with opportunities in the Pacific Rim:

Earthwatch
680 Mt. Auburn St.
Watertown, MA 02272
Earthwatch recruits volunteers to work with conservation and science projects around the world. Volunteers must pay for their own expenses.

Ecumenical Youth Action
WCC, P.O. Box 2100
1211 Geneva 2, Switzerland
Offers positions of manual work in camps througout Asia, Africa, and the Middle East. Projects usually last two to three weeks, with daily biblical readings and reflections. Participants pay for their own travel and insurance costs in addition to contributing three dollars per day toward maintenance costs. Ages 18-30.

Foundation for Field Research
P.O. Box 2010
Alpine, CA 92001-0020
Volunteers assist scientists in field research around the world. Previous projects have been in archaeology, biology, and paleontology. Projects vary widely in length of time, and volunteers are expected to contribute to the costs of the project. No age restrictions apply and no experience is required.

Getting a Job in the Pacific Rim

GAP Activity Projects Limited
44 Queen's Road, Reading,
Berkshire RG1 4BB, England
Tel.: 44 0734 594914
Arranges work in foreign countries for students taking a year of leave from their studies ("gap" year). GAP requires that participants work full time for a minimum of six months. In return for their work in various fields such as teaching, community projects, and conservation work, students are provided with room and board and limited pocket money.

The Missions to Seamen
St. Michael Paternoster Royal
College Hill, London EC4R 2RL, England
Volunteers assist chaplains in a variety of duties, including running clubs, visiting ships, counseling, and welfare work. Missions are located in Australia, the Far East, Africa, and North America. Fare is paid, and projects last around 12 months. A driver's license is required and all applicants must be practicing members of any Christian denomination. Address applications to the Deputy General Secretary.

Operation Raleigh
The Power House, Alpha Place, Flood St.
London SW3 5SZ, England
Tel.: 44 071 3517541
Expeditions of ten weeks involve community and conservation projects in remote parts of the world. For ages 17-25. No qualifications except the ability to swim 500 meters and pass a selection weekend. Applicants must pay for the cost of the trip.

The Project Trust
Breacachadh Castle, Isle of Coll
Argyll PA78 6TB, England
Tel.: 44 087 93444
This educational trust sends students (ages 17-19) overseas before they go to college or find employment. Participants work in a variety of positions, ranging from teaching English and medical work to agricultural work in order to gain understanding of cultures outside of Europe. Food is provided, but other costs must be paid by participants.

Tear Fund
100 Church Road, Teddington
Middlesex TW11 8QE, England
Summer assignments of six to eight weeks to do manual labor (carpentry, plumbing, etc.) in foreign countries. Skills in the above categories are helpful but not necessary. Volunteers pay for their travel, with food and accommodation provided by Tear Fund. Must be at least 20 years of age and a committed Christian, active in a home church.

Temporary Jobs in the Pacific Rim, by Country

For more complete information about available jobs, language requirements, and specific employment and travel regulations in each country, check the individual countries listings in Part II of this book.

Employment agencies can sometimes assist you in the job search. Keep in mind that some of these agencies are state owned and therefore much more likely to supply help to one of their own nationals than to a foreigner. Some agencies, however, will assist foreigners who possess desirable skills. You are most likely to benefit from these government agencies if you are in the country and can regularly visit their offices to look for job postings. You can then contact a potential employer directly. In some countries, the agencies may be more helpful if you ingratiate yourself with someone in their offices.

Other routes for finding temporary employment are the same as in America: check the advertisements in the local paper, look at listings in the Yellow Pages, and check notice boards. The individual country listings in Part II of this book contain useful information such as the names of major daily newspapers that may be helpful in the temporary or summer job search.

AUSTRALIA

Depending on the unemployment rate at the time, temporary and casual jobs are usually readily available in Australia. Agricultural and farm jobs are, for the most part, easily obtained in the rural areas. Resorts are another option. Queensland, the Great Barrier Reef, and the Australian Alps are hot spots for vacationers, and a number of resorts are located in these places.

The government's Commonwealth Employment Service is one of the best routes for finding a job throughout the country, although other employment agencies also locate sources of employment in urban areas. Other routes for finding employment are newspaper advertisements and notice boards (located at youth hostels and other visible places). Nanny agencies (listed in the Yellow Pages) also offer decent summer work.

Working holiday visas that allow for casual employment during vacations are available to people aged 18-25. Both AIESEC and IAESTE offer programs in Australia, as does the GAP Project (addresses listed at the end of this chapter).

GENERAL WORK:

Work Australia: BUNAC Travel
16 Bowling Green Lane
London EC1R 0BD, England
Tel.: 44 071 2513472
This company, for fees of 775 British pounds if departing from California and 1,060 if from London, provides participants with a round trip flight, a working holiday visa, two nights' accommodation in Sydney, and an orientation on living and working in Australia. Must be aged 18-25 and be able to show reserve funds of 2,000 British pounds.

VOLUNTEER WORK:

Australian Education Alternatives
Field Biosearch Pty., Ltd., P.O. Box 185
St. Lucia, Queensland 4067, Australia
Arranges internships in a variety of careers.

Australian Trust For Conservation Volunteers
P.O. Box 423
Ballarat, Victoria 3350, Australia
Arranges short- and long-term placements in conservation work. Short-term (six weeks) placement costs A$450, which includes accommodation, food, and travel.

Ecumenical Work Camps
Australian Council of Churches
P.O. Box C199, Clarence St. Post Office
Sydney, New South Wales 2000, Australia
Holds three-week work camps in New South Wales and Central Australia commencing December 26 (summer there) each year. Camp fees run approximately A$150, and volunteers pay their own travel costs.

Involvement Volunteers
P.O. Box 218
Port Melbourne, Victoria 3207, Australia
Tel.: 61 3 6465504
Placements in either single or team operations in work varying from conservation to social welfare, lasting for periods of 2-12 weeks. There is a fee, but programs vary in the amount of money that volunteers are expected to contribute to their expenses (ranging from nothing to 30 dollars per week).

EMPLOYMENT AGENCIES:

Accountancy Placements Ltd.
Levels 16 & 18, 25 Bligh St.
Sydney, New South Wales 2000, Australia
Tel.: 61 02 2235344

Centacom
72 Pitt St.
Sydney, New South Wales, Australia
Tel.: 61 02 2315555

Cocktail Bartenders Staff Agency
28 Elizabeth
Melbourne, Victoria, Australia
Tel.: 61 3 6457035

Commonwealth Employment Service
128 Bourke St.
Melbourne, Victoria 3000, Australia
Tel.: 61 03 6661222

Commonwealth Employment Service
Templine, 9th Floor, Santos House, 215 Adelaide St.

Brisbane, Queensland 4002, Australia
Tel.: 61 07 2295188

Drake Industrial
2nd Floor, 9 Queen St.
Melbourne, Victoria, Australia

Hospitality Personnel
Suite 17, The Russell Centre
159 Adelaide Tce.
Perth, Western Australia, Australia
Tel.: 61 9 2212468
Places people in hotels, motels, restaurants, and clubs.

Kelly Services
Level 15, 115 Pitt St.
Sydney, New South Wales, Australia
Tel.: 61 2 2327111

Labstaff
Suite 607, Harley Place
251 Oxford St., Bondi Junction
Sydney, New South Wales, Australia
Tel.: 61 2 3893722

Pollitt's Employment Agency
Fl. 15, Natwest House
251 Adelaide Tce.
Perth, Western Australia, Australia
Tel.: 61 9 3252544
Places hotel/motel, restaurant, farm, and household help.

Staffing Centre Personnel Services
Suite 3403, 60 Margaret St.
Sydney, New South Wales, Australia
Tel.: 61 021 2612777

Waiter & Waitresses Agency
113 Swanston
Melbourne, Victoria, Australia
Tel.: 61 3 6509030

Western Personnel Services Ltd.
7th Floor, 288 Edward St.
Brisbane, Queensland 4001, Australia
Tel.: 61 7 452 410841

CHINA

Teaching English is about the only field available for the temporary worker in China. Travelers in China have reported being approached on the street to teach English; obviously, teachers are needed. To arrange for a position before you arrive, contact either of the government offices listed below. If you are already in the country, check at local colleges to inquire whether or not they need instructors.

Bureau of Foreign Affairs
Ministry of Education
Beijing, 10086 People's Republic of China

External Relations Secretary
Chief of Recruiting and Placement Division
P.O. Box 300
Beijing, People's Republic of China

HONG KONG

English teaching opportunities abound for the summer traveler in Hong Kong. Check the *South China Morning Post* or the Yellow Pages for a listing of private language institutions and jobs available. Most schools ask for only a three-month commitment. Some of the better private schools are listed below.

Hong Kong English Club
1/F 190 Nathan R.
Kowloon, Hong Kong
Tel.: 852 3 666961

First Class Languages Centre
22A Bank Tower, 351-353 King's Rd.
North Point, Hong Kong
Tel.: 852 8877555

VOLUNTEER WORK:

Summer with a Purpose (SWAP)
Reformed Church in America
Box 803, Orange City, IA 51041
Tel.: (712) 737-4952
Participants teach English for a month to Chinese youth in a Christian residential summer camp. Must be a committed Christian college upperclassman. Application deadline is February 15.

EMPLOYMENT AGENCIES:

Manpower, Inc.
2207 Alexandra House, 16-20 Chater
Hong Kong

JAPAN

Short-term assignments in Japan are very limited. Opportunities are better for longer-term jobs, especially in the field of teaching English. Such jobs may be found either through a language institution or through individuals seeking private tutors. Also, the employment agencies below may be able to locate work for those who speak Japanese fluently.

VOLUNTEER WORK:

Shin-Shizen-Juku
Tsurui, Akan-gun
Hokkaido 085-12, Japan
Tel.: 81 0154 642821
This organic farm, located on the northern island of Hokkaido, provides free room and board in exchange for eight hours of work per day.

EMPLOYMENT AGENCIES:

Able Corp.
Time Life Bldg., 2nd Floor
3-6, Ohte-machi 2-chome
Chiyoda-ku, Tokyo 100, Japan
Tel.: 81 03 2426506
Fax: 81 03 2422802

Beststaff Japan
5th Floor, Sakura Bldg.
31-15, Yoyogi 1-chome
Shibuya-ku, Tokyo 151, Japan
Tel.: 81 03 3797631
Fax: 81 03 3797635

Borgnan Human Development Institute
Daisan Taihei Bldg.
25-3, Higashi Ikebukuro 1-chome
Toshima-ku, Tokyo 170, Japan
Tel.: 81 03 9898151
Fax: 81 03 9834897

JKC Recruiting Co.
4th Floor, Yamagata Bldg.
14-7, Nishi Shinbashi 1-chome
Minato-ku, Tokyo 105, Japan
Tel.: 81 03 5023991
Fax: 81 03 5970447

Oak Associates
5-21-5 Sendagaya
Shibuya-ku, Tokyo 151, Japan
Tel.: 81 03 3549502

Veritas International
17-2, Kamiyama-cho
Shibuya-ku, Tokyo 150, Japan
Tel.: 81 03 4687889
Fax: 81 03 4687877

Worldwide Freelance Hands
Rm. 407, Primera Dogenzaka
15-3, Dogenzaka 1-chome
Shibuya-ku, Tokyo 150, Japan
Tel.: 81 03 4762142

Young Abroad Club
Sato Bldg.
25 Daikyo-cho
Shinjuku-ku, Tokyo 160, Japan
Places young women in homes as au pairs to do housekeeping and childcare tasks.

INDONESIA

Work permits for casual work are impossible to obtain here. However, internships are available through AISEC. Summer employment in Indonesia is difficult to find because of the country's large labor force, but in some parts of Java, there are more jobs available than can be filled.

VOLUNTEER WORK:

Trekforth
58 Battersea Park Rd.
London SW11 4JP, England
Tel.: 44 071 4980855
Trekforth organizes scientific expeditions to Sulawesi, Indonesia, between the months of July and September. Program costs must be paid by the participant.

KOREA (SOUTH)

Teaching English opportunities are good for the casual worker. However, a work permit must be obtained before entering the country, which requires a university degree certificate. The IAESTE and AIESEC both operate programs in South Korea.

MALAYSIA

An AISEC program operates in Malaysia. Opportunities are also available teaching English in the capital city of Kuala Lumpur. Most economic growth and, therefore, construction work is found on the western coast of the Malay Peninsula.

NEW ZEALAND

Due to high unemployment, the government of New Zealand is not inclined to give out working permits. If you find employment, you must be able to convince the authorities that your job would not take one away from a national. Unofficial farm work is the best bet for working in New Zealand, as the economy is centered around fruit and sheep farming. Tourism is also a rapidly growing business, and jobs can be found in this sector. An agreement with the Department of Labor of New Zealand and the Student Travel Bureau of the New Zealand University Students Assoc. (NZUSA) enables U.S. students to work through CIEE (up to six months). AIESEC operates internships in New Zealand.

EMPLOYMENT AGENCY:

Western Staff Services (NZ) Ltd.
Westoff Employment, 37 Titara Ave.
New Lynn, Auckland 7, New Zealand
Tel.: 64 9 875814

PHILIPPINES

Both AIESEC and IAESTE operate in the Philippines (addresses at end of chapter). The country has a large and varied economy, meaning that temporary and summer jobs are available for those resourceful enough to hunt them out. Americans should also find the Philippines comfortable because English is the common language. The Philippines have been exposed to American culture for a long time and provide a very different atmosphere from the rest of East Asia.

EMPLOYMENT AGENCIES:

Aimstaffs, Inc.
ENZO Bldg., Makati
Metropolitan Manila, Philippines
Tel.: 63 2 8162641
Temporary placement.

Corporate Executive Search
Insular Life Bldg.
Makati, Metro Manila, Philippines
Tel.: 63 2 8175927

Corporate Macro-Management Resources
Rajah Sulayman Bldg.
Makati, Metro Manila, Philippines
Tel.: 63 2 8158451

Livicor Staffing Assistance
BF Topman Centre
Makati, Metro Manila, Philippines
Tel.: 63 2 8173629

Manpower Philippines,
Valgosons Realty Bldg. , 5th Floor
2151 Pasong Tamo, P.O. Box 549
Makati, Rizal 3117, Philippines

Miling's Employment Center
1830 Laon-Laan St.
Sampaloc, Manila, Philippines
Tel.: 63 2 7314272
Household help.

Optimim Manpower Corp.
Campos Rueda Bldg., Suite 403
Makati, Metro Manila, Philippines
Tel.: 63 2 862893

SINGAPORE

Teaching English is a good way to earn money in Singapore. An AIESEC program operates in this country. Singapore constantly experiences shortages of unskilled labor. The national language is English, so you should be able to find casual work if you're persistent.

TAIWAN

For those looking for shorter-term employment, teaching English is the best bet. The demand for such teachers is high, and jobs can be found with ease. Newspapers, such as the *China Post,* and notice boards are a good source of job openings. Notice boards can be found at youth hostels or at the Taiwan Normal University. Also, AIESEC operates internships in Taiwan. Some English schools are:

YES English Institute
Room 2, 10th Floor, 213 Fu Hsin S. Rd.
Taipei, Taiwan
Tel.: 886 2 7510259

Hess Language School
51 Ho Ping East Rd., Section 2
3F Taipei, Taiwan
Tel.: 886 2 7031118

THAILAND

Both AIESEC and IAESTE operate in Thailand (addresses below). Neither casual work nor the permits for such work are easily available. But for those who teach English illegally, the goverment seems to look the other way. Thailand also has a booming economy, making casual labor for foreigners available even if illegal.

Pacific Rim Student Employment Sources

Non-profit organizations are yet another route for the aspiring summer traveler. Some operate on an employment exchange basis and charge a small fee for their services. They usually will arrange all paperwork and working permits for you.

AIESEC
841 Broadway, Suite 608

New York, NY 10003
Tel.: (212) 979-7400
The AIESEC (a French acronym for the International Association of Students in Economics and Commerce) operates as an employment exchange program for college students in 69 countries worldwide. In exchange for developing positions in America for international students, American students in the business and computer fields are then eligible themselves for overseas placement. Participants must be sophomores, juniors, or seniors in college, attending one of the 77 U.S. AIESEC member universities.

American Youth Hostels
American Youth Hostels
P.O. Box 36713
Washington, DC 20013-7613
Youth hostels around the world will employ young travelers for many different jobs during the summer. The compensation for the work is usually free room and board and a small amount of money. To obtain addresses of youth hostels around the world, contact the address above.

Council on International Educational Exchange (CIEE)
205 E. 42nd St.
New York, NY 10017
Tel.: (212) 661-1450
The CIEE, a non-profit organization, arranges working holiday programs abroad for American college students. Although they deal primarily with European countries, they do operate a program in New Zealand. They may also be able to provide help obtaining permits for other countries.

Experiment in International Living
Kipling Rd.
Brattleboro, VT 05301
The Experiment in International Living is an organization that sends high school and college students to countries around the world. Summer group leader and semester academic director positions are available to people at least 24 years of age who have experience working with American teenagers. The EIL also works in conjunction with the U.S. Agency for International Development to teach English in Thailand and Indonesia.

IAESTE
International Association for the Exchange of Students for Technical Experience
Park View Bldg., Suite 320
10480 Little Patuxent Parkway
Columbia, MD 21044-3502
Tel.: (301) 997-2200
The IAESTE provides students of engineering, architecture, and the sciences with training in 50 countries worldwide. College juniors, seniors, and graduate students are eligible for the program, which pays an allowance for living expenses while training. Some countries require fluency in the language.

YMCA
International Camp Counselor Program/Abroad
356 W. 34th St., 3rd Floor

New York, NY 10001
Summer camp counselor positions are available through the YMCA in 24 countries throughout the world, including Australia, New Zealand, Japan, and the U.S.S.R. Other positions at YMCA centers may also be obtained. Contact:

YMCA of the USA
Personnel and Training
Overseas Personnel Programs
101 N. Wacker Dr.
Chicago, IL 60606

PUBLICATIONS:

Directory of Overseas Summer Jobs
Lists 50,000 summer jobs worldwide. Includes contact name, rate of pay, length of employment, application dates and procedures, and qualifications. Annual. The cost is $9.95 (plus $2.50 for postage) from Writer's Digest Books, 1507 Dana Ave., Cincinnati, OH 45207.

Volunteer! The Comprehensive Guide to Voluntary Service in the U.S. and Abroad
This guide, published by the CIEE, lists more than 170 organizations that handle placements in voluntary service projects. The publication costs $6.95 (plus $1.00 for postage) and can be obtained from the CIEE at 205 E. 42nd St., New York, NY 10017.

PART II
WHERE THE JOBS ARE: COUNTRY-BY-COUNTRY LISTINGS

Japan

Japan forms a 123,000 square mile archipelago off the coast of East Asia. The Soviet Union, North Korea, and South Korea, to the west across the Sea of Japan, are the closest neighbors. Four main islands make up Japan: Honshu, the main island, Hokkaido, Kyushu, and Shikoku. Approximately 70% of the territory is mountainous. Minor earthquakes occur fairly frequently. Over 99% of the people are Japanese and about 0.5% are Korean. Japanese is the sole language. Buddhism and Shintoism have traditionally been the major religious affiliations.

Japanese tradition ascribes the founding of the empire to the Emperor Jimmu in 660 B.C.E., but records of unified Japan can be found from 1600 B.C.E. Chinese influence strongly affected the development of early Japanese culture. By the late twelfth century, a feudal system had been established in Japan. Military dictators, called shoguns, exercised political power from 1192 to 1868, when the Emperor Meiji recovered effective control. The Meiji period initiated a series of significant reforms aimed at modernizing the country.

Portugal and Holland maintained a very limited trade with Japan beginning in the sixteenth century. The country did not open to foreigners until 1854, however, when U.S. Commodore Matthew Perry forced Japan to sign a treaty permitting new trade and commerce. In the late nineteenth century, Japan began to industrialize and to imitate Western technology. By the 1930s, Japan had established itself as a major economic power.

Japanese military power and economic development allowed the country to defeat China in 1895, capturing Taiwan and gaining influence over former Chinese protectorates. In 1905, Japan defeated Russia, gained part of Sakhalin Island, and forced Russia to withdraw from most of China. Korea was annexed in 1910. Germany lost its Pacific territories and Chinese concessions to Japan during World War I. Manchuria was taken in 1931 and China was invaded in 1932. Japan attacked the U.S. at Pearl Harbor in 1941 and fought a long and bloody Pacific war until 1945, when the U.S. employed nuclear weapons.

The 1947 constitution, basically written by Americans, renounced the right to war and the emperor's divinity. A parliamentary model, featuring a sovereign legislature, the Diet, was introduced. Japan and the U.S. signed a peace treaty in 1951. Japan has since signed treaties ending the state of war with its other World War II opponents. The U.S. has also returned several Pacific territories captured during the war, although it maintains a military base at Okinawa. The Soviet Union and Japan still disagree over the status of the Kuril Islands.

Since World War II, Japan has become one of the world's leading economies, especially in electronics technology. Japan's huge trade surpluses have also led the U.S. and the European Community to complain that unfair practices prevent their companies from gaining entrance into the Japanese market. The U.S. has at times imposed trade sanctions in retaliation and threatens to do so again unless Japan reforms its trade and investment policies.

Since the mid-1950s, the Liberal Democratic Party, supported by the business and agricultural communities, has governed Japan. The LDP maintains pro-American foreign and pro-growth economic policies. As a result of tremendous economic prosperity, the LDP enjoyed public confidence until 1989, when the Recruit scandal forced Prime Minister

Takeshita to resign. Other unpopular measures, such as a proposed cut in the rice subsidy, allowed the opposition Japan Socialist Party to capture the upper house of the Diet. Current Prime Minister Kaifu has endeavored to improve U.S.-Japan relations.

Largest stock brokerage firms in Japan

American Firms:
1. Salomon Brothers
2. Goldman Sachs
3. Morgan Stanley
4. Merrill Lynch
5. Lehman Brothers
6. First Boston

Japanese Firms:
1. Nomura
2. Daiwa
3. Nikko
4. Yamaichi■

Current Economic Climate

Japan's gross national product of $2 trillion is the world's third largest, behind the U.S. and the Soviet Union. With a per capita income of over $15,000, the Japanese also enjoy one of the world's highest living standards; but the cost of living in Japan is also one of the world's highest. Japanese families save about 15% of their annual income, contributing to a large capital pool for investment. The unit of currency is the yen, which generally trades at a rate of 140-150 to the U.S. dollar.

Japan has a very high population density, as over 123 million people live in an area about the size of California. About 77% of the population live in urban areas. The largest cities are Tokyo with 9 million inhabitants, Osaka with 3 million, Yokohama with 3 million, Nagoya with 2 million, and Kyoto with 2 million. Approximately 10% of the population lives in the area around Tokyo.

The country's leading industries include electronics technology, automobiles, industrial machinery, chemicals, and shipbuilding. Rice and other grains are the major agricultural products. Japan must import nearly all of its oil, over 75% from the Middle East. Business hours are from 9:00 am to 5:00 pm, Monday through Friday; some businesses are open on Saturday until noon. Banks close at 3:00 pm and are closed on Saturday. Retail stores are often open on weekends.

Japan's growth rate has been slowing in late 1990 and early 1991. In the last quarter of 1990, the economy only grew 0.5%, leading to an overall growth rate of 2.1% in 1990. The economy grew by about 5% each of the preceding four years. Growth probably decreased in late 1990 because of uncertainty over the war in the Persian Gulf. The economy is expected to expand again in 1991 as nationwide local elections draw near. LDP politicians are pressuring the Bank of Japan to ease interest rates.

Japanese foreign investment is well-known in the U.S, but is perhaps more important in Southeast Asia. While most Japanese investment in the United States originally took place to placate American protectionism by setting up new enterprises employing Americans, investment in Southeast Asia has occurred for longer-term, economically strategic reasons. The Japanese believe that developing the economic resources of Southeast Asia will ultimately benefit their own economy. The countries of the region provide both cheap sources of labor and materials and growing new markets.

By the end of 1990, over 50% of Japanese foreign investment was in the U.S. and Canada, whereas 25% was in Southeast Asia. Nonetheless, annual Japanese investment in the region increased by 13% in 1989 and by 17% in 1990 and is expected to continue increasing. In 1990, Japanese companies invested over $2 billion in Hong Kong, $1.3 billion in Singapore, $1.1 billion in Thailand, and $700 million in Indonesia. Japan has invested especially heavily in Malaysia, where costs are still quite low. Mitsubishi, for example, is building an elevator plant in Thailand, and Matsushita will build a new television plant in Malaysia. Unlike previous investment, which was export-oriented, these projects are aimed at domestic and regional markets. Additionally, Japanese companies are now opening offices in Indochina: Mitsubishi in Vietnam and Mitsui in Laos.

Meanwhile, Japan-U.S. relations have been troubled over investment and trade issues. In 1990, Japanese firms spent $17 billion to acquire over 200 American companies, but U.S. firms only spent $3.7 million to buy three Japanese companies. American companies complain that their ability to invest in Japan is severely limited by unfair practices. The Japanese *keiretsu* system, for instance, results in cross-holding of stocks, interlocking directorates, and other corporate interchange that makes mergers and acquisitions extremely difficult.

American corporate raider, T. Boone Pickens, experienced the difficulties of breaking into corporate Japan when he purchased 26.4% of Koito Manufacturing, making him the company's largest stockholder. Despite his investment, Pickens was not allowed a seat on Koito's board of directors. Likewise, the Japanese patent office often fails to recognize a foreign company's patent on a product until Japanese firms can also develop it. Monsanto, Motorola, and Allied-Signal have all lost market opportunities in this way.

On the other hand, Eastman Kodak has successfully penetrated Japan, edging out Fuji Film in several markets. Kodak sells over $18 billion of film annually in Japan, and Fuji sells about $7 billion. Kodak has been able to compete effectively in Japan by hiring Japanese staff, advertising extensively and aggressively, packaging in Japanese, and adjusting to consumer preferences in quality and type of film. Most American firms simply expect to do business in Japan the same way as in the U.S. and thus fail to adust to a very different marketplace.

In addition, the U.S. trade deficit with Japan has been showing signs of improvement. The U.S. exported about $48 billion worth of goods and services to Japan in 1990, up from $28 billion in 1987. At the same time, Japanese demand for American products has been increasing while American demand for Japanese products has been decreasing. These trends indicate that over the long term the U.S. will probably be able to compete with Japan in international trade, but only if American firms adust to new market realities and if the Japanese consumers are allowed to buy their products in a fair market.

JAPAN'S 25 LARGEST COMPANIES

1. Nippon Telephone & Telegraph (Communications)
2. Industrial Bank of Japan (Banking)
3. Sumitomo Bank (Banking)
4. Fuji Bank (Banking)
5. Toyota Motor (Automobile manufacturing)
6. Mitsui Taiyo Kobe Bank (Banking)
7. Dai-Ichi Kangyo Bank (Banking)
8. Mitsubishi Bank (Banking)
9. Tokyo Electric Power (Utility)
10. Sanwa Bank (Banking)
11. Hitachi (Electronic equipment)
12. Nomura Securities (Financial services)
13. Long-Term Credit Bank of Japan (Banking)
14. Matsushita Electric Industrial (Household electronics)
15. Kansai Electric Power (Utility)
16. Nippon Steel (Industrial manufacturing)
17. Tokai Bank (Banking)
18. Mitsubishi Heavy Industries (Industrial manufacturing)
19. Toshiba (Electronic equipment)
20. NEC (Electronic equipment)
21. Nissan Motor (Automobile manufacturing)
22. Japan Air Lines (Air transportation)
23. Nippon Credit Bank (Banking)
24. Bank of Tokyo (Banking)
25. Sony (Electronic equipment)

Getting Around in Japan

Japan Airlines maintains international connections between Tokyo and other major cities, as well as limited flights between the larger cities. For service within Japan, as well as some regional international flights, All Nippon Airways, Japan Air System, Japan Asia Airways, and Toa Domestic Airlines are generally more convenient.

Japanese rail services are excellent and very efficient. Various options range in price from least to most expensive: the local trains, which stop at every station in the metropolitan areas; express trains, with more direct routes; limited express trains, which are almost non-stop; and the bullet trains, which link Tokyo to several parts of the country and can reach speeds of 130 miles per hour. The Japan Rail Pass is valid throughout the country and can be bought at most rail stations.

Subways can be found in Tokyo, Osaka, Nagoya, Yokohama, Kyoto, Fukuoka, and Sapporo. The subway system in Tokyo is extremely comprehensive. All mass transit stops operating around midnight, making taxis the only way to get about after that time. The bus system is also comprehensive, especially within the major urban areas. Buses are very crowded and not nearly as fast as the rail system and should therefore be avoided whenever the subway is available. Rental cars are available and the highway system is good, but traffic signs are, of course, in Japanese. Ferries also link the major and minor islands.

Using the Phone

Japan's country code is "81," and Tokyo's city code is "03." All city codes begin with a zero. Other city codes include: Osaka "06"; Nagoya "052"; Kyoto "075"; Yokohama "045"; and Narita "0476." Yellow and green public phones accept 10 yen and 100 yen coins. Blue and red public phones only accept 10 yen coins. The green phones also accept a phone credit card. Local calls are currently 10 yen for three minutes. The overseas operator is "0051." The national police number is "110," and the fire and ambulance number is "119." You need to push a red button before dialing these emergency numbers, but the 10 yen coin is unnecessary.■

Employment Regulations for Americans

Americans do not need a visa for stays of less than 90. For longer stays, and just to be safe in case the authorities choose to change the regulations, you should apply for a regular tourist visa. The regular visa can also be upgraded into a work permit so that you can find legal employment. Visas can usually be obtained rather easily, but to enter the country with a work permit, you must provide proof of employment in Japan and demonstrate that the job can not be filled by a Japanese national.

The Ministry of Foreign Affairs has frequently changed its visa requirements for different groups in the past. You should contact the ministry before making any plans.

Ministry of Foreign Affairs—Visa Section
2-2-1 Kasumigaseki
Chiyoda-ku, Tokyo 100
Japan
Tel.: 81 03 5803311

Using the language

Japanese is the sole language spoken in Japan. A standard dialect is used throughout the country and although some local variations may occasionally be found, they are not very significant. Most young people are quite familiar with English at the conversational level. Many older adults have studied English in language schools and are also conversant. Business people usually speak English quite well. Despite people's familiarity with English, it is always appropriate to at least begin your conversations in Japanese and then ask if you can shift into English. The Japanese are generally willing to speak with you in English, but you should demonstrate an effort to communicate in their language. ■

Teaching English in Japan

The Japan Exchange and Teaching Program (JET) is sponsored by several Japanese government agencies and offers 12-month English teaching positions to college graduates. Some teaching or Japanese language experience is preferred. Contact a consulate or the Japanese embassy for more information and application forms. YMCA language schools are located throughout the country and offer English teaching positions. YMCA wages are usually lower than the language schools, but you can always tutor private individuals for more money.

Embassy of Japan-JET Program
2520 Massachusetts Ave. N.W.
Washington, DC 20008
Tel.: (202) 939-6700

Country-by-Country Listings

Overseas Service Corps
International Division, YMCA
101 N. Wacker Dr.
Chicago, IL 60606
Tel.: (312) 977-0031

Or write to:

International Office for Asia-YMCA
909 4th Ave.
Seattle, WA 98104

Language schools also employ Americans to teach English throughout Japan. Many Americans find that teaching English in Japan, either at a school or through private tutoring, is a relatively easy way to make some money. Informal tutoring can generally be found without difficulty to augment the salary earned at the school. The following list includes several of the larger language schools, but there are hundreds of such schools in Tokyo alone.

ASA Community Salon
Tanaka Bldg.
2-11-12 Yoyogi
Shibuya-ku, Tokyo 151
Tel.: 81 03 3208649

Atty Language Institute
Osaka Ekimae Daichi Bldg.
1-3-1 Umeda
Kita-ku, Osaka 530
Tel.: 81 06 3462323

Berlitz
Daini Koa Bldg.
1-11-39 Akasaka
Minato-ku, Tokyo 107
Tel.: 81 03 5893525

ECC Foreign Language Institute
Dairuoku Arai Bldg.
1-5-4 Kabuki-cho
Shinjuku-ku, Tokyo 16
Tel.: 81 03 2093733

ELEC
3-8 Jimbocho
Chiyoda-ku, Kanda, Tokyo 101
Tel.: 81 03 2658911

Gregg Gaigo Gakko
1-14-16 Jugaoka
Meguro-ku, Tokyo 152
Tel.: 81 03 7240552

Interac
2-10-28 Fujimi-cho
Chiyoda-ku, Tokyo 160
Tel.: 81 03 2347814

International Education Center
(Nichibei Kaiwa Gakuin)
1-21 Yotsuya
Shinjuku-ku, Tokyo 160
Tel.: 81 03 3599621

International Language Center
Iwanami Jimbocho Bldg.
2-1 Kanda-Jimbocho
Chiyoda-ku, Tokyo 101
Tel.: 81 03 2645935

Kanda
1-13-13 Uchikanda
Chiyoda-ku, Tokyo 101
Tel.: 81 03 2542731

You should also contact professional organizations such as the Japan Association of Language Teachers (JALT) or the Association of English Teachers of Children. These associations can provide valuable networking contacts who can recommend you to teaching positions. JALT is the largest group and maintains branches throughout the country.

Association of English Teachers of Children
2-7-11 Takaido Higashi
Suginami-ku, Tokyo 168

Japan Association of Language Teachers
6-27 Hirakata Motomachi
Hirakata-shi, Osaka 573

If you're interested in volunteering in various service projects, which may or may not involve teaching, contact Service Civil International. This international organization can place Americans in workcamps in Japan, working with the mentally or physically disabled or in agricultural projects.

Service Civil International
2-31-16 Minami-urawa, Urawa-shu
Saitama-ken, Tokyo 336

Japanese Newspapers and Periodicals in English

Japan Economic Daily
Kyodo News International
50 Rockefeller Plaza, Suite 832
New York, NY 10020
Tel.: (212) 586-0152
Ed. Kenichi Sasaki

Tokyo Business Today
Toyo Keizai Inc.-Oriental Economist
1-2-1 Hongokucho, Nihonbashi
Chuo-ku, Tokyo 103
Ed. Nozomu Nakaoka

Economic Survey of Japan
Annual Economic White Paper of Economic Planning Agency, Japan
Japan Times,
4-5-4 Shibaura
Minato-ku, Tokyo 108

Kansai University Economic Review/Kansai Daigaku Keizai Ronshu
Kansai Unversity Economic Society
Osaka, Japan

Keidanren Review
Japan Federation of Economic Organizations
Keizai Dantai Rengokai
9-4 Otemachi, 1-chome
Chiyoda-ku, Tokyo 100

Keio Business Review
Keio University Society of Business and Commerce
c/o Faculty of Business and Commerce
Mita Minato-ku,Tokyo 108
Ed. Tadahiro Yamamasu

Keizai Ohrai/Economic Review
11 Yotsuya
Shinjuku-ku, Tokyo
Ed. Yoshiya Sekine

Kobe Economic and Business Review
Kobe University
Research Institute for Economics and Business Administration
Rokko, Nada, Kobe

Organizations for Further Information

The following organizations, both in the U.S. and Japan, may be helpful in the job search. American embassies and consulates have commercial and/or economic sections that can provide you with business information and explain aspects of the local economy. World Trade Centers usually include many foreign companies operating in the country. Foreign government missions in the U.S. such as National Tourist Offices, embassies, and consulates can furnish visas and information on work permits and other important regulations. They may also offer economic and business information about the country.

CHAMBERS OF COMMERCE

American Chambers of Commerce in Japan
Fukide Bldg, No. 2,
4-1-21 Toranomon 4-chome,
Minato-ku
Tokyo 150, Japan
Tel.: 81 03 4335381
Fax.: 81 03 4361446

Hiroshima Chamber of Commerce
44 Matomachi 5-chome
Hiroshima, Japan
Tel.: 81 21 9191/4221

Japan Business Assn. of Southern California
345 Figueroa St., #206
Los Angeles, CA 90071
Tel.: (213) 485-0160

Japanese Chamber of Commerce of Chicago
401 N. Michigan Ave., Rm. 602
Chicago, IL 60611
Tel.: (312) 332-6199

Japanese Chamber of Commerce of Honolulu
2454 S. Beretania St.
Honolulu, HI 96826
Tel.: (808) 949-5531

Japanese Chamber of Commerce of New York
145 W. 57th St.
New York, NY 10019
Tel.: (212) 935-0303

Japanese Chamber of Commerce of Northern California
World Affairs Center, 312 Sutter St., Rm. 408
San Francisco, CA 94108
Tel.: (415) 986-6140

Japanese Chamber of Commerce of Southern California
244 S. San Pedro St., Rm. 504
Los Angeles, CA 90012
Tel.: (213) 626-3067

Kyoto Chamber of Commerce
240 Shoshoicho
Ebisugawa-Agaru, Kyoto 604, Japan
Tel.: 81 75 2310181/8

Nagoya Chamber of Commerce
2-10-19 Sakaie
Naka-ku, Nagoya 460, Japan

Osaka Chamber of Commerce
58-7 Uchi Homachi, Hashizume-cho
Osada 540, Japan
Tel.: 81 06 9426151

Sopporo Chamber of Commerce
2-2-1 Kita Ichijo-nishi, Chuo-ku
Sapporo, Hokkaido 060, Japan

Tokyo Chamber of Commerce
2-2 Marunouchi 3-chome
Tokyo 100, Japan
Tel.: 81 03 2114411

Yokohama Chamber of Commerce
2 Yamashita-cho
Naka-ku, Yokohama 231, Japan

U.S. CONSULAR OFFICES
Check your local telephone book white pages under "Consulate General of Japan" for consulates in major U.S. cities.

American Consulate General, Osaka-Kobe
11-15, Nishitenma 2-chome
Kita-Ku, Osaka 530. Japan
Tel.: 81 06 3155900
Michael J. Benefeil, Commercial Officer

American Consulate General, Sapporo
Kita 1-Jo Nishi 28-chome
Chuo-Ku, Sapporo 064, Japan
Tel.: 81 1 6411115/7
Mark J. Bezner, Consular Officer

American Consulate, Fukuoka
5-26 Ohori 2-chome
Chuo-ku, Fukuoka-810, Japan
Tel.: 81 92 7519331/4
Alec Wilczynski, Consular Officer

American Embassy Commercial Section
10-1 Akasaka, 1-chome
Minato-ku, Tokyo 107, Japan
Tel.: 81 03 5837141
Keith R. Bovett, Commercial Officer

WORLD TRADE CENTER IN JAPAN

The World Trade Center of Japan
P.O. Box 57, World Trade Center Bldg.
No. 4-1, 2-chome, Hamamatsu-cho
Minato-ku, Tokyo 105, Japan
Tel.: 81 03 4355651

OTHER INFORMATIONAL ORGANIZATIONS

Embassy of Japan
250 Massachusetts Ave. N.W.
Washington, DC 20008
Tel.: (202) 939-6700

Fukuoka Int'l. Exchange Center
c/o Fukuoka Sun Palace
2-1, Chikko-Honmachi
Hakata-ku, Fukuoka, Japan
Tel.: 81 092 2910777

Hiroshima Tourist Association
1-1, Nakajima-cho
Naka-ku, Hiroshima, Japan
Tel.: 81 082 2499324

Japan External Trade Organization
1221 Ave. of the Americas
New York, NY 10020
Tel.: (212) 997-0400

Japan Information Service
235 E. 42nd St.
New York, NY 10017

Japan Foundation
600 New Hampshire Ave. N.W.
Suite 430
Washington, DC 20008

Japan National Tourist Organization in Chicago
333 N. Michigan Ave.
Chicago, IL 60601
Tel.: (312) 332-3975

Japan National Tourist Organization in Dallas
1519 Main St., Suite 200
Dallas, TX 75201
Tel.: (214) 741-4931

Japan National Tourist Organization Headquarters
Tokyo Kotsu Kaikan Bldg., 10th Floor
10-1 Yuraku-cho, 2-chome
Chiyoda-ku, Tokyo, Japan

Japan National Tourist Organization in Los Angeles
624 S. Grand Ave., Suite 2640
Los Angeles, CA 90017
Tel.: (213) 623-1952

Japan National Tourist Organization in New York
Rockefeller Plaza, 630 Fifth Ave.
New York, NY 10111
Tel.: (212) 757-5640
Fax.: (212) 307-6754

Japan National Tourist Organization in San Francisco
360 Post St., Suite 401
San Francisco, CA 94108
Tel.: (415) 989-7140
Fax.: (415) 398-5461

Japan Society
333 E. 47th St.
New York, NY 10017

Kobe Tourist Association
Kobe Shoko Boeki Center
5-1-14 Hamabe-dori
Fukiai-ku, Kobe, Japan
Tel.: 81 78 2321010

Nagoya International Center
4F, Nagoya Kokusai Center Bldg.
Nagono 1-chome
Nakamura-ku, Nagoya, Japan
Tel.: 81 052 5815678

Okayama International Exchange Plaza
3-1-15, Koseicho, Okayama, Japan
Tel.: 81 0862 322255

Osaka Tourist Association
Semba Center Bldg. 2, 1-4 Semba-sho
Hihashi-ku, Nagoya, Japan
Tel.: 81 06 3452189

Sapporo Tourist Association
City Hall, 2nd Fl.
Chuo-ku, Sapporo, Japan
Tel.: 81 011 2113341

Tourist Information Center in Narita
Airport Terminal Bldg.
Narita City, Japan
Tel.: 81 0476 328711

Tourist Information Center in Tokyo
Kotani Bldg.
1-6-6, Yurakucho
Chiyoda-ku, Tokyo, Japan
Tel.: 81 03 5021461

United Nations Information Center
Shin Aoyama Bldg., Nishi-kan 22F
1-1-1 Minami Aoyama, Minato-ku, Tokyo, Japan
Tel.: 81 03 4751611

U.S. Export Development Office
7th Floor, World Import Mart
1-3 Higashi Likebukuro 3-chome
Toshima-ku, Tokyo 170, Japan
Tel.: 81 3 9872441
Thomas W. Callow, Consular Officer

Yokohama International Welcome Association
Silk Center, 1 Yamashita-cho
Naka-ku, Yokohama, Japan
Tel.: 81 45 6415824

Business Directories

Although not always easy to find, business directories can prove invaluable in the international job search. Most directories list company names, addresses, products, and phone numbers. Some directories include executive names and titles and financial information about the company. These sources provide you with the names of the people to contact for employment information as well as financial data.

Affiliates & Other Offices of Japanese Firms in the U.S.A. and Canada. Japan External Trade Organization, 1221 Ave. of the Americas, New York, NY 10020. Published occasionally by JETRO. Lists basic information about over 5,000 Japanese firms operating in the U.S. and Canada.

American Chamber of Commerce in Japan Directory of Members. Published annually by the chamber. Lists over 1,500 companies involved in bilateral trade.

Diamond's Japan Business Directory. Annual publication of Diamond Lead Co., 1-4-2 Kasumigaseki, Chiyoda-ku, Tokyo 100, Japan. Provides detailed financial information on over 1,000 companies.

Economic World Directory of Japanese Companies in USA. Economic Salon, Ltd., 60 E. 42nd St., New York, NY 10165. Annual publication listing financial data on nearly 1,000 Japanese businesses in the U.S.

Industrial Groupings in Japan. Dodwell & Co., C.P.O. Box 297, Tokyo 100-91, Japan. Biennial publication providing detailed financial information on nearly 3,000 Japanese companies, divided by major industrial group companies.

Japan Company Handbook. Toyo Keizai Shinposha Ltd., 1-4 Hongokucho, Nihonbashi Chuo-ku, Tokyo 103, Japan. Semiannual publication containing detailed financial information on over 1,000 Japanese firms.

Japan Directory. Published annually by Japan Press Ltd., 12-8 Kita Aoyama, 2-Chrome, Minato-ku, Tokyo 107, Japan. Contains basic information on over 22,000 Japanese companies.

Japan Trade Directory. Published annually by Japan External Trade Organization, 1221 Ave. of the Americas, New York, NY 10020. Lists over 2,000 trade associations and detailed financial information for companies engaging in international trade.

Japan Yellow Pages. Published semiannually by Japan Yellow Pages, Ltd., ST Bldg., 6-9 Lidabashi, 4-chome, Chiyoda-ku, Tokyo 102, Japan. Lists basic information about 28,000 manufacturers and other businesses.

Retail Distribution in Japan. Dodwell & Co., C.P.O. Box 297, Tokyo 100-91, Japan. Irregularly published listing of over 500 retailers and wholesalers.

Standard Trade Index of Japan. Annual publication of Nippon Shoko Kaigi-sho, 2-2 Marunouchi, Chiyodaku, 3-chome, Tokyo, Japan. Basic information on over 8,000 Japanese companies engaged in trade.

2,000 Importers of Japan. Published irregularly by Japan External Trade Organization, 1221 Ave. of the Americas, New York, NY 10020. Detailed financial data on 2,000 Japanese firms engaged in importing foreign products.

Making a good first impression

Bowing is a traditional form of greeting used in a variety of contexts to greet almost everyone. Most Japanese, however, will greet foreigners with a handshake instead of a bow. The more international experience someone has, the more likely it is that a handshake will be offered. You should generally let the Japanese person lead the greeting and respond with the same gesture. The speed and depth of the bow vary with the amount of respect being demonstrated. Always use a title and surnames when introduced to someone for the first time. It is not customary to use first names when meeting someone.

It is very important to exchange business cards in Japan. The cards should contain one's name, full title or position, company or organization, phone number, and address. You should print this information in Japanese on one side and in English on the other. When you recieve a card, keep it in front of you to check for pronunciations if you forget. Even if you can remember Japanese pronunciations, it is considered rude to immediately put the card away. Japanese who meet Americans or other foreigners frequently will have similar business cards. When presenting the card, use both hands and make sure the type is facing upward toward the recipient.■

MAJOR AMERICAN COMPANIES IN JAPAN

Many American firms operate in Japan. The following companies are classified by business area: Banking and Finance; Industrial Manufacturing; Retailing and Wholesaling; and Service Industries. The company information includes type of business, American parent company, and contact name where possible. Your chances of achieving employment are substantially greater if you contact the subsidiary company in Japan rather than the parent company in the U.S.

BANKING AND FINANCE

American International Underwriters
P.O. Box 951
Tokyo 100-91, Japan
(Insurance)
P. Hammer, Chairman
American International Underwriters Overseas

Bankers Trust International
Chiyoda-ku, Tokyo 100-91, Japan
(Banking)
Bankers Trust New York Corp.

Citicorp Services Co.
8-11 Nishi Shinbashi 2-chome
Tokyo, Japan
(Banking)
Citicorp

Cititrust & Banking Corp.
1-3 Otemachi 1-chome
Tokyo, Japan
(Banking)
Citicorp

Goldman Sachs Corp.
ARK Mori Bldg., 10th Floor
12-32 Akasaka 1-chome
Minato-ku, Tokyo 107, Japan
Tel.: 81 3 5897000
Fax.: 81 3 5879260
(Investment banking)
Goldman Sachs & Co.

Manufacturers Hanover Tokyo
Ashai Tokai Bldg. 21st, Floor
2-6-1 Otemachi
Chiyoda-ku, Tokyo, Japan
Tel.: 81 3 2426511
(Banking and finance)
Manufacturers Hanover Trust Corp.

Merril Lynch
1-1-3 Otemachi Bldg.
Chiyoda-ku, Tokyo 100, Japan
Tel.: 81 3 2137000
Fax.: 81 3 2137007
(Investment banking, brokerage firm)
Merril Lynch & Co.

Morgan Stanley
Otemachi Center Bldg., 8-9 Floor
1-3 Otemachi 1-chome
Chiyoda-ku, Tokyo 100, Japan
(Brokerage firm)
Morgan Stanley Group

Prudential Life Insurance Co.
1-7 Kojimachi Sogo Hanzomon Bldg.
Chiyoda-ku, Tokyo 102, Japan
(Life insurance)
Joseph F. Dunn, Chairman
Prudential Life Insurance Co. of America

Prudential-Bache Securities
AIU Bldg., 14th Floor
1-3 Marunouchi 1-chome
Chiyoda-ku, Tokyo 100, Japan
Tel.: 81 3 5970567
(Business services)
William Custard, President
Prudential-Bache Securities

Security Pacific Capital Markets
Ark Mori Bldg., 15th Floor
12-32 Akasaka 1-chome
Minato-ku, Tokyo 107, Japan
Tel.: 81 3 5874830
Taoashi Kano, Managing Director, CEO
Security Pacific Hoare Govett (Asia)

Shearson-Lehman Brothers
ARK Mori Bldg., 36th Floor
12-32 Minato-k 1-chome
Akasaka, Tokyo 107, Japan
Tel.: 81 3 5059000
Fax.: 81 3 5055725
(Brokerage firm)
Shearson-Lehman Brothers Intl.

INDUSTRIAL MANUFACTURING

Albany International Japan
Akasaka Sanno Bldg., 3rd Floor
#5-11 Akasaka 2-chome
Minato, Tokyo 107, Japan
Sadeo Yoshakawa
Albany International Corp.

Allied-Signal Inc. Asia
Mori Bldg.
3 13-16 Mita 3-chome, Minato-ku
Chiyoda-ku, Tokyo 108, Japan
(Electrical appliances)
Allied-Signal Inc.

Country-by-Country Listings

AMP
87 Hisamoto, Takatsu-ku
Kawasaki, Kanagwa 213, Japan
Tel.: 81 44 8448111
(Solderless terminals)
M. Komatsu, Manager
AMP Inc.

Avon Products Co.
Nagai International Bldg.
12-19 Shibuya 2-chome
Shibuya-ku, Tokyo 150, Japan
(Cosmetics)
Akitomo Kato, Manager
Avon International Operations

Bell & Howell Japan
Ando Fukuyoshi Bldg., 8th Fl.
11-28, Akasaka 1-chome
Minato-ku, Tokyo 107, Japan
Tel.: 81 3 35824691
Fax.: 81 3 5821748
(Audio/visual film products)
Bell & Howell Co.

Bristol-Myers
Nihon Smi Akska Dni Bldg.
1-16 Akasaka 7-chome
Minato-ku, Tokyo 107, Japan
(Pharmaceuticals)
Bristol-Myers Squibb Co.

Campbell Japan
13-40 Konan 2-chome
Tokyo 108, Japan
(Canned foods)
John W. Argabright, President
Campbell Soup Co.

Champion Spark Plug Co.
908 Maersk Bldg.
8 Nippon Odori
Naka-ku, Yokahama, Kanagawa
231-91, Japan
(Spark plugs)
Champion Spark Plug Co.

Coca-Cola Co.
6-3 Shubuya 4-C chome
Shibuya-ku, Tokyo 150, Japan
Tel.: 81 3 4076311
(Soft drink beverages)
Coca-Cola Export Corp.

Dow Chemical Japan
Hibiya Chunichi Bldg., 6th Floor
1-4 Uchisaiwaicho 2-chome
Chiyoda-ku, Tokyo 100, Japan
(Silicone products)
Dow Chemical Co.

Dr. Pepper Japan Co.
New Aoyama Bldg., W. 1960
1-1-1 Minami Aoyama
Minato-ku, Tokyo 107, Japan
Tel.: 81 3 5917361
(Soft drinks)
Dr. Pepper Co.

Du Pont Japan
Shin-Nikko Bldg.
10-1 Toranomon 2-chome
Minato-ku, Tokyo 105, Japan
(Photographic equipment)
Du Pont, E. I., De Nemours & Co.

Ford Motor Co.
Toranomon Bldg.
26 Shiba Fukide-Cho
Minato-ku, Tokyo, Japan
(Automobiles and parts)
B.R. Lever, President
Ford Motor Co.

Fuji Xerox Co.
3-5 Akasaka 3-chome
Minato-ku, Tokyo 107, Japan
Tel.: 81 3 5853211
(Copiers)
Xerox Corp.

Gillette Inc.
13-31 Kohnan 2-chome
Minato-ku, Tokyo 108, Japan
Tel.: 81 3 4582501
Norman Roberts, Manager
Gillette Co.

B F Goodrich Co. of Japan
36-11 Shinbashi 5-chome
Minato-ku, Tokyo, Japan
Tel.: 81 34 343591
(Plastics, rubber, chemicals)
D.G. Barger, President
B. F. Goodrich Co.

Heinz Japan
13 Hachiman-Cho
Ichigaya Shiniuku, Tokyo 162, Japan
Tel.: 81 3 2698161
(Food products)
H. J. Heinz Co.

Japan Tupperware Co.
Bungei Shunju Bldg.
3-23 Kioi-Cho
Chiyoda-ku, Tokyo 102, Japan
Tel.: 81 3 2655252
(Plastic products)
Dart Industries

Johnson & Johnson Japan
CPO Box 1810
Tokyo 100-91, Japan
Tel.: 81 3 4382911
(Pharmaceuticals, toiletries)
Masami Atarashi, President
Johnson & Johnson

Kellogg
Shinjuku Nomura Bldg.
26-2 Nishi-Shinjuku
Tokyo 160, Japan
(Cereal products)
Kellogg Co.

Kodak Imagica
Tokyo, Japan
(Photofinishing laboratories)
Eastman Kodak Co.

Lilly Eli Japan
9 F Kobe Kanden Bldg.
Ikuta-ku
15 Kano-Cho 6-chome
Kobe, Hyogo 650, Japan
(Pharmaceuticals)
Lilly Eli SA

Philip Morris Kabushiki Kaisha
Akasaka Twin Tower
17-22 Akasaka Choma
Minato-ku, Tokyo 107, Japan
(Tobacco products)
Philip Morris Inc.

Polaroid Asia Pacific
Akasaka Twin Towers, 15th Floor
2-17 Arasako
Minato-ku, Tokyo, Japan
(Photographic equipment)
Polaroid Corp.

Texas Instruments Japan
Aoyama Fuji Bldg.
6-12 Kita Aoyama 3-chome
Minato-ku, Tokyo 107, Japan
(Semiconductors)
Kenneth Sanders, Managing Director

Warner-Lambert
31 Kowa Bldg.
19-1 Shiroganedai 3-chome
Minato-ku, Tokyo, Japan
(Pharmaceuticals)
Parke Davis & Co.

RETAILING AND WHOLESALING

Associated Press
Asahi Shinbun Bldg.
5-3-2 Tsukuji
Chuo-ku, Tokyo 104, Japan
Tel.: 81 03 5455901
Fax.: 81 03 5450895
(Publishing)
Associated Press

Burroughs Co.
13-1 Shimomiyabi-cho
Shinjuku-ku, Tokyo 162, Japan
(Business machines)
Herbert F. Hayde, Chairman
Unisys Corp.

Control Data Japan
Sunshine Bldg., 27th Floor
1-1 Higashi-Ikebukuro 3-chome
Tokyo 170, Japan
(Computer leasing)
Control Data Corp.

GAF
Kogen Bldg. 6F
Tokyo, Japan
(Chemicals)
GAF Corp.

Country-by-Country Listings

Harcourt Brace Jovanovich Japan
Ichibango Central Bldg.
22-1 Ichibancho
Chiyoda-ku, Tokyo 102, Japan
Tel.: 81 3 2343911
(Publishing)
Junichiro Minagawa, Managing Director
Harcourt Brace Jovanovich Inc.

Helene Curtis Japan
Shinjuku Daiichi Seimei Bldg.
7-1 Nishi-Shinjuku 2-chome
Shinjuku-ku, Tokyo 160, Japan
(Hair care products)
Hiroya Yano, President
Helene Curtis Co.

Hokkai Ford Tractor Co.
661 Kotoni Sanjo 7-chome
Nishi-ku, Sapporo, Hokkaido 063, Japan
(Farm machinery)
Toshio Takasusuki, Chairman
Ford Motor Co.

Knight-Ridder Financial News
Ichibancho F.S. Bldg.
8 Ichibancho
Chiyoda-ku, Tokyo 102, Japan
Tel.: 81 03 2301155
Fax.: 81 03 2304828
(Publishing)
Knight-Ridder Inc.

Moody's Japan
Imperial Tower, 13th Floor
1-1 Uchisaiwai-Cho 1-chome
Chiyoda-ku, Tokyo 100, Japan
Tel.: 81 35930921
(Publisher)
Jon Michael McMullen, Vice President
Moody's Investors Service

Tandem Computers
Bingei Shinju Shinkan Bldg.
Kioi-Cho
Chiyoda-ku, Tokyo 102, Japan
Tel.: 81 32346000
(Computer systems)
Tandem Computers

United Press International
Palaceside Bldg.
1-1-1 Hitotsubashi
Chiyoda-ku, Tokyo 100, Japan
Tel.: 81 03 2127911
Fax.: 81 03 2135053
(Publishing)
United Press International

Walt Disney Enterprises of Japan
Horaiya Bldg.
2-1 Roppongi 5-chome
Minato-ku, Tokyo 105, Japan
(Consumer products)
Matsuo Yokyama
The Walt Disney Company

Wang Computer
Shindaiso Bldg. No.5
2-10-7 Dohgenzaka Shibuyaku
Tokyo 104, Japan
(Data processing equipment)
Wang Labs

Wrigley & Co. Japan
1-2-1 Otemachi
Chiyoda-ku, Tokyo 100, Japan
(Chewing gum)
J.E. Dy-Liacco, President
Wrigley, Wm., Jr. Co.

SERVICE INDUSTRIES

A.C. Nielson Company of Japan
Neilson Bldg.
1-1-71 Nakameguro 1-chome
Meguro-ku, Tokyo 153, Japan
Tel.: 81 3 7106551
(Marketing research)
R.B. Norris
Nielson Marketing Research

Booz Allen & Hamilton
1-1-1 Uchisaiwai-Cho
Chiyoda-ku, Tokyo 100, Japan
(Consulting)
Booz Allen & Hamilton

Korn/Ferry International Japan
AIU Bldg., 7th Floor
1-3 Marunouchi 1-chome
Chiyoda-ku, Tokyo 100, Japan
Tel.: 81 3 2116851
(Management consultant)
Andrew Knox, Managing Vice-President
Korn/Ferry International

Little, Arthur D., Inc.
Fukide Bldg.
4-1-13 Toranomon
Minato-ku, Tokyo 105, Japan
Tel.: 81 3 4362196
(Management consulting)
Yoshimichi Yamashita, President
Little, Arthur D., International

Ogilvy & Mather
MSK Bldg., 5th Floor
Nihonbashi Honch 4-15-4
Chuo-ku, Tokyo 103, Japan
Tel.: 81 3 2412841
(Advertising agency)
Kenneth L. Brady, President
Ogilvy & Mather Worldwide

Phillips Petroleum International
606 Shin Tokyo
3-1 Marunouchi 3-chome
Chiyoda-ku, Tokyo 100, Japan
(Sales advising)
Phillips Petroleum Internatinal Corp.

DOMESTIC COMPANIES IN JAPAN

The following is a listing of the major domestic companies of Japan. They are classified by business area: Banking and Finance; Industrial Manufacturing; Retailing and Wholesaling; Service Industries. Company information includes type of business and contact name. These companies will generally hire their own nationals first but may employ Americans.

BANKING AND FINANCE

Bank of Fukuoka
13-1 Tenjin 2-chome
Chuo-ku, Fukuoka 810, Japan
Tel.: 81 92 7111315
Fax.: 81 92 7232441
(Banking)
Toshiaki Yamashita, Chairman

Bank of Tokyo
3-2 Nihonbashi Hongoku-Cho 1-chome
Chuo-ku, Tokyo 103, Japan
(Banking)
Yusuke Kashiwagi, Chairman

Bank of Yokahama
8-2 Nihonbashi 2-chome
Chuo-ku, Tokyo 103, Japan
Tel.: 81 3 2724171
Fax.: 81 3 2816940
(Banking)
Jiro Yoshikuni, Chairman

Chiba Bank
1-2 Chiba-minato
Chiba 260, Japan
Tel.: 81 472 451111
(Commercial banking)
Taro Ogata, Chairman

Dai-Ichi Kangyo Bank
1-5 Uchisaiwaicho 1-chome
Chiyoda-ku, Tokyo 100, Japan
Tel.: 81 3 5961111
(Commercial and international banking, finance)
Ichiro Nakamura, Chairman

Daido Mutual Life Insurance Co.
1-23-101 Esaka
Sulta, Osaka 564, Japan
Tel.: 81 6 3851130
(Insurance)
E. Fukumoto, President

Daiwa Bank
1-8 Bingomachi
Chuo-ku, Osaka 541, Japan
Tel.: 81 6 2711221
Fax.: 81 6 2221880
(Commercial and trust bank)
Sumio Abekawa, Chairman and President

Daiwa Securities Co.
6-4 Otemachi 2-chome
Chiyoda-ku, Tokyo 100, Japan
Tel.: 81 3 2432111
(Securities broker)
Chino Yoshitoki, Chairman

Export-Import Bank of Japan
4-1 Otemachi 1-chome
Chiyoda-ku, Tokyo 100, Japan
Tel.: 81 3 2871221
Fax.: 81 3 2871831
(Banking)
Takashi Tanaka, President

Fuji Bank
5-5 Otemachi 1-chome
Chiyoda-ku, Tokyo 100, Japan
Tel.: 81 3 2162211
Fax.: 81 3 2144150
(Commercial banking)
Taizo Hashida, President

Fuji Fire and Marine Insurance Co.
1-18-11 Minamisenba
Chuo-ku, Osaka 542, Japan
Tel.: 81 6 2667007
Fax.: 81 6 2667102
(Insurance)
Yasuo Oda, Director, Personnel Division

Gunma Bank
194 Motosoja-machi
Maebashi, Gunma 371, Japan
Tel.: 81 27 521111
Fax.: 81 272 529721
(Banking)
Kazuo Yamazaki, Chairman

Hiroshima Bank
3-8 Kamiya-cho 1-chome
Naka-ku, Hiroshima 730, Japan
Tel.: 81 82 2475151
Fax.: 81 82 2477399
(Banking)
Osamu Hashiguchi, President

Japan Development Bank
9-1 Otemachi 1-chome
Chiuoda-ku, Tokyo 100, Japan
Tel.: 81 3 2703211
Fax.: 81 3 2451938
(Development bank)
Gen Takahashi, Governor

Long-Term Credit Bank of Japan
2-4 Otemachi 1-chome
Chiyoda-ku, Tokyo 100, Japan
Tel.: 81 3 2115111
(Commercial banking)
Binsuke Sugiura, Chairman

Mitsubishi Bank
7-1 Marunouchi 2-chome
Chiyoda-ku, Tokyo 100, Japan
Tel.: 81 3 2401111
Fax.: 81 3 2116645
(Commercial banking)
Hajime Yamada, Chairman

Mitsubishi Trust and Banking Corp.
4-5 Marunouchi 1-chome
Chiyoda-ku, Tokyo 100, Japan
Tel.: 81 3 2121211
Fax.: 81 3 2012917
(International banking)
Tadashi Yasui, Chairman

Mitsui Bank
1-2 Yurakucho 1-chome
Chiyoda-ku, Tokyo 100, Japan
Tel.: 81 3 5011111
Fax.: 81 3 5018538
(Commercial banking)
Keno Yamamoto, Director, Human Resources Division

Mitsui Trust & Banking Co.
1-1 Nihonbashi-Muromachi 2-chome
Chuo-ku, Tokyo 103, Japan
Tel.: 81 3 2461541
Fax.: 81 3 2450459
(International banking and finance)
Seiichi Kawasaki, Chairman

Nikko Securities Co.
Shin Tokyo Bldg.
3-1 Marunouchi 3-chome
Chiyoda-ku, Tokyo 100, Japan
Tel.: 81 3 2832211
(Securities broker, underwriter)
Shogo Watanabe, Chairman
Nikko Securities Co.

Nippon Trust Bank
1-8 Nihonbashi 3-chome
Chuo-ku, Tokyo 103, Japan
Tel.: 81 3 2458111
Fax.: 81 3 2744260
(Commercial banking)
Kinichiro Shimada, President

Nippon Life Insurance Co.
7 Imabahi 4-chome
Higashiku, Osaka 541, Japan
Tel.: 81 6 2094500
(Life insurance)
Gentaro Kawase, President

Nomura Securities Co.
9-1 Nihonbashi 1-chome
Chuo-ku, Tokyo 103, Japan
Tel.: 81 3 2111811
(Securities broker)
Setsuya Tabuchi, Chairman

Sanwa Bank
4-10 Fushimimachi
Higashi-ku, Osaka 541, Japan
Tel.: 81 6 2022281
Fax.: 81 6 2291066
(Commercial banking)
Kenji Kawakatsu, Chairman and President

Sumitomo Bank
3-2 Marunouchi 1-chome
Chiyoda-ku, Tokyo, Japan
Tel.: 81 3 2825111
Fax.: 81 3 2871640
(Commercial banking)
Ichiro Isoda, Chairman

Taiyo Kobe Bank
56 Naniwa-machi
Chuo-ku, Kobe 650, Japan
Tel.: 81 78 3318101
(Commercial banking)
Teruyuki Okumura, Chairman

Tokai Bank
21-24 Nishiki 3-chome
Naka-ku, Nagoya 460, Japan
Tel.: 81 5 2211111
(Banking)
Ryuichi Kato, Chairman

Toyo Trust and Banking Co.
4-3 Marunouchi 1-chome
Chiyoda-ku, Tokyo 100, Japan
Tel.: 81 3 2872211
Fax.: 81 3 2011448
(Commerical banking)
Mitsuo Imose, President

Yamaguchi Bank
2-36 4-chome
Takezaki-cho, Shimoneseki City
Yamaguchi Prefecture 750, Japan
Tel.: 81 83 2233411
Fax.: 81 83 2223233
(Commercial banking)
Takeshi Kuwabara, Personnel Department

Yamaichi Securities Co.
4-1 Yaesu 2-chome
Tokyo 104, Japan
Tel.: 81 2 2763181
(Securities underwriter)
Yoshio Yokota, Chairman

Yasuda Trust and Banking Co.
2-1 Yaesu 1-chome
Chuo-ku, Tokyo 103, Japan
Tel.: 81 3 2788111
Fax.: 81 3 2816947
(Commercial banking)
Yoshio Yamaguchi, Chairman

Country-by-Country Listings

INDUSTRIAL MANUFACTURING

Aisin Seiki Co.
2-1 Asahimachi, Kariya City
Aichi Prefecture 448, Japan
Tel.: 81 56 6248687
Fax.: 81 56 6225097
(Auto parts, household appliances, industrial sewing machines)
Kiyoshi Ito, Chairman

Ajinomoto Co.
1-5-8 Kyobashi
Chuo-ku, Tokyo 104, Japan
Tel.: 81 3 2721111
Fax.: 81 3 2978720
(Food products, amino acids, pharmaceuticals, chemicals)
Saburosuke Suzuki, Chairman

Asahi Breweries
7-1 Kyobashi 3-chome
Chuo-ku, Tokyo 104, Japan
Tel.: 81 3 5675111
Fax.: 81 3 5630327
(Beverages, food, pharmaceuticals)
Tsutomu Murai, Chairman

Bridgestone Corp.
10-1 Kyobashi 1-chome
Chuo-ku,Tokyo 104, Japan
Tel.: 81 3 5670111
Fax.: 81 3 5352553
(Chemicals, marine equipment, sporting goods)
Teiji Eguchi, Chairman

Brother Industries
35 Horita-dori 9-chome
Mizuho-ku, Nagoya 467, Japan
Tel.: 81 52 8242511
Fax.: 81 52 8217628
(Business machines, electronic appliances, machine tools)
Tamotsu Shimizu, Managing Director, Personnel Department

Canon Inc.
7-1 Nishi Shinjuku 2-chome
Shinjuku-ku, Tokyo 163, Japan
Tel.: 81 3 3482121
Fax.: 81 3 3498164
(Copying machines, chemicals, business systems, optical products)
Ryuzaburo Kazu, Chairman

Casio Computer
New Sumitomo Bldg.
2-6 Nishi-Shinjuku
Shinjuku-ku, Tokyo 160, Japan
Tel.: 81 3 3474800
(Computing equipment)
Tadao Kashio, Chairman

Citizen Watch Co.
2-1-1, Nishishinjuku
Shinjuku-ku, Tokyo 163, Japan
Tel.: 81 3 3421231
Fax.: 81 3 3421280
(Wristwatches, industrial and office equipment)
Rokuya Yamazaki, Chairman

Daihatsu Motor Co.
1-1 Daihatsu-cho, Ikeda City
Osaka Prefecture 563, Japan
Tel.: 81 72 7518811
Fax.: 81 72 7536880
(Automobiles and parts)
Tomonaru Eguchi, Chairman

Fuji Electric Co.
12-1 Yurakucho 1-chome
Chiyoda-ku, Tokyo 100, Japan
Tel.: 81 3 3337111
Fax.: 81 3 2158321
(Electronic systems, sewage treatment systems, vending machines)
Hideo Abe, Chairman

Fuji Heavy Industries
Subaru Building
7-2 Nishishinjuku 1-chome
Tokyo 160, Japan
Tel.: 81 3 3472008
Fax.: 81 3 3472388
(Transportation equipment, commercial/military aircraft and parts)
Hiroshi Sawai, Managing Director and General Manager, Personnel

Fuji Photo Film Co.
26-30 Nishiazabu 2-chome
Minato-ku, Tokyo 106, Japan
Tel.: 81 34062111
Fax.: 81 34864291
(Photographics, magnetic and industrial products)
Minoru Ohnishi, President

Furukawa Electric Co.
6-1 Marunouchi 2-chome
Chiyoda-ku, Tokyo 100, Japan
Tel.: 81 3 2863276
Fax.: 81 3 2863747
(Power cables, telecommunication fibers)
Masao Funahashi, Chairman

Hattori Seiko Co.
6-21 Kyobashi 2-chome
Chuo-ku, Tokyo 104, Japan
Tel.: 81 3 5632111
Fax.: 81 3 5353594
(Watches, clocks, lenses, computers)
Reijiro Hattori, Chairman

Hitachi
6 Kanda-Surugadai 4-chome
Chiyoda-ku, Tokyo 101, Japan
Tel.: 81 32581111
Fax.: 81 32582375
(Electronics, industrial machinery, metals, chemicals)
Katsushige Mita, President

Hitachi Sales Corp.
2-15 Nishi-Shimbashi 2-chome
Minato-ku, Tokyo 105, Japan
Tel.: 81 3 5022111
Fax.: 81 3 5082856
(Electronics, household appliances)
Yasuja Miyoshi, President

Hitachi Zosen Corp.
1-6-14 Edobori
Nishi-ku, Osaka 550, Japan
Tel.: 81 6 4438051
Fax.: 81 6 4485072
(Steel constructions, diesel engines, ship repair)
Yoshihiro Fujii, President

Honda Motor Co.
1-1 Minami-Aoyama 2-chome
Minato-ku, Tokyo 107, Japan
Tel.: 81 3 4234111
Fax.: 81 3 4230511
(Transportation vehicles, engines)
Satoshi Okubo, Chairman

Honshu Paper Co.
12-8 Ginza 5-chome
Chuo-ku, Tokyo 104, Japan
Tel.: 81 35431801
Fax.: 81 35459035
(Paper products)
Kenji Noda, Personnel

Isuzu Motors
22-10 Minami-Oi 6-chome
Shinagawa-ku, Tokyo 140, Japan
Tel.: 81 3 7611111
Fax.: 81 3 7614236
(Automobiles and parts)
Yozo Tajiri, Personnel Administration

Japan Steel Works
Hibiya-Mitsui Bldg.
1-1-2 Yuraku-Cho 1-chome
Chiyoda-ku, Tokyo 100, Japan
Tel.: 81 3 5016111
(Steel)
Mankichi Tateno, President

Kanematsu-Gosho
14-1 Kyobashi 2-chome
Chuo-ku, Tokyo 104, Japan
Tel.: 81 3 5628111
Fax.: 81 3 5628127
(Electronic equipment, textiles, metals, foodstuffs, petroleum, machinery)
Hideo Suzuki, Chairman

Kawasaki Heavy Industries
1-18 Nakamachi-dori 1-chome
Chuo-ku, Kobe 650, Japan
Tel.: 81 78 3419120
Fax.: 81 78 3419120
(Machinery, aircraft, shipbuilding, engines, motorcycles)
Kenko Hasegawa, Chairman

Kawasaki Steel Corp.
Hibiya Kokusai Building
2-2-3 Uchisaiwaicho
Tokyo 100, Japan
Tel.: 81 3 5973111
Fax.: 81 3 5974868
(Steel, semiconductors, chemicals, magnets, computer services)
Einosuke Murakami, Executive Vice-President, Personnel

Kenwood Corp.
17-5 Shibuya 2-chome
Shibuya-ku, Tokyo 150, Japan
Tel.: 81 3 486551
(Radio and television, electronics)
Kazyoshi Ishizaka, President

Kirin Brewery Co.
26-1 Jingumae 6-chome
Shibuya-ku, Tokyo 150, Japan
Tel.: 81 3 4996111
Fax.: 81 3 4996151
(Beverages)
Masashige Ohzeki, Senior Managing Director, Personnel

Kobe Steel
Tekko Building
8-2 Marunouchi 1-chome
Chiyoda-ku, Tokyo 100, Japan
Tel.: 81 3 2187111
Fax.: 81 3 2872278
(Steel, metals, construction machinery)
Takahiko Shiraishi, Executive Officer, Personnel Group

Komatsu
2-3-6 Akasaka
Minato-ku, Tokyo 107, Japan
Tel.: 81 3 564711
Fax.: 81 3 5872005
(Construction equipment, farm machinery, industrial machinery)
Ryoichi Kawai, Chairman

Konica Corp.
Nomura Bldg.
26-2 Nishi-Shinjuku 1-chome
Shinjuku-ku, Tokyo 163, Japan
Tel.: 81 3 3495251
(Business machines, photographic equipment)
Megumi Ide, President

Matsushita Electric Industrial Co.
1006 Kadoma
Kadoma City, Osaka 571, Japan
Tel.: 81 6 9081121
Fax.: 81 6 9061762
(Video and audio equipment, home appliances, communication equipment)
Masaharu Matsushita, Chairman

Mazda Motor Corp.
3-1 Shinchi, Fuchu-cho
Aki-gun, Hiroshima 730-91, Japan
Tel.: 81 822821111
Fax.: 81 822851223
(Automobiles)
Akira Fujii, Senior Managing Director, Personnel and Human Development

Minolta Camera Co.
2-30 Azuchi-Machi
Higashi-ku, Osaka 541, Japan
Tel.: 81 6 2712251
Fax.: 81 6 2661010
(Office equipment, medical equipment, video systems)
Hideo Tashima, President

Mitsubishi Electric Corp.
Mitsubishi Denki Bldg.
2-3 Marunouchi 2-chome
Tokyo 100, Japan
Tel.: 81 3 2182111
Fax.: 81 3 2183638
(Electronics, electrical appliances)
Shinzaburo Amano, Director, Personnel

Mitsubishi Heavy Industries
5-1 Marunouchi 2-chome
Chiyoda-ku, Tokyo 100, Japan
Tel.: 81 32123111
Fax.: 81 32872438
(Industrial machinery, aircraft, construction, engines)
Yotaro Iida, Chairman

Mitsubishi Motors Corp.
33-8 Shiba 5-chome
Minato-ku, Tokyo 108, Japan
(Automobiles)
Toyoo Tate, President

Mitsubishi Oil Company
1-2-4 Toronomon
Minato-ku, Tokyo 105, Japan
Tel.: 81 3 5957663
Fax.: 81 3 5082521
(Petrochemicals)
Kiyoshi Ishikawa, Chairman

Mitsubishi Petrochemical Co.
5-2 Marunouchi 2-chome
Chiyoda-ku, Tokyo 100, Japan
Tel.: 81 3 2835700
Fax.: 81 3 2130407
(Plastics, chemicals, medical products)
Masaki Yoshida, President

NEC Corp.
33-1 Shiba 5-chome
Minato-ku, Tokyo 108, Japan
Tel.: 81 3 4541111
Fax.: 81 3 7981510
(Communication systems, industrial electronic systems)
Atsuyoshi Ouchi, Chairman

Nikon Corp.
Fuji Bldg. 2
3 Marunouchi 3-chome
Chiyoda-ku, Tokyo 100, Japan
Tel.: 81 3 12145311
(Photographic equipment, lenses)
Shigetada Fukuoka, President

Nintendo Co.
60 Kamitakamatsu
Higashiyama-ku
Kyoto 605, Japan
Tel.: 81 75 5416112
(Video games)
Hiroshi Yamauchi, President and CEO

Nippon Sanso
16-7 Nishi-Shinbashi 1-chome
Minato-ku, Tokyo 105, Japan
Tel.: 81 3 5818336
(Industrial gases)
Hideo Mabuchi, President

Nippon Seiko
1-6-3 Ohsaki
Shinagawa, Tokyo 141, Japan
Tel.: 81 3 7797111
Fax.: 81 3 7797120
(Machinery components)
Masao Hasewawa, Chairman

Nippon Steel Corp.
6-3 Otemachi 2-chome
Chiyoda-ku, Tokyo 100, Japan
Tel.: 81 3 2424111
Fax.: 81 3 2755607
(Seel products)
Akira Miki, Chairman

Nippondenso Co.
1-1 Showa-cho, Kariya City
Aichi Prefecture 448, Japan
Tel.: 81 56 6255511
Fax.: 81 56 6254520
(Electronic goods, automobile parts)
Kengo Toda, Chairman

Nissan Motor Co.
17-1 Ginza 6-chome
Chuo-ku, Tokyo 104, Japan
Tel.: 81 3 5435523
Fax.: 81 3 15451040
(Vehicles, boats, marine engines, rockets, textile machinery)
Takashi Ishihara, Chairman

Osaka Gas Co.
1 Hiranomochi 4-chome
Chuo-ku, Osaka 541, Japan
Tel.: 81 6 2022221
Fax.: 81 6 2261681
(Natural gas)
Masafumi Ohnishi, President

Pioneer Electronic Corp.
4-1 Meguro 1-chome
Meguro-ku, Tokyo 153, Japan
Tel.: 81 3 4941111
Fax.: 81 3 7792163
(Audio and video equipment)
Katsuhiro Abe, Director, Personnel

Ricoh Company
15-5 Minami-Aoyama 1-chome
Minato-ku, Tokyo 107, Japan
Tel.: 81 3 4793111
Fax.: 81 3 4792900
(Office equipment)
Hiroshi Hamada, President

Sansui Electric Co.
14-1 Izumi 2-chome
Suginami-ku, Tokyo 168, Japan
Tel.: 81 3 3248891
(Transformers, amplifiers)
Keizo Fujiwara, President

Sanyo Electric Co.
18 Keihan-hondori 2-chome
Moriguchi-shi, Osaka 570, Japan
Tel.: 81 6 9911181
Fax.: 81 6 9915411
(Audio and video equipment, home appliances)
Yasuaki Takano, Vice President, Personnel

Sanyo-Kokusaku Pulp Co.
1-4-5 Marunouchi
Chiyoda-ku, Tokyo 100, Japan
Tel.: 81 3 2113411
Fax.: 81 3 2876480
(Paper and pulp, chemicals, building materials, lumber)
Shiro Uchikoshi, Director, Personnel

Sharp Corp.
22-22 Nagaike-cho
Abeno-ku, Osaka 545, Japan
Tel.: 81 6 6211221
Fax.: 81 6 6281667
(Audio and video systems, appliances, office equipment)
Haruo Tsuji, President

Sony Corp.
6-7-35 Kita-Shinagawa
Shinagawa-ku, Tokyo 141, Japan
Tel.: 81 3 4482111
Fax.: 81 3 4482244
(Electronic equipment)
Akio Morita, Chairman

Sumitomo Chemical Co.
5-33 Kitahama 4-chome
Chuo-ku, Osaka 541, Japan
Tel.: 81 6 2203272
Fax.: 81 6 2203345
(Chemicals, plastics, electronics, aluminum)
Takeshi Hijikata, Chairman

Sumitomo Corp.
2-2 Hitosubashi 1-chome
Chiyoda-ku, Tokyo 100, Japan
Tel.: 81 3 2175000
Fax.: 81 3 2177860
(Steel and iron products, industrial equipment)
Tadashi Itoh, President

Sumitomo Metal Industries
1-1-3 Otemachi
Chiyoda-ku, Tokyo 100, Japan
Tel.: 81 3 2826111
Fax.: 81 3 2230305
(Steel products)
Hisaharu Hara, Director, Personnel

Susuki Motor Co.
Hamamatsu-Nishi, P.O. Box 1
Hamamatsu 432-91, Japan
Tel.: 81 53 4402342
Fax.: 81 53 4560002
(Motorcycles, four-wheeled vehicles, engines)
Seiichi Inagawa, Chairman

Takeda Chemical Industries
3-6 Doshomachi 2-chome
Chuo-ku, Osaka 541, Japan
Tel.: 81 6 2042111
Fax.: 81 6 2042943
(Pharmaceuticals, chemicals)
Hiroshi Nakanishi, Personnel

Toshiba Corp.
1-1 Shibaura 1-chome
Minato-ku, Tokyo 105, Japan
Tel.: 81 3 4574511
Fax.: 81 3 4561631
(Electronics)
Joichi Aoi, President and CEO

Toyoda Automatic Loom Works
2-1 Toyodacho
Kariya-shi, Aichi Prefecture
448, Japan
Tel.: 81 56 6222511
Fax.: 81 56 6233255
(Textile machinery, industrial vehicles and parts)
Yoshitoshi Yoyoda, President

Toyota Motor Corp.
1 Toyota-cho
Toyota City, Aichi Prefecture
471, Japan
Tel.: 81 56 5282121
Fax.: 81 56 5801116
(Automobiles, industrial vehicles, parts)
Eiji Toyoda, Chairman

Victor Company of Japan (JVC)
8-14 Nihonbashi-Honcho 4-chome
Chuo-ku, Tokyo 103, Japan
Tel.: 81 3 2417811
Fax.: 81 3 2460780
(Audio/visual equipment, electronics)
Toshiro Furichi, Director, Personnel

Yamaha Corp.
10-1 Nakazawamachi,
Hamamatsu City
Shizuoka Prefecture 430, Japan
Tel.: 81 53 4602850
Fax.: 81 53 4652798
(Musical instruments, electronics)
Genichi Kawakami, Chairman

Yamaha Motor Co.
2500 Shingai, Iwata City
Shizuoka Prefecture 438, Japan
Tel.: 81 53 8321138
Fax.: 81 53 8321131
(Motorized vehicles, engines)
Hideto Eguchi, President

Yokohoma Rubber Co.
36-11 Shimbashi 5-chome
Minato-ku, Tokyo 105, Japan
Tel.: 81 3 4327111
Fax.: 81 3 4325616
(Rubber products)
Hisaaki Suzuki, Chairman

RETAILING AND WHOLESALING

Asahi Breweries
7-1 Kyobashi 3-chome
Chuo-ku, Tokyo 104, Japan
Tel.: 81 3 5675111
Fax.: 81 3 5630327
(Beverages, food, pharmaceuticals)
Tsutomu Murai, Chairman

Asics Corp.
1-1 Minatojima Nakamachi 7-chome
Chuo-ku, Kobe, Hyogo 650, Japan
Tel.: 81 78 3033333
(Sporting goods)
Kihachiro Onitsuka, President

Canon Inc.
7-1 Nishi Shinjuku 2-chome
Shinjuku-ku, Tokyo 163, Japan
Tel.: 81 3 3482121
Fax.: 81 3 3498164
(Copying machines, chemicals, optical products)
Ryuzaburo Kazu, Chairman

Diesel Kiki Co.
6-7 Shibuya 3-chome
Shibuya-ku, Tokyo 150, Japan
Tel.: 81 3 4001551
Fax.: 81 3 7974774
(Fuel systems, auto air conditioners)
Shunji Egi, Senior Director, Personnel

Fuji Electric Co.
12-1 Yurakucho 1-chome
Chiyoda-ku, Tokyo 100, Japan
Tel.: 81 3 3337111
Fax.: 81 3 2158321
(Electronic systems, sewage systems, vending machines)
Hideo Abe, Chairman

Hattori Seiko Co.
6-21 Kyobashi 2-chome
Chuo-ku, Tokyo 104, Japan
Tel.: 81 3 5632111
Fax.: 81 3 5353594
(Watches, clocks, lenses, computers)
Reijiro Hattori, Chairman

Ito-Yokado Co.
4-1-4 Shibakoen
Minato-ku, Tokyo 105, Japan
Tel.: 81 3 4592111
Fax.: 81 3 4348373
(Supermarkets, department stores)
Masao Nakamura, Personnel Affairs Officer

Jusco Co.
1 Kanda Nishiki-cho 1-chome
Chiyoda-ku, Tokyo 101, Japan
Tel.: 81 3 2967895
Fax.: 81 3 2922745
(Stores, restaurants)
Takuya Okada, Chairman

Kirin Brewery Co.
26-1 Jingumae 6-chome
Shibuya-ku, Tokyo 150, Japan
Tel.: 81 3 4996111
Fax.: 81 3 4996151
(Brewery, beverages)
Masashige Ohzeki, Senior Director, Personnel

Kyodo News Service
2-2-5 Toranomon
Minato-ku, Tokyo 105, Japan
Tel.: 81 03 5844111
Fax.: 81 03 5056630
(Publishing)

Nichimen Corp.
13-1 Kyobashi 1-chome
Chuo-ku, Tokyo 104, Japan
Tel.: 81 3 2775111
Fax.: 81 3 2817980
(Trading company.)
Hiroichi Yamada, Senior Director, Personnel

Nippon Telegraph and Telephone Corp.
1-6 Uchisaiwaicho 1-chome
Chiyoda-ku, Tokyo 100, Japan
Tel.: 81 3 5093101
Fax.: 81 3 5809104
(Telecommunications)
Haruo Yamaguchi, President

Nomura Trading Co.
15 Bingomachi 1-chome
Higashiku, Osaka 541, Japan
Tel.: 81 6 2688111
(Seafoods, chemicals)
Takaaki Kikuyama, President

TDK Corporation
1-13-1 Nihonbashi
Chuo-ku, Tokyo 103, Japan
Tel.: 81 3 2785111
Fax.: 81 3 2785358
(Magnetic tapes, electronics)
Yutaka Otoshi, Chairman

Tokyu Department Group
24-1 Dogenzaka 2-chome
Shibuya-ku, Tokyo 150, Japan
Tel.: 81 3 47731111
(Department stores)
Mamoru Miura, President

Toppan Printing Co.
1 Kanda Izumi-cho
Chiyoda-ku, Tokyo 101, Japan
Tel.: 81 3 8355741
(Publishing, printing, electronics)
Kazuo Suzuki, President

Yaohan Department Store Co.
1256-1 Terabayashi Okanomiya
Numazu, Shizuoka 410, Japan
Tel.: 81 55 9233234
(Grocery and department stores)
Kazuo Wada, President

SERVICE INDUSTRIES

All Nippon Airways Co.
Kasumigaseki Bldg.
3-2-5 Kasumagaseki
Chiyoda-ku, Tokyo 100, Japan
Tel.: 81 3 5923048
Fax.: 81 3 5923039
(Airline travel)
Takashi Ijichi, Senior Vice President, Personnel

Computer Services Corp.
2-12 Haneda 1-chome
Ohta-ku, Tokyo 144, Japan
Tel.: 81 3 7423171
(Data processing)
Issao Okawa, President

Fujita Corp.
6-15 Sendagaya 4-chome
Shibuya-ku, Tokyo 151, Japan
Tel.: 81 3 4021911
Fax.: 81 3 4971064
(Engineering and construction)
Kazuaki Fujita, Chairman

Japan Air Lines Co.
7-3 Marunouchi 2-chome
Tokyo 100, Japan
(Passenger and freight carrier)
Susumu Yamji, President

Japan Line
Kokusai Bldg.
1-1 Marunouchi 3-chome
Chiyoda-ku, Tokyo 100, Japan
Tel.: 81 3 2866599
(Steamship agent)
H. Naoi, President

Japan Travel Bureau
6-4 Marunouchi 1-chome
Chiyoda-ku, Tokyo 100, Japan
(Passenger transportation)
Hiroshi Ishida, President

Kansai Electric Power Co.
3-22 Nakanoshima 3-chome
Kita-ku, Osaka 530, Japan
Tel.: 81 6 4418598
Fax.: 81 6 4477174
(Electric utility)
Shoichiro Kobayashi, Chairman

Kinki Nippon Tourist Co.
19-2 Kanda Matsunaga-Cho
Chiyoda-ku, Tokyo 101, Japan
Tel.: 81 3 2557111
(Travel agency)
Eiichi Kojima, President

Kyushu Electric Power Co.
2182 Watanabe-dori
Chuo-ku, Fukuoka 810, Japan
Tel.: 81 92 7613031
Fax.: 81 92 7614622
(Electric power)
Tatsuo Kawai, Chairman

Mitsui & Co.
2-1 Ohtemachi 1-chome
Chiyoda-ku, Tokyo 100, Japan
Tel.: 81 3 2851111
Fax.: 81 3 2859819
(Trade)
Toshikuni Yahiro, Chairman

Nippon Express Co.
12-9 Soto-Kanda 3-chome
Chiyoda-ku, Tokyo 101, Japan
Tel.: 81 3 2531111
Fax.: 81 3 2571297
(Transportation, distribution, warehousing, construction)
Takeshi Nagoaka, President

Nissho Iwai Corp.
4-5 Akasaka 2-chome
Minato-ku, Tokyo 107, Japan
Tel.: 81 3 5882111
Fax.: 81 3 5884571
(International trade, management)
Masaru Hayami, Chairman

Ohbayashi Corp.
2-3 Kanda Tsukasa-cho
Chiyoda-ku, Tokyo 101, Japan
Tel.: 81 3 2921111
Fax.: 81 3 2330085
(Construction and engineering)
Yoshiro Ohbayashi, Chairman

Tokyo Electric Power Co.
1-3 Uchisaiwai-cho 1-chome
Chiyoda-ku, Tokyo 100, Japan
Tel.: 81 3 5018111
Fax.: 81 3 5194609
(Electric utility)
Gaishi Hiraiwa, Chairman

Tokyo Gas Company
5-20 Kaigan 1-chome
Minato-ku, Tokyo 105, Japan
Tel.: 81 3 4332111
Fax.: 81 3 4379190
(Gas utility)
Yoichi Akiyama, Director, Personnel

MAJOR INTERNATIONAL COMPANIES IN JAPAN

There are many international firms operating in Japan. These companies will be classified by business area: Banking and Finance; Industrial Manufacturing; Retailing and Wholesaling; and Service Industries. The company information includes type of business, international parent company, and contact name where possible. Your chances of achieving employment are substantially greater if you contact the subsidiary company in Japan rather than the parent company in the home country.

BANKING AND FINANCE

Algemene Bank Nederland-Tokyo
Fuji Bldg., 2-3 Marunouchi 3-chome
Chiyoda-ku, Tokyo, Japan
Tel.: 81 3 32114858
Fax.: 81 3 2165420
(Banking)
W.A.J. Kortekaas, General Manager
Algemene Bank, Netherlands

Australia and New Zealand Bank Group
Yanmar Tokyo Bldg., 8th Floor
1-1 Yaesu 2-chome
Chuo-ku, Tokyo 104, Japan
Tel.: 81 3 2171151
Fax.: 81 3 2818417
(Banking)
Australia and New Zealand Banking Group, Australia

Banco Nacional de Mexico
Kokusai Bldg., No. 710
3-1-1 Marunouchi
Chiyoda-ku, Tokyo 100, Japan
Tel.: 81 3 32135257
(Banking)
Banco Nacional de Mexico

Baring Brothers & Co.
Shin-Kasumigaseki Bldg., 10th Floor
3-2 Kasumigaseki 3-chome
Chiyoda-ku, Tokyo 100, Japan
Tel.: 81 3 35015507
Fax.: 81 3 5016607
(Finance)
Barings PLC, England

Commonwealth Bank-Tokyo
AIU Bldg., 4th Floor
1-3 Marunouchi 1-chome
Chiyoda-ku, Tokyo 100, Japan
Tel.: 81 3 32137311
Fax.: 81 3 2137315
(Banking)
R.L. Potter, General Manager
Commonwealth Bank Group, Australia

Credit Agricole-Japan
Ando Fukuyoschi Bldg., 10th Floor
1-11-28 Akasaka
Minato-ku, Tokyo 107, Japan
Tel.: 81 3 35871617
Fax.: 81 3 6871223
(Banking)
Michael Bovy, Manager
Caisse Nationale de Credit Agricole, France

Deutsche Bank
ARK Mori Bldg.
1-12-32 Akasaka
CPO Box 1430
Minato-ku, Tokyo 107, Japan
(Banking)
Gunter P. Bartel, General Manager
Deutsche Bank, Germany

Dresdner Bank
Ninonbashi Muromachi Center Bldg.
2-15 Nihonbashi-Muromachi 3-chome
Chuo-ku, Tokyo, Japan
Tel.: 81 3 32145961
(Banking)
Dr. Peter-Jorg Klein, Chief Operations Officer
Dresdner Bank, Germany

Harris Trust & Savings Bank
7-1 Yorakucho 1-chome
Chiyoda-ku, Tokyo, Japan
Tel.: 81 3 32153465
(Banking)
Toshio Asanuma, Vice President
Bank of Montreal, Canada

Morgan Grenfell Japan
Hibiya Kokusai Bldg., 4th Floor
2-3 Uchisaiwaicho 2-chome
Chiyoda-ku, Tokyo 100, Japan
Tel.: 81 3 35818950
Fax.: 81 3 5818970
(Securities)
Y. Amano, Chairman
Deutsche Bank, Germany

National Australia Bank
1-1 Nihonbashi Muromachi 2-chome
Chuo-ku, Tokyo 103, Japan
Tel.: 81 3 32418781
Fax.: 81 3 2415369
(Banking)
P.A. Crutchley, General Manager
National Australia Bank, Australia

Nationale-Nederlanden Life Insurance Co.
Kasumigaseki Bldg., 16th Floor
2-5 Kasumigaseki 3-chome
Chiyoda-ku, Tokyo 100, Japan
Tel.: 81 3 35050121
Fax.: 81 3 35030130
(Insurance)
Nationale-Nederlanden, Netherlands

Standard Chartered Bank
Fuji Bldg., 2-3 Marunouchi 3-chome
CPO Box 906
Chiyoda-ku, Tokyo 100-91, Japan
Tel.: 81 3 32136541
Fax.: 81 3 2152448
(Banking)
Standard Chartered, England

Westpac Banking Corp.
Imperial Tower, 8th Floor
1-1-1 Uchisaiwai-Cho
Chiyoda-ku, Tokyo 100, Japan
Tel.: 81 3 35014101
Fax.: 81 3 5014100
(Banking)
Richard Pyvis, General Manager
Westpac Banking Corp., Australia

INDUSTRIAL MANUFACTURING

BASF Japan
3-3 Kioicho
Chiyoda-ku, Tokyo 102, Japan
Tel.: 81 3 32382222
Fax.: 81 3 2635710
(Audio equipment)
Dr. Harold Kohl, Managing Director
BASF Group, Germany

Bayer Japan
Seiwa Bldg.
12-15 Shiba Daimon 1-chome
Minato-ku, Tokyo 105, Japan
(Chemicals)
Oscar Rhode, President
Bayer, Germany

Country-by-Country Listings

Bosch
10-5 Shiba 4-chome
Minato-ku, Tokyo 108, Japan
Tel.: 81 3 34579401
Fax.: 81 3 465423138
(Automotive products)
Robert Bosch GMBH, Germany

Electrolux Ltd.
Gadelius Bldg., 7-8 Moto
Akasaka 1-chome
Tokyo, Japan 107
Tel.: 81 3 34793411
(Automotive parts)
Gunnar Kniberg, Chief
Operations Officer
Electrolux AB, Sweden

Falconbridge Ltd.
Daiichi Seimei Sohgokan Bldg.,
No. 7-1
3-chome Kyobashi
Chuo-ku, Tokyo 104, Japan
Tel.: 81 3 35623971
Fax.: 81 3 5620566
(Mining)
Hajime Amano, President
Falconbridge Ltd., Canada

John Crane Inc.
Tenroku Hankyu Bldg.
1-10 Tenjinbashi 7-chome
Oyodo-ku, Osaka 531, Japan
Tel.: 81 6 3520212
Fax.: 81 6 3586094
(Industrial/mechanical seals)
TI Group, England

Nestle
Nihonbashi Toho Seimei Bldg.
4-10 Nihonbashi Muro-machi 4-chome
Chuo-ku, Tokyo, Japan
Tel.: 81 3 32425231
(Foods)
Nestle, Switzerland

Rhone-Poulenc Japan
No. 16 Kowa Bldg. Annex
9-20 Akasaka 1-chome
Minato-ku, Tokyo, Japan
Tel.: 81 3 35854691
(Chemicals)
Rhone-Poulenc, France

SmithKline & Fujisawa
SKB Bldg., 6 Sanbancho
Chiyoda-ku, Tokyo 102, Japan
(Pharmaceuticals)
SmithKline Beecham, England

Ssangyong Japan Corp.
Matsuoka Tamuracho Bldg.
22-10 Shimbashi 5-chome
Minato-ku, Tokyo, Japan
Tel.: 81 3 34337557
Fax.: 81 3 4343856
(Cement, trading, securities, motors)
Ssangyong Group, South Korea

Tyton Co. of Japan
Kaiko-Bldg., No. 11-15 Ebisu-Minami 1-chome
Shibuya-ku, Tokyo 150, Japan
Tel.: 81 3 37924171
Fax.: 81 3 7108218
(Industrial cable products)
T. Kojima, Chief Operations
Officer
Bowthorpe Holdings, England

Vivitar Japan
Marusho Bldg., 6th Floor
12 Yotsuya 3-chome
Shinjuku-ku, Tokyo 160, Japan
Tel.: 81 3 3576021
(Photographic equipment, electronics)
Noboru Muraoka, President
Franz Haniel & Cie, Germany

RETAILING AND WHOLESALING

Alron Chefaro
Ueno Bldg., No. 1
1-19 1-chome Yotsuya
Shinjuku-ku, Tokyo 160, Japan
Tel.: 81 3 33415811
Fax.: 81 3 511174
(Diagnostic equipment)
Akzo N.V., Netherlands

Arianespace Inc.
Hibiya Central Bldg.
1-2-9 Nishi-Shimbashi
Minato-ku, Tokyo 105, Japan
Tel.: 81 3 592766
Fax.: 81 3 5922768
(Space technology)
Jean-Louis Claudon, Director
Arianspace Participation, France

Bang & Olufsen of Japan
Kudan-New Central Bldg.
4-5 Kudan-Kita 1-chome
Chiyoda-ku, Tokyo 102, Japan
Tel.: 81 3 32614431
(Electronics)
Kazuhiko Okamoto, Managing Director
Bang & Olufsen A/S, Denmark

BMW Japan Corp.
15-17 Takanawa 2-chome
Minato-ku, Tokyo, Japan
Tel.: 81 3 34433231
(Automobiles)
Bayerische Motoren Werke Aktiengesellschaft, Germany

EMI Music International Services
Toshiba-EMI Bldg.
2-17 Akasaka 2-chome
Tokyo, Japan 107
Tel.: 81 3 35858780
(Music products)
G. Collins, Resident Director
Thorn EMI, U.K.

Haagen-Dazs Japan
Arai Bldg., 3rd Floor, #15
19-20 Jungumae 6-chome
Shibuya-ku, Tokyo 150, Japan
Tel.: 81 3 34982911
(Ice cream stores)
Hank Wendler, Chief Operations Officer
Grand Metropolitan, England

Laura Ashley Japan Co.
1-1 Kanda-Nishikicho
Chiyoda-ku, Tokyo 101, Japan
Tel.: 81 3 32967303
(Clothes)
Laura Ashley, England

Lion Henkel Corp.
1-3-7 Honjo
Sumida-ku, Tokyo 130, Japan
Tel.: 81 3 36216211
Fax.: 81 3 6216328
(Detergents, chemicals)
Hiroshi Kobayashi, Chairman
Henkel KGAA, Germany

McCain Japan
Hongo-House 1307
1-27-8 Hongo
Bunkyo-ku, Tokyo, Japan
(Food products)
Carl Morris, President
McCain Foods, Canada

Sandoz Yakuhin
Nishi Azabu Mitsui Bldg.
17-30 Nishi Azabu 4-chome
Minato-ku, Tokyo, Japan
Tel.: 81 3 37978000
(Pharmaceuticals)
Sandoz Ltd., Switzerland

SEB Japan Co.
T.O.C. Bldg.
7-22-17 Nishigotanda
Shinagawa-ku, Tokyo 141, Japan
Tel.: 81 3 34945951
Fax.: 81 3 34902190
(Electronics)
Group SEB, France

SERVICE INDUSTRIES

BHP Nominees
Kishimoto Bldg., 10th Floor
2-1 Marunouchi 2-chome
Chiyoda-ku, Tokyo, Japan
(Investment)
B.W. O'Flynn, Chief Representative
Broken Hill Co., Australia

Club Mediterranee
Banque Indosuez Bldg., 9th Floor
1-1-2 Akasaka
Minato-ku, Tokyo 107, Japan
(Resort hotels)
Alexis Agnello, Chief Operations Officer
Club Mediterranee, France

Hoechst Japan
New Hoechst Bldg.
10-16 Akasaka 8-chome
Minato-ku, Tokyo 107, Japan
Tel.: 81 3 34795111
Fax.: 81 3 4795157
(Holding company)
H.Waesche, Chief Executive Officer
Hoechst AG, Germany

Saatchi & Saatchi Advertising
Izumikan Sanbancho Bldg., 4th Floor
3-8 Sanbancho
Chiyoda-ku, Tokyo 102, Japan
Tel.: 81 3 2218600
Fax.: 81 3 2648610
(Advertising)
Ian Hamilton, Chairman
Saatchi & Saatchi Advertising International, England

Toppan Moore Co.
Shufunotomo Bldg.
1-6 Surugadai, Kanda
Chiyoda-ku, Tokyo 101, Japan
Tel.: 81 3 32952411
(Printing)
K. Kinami, President
Toppan Printing Co., Japan

Universal Public Relations
BR Shinagawi Bldg. 1
20-9 Kitashinagawa 1-chome
Shinagawa-ku, Tokyo 140, Japan
Tel.: 81 3 54795001
Fax.: 81 3 54795218
(Public relations)
Hiromichi Kubota, Senior Managing Director
Shandwick, U.K.

MAJOR INTERNATIONAL NON-PROFIT ORGANIZATIONS IN JAPAN

Asia Electronics Union
4-2, Uchisaiwaicho, 1-chome
Chiyoda-ku, Tokyo 100, Japan
Tel.: 81 3 5917161

Asian Pacific Youth Forum
6-12 Izumi, 3-chome
Suginami-ku, Tokyo 168, Japan
Tel.: 81 3 3225164

Asian Patent Attorneys Assoc.
c/o Asamura Patent Office
331 New Ohtemachi Bldg.,
Tokyo 100, Japan
Tel.: 81 3 2113651

Asian Productivity Organization
4-14 Akasaka 8-chome
Minato-Ku, Tokyo 107, Japan
Tel.: 81 3 4087221

East-West Sign Language Assoc.
Department of Linguistics
International Christian University
10-2, 3-chome, Osawa
Mitaka, Tokyo 181, Japan

Ikebana International
c/o Mrs. Kaeko Nakashima
1-6 Surugadai Kanda
Chiyoda-Ku, Tokyo 101, Japan

International Association of Agriculture Medicine and Rural Health
c/o Saku Central Hospital 197, Usuda
Minami-Saku, Negano
Prefecture 384-03, Japan
Tel.: 81 267 823131

International Assoc. of Ports and Harbors
Kotohira-Kaikan Bldg., 2-8
Toranomon 1-chome Minato-Ku, Tokyo 105, Japan
Tel.: 81 3 483535

International Congress on Fracture
c/o Institute for Fracture
Tohoku University, Aramaki
Aoba, Sendai, Japan
Tel.: 81 222 221800

Pan-Pacific and South-East Asia Women's Assoc.
2-20-2 Higashi Nakano
Nakano-ku, Tokyo 164, Japan
Tel.: 81 3 3611490

Universal Medical Esperanto Assoc.
c/o Saburo Yamazoe, M.D.
371 Maebashi-Shi
Iwagami-Machi 4-8-9, Gunma
Ken, Japan
Tel.: 81 272 317839

World Assoc. of Societies of Pathology -Anatomic and Clinical
c/o Tadashi Kwai, M.D.
Jichi Medical School
Minamikawachi mach, Tochigi
3311-1, Japan
Tel.: 81 285 442111

World Friendship Centre
5-8-20 Midori Machi
Minmi-Ku, Hiroshima 734,
Japan
Tel.: 81 82 2515529

MAJOR HOTEL EMPLOYERS IN JAPAN

Akasaka Prince
1-2 Kioi-cho
Chiyoda-Ku, Tokyo 102, Japan
Tel.: 81 03 2341111

Akasaka Tokyo Hotel
2-14-3, Nagatacho
Chiyoda-ku 107, Tokyo, Japan
Tel.: 81 03 5802311

ANA Hotel Tokyo
1-12-33, Akasaka
Minato-ku 107, Tokyo, Japan
Tel.: 81 03 5051111

ANA Sheraton Hotel Osaka
1-3-1, Dojimahama
Kita-ku, Osaka 530, Japan
Tel.: 81 06 3471112

Capital Tokyu Hotel
2-10-3, Nagata-Cho
Chiyoda-ku, Tokyo 100, Japan
Tel.: 81 03 5814511

Century Hyatt Tokyo
2-7-2, Nishi-Shinjuku
Shinjuku-ku, Tokyo 160, Japan
Tel.: 81 03 3490111

Fairmont Hotel
2-1-17, Kudan-Minami
Chiyoda-ku 102, Tokyo, Japan
Tel.: 81 03 2621151

Holiday Inn Nankai Osaka
28-1, Kyuzaemon-Cho
Minami-ku, Osaka 542, Japan
Tel.: 81 06 2138281

Holiday Inn Tokyo
1-13-7, Hatchobori
Chuo-ku, Tokyo 104, Japan
Tel.: 81 03 5536161

Hotel Grand Palace
1-1-1, Uchisaiwaicho
Chiyoda-ku , Tokyo 100, Japan
Tel.: 81 03 2641111

Hotel Metropolitan
1-6-1, Nishi-lkebukuro
Toshima-ku, Tokyo 171, Japan
Tel.: 81 03 9801111

Hotel Pacific Meridien Tokyo
3-13-3, Takanawa
Minato-ku, Tokyo 954, Japan
Tel.: 81 03 4456711

Imperial Hotel
1-1-1, Uchisaiwai-Cho
Chyoda-ku, Tokyo 100, Japan
Tel.: 81 03 5041111

Keio Plaza Inter-Continental Hotel
2-2-1, Nishi-Shinjuku, 2-chome
Tokyo 160, Japan
Tel.: 81 03 3440111

Kyoto Takaragaike Prince Hotel
Takaragaike
Sankyo-ku, Kyoto 606, Japan
Tel.: 81 075 7121111

Narita Tokyu Inn
31, Ohyama
Chiba Prefecture, Narita 286-01, Japan
Tel.: 81 0476 330109

New Takanawa Prince Hotel
3-13-1, Takanawa
Minato-ku, Tokyo 108, Japan
Tel.: 81 03 4421111

Nigata Grand Hotel
5-11-20, Bandai
Nigata City 950, Japan
Tel.: 81 025 2453331

Osaka Riverside Hotel
5-10-160, Nakanocho
Miyakojima-ku, Osaka 534, Japan
Tel.: 81 06 9283251

Osaka Terminal Hotel
3-1-1, Umeda
Kita-ku, Osaka 530, Japan
Tel.: 81 06 3441235

Ramada Renaissance Ginza Tobu Hotel
14-10, Ginza 6-chome
Chuo-ku, Tokyo 104, Japan
Tel.: 81 03 5460111

Royal Hotel
5-3-68, Nakanoshima, Kita-Ku
Osaka 530, Japan
Tel.: 81 06 4481121

Sheraton Grand Tokyo Bay Hotel and Towers
1-9, Maihama
Urayasu, Chiba 279, Japan
Tel.: 81 0473 555555

Shiba Park Hotel
1-5-10, Shiba Koen
Minato-Ku, Tokyo 105, Japan
Tel.: 81 03 4334141

Takanawa Prince Hotel
3-13-1, Takanawa
Minato-Ku, Tokyo 108, Japan
Tel.: 81 03 4471111

Tokyo Hilton International
6-6-2, Nishi-Shinjuku
Shinjuku-ku, Tokyo 160, Japan
Tel.: 81 03 3445111

Tokyo Prince Hotel
3-3-1, Shiba-Kohen
Minato-Ku, Tokyo 105, Japan
Tel.: 81 03 4321111

INTERNATIONAL SCHOOLS IN JAPAN

International Schools Services
P.O. Box 5910
Princeton, NJ 08543
American teachers seeking employment abroad may contact this recruitment service.

American School In Japan
1-1-1, Nomizu
Chofu-dhi, Tokyo 182, Japan
Tel.: 81 422 316351
(U.S. school, Nursery-13)

Aoba International School
2-10-34 Aobadai
Meguro-ku, Tokyo, Japan
Tel.: 81 3 4611442
(U.S. bilingual school, Nursery-1)

Canadian Academy
Nagminedai 2-chome
Nada-ku, Kobe 657, Japan
Tel.: 81 78 8815211
(U.S. International Baccalaureate school, pre-K-13)

Christ the King International School
14 Maehara
Ginowan City, Okinawa, Japan
Tel.: 81 9889 73393/72366
(U.S. school, K-12)

Christian Academy in Japan
1-2-14 Shinkawa-cho
Higashi Kurume-shi, Tokyo 203, Japan
Tel.: 81 424 710022
(U.S. school, K-12)

Fukuoka International School
4-1-28 Maidashi
Higashi-ku, Fukuoka-shi 812, Japan
Tel.: 81 92 6410326
(U.S. school, K-9)

Hiroshima International School
Koyo New Town "C"
Koyo-cho, Hiroshima 739, Japan
Tel.: 81 82 2216202
(U.S.-U.K.-Australian-New Zealand school, K-9)

Hokkaido International School
5-35, 3-jo, 2-chome, Fukuzumi
Toyohira-ku, Sapporo 062, Japan
Tel.: 81 11 8511205
(U.S. school, 1-9)

International School of the Sacred Heart
4-3-1 Hiroo
Shibuya-ku, Tokyo 150, Japan
Tel.: 81 3 4003951
(U.S.-U.K.-Japanese, International Baccalaureate, K-12)

Japan International School
5-20 Kamiyama-cho
Shibuya-ku, Tokyo, Japan
Tel.: 81 3 4688476
(U.S. bilingual school, 1-9)

Kyoto International School
11-1 Ushinomiya-cho, Yoshida
Sakyo-ku, Kyoto 606, Japan
Tel.: 81 75 7714022
(U.S.-U.K. school, K-9)

Marist Brothers International School
2-1 1-chome, Chimori-cho
Suma-ku, Kobe 654, Japan
Tel.: 81 78 73266/73267
(U.S. school, pre-K-12)

Nagoya International School
2686 Minamihara, Nakashidami
Moriyama-ku, Nagoya 463, Japan
Tel.: 81 52 7362025
(U.S. school, pre-K-12)

Nishimachi International School
2-14-7 Moto Azabu
Minato-ku, Tokyo, Japan
Tel.: 81 3 4515520
(U.S. school, K-9)

Okinawa Christian School
1300 Aza Makiminato
Urasoe, Okinawa, Japan
Tel.: 81 988 773661
(U.S. school, pre-K-12)

Saint Maur International School
83 Yamate-cho
Naka-ku, Yokohama 231, Japan
Tel.: 81 45 6415751
(U.S., International Baccalaureate school, pre-K-12)

Seisen International School
12-15 Yoga 1-chome
Setagaya-ku, Tokyo 158, Japan
Tel.: 81 3 7042661
(U.S., International Baccalaureate school, pre-K-12)

St. Joseph International School
85 Yamate-cho
Naka-ku, Yokohama 231, Japan
Tel.: 81 45 6410065
(U.S. school, pre-K-12)

St. Mary's International School
6-19, Seta 1-chome
Setagaya-ku, Tokyo 158, Japan
Tel.: 81 3 7093411
(U.S., International Baccalaureate school, K-12)

St. Michael's International School
17-2 Nakayamate-dori 3-chome
Chuo-ku, Kobe 650, Japan
Tel.: 81 78 2318885
(U.K. school, pre-K-6)

Yokohama International School
258 Yamate-cho
Naka-ku, Yokohama 241, Japan
Tel.: 81 045 6220084
(U.S.-U.K., International Baccalaureate school, pre-K-13)

China: The People's Republic, Taiwan, Hong Kong, Macau

The People's Republic of China

The People's Republic of China (PRC), with nearly 4 million square miles, is larger than the contiguous United States and ranks as the third largest country in the world. Over two-thirds of China, however, is either mountainous or desert. China is bordered by Mongolia and the Soviet Union on the north; the Soviet Union, Afghanistan, Pakistan, and India on the west; Vietnam, Laos, Burma, Bhutan, Nepal, and India on the south;

and North Korea, the East China Sea, and the South China Sea on the east.

The northeastern portion of the country is China's industrial heartland, with plentiful supplies of raw materials and fuel products, including oil and coal. The northern region is a large plain that contains Beijing and several other large industrial cities, and it is also a well-cultivated agricultural center. Southern China is intensely cultivated, especially around the major river basins. This is the most densely populated section of the country. The western parts of China, Tibet, and Xinjiang, contain over 40% of the land but less than 1% of the people.

Han Chinese provide 95% of the population, while Mongols, Koreans, Manchus, and a variety of other minorities comprise the rest. Tibet's population of 4 million includes over 500,000 Han Chinese. Tibetans have rebelled against Chinese rule several times. The Xinjiang Uygur region in Central Asia is only one-quarter Chinese. Mandarin Chinese is the official national language, but different dialects predominate in various regions. China is officially atheist but has traditionally included Confucian, Buddhist, and Taoist groups.

Human bone remnants from the Neolithic Age and earlier have been located in China. Moreover, the fossilized remains of Peking Man are estimated to be over 400,000 years old. A recognizable Chinese civilization achieved prominence by 1500 B.C.E. After a long series of dynasties, the Manchu Ch'ing Dynasty established itself in 1644 and ruled until 1911. The last decades of Ch'ing imperial rule featured massive internal instability and increasing foreign exploitation. The republic was finally declared in 1912.

While European powers and the U.S. were creating spheres of influence on China's coast in the late nineteenth and early twentieth centuries, Japan was aggressively acquiring Chinese territories and dependencies. By 1933, Japan had taken Korea, Taiwan, Manchuria, and several islands. Japan invaded China proper in 1937. Following World War II, China regained most of its territory but continued to suffer from a civil war between the Communist Red Army and the Nationalist Kuomintang. The Communists eventually forced the Nationalists to flee to Taiwan in 1949.

The People's Republic of China was proclaimed in 1949 with Mao Zedong as its leader. China and the Soviet Union initially enjoyed cordial relations while the U.S. refused to recognize the new regime. Chinese and American troops actually fought against each other during the Korean War in the early 1950s. Chinese relations with the U.S.S.R. deteriorated in the 1960s and remain distant today.

Economic development in the 1950s progressed significantly under central planning. At the same time, at least 800,000 people were executed for political reasons. Mao instituted the Great Leap Forward in 1958 as an attempt to accelerate Chinese development. Instead, the program's collectivization policies led to food shortages and was consequently abandoned in 1960.

The Great Proletarian Cultural Revolution was launched in 1965 in order to restore ideological purity and revolutionary fervor. Massive repression ensued and thousands of Communist Party leaders, including Deng Xiaoping, were sent to the countryside. By the early 1970s the movement had exhausted its sources of support, and many formerly purged officials returned to power.

Political turmoil continued, and following Mao's death in 1976, the new group in power moderated most national policies and sought to improve foreign relations. Except for a brief border war with Vietnam in 1979, China enhanced its international position. The PRC gained recognition as the Chinese representative to the United Nations in 1971 as Taiwan was expelled. President Nixon visited China in 1972, and in 1979 formal relations with the U.S. were restored.

China has focused domestically upon renewing economic expansion, controlling population growth, and maintaining stability. Under Deng Xiaoping, China pursued a policy of dramatic economic reforms. Growth rates increased throughout the 1980s as private enterprises and foreign investment boosted the Chinese economy. Although economic reforms apparently succeeded in improving living standards, political reform stagnated, leading to a massive student protest in Tiananmen Square in Beijing in 1989. The army was called to crush the protest, and at least 5,000 students were killed. Deng is believed to have formed political alliances with conservatives in order to hold power during the protests.

The U.S. and China enjoyed cordial relations until the Tiananmen massacre. Various multilateral agencies and most of the international community severely condemned the Chinese government's behavior. Foreign investment decreased significantly during the next year. Since then, however, foreign relations have improved again. China has attempted to improve relations with the Soviet Union and is negotiating for greater influence in Hong Kong prior to repatriation in 1997.

Most sinologists expect Chinese policies to liberalize after the deaths of Deng and the rest of the current octogenarian leadership. Nonetheless, current Prime Minister Li Peng and other younger conservatives seem well entrenched. At the opening session of the 1991 National People's Congress, Li Peng emphasized stability over economic growth. He also promised to expand the role of the market in the economy but intends to preserve central planning. Notwithstanding oppostition from Congress, China received "most favored nation" status in 1991, so commerce and trade between the U.S. and China should remain healthy, with a positive effect on employment.

Using the language

Mandarin Chinese is the official language, but several other dialects are found in different regions: Cantonese, Fukiense, Wu, and Hakka. A few words in Chinese will always ingratiate you with the people you meet, but be careful to use the proper pronunciation, as the same word will often mean different things, depending on intonation.

Despite the variety in spoken Chinese, the written language is uniform throughout the country. In translating Chinese into the Roman alphabet, several systems have been used. In the West, the Wade-Giles system predominated until 1979, when China began translating documents and public materials using the Pinyin system. Pinyin generally reflects the Beijing pronunciation. Most references to China today utilize the Pinyin system. China's capital, for example, is Beijing in Pinyin but Peking in Wade-Giles, and the name of the founder of the People's Republic is spelled Mao Tse-tung in Wade-Giles but Mao Zedong in Pinyin.■

Current Economic Climate

China's gross national product, about $350 billion, is one of the world's largest. Population pressures, however, reduce per capita income to about $300, one of the world's lowest. China currently contains 1.5 billion people, about one-quarter of the world's people, although the growth rate has been decreasing. Only 45% of the population lives in urban areas. China's largest cities are Shanghai, with 12 million inhabitants, Beijing with 9 million, Tianjin 5 million, Guangzhou 4 million, Shenyang 4 million, and Wuhan 3 million.

The nation's leading industries include steel, textiles, motor vehicles, and agricultural machinery and implements. China possesses large deposits of coal, iron, lead, tin, and many other minerals. Wheat, rice, and cotton are the principal agricultural products. Most-favored-nation status allowed China to amass a $10.4 billion trade surplus with the U.S. in 1990. Chinese trade barriers, however, can run as high as 170% tariffs. The total value of Chinese trade in 1990 was $115 billion.

Most foreign investment takes place in the coastal provinces. Guangdong, bordering Hong Kong, is the primary location for Hong Kong and many U.S. firms. Japanese companies concentrate in Liaoning; South Koreans in Liaoing and Shandong; and Taiwanese in Fujian. Foreign investment at the beginning of 1990 was less than $1 billion, reflecting tension following the Tiananmen massacre, but climbed to nearly $2 billion by early 1991. Firms that have announced new investment in China include IBM, Proctor & Gamble, Heinz, and DuPont from the U.S., Volkswagen from Germany, and Citroen from France.

Concerned over the establishment of European and North American trading blocs, China has attempted to pursue closer economic and trade relations with Japan. China has also requested more development aid. Japanese investment fell by 45% in the six months after the Tiananmen crackdown but rose again in late 1990. Nearly $25 billion has been invested by foreign companies in China in the last five years.

Inflation has been a problem in recent years. In 1990, inflation was reduced to 6% from about 15% in 1989. The government's generous credit policies, however, are pushing inflation back up into double-digits in 1991. Unemployment is currently at 5%, and the government is granting credit to large, inefficient enterprises to keep the jobless rate from rising further. Over one-third of Chinese state-owned enterprises operate at a loss and would likely fail without government support.

The private economy, however, is thriving. In 1980, state-owned enterprises accounted for 80% of China's economic output. Today, the state-controlled economy produces less than half of the national output. In the countryside, the private economy has essentially overwhelmed the state sector. Most private businesses are in the form of "collective enterprises." Some are more private than others, but they operate independently of the state and may soon produce virtually all of China's industrial output.

CHINA'S LARGEST TRADING PARTNERS
(In annual trade value in billions of U.S. dollars)

Hong Kong	$20
Japan	$18
United States	$8.2
European Community	$7.7
Taiwan (indirect)	$4.1
Southeast Asia	$3.1
Soviet Union	$2.4
Canada	$1.9
Australia	$1.7

Getting Around in China

The national airline, CAAC (Civil Aviation Administration of China), provides service between most major cities but is rather inefficient and expensive for foreigners. The train system also provides special cars for tourists but at much higher fares than usual. Tickets can only be bought for trains departing from the city of purchase. In the cities, buses are a convenient way to get around. Beijing and Shanghai also have subway systems. Bicycles are certainly the most common means of transportation and can be rented easily.

Using Chinese currency

Renminbi, or people's money, is the currency normally used in China. Foreign Exchange Certificates, or FECs, have been developed for foreigners to use for all expenses. FECs should be used for hotels, train tickets, airline tickets, and in special shops called Friendship Stores. In practice, renminbi can be used by foreigners for these purposes if the clerk is willing. Renminbi and FECs are both subdivided into smaller units: 10 fen equal 1 jiao, 10 jiao equal 1 yuan. It is illegal to circulate foreign currency.■

Employment Regulations for Americans

Americans must provide a visa to enter China. Tour groups can acquire visas more easily than individuals. If applying as an individual, you should expect to wait several months to obtain a visa. Write to the China International Travel Service to explain in detail why you want to enter the country and what you will be doing there. This agency is responsible for all foreign tourism in China. Then write to the Chinese Embassy, which will provide you with an application.

China International Travel Service (Luxingshe)
6 Ch'ang an Ave. East
Beijing, China

Embassy of the People's Republic of China
2300 Connecticut Ave. N.W.
Washington, DC 20008
Tel.: (202) 328-2500

Foreigners are generally not allowed to work in China unless they have received special permission from a government agency. Chinese colleges and universities do offer year-long teaching positions to foreigners who have at least a master's degree and five years' teaching experience. Although many young people now learn English, to communicate with the vast majority of Chinese, you should know at least a few phrases in the language.

Business cards

It is a good idea to carry business cards in China. The cards should contain one's name, full title or position, employer or organization, phone number, and address. You should have this information in Chinese on one side and in English on the other. Presenting business cards is a common custom in East Asia and will help potential employers, customers, clients, or anyone else you may meet remember you. Chinese society is much more formal than ours, and full titles and positions are important to know. Punctuality for meetings is also very important.■

Teaching English in China

Teaching positions, particularly in English, can be found in China. Checking with local colleges for openings may present an opportunity. A few programs specifically place Americans in teaching positions. World Teach sponsors a year-long volunteer teaching program in China for college graduates. The Chinese Education Association for International Exchange, at the Chinese Embassy, recruits foreigners for teaching jobs. In addition, the Bureau of Foreign Affairs at the Ministry of Education may also be of assistance. You may also be interested in volunteer work. Although traditional workcamps do not exist in China, International Christian Youth Exchange places people aged 18 to 24 in services covering education, construction, and health care.

Bureau of Foreign Affairs
Ministry of Education
Beijing 10086, China

Education Division
Embassy of the People's Republic of China
2300 Connecticut Ave. N.W.
Washington, DC 20008

International Christian Youth Exchange
134 W. 26th St.
New York, NY 10001

World Teach
Institute for International Development
1 Eliot St., Harvard University
Cambridge, MA 02138

Organizations for Further Information

The following organizations, both in the U.S. and China, may be helpful in the job search. American embassies and consulates have commercial and/or economic sections that can provide you with business information and explain aspects of the local economy. World Trade Centers usually include many foreign companies operating in the country. Foreign government missions in the U.S. such as National Tourist Offices and embassies and consulates can furnish visas and information on work permits and other important regulations. They may also offer economic and business information about the country.

CHAMBERS OF COMMERCE

American Chambers of Commerce in China
Weyerhaeuser Ching Ltd.
Noble Tower No. 907, 22 Jianguo Menwai, Daijie
Beijing, China
Tel.: 86 5122288, ext. 2907

Chinese Chamber of Commerce of New York
Confucius Plaza, 33 Bowery, Room C203
New York, NY 10002
Tel.: (212) 226-2795

Chinese Chamber of Commerce of San Francisco
730 Sacramento St.
San Francisco, CA 94108
Tel.: (415) 982-3000

China Council for Promotion of International Trade
1 Fu Xing Men Wai St.
Beijing, China
Tel.: 86 89 61

U.S. CONSULAR OFFICES

American Consulate General, Chengdu
Jinjiang Hotel, 180 Renmin Rd.,
Chengdu, Sichuan, Box 85
Chengdu, China
Tel.: 86 028 24481, ext.131
Glen Carey, Consular Officer

American Consulate General, Guangzhou
Dong Fang Hotel, Liu Hua Rd.,
Box 100
Guangzhou, China
Tel.: 86 20 669900, ext.1000
Todd N. Thurwachter,
Commercial Officer

American Consulate General, Shanghai
1469 Huai Hai Middle Rd., Box
200
Shanghai, China
Tel.: 86 21 336880
Nora Sun, Commercial Officer

American Consulate General, Shenyang
40 Lane 4, Section 5, Sanjing
St., Heping District
Shenyang, China
Tel.: 86 24 290000
Richard Mohr, Commercial
Officer

China Embassy Commercial Section
Xiu Shui Bei Jie 3
100600, PRC. Box 50
Beijing, China
Tel.: 86 1 5323831
Timothy P. Stratford,
Commercial Officer

Consulate General of the PRC, Houston
3417 Montrose Blvd.
Houston, TX 77006

Consulate General of the PRC, New York
520 12th Ave.
New York, NY 10036

Consulate General of the PRC, San Francisco
1450 Laguna St.
San Francisco, CA 94225

Embassy of the People's Republic of China
2300 Connecticut Ave. N. W.
Washington, DC 20008
Tel.: (202) 328-2500

National Committee on U.S.-China Relations
777 United Nations Plaza
New York, NY 10017

National Council for U.S.-China Trade
1818 N St. N.W.
Washington, DC 20036
Tel.: (202) 429-0340

WORLD TRADE CENTERS IN CHINA

Convention Center of Shenzhen
Parker Hill
Shenzhen, China
Tel.: 86 22834

Jiansu Provincial Travel and Tourism Corp., PRC
North Zhong Shan Road
Nanjing, China
Tel.: 86 34121

Prepatatory Office of Shanghai World Trade Centre
c/o CCPIT Shanghai Sub-Council
33 Zhong Shan Dong yi Lu
Shanghai, China
Tel.: 86 232348

OTHER INFORMATIONAL ORGANIZATIONS

China International Travel Service
60 E. 42nd St., Rm. 465
New York, NY 10165
Tel.: (212) 867-0271

China International Travel Service (Luxingshe)
6 Ch'ang an Ave. East
Beijing, China

China National Tourist Office
60 E. 42nd St., Suite 3216
New York, NY 10165

Business Directories

Although not always easy to find, business directories can prove invaluable in the international job search. Most directories list company names, addresses, products, and phone numbers. Some directories include executive names and titles and financial information about the company. These sources provide you with the names of the people to contact for employment information as well as financial data.

China Business Manual. Published irregularly by the National Council for U.S.-China Trade, 1818 N St. N.W., Washington, DC 20036. Provides information on a variety of agencies related to foreign trade.

China Directory. Annual publication of Radiopress, Inc., Fuji Television Bldg., 7 Kawada-cho, Shinjuku-ku, Tokyo 162, Japan. Detailed listing of 2,000 agencies, government bodies, and companies.

China Directory of Industry and Commerce. Biennial publication distributed by Professional Book Center, 5600 NE Hassado St., Portland, OR 97213. Provides information on 10,000 firms, both private and state controlled.

China Facts and Figures Annual. Academic International Press, Box 1111, Gulf Breeze, FL 32561. Provides basic information on various government agencies and companies.

China Phone Book & Address Directory. Annual publication of China Phone Book Co., GPO Box 11581, Hong Kong. Lists basic information on foreign companies and enterprises in China as well as various agencies and institutions.

China Telephone Directory. Published irregularly by the China Ministry of Posts and Telecommunications, 129 Xidan Bei Dajie, Beijing, China. Lists basic information on 22,000 Chinese businesses and agencies.

MAJOR AMERICAN COMPANIES IN CHINA

Some American firms operate in China. The following companies are classified by business area: Banking and Finance; Industrial Manufacturing; Retailing and Wholesaling; and Service Industries. The company information includes type of business, American parent company, and contact name where possible.Your chances of achieving employment are substantially greater if you contact the subsidiary company rather than the parent company in the U.S.

BANKING AND FINANCE

American Express Co.
Hotel Beijing, Rm. 410, East Chang An Ave.
Beijing, China
(Financial and credit services)
American Express Co.

Bank of America
23 Qianmen Dong Dajie, West Bldg.
Beijing, China
Tel.: 86 1 542943
(Banking)
Frederick Chan, Vice President
Bank of America

Chase Manhattan Bank
(Representative office)
RMS 1629-31, Great Wall Sheraton Hotel
Beijing, China
(Banking)
Chase Manhattan Corp.

China-America Insurance
Hotel Beijing
Beijing, China
(Insurance)
American International Group

Citibank
P.O. Box 14
Beijing, China
(Banking)
Citibank

First Interstate Bank
Room 505, Hepingmen Wai Kaoyadian
Beijing, China
Tel.: 86 1 330322
Chepa Wang, Representative
First Interstate Bancorp

Manufacturers Hanover Trust
Noble Tower, 22 Jianguo Men Wai Dajie
Room 1911, Beijing, China
Tel.: 86 1 501986
(Banking)
Sumner Gerard, Vice President
Manufacturers Hanover

INDUSTRIAL MANUFACTURING

Allied-Signal China
Block A2, Commercial Bldg., 5th Floor
Lido Centre, Jichang Rd., Jiang Tai Rd.
Beijing, China
Tel.: 86 1 5006763
Fax.: 86 1 5006616
(Aerospace and engineering technology)
Allied-Signal International

ARCO China
Box 18, Potou, Zhanjiang City
Guangdong Province, China
Tel.: 86 23111, ext. 21218
(Oil production)
E.F. Dean, General Manger
Atlantic Richfield Co.

Control Data Corp.
Beijing Hotel, Room 3009
Beijing, China
(Data and computer systems equipment)
James F. Kilian, Manager China Marketing
Control Data Corp.

John Deere
c/o The East Asiatic Co.
Minzu Wen Hua, Gong Ju, LaBu Xi, Dan
Beijing, China
(Agricultural and construction equipment)
Deere & Co.

Grace China
Minhang Economic &
Technological Dev. Zone
30 Jing Yi Rd.
Shanghai, China
Tel.: 86 21 4300950
Fax.: 86 21 4300425
(Sealants, construction products)
Leo Ngai, General Manager
W.R. Grace & Co.

General Electric Co.
International Club, Jianguo Men Wai
Beijing, China
(High technology, electrical products)
General Electric Co.

Geosource Ltd.
P.O. Box 2823
Beijing, 1000044, China
(Petroleum)
Geosource Inc.

China Hewlett-Packard Co.
Beijing Second Watch Factory, 4th Floor
Shuang Yu Shu, Bei San Huan Rd., Hai Dian Dist.
Beijing, China
(Computation products)
Hewlett-Packard Co.

Heinz-UFE
Heinz UFE Mansion 33, Tienho Rd.
Guangzhou, Guangdong, China
(Food products)
Wah-Hui Chu, General Manager
H.J. Heinz Company

Lockheed Corp.
Beijing Hotel, Rm. 6036
Beijing, China
(Aircraft, missiles)
Lockheed Corp.

Martin Marietta Intl.
Liason Office
Level 29, Unit 1-2 China World Tower
China World Trade Center, 1 Jian guo Men Wai
Beijing 1000020, China
Tel.: 86 1 5051501
Fax.: 86 1 5051507
(Operating systems, aerospace, electronics)
Marvin L. Duke, Vice President
Martin Marietta Corp.

McDonnell-Douglas China Technical Sevices
P.O. Box 7840
Shanghai, China
(Aircraft, missiles, electronics)
McDonnell-Douglas Corp.

3M China
40 Min Sheng Rd.
Shanghai, China
Tel.: 86 21 410661
(Business, electrical, and health care products)
William G. Allen, Managing Director
3M

SmithKline Corp.
SKC China, 23 Qianman Dong Dajie, West Bldg.
Beijing, China
(Pharmaceuticals, laboratory services)
SmithKline Corp.

RETAILING AND WHOLESALING

Boeing China
Lido Holiday Inn Jichang Rd., Jiang Tai Rd.
4F, Block A-1, Rm. 418
Beijing, 100004 China
Tel.: 86 1 5002233
Fax.: 86 1 5006390
(Airplanes, missiles)
Boeing Corp.

China Hewlett-Packard Co.
18 Bei San Huan Xi Rd. Shuang Yu Shu, Hai Dian District
Beijing, China
Tel.: 86 1 256 6888
(Computer products)
Hewlett-Packard Co.

Fuqua World Trade Corp.
Xiyuan Hotel, Bldg. N8, Suite 840-841
Erligou, Beijing, China
Tel.: 86 1 896770
(Sporting goods)
Fuqua Industries

SERVICE INDUSTRIES

Coopers & Lybrand Intl.
International Club, Suite 409, 65 Yanan Xi Lu
Shanghai, China
(Accountants)
Coopers & Lybrand International

Hill & Knowlton Asia
Jingiun Hotel, Suite 3045, Jianguo Men Wai Ave.
Beijing, China
(Public relations and affairs)
Hill & Knowlton Inc.

McCann-Erickson
Beijing Hotel, Rm. 5035
Beijing, China
(Advertising)
McCann-Erickson

Price Waterhouse Intl.
Beijing Hotel, Rm. 4056, Middle Wing
Beijing, China
(Accountants)
Price Waterhouse & Co.

DOMESTIC COMPANIES IN CHINA

These companies are owned by the state and are not at all likely to employ foreigners. Nonetheless, the following is a listing of the major domestic companies of China. Company information includes type of business and contact name.

Bank of China
410 Fu Cheng Men Nei Dajie
Beijing, 100818 China
Tel.: 86 1 6016688
Fax.: 86 1 6016869
(Banking)
Au Chingping, Managing Director

China International Finance Co.
International Trade Center, 33rd Floor, Renmin Nan Rd.
P.O. Box 0072, Shenzhen 518014, China
Tel.: 86 237567
Fax.: 86 237566
(Banking)
Shoji Moriguchi, General Manager

People's Bank of China
San Li He St.
Beijing, China
Tel.: 86 1 863907
(Banking)
Chen Muhua, Chairman

MAJOR INTERNATIONAL COMPANIES IN CHINA

There are many international firms operating in China. These companies will be classified by business area: Banking and Finance; Industrial Manufacturing; Retailing and Wholesaling; and Service Industries. The company information includes type of business, international parent company, and contact name where possible. Your chances of achieving employment are substantially greater if you contact the subsidiary company in China rather than the parent company in the home country.

BANKING AND FINANCE

ANZ Grindlays Bank
China World Tower, Suite 1530
1 Jianguomenwai Dajie
Beijing, China
Tel.: 86 1 5051602
Fax.: 86 1 5051604
(Banking)
Australia and New Zealand Bank Group, Australia

Bank of East Asia
China Hotel, North Tower, Rm. 414-15
Guangzhou, China
Tel.: 86 678808
Fax.: 86 678538
(Banking)
Wong Chung-Sang, Representative
Bank of East Asia, Hong Kong

Banque Indosuez
Nanyang Bldg., Block B
Shenzhen, PRC
Tel.: 86 755 39085
(Banking)
Bertrand Viriot, Manager
Banque Indosuez, France

Banque Nationale de Paris
Jing Jiang Foreign Traders Bldg.
Suite 58142, 58 Maoming Rd. S.
Shanghai, China
Tel.: 86 20 370115
(Banking)
Banque Nationale de Paris, France

Barclays Bank
China Science & Technology Exchange Commercial Bldg.
12th Fl., Rm. 1211
22 Jianguo Men Wai Dajie
Beijing, China
Tel.: 86 1 5122288, ext. 1211
Fax.: 86 1 5127889
(Banking)
Barclays Bank, U.K.

Credit Agricole (CNCA)
1207 Noble Tower
Beijing, China
Tel.: 86 1 5122288, ext. 1207
(Banking)
Francis Lai, Manager
Caisse Nationale de Credit Agricole, France

Credit Lyonnais
CITIC Bldg., 19 Jianguo Men Wai Dajie, Suite 2004
Beijing, China
Tel.: 86 1 5002255, ext. 2040
(Banking)
Credit Lyonnais, France

Credit Suisse
Noble Tower, Rm. 911, 22 Jianguo Men Wai
Beijing, China
Tel.: 86 1 5123655
Fax.: 86 1 5123757
(Banking)
Credit Suisse, Switzerland

Deutsche Bank
(Representative office in China)
2620-24 China World Tower
China World Trade Center, No. 1
Jianguo Men Wai Dajie, Beijing 100004, China
(Banking)
Christoph M. Ewerhart, General Manger
Deutsche Bank, Germany

Dresdner Bank
International Bldg, 19 Jianguo Men Wai Dajie
6th Floor, Office 1
Beijing, China
Tel.: 86 1 5003588
(Banking)
Johannes Graf von Ballestrem, Representative
Dresdner Bank, Germany

Fuji Bank
CITIC Bldg., Rm. 802, 19 Jianguo, Men Wai Dajie
Beijing, China
Tel.: 86 1 5004694
(Banking)
Yoshimochi Kuwata, Chief Representative
Fuji Ltd., Japan

Hongkong and Shanghai Banking Corp.
Jianguo Hotel, Suite 149
Jianguo Men Wai Dajie
Beijing, China
Tel.: 86 1 5002233, ext. 145
Fax.: 86 1 5001074
(Banking)
Lau Kan Kwan, Representative
Hongkong and Shanghai Banking Corp., Hong Kong

Mitsubishi Trust and Banking Corp.
24-04 Rui Jin Bldg., 205 Mao Ming Rd.
Shanghai, PRC
Tel.: 86 021 336270
Fax.: 86 021 336281
(Banking)
Mitsuo Sugino, Representative
Mitsubishi Trust and Banking Corp., Japan

Mitsui Trust & Banking Co.
Chang Fu Gong Office Bldg, A-26
Jianguo Men Wai Dajie, Chang Yang District
Beijing, China
Tel.: 86 1 5139234
Fax.: 86 1 5139235
(Banking)
Takashi Imachi, Manager
Mitsui Trust & Banking Co., Japan

National Australia Bank
Office 1, 11th Floor, CITIC
19 Jianguo Men Wai Dajie
Beijing, China
Tel.: 86 1 500 225, ext. 1110-2
Fax.: 86 1 500 3642
(Banking)
P J Murray, Representative
National Australia Bank, Australia

Oversea Chinese Banking Corp.
120 Kiukiang Rd., P.O. Box 3030
Shanghai, China
Tel.: 86 21 3233888
Fax.: 86 21 3290888
(Banking)
Lee Yeoh Nguan, Manager
Oversea Chinese Banking Corp., Singapore

Societe Generale
Scite Tower, Rm. 1504-06
22 Jianguo Men Wai Dajie
Beijing, China
Tel.: 86 1 5123366
Fax.: 86 1 5127485
(Banking)
Andre Kowalski, Representative
Societe Generale, France

Standard Chartered Bank
China Science & Technology Exchange Center
Commercial Bldg., Rm. 701
22 Jianguo Men Wai Dajie
Beijing, China
Tel.: 86 1 5123661
Fax.: 86 1 5123660
(Banking)
T. Hooper, Chief Representative
Standard Chartered Bank, U.K.

Westpac Banking Corp.—China
Suite 506, Tower of Science & Technology
Exchange Corp. Ltd.
23 Jianguo Men Wai Dajie
Beijing, China
Tel.: 86 1 5122288
Fax.: 86 1 5123780
(Banking)
Roy Hammill, Chief Representative
Westpac Banking Corp., Australia

INDUSTRIAL MANUFACTURING

Mitsui & Co.
1702 International Bldg., 19 Jianwai Street
Beijing, China
Tel.: 86 1 5003331
(Metals, machinery)
Mitsui & Co., Japan

RETAILING AND WHOLESALING

Toyota Motor Corp.
China Science and Technology Exchange Center Commercial Bldg.
22 Jianguo Menwai Dajie
Beijing, China
Tel.: 86 1 5122288
Fax.: 86 1 5127551
(Automobiles)
Toyota Motor Corp., Japan

SERVICE INDUSTRIES

Ogilvy & Mather Marketing Services
Ruijin Bldg., Suite 2411, 205 Mao Ming Rd., South
Shanghai, China
Tel.: 86 21 331330
Fax.: 86 21 330972
(Advertising)
Tony Tse, General Manager
WPP Group, U.K.

Saatchi & Saatchi Advertising
Guangdong Trade Center, Rm. 531
Haizhe Square, Guangzhou, China
Tel.: 86 20 338293
(Advertising)
Gordon Greig, Managing Director
Saatchi & Saatchi Advertising International, U.K.

MAJOR HOTEL EMPLOYERS IN CHINA

Great Wall Sheraton Hotel
North Dong Huan Road
Beijing, China
Tel.: 86 1 5005566

Holiday Inn City Centre, Guangzhou
Huanshi Dong Lu
Guangzhou, China
Tel.: 86 20 753141

Holiday Inn, Dalian
18 Sheng Li Square
Zhong Shan Ward
Dalian, China
Tel.: 86 809705/803802

Holiday Inn, Guilin
14 S. Ronghu Rd.
Guilun, China
Tel.: 86 223950

Holiday Inn, Xian
8 S. Section, Huang Cheng, E. Rd.
Xian, China
Tel.: 86 29 721962

Holiday Inn, Yangtze Chongqing
Dian Zi Ping, Nan An District
Chongqing, Sichuan, China
Tel.: 86 483380

Holiday Lido, Beijing
Jichang Rd., Jiang Tai Rd.
Beijing, China 100004
Tel.: 86 1 5006688

Hua Ting Sheraton, Shanghai
1200 Cao Xi Bei Lu
Shanghai, China 0703
Tel.: 86 29 386000

Shanghai Hilton International
250 Hua Shan Rd.
Shanghai, China
Tel.: 86 563343

Shangri-La Hotel
29 Zizhuyan Rd.
Beijing, China
Tel.: 86 8312211

Sheraton Guilin Hotel
Bing Jiang Nan Rd.
Guilun, China
Tel.: 86 223855

Sheraton Tianjin Hotel
Zi Jin Shan Rd.
He Xi District
Tianjin, China
Tel.: 86 313388

White Swan Hotel
Southern St., No. 1
Shamiam Island
Guangzhou, China 510133
Tel.: 86 20 886968

INTERNATIONAL SCHOOLS IN CHINA

International Schools Services
P.O. Box 5910
Princeton, NJ 08543
American teachers seeking employment abroad may contact this recruitment service.

American School of Guangzhou
Garden Hotel Office Tower, Rm. 902
368 Huanshi Dong Lu
Guangzhou, China
Tel.: 86 20 773899
(U.S. school, K-8)

International School of Beijing
Xui Shui Bei Jie No. 3
Beijing, China
Tel.: 86 1 523831, ext. 445
(U.S. school, K-8)

Shanghai American School
1469 Huai Hai Zhong Lu
Shanghai, China
Tel.: 86 21 379880, ext. 218
(U.S. school, pre-K-8)

Shenyang American Academy
No. 41, Lane 4, Section 5
Sanjing St., Heping District
Shenyang, China
Tel.: 86 24 290012
(U.S. school, K-8)

TAIWAN

The Republic of China is more commonly referred to as Taiwan. Formosa is an older name for the island. Taiwan measures 14,000 square miles, a little larger than Maryland. China is 100 miles to the west, and Japan is 700 miles to the north. Over two-thirds of Taiwan is mountainous or hilly. Most of its 20 million people live in the western part of the country, where a coastal plain contains arable land.

Most residents are descendants of immigrants from Fukien and Kwantung provinces who arrived in the seventeenth and eighteenth centuries. About 250,000 aboriginal people, descended largely from Malays, live in the central mountains and along the east coast. Taiwan is religiously very diverse, with Buddhist, Taoist, Christian, and Muslim communities.

China established a protectorate over the island in 1206. Spain and Holland both gradually established settlements on Taiwan. The Dutch expelled the Spanish and took control of the island in 1620. Following the collapse of the Ming Dynasty on the mainland in 1661, resistors to the new Ch'ing rulers fled to the island in 1662. Ming loyalists held Taiwan until 1682, when the mainland recovered the territory. In 1684, Taiwan was declared a prefecture of Fukien province. Taipei was built by the Ch'ing dynasty in 1709. The island finally became a province in 1887.

Japan gained control in 1895, after defeating China in the Sino-Japanese War. The islanders revolted and declared the first republic in Asia, but they were crushed by the Japanese. Taiwan, renamed Formosa, became Japan's base of operations for expansion into Southeast Asia. In 1945, after World War II, Taiwan reverted to Chinese sovereignty.

Following the collapse of China's Kuomintang government in 1949, over 2 million Chinese fled to Taiwan. The government of the Republic of China maintained its structure and established itself in Taipei in 1950. The Republic of China government on Taiwan still refuses to recognize the legitimacy of the People's Republic of China on the mainland. The government in Taipei officially refers to itself as the government of all China.

Upon establishing diplomatic relations with the People's Republic in 1978, the United States severed official relations with Taiwan. Both countries nonetheless maintain legations in each capital and significant trade relations remain uninterrupted. In Washington, Taiwan's office is called the Coordination Council for North American Affairs. Taiwan maintains consular offices in other countries as well.

Taiwan's ruling Nationalist Party, or Kuomintang, lifted martial law in 1987 and initiated several reforms to modernize the country's economy. Since 1988, President Lee Teng Hui has accelerated the government's policy of economic and political liberalization. Moreover, Taiwan has been gradually improving its relations with the Soviet Union, Eastern Europe, and the European Community in order to break out of its diplomatic isolation.

Taiwan is also attempting to improve relations with the People's Republic of China. In 1991, the government of the People's Republic of China was reclassified from "rebels" to "communist/mainland authorities," and the Period of National Mobilization for Suppression of the Communist Rebellion was officially ended. A National Unification Council was set up to draft procedures for unification, to be carried out by the newly created Mainland Affairs Council. The Straights Exchange Foundation was also created as a private business group to pursue closer economic relations with China.

Taiwan's exports and imports (1990)

Export Partners:	United States	35%
	Japan	15%
	Hong Kong	10%
Major Exports:	Electronic Equipment	28%
	Textiles	14%
	Plastic Products	12%
Import Partners:	Japan	32%
	United States	30%
	European Community	10%
Major Imports:	Metals	20%
	Electronic Equipment	18%
	Chemical Products	15%

Current Economic Climate

Taiwan has the 25th largest economy in the world and is the 13th largest trading nation. Its gross national product increased from $100 billion in 1987 to $160 billion in 1990. During the same period, per capita income increased from $5,000 to $8,000. In 1990, Taiwan's economy grew 5%, a fairly strong rate but much lower than the 11% peak in 1987. Inflation averaged about 4% during the last three years. Unemployment averages 1.5%. The currency is the New Taiwan dollar, which generally trades at a rate of 25 to the U.S. dollar.

As a result of rising labor and production costs in Taiwan, the trade surplus has shrunk from $20 billion in 1987 to $12 billion in 1990. Exports totalled $67 billion, while imports reached $55 billion in 1990. Both imports and exports are growing, but imports are growing at a faster rate. Over $22 billion of Taiwan's 1990 exports went to the United States. Taiwan also had an $8 billion trade deficit with Japan. Total trade with Asia amounted to $26 billion. Indirect trade with China provided $4 billion. Trade with the Soviet Union in 1990 was valued at $100 million.

The government has relaxed financial and investment regulations over the past few years in order to encourage more foreign investment. The Taipei stock market, for example, is one of the world's most active, but it is also heavily regulated and restricts foreigners. The government also maintains an active role in developing Taiwanese industry by investing heavily in research and development projects.

Taiwan itself is Asia's third largest foreign investor, after Japan and Hong Kong. In 1990, Taiwanese firms invested $600 million in Thailand, $450 million in Indonesia, $300 million in China, and $200 million in Malaysia. Rising standards and costs of living in Taiwan encourage the island's companies to invest in Southeast Asia's cheaper labor markets.

Taiwan is preparing to embark upon a massive infrastructure program costing over $300 billion. The government normally runs surpluses and possesses over $75 billion in foreign currency reserves, less only than Japan and Germany. The plan, including 779 projects, is three times larger than the rebuilding of Kuwait. Infrastructure projects include over $98 billion for roads, bridges, subways, and rail systems; $40 billion in new housing units; $35 billion for energy and utility improvement; $20 billion for industry and research; and $16 billion for irrigation.

American companies should benefit from the projects by successfully bidding for many of the contracts. De Leuw Cather International, for example, won a $35 million contract in the Kaohsiung transit system project. Japanese firms, however, are also aggressively pursuing the new contracts. The government favors American over Japanese firms in order to decrease Taiwan's trade deficit with Japan. Nonetheless, Japanese companies have a longer record in Taiwan than their American competitors and have cultivated strong ties to Taiwanese business people.

The government has pinned very high hopes on the infrastructure plan. Taiwan expects to raise its living standards by improving the quantity and quality of transportation, communication, and housing. Enhancing the country's infrastructure is also likely to attract further foreign investment. More significantly, the government intends to play politics in awarding large contracts. Those countries that maintain favorable trade and political relations with Taiwan will find their firms winning large projects.

The economy is currently suffering from a labor shortage, especially lacking in unskilled workers, which can only become worse as the infrastructure program begins. An estimated 200,000 unskilled laborers are needed. Immigrants, often illegal, from Southeast Asia and the Philippines are employed throughout the economy. Illegal workers in Taiwan may number as high as 100,000. Wages in Taiwan for unskilled labor are considerably higher than in nearby countries.

Over 20 million people live in Taiwan, making it one of the most densely populated countries in the world. Taipei is the largest city, with 3 million people. Kaohsiung is the largest industrial center, with over 2 million inhabitants. Taichung, the provincial capital, has a population of slightly less than 1 million, and Tainain, a major historical site, has about 700,000 people. Over 74% of the population lives in urban centers.

Regular business hours are from 9:00 am to 5:30 pm, Monday through Friday, and 9:00 am to 12:30 pm Saturday. Banks close two hours earlier during the week but still open on Saturday. Government offices close one-half hour earlier each day.

TAIWAN'S MOST PROFITABLE COMPANIES
(figures rounded in millions of U.S. dollars)

1.	China Steel	$700
2.	Cathay Life Insurance	$150
3.	Nan Ya Plastics	$140
4.	First Commercial Bank	$120
5.	Hua Nan Commercial Bank	$80

Getting Around Taiwan

China Airlines provides international service to Taiwan. The People's Republic of China bans any air carrier that flies to Taiwan, so international flights are occasionally difficult to find. KLM provides international flights into Taipei. The rail and bus systems link Taipei with cities on both coasts and some in the central part of the country. A wide variety of travel accommodations is available, including luxury express trains and buses. In Taipei, taxis are probably the best way to get around, although the bus system is generally convenient. Rental cars are available, but road signs are in Chinese, of course.

Using the language

Mandarin Chinese is the official language. Taiwanese, a dialect originating in Fukien province, is widely spoken as well. English is the most commonly spoken foreign language and is taught in the schools. Many young people and most people in the tourist industry speak English. Japanese is also spoken by many, especially of the older generation. As always, you should at least attempt to begin a conversation in the local language before shifting into English.■

Employment Regulations for Americans

Americans need a visa to enter Taiwan. Although the U.S. and Taiwan no longer maintain diplomatic relations, visas may be obtained from trade missions, cultural centers, and information centers. These organizations may be able to provide a letter allowing you to obtain a visa upon arrival at one of Taiwan's international airports. Visas are also available at consular offices in other countries. Tourist visas are valid for six months and can be extended. Transit visas are valid for two weeks and cannot be extended. Documents can be acquired at a Coordination Council for North American Affairs office.

Americans who intelligently market themselves may be able to find employment in Taiwan because of the current labor shortage. Although unskilled labor is in very short supply, Americans with business experience and marketable skills may also be able to find employment. Tourism is a growing industry, with 2 million visitors per year. Employment may be possible as tour guides or as casual laborers. English language schools are not as plentiful as in Japan or Hong Kong but still provide a good source of income for Americans. Private tutoring to individuals can raise money as well.

Additionally, the $300 billion infrastructure program will provide thousands of new jobs. Most of these jobs will be in unskilled labor positions. You should keep in mind, however, that Southeast Asians are likely to work longer hours for lower wages than you would.

Making a good first impression

It is a good idea to carry business cards in Taiwan. The cards should contain one's name, full title or position, employer or organization, phone number, and address. You should have this information in Chinese on one side and in English on the other. Presenting business cards is a common custom in East Asia and will help potential employers, customers, clients, or anyone else you may meet remember you. Chinese society is much more formal than ours, and full titles and positions are important things to know about people.■

Organizations for Further Information

The following organizations, both in the U.S. and Taiwan, may be helpful in the job search. American embassies and consulates have commercial and/or economic sections that can provide you with business information and explain aspects of the local economy. World Trade Centers usually include many foreign companies operating in the country. Foreign government missions in the U.S. such as National Tourist Offices and embassies and consulates can furnish visas and information on work permits and other important regulations. They may also offer economic and business information about the country.

CHAMBER OF COMMERCE

American Chamber of Commerce
Chungshan N. Rd., Sec. 2, P.O. Box 17-277, M 750
Taipei, Taiwan
Republic of China
Tel.: 886 2 5512515, ext. 327
Fax.: 886 2 5423376

CONSULAR OFFICE

American Institute in Taiwan
7 Lane 134, Hsin Yi Rd., Section 3
Taipei, Taiwan
Republic of China
Tel.: 886 2 7092000
(Serves as the U.S. Embassy in Taiwan)

OTHER INFORMATIONAL ORGANIZATIONS

Chinese Information and Culture Center
1230 Ave. of the Americas
New York, NY 10020-1579
Tel.: (212) 373-1880

Chinese Information Service
159 Lexington Ave.
New York, New York 10016
Tel.: (212) 373-0155
Fax.: (212) 373-1866

Taiwan Coordination Council for North American Affairs
Information and Communications Divisions
4201 Connecticut Ave. N.W.
Washington, D.C. 20008

Taiwan Visitors Association
111 Mingchuan Rd., 5th Floor
Taipei, Taiwan
Republic of China

Tourism Bureau
280 Chunghsiao East Rd., Sec. 2
Taipei, Taiwan
Republic of China

Business Directories

Although not always easy to find, business directories can prove invaluable in the international job search. Most directories list company names, addresses, products, and phone numbers. Some directories include executive names and titles and financial information about the company. These sources provide you with the names of the people to contact for employment information as well as financial data.

American Chamber of Commerce Roster. Annual publication of the American Chamber of Commerce in the Republic of China, Box 17-277, Taipei, Taiwan, Republic of China. Provides basic information on companies engaged in bilateral trade.

Directory of Taiwan. Published annually by the China News, 110 Yenping S. Rd., 11th Floor, Taipei, Taiwan, Republic of China. Lists basic information on government, trade, and business organizations.

Exports of the Republic of China. Annual publication of the China External Trade Development Council, 201 Tun Hwa N. Rd., Taipei 105, Taiwan, Republic of China. Lists detailed information on over 10,000 firms engaged in export.

Imports of the Republic of China. Annual publication of the China External Trade Development Council, 201 Tun Hwa N. Rd., Taipei 105, Taiwan, Republic of China. Lists detailed information on over 4,000 firms engaged in import.

Taiwan Business Directory. Biennial publication of China Credit Information Service, 30 Kung Yuan Rd., 9th Floor, Taipei 100, Taiwan, Republic of China. Provides basic information on 25,000 companies.

Taiwan Buyers Guide. Published biennially by China Productivity Center, 201-26 Tun Hwa N. Rd., 11th Floor, Taipei, Taiwan, Republic of China. Lists detailed information on 15,000 businesses and government agencies.

Taiwan Importers Directory. Semiannual publication of the Taiwan Yellow Pages Corp., Box 84-84, Taipei, Taiwan, Republic of China. Lists basic information on about 7,000 companies engaged in import.

Taiwan Yellow Pages. Annual publication of the Taiwan Yellow Pages Corp., Box 84-84, Taipei, Taiwan, Republic of China. Lists basic information on 40,000 manufacturers and trading companies.

Top 500 Largest Industrial Corporations in the Republic of China. Annual publication of China Credit Information Service, 30 Kung Yuan Rd., 9th Floor, Taipei 100, Taiwan, Republic of China. Provides detailed financial information on Taiwan's 500 largest companies as well as detailed data on over 500 more.

MAJOR AMERICAN COMPANIES IN TAIWAN

Many American firms operate in Taiwan. The following companies are classified by business area: Banking and Finance; Industrial Manufacturing; Retailing and Wholesaling; and Service Industries. The company information includes type of business, American parent company, and contact name where possible. Your chances of achieving employment are substantially greater if you contact the subsidiary company in Taiwan rather than the parent company in the U.S.

BANKING AND FINANCE

Aetna Life Insurance Co. of America
3/F, 658 Tun Hwa S. Rd.
Taipei, Taiwan
Republic of China
Tel.: 886 2 3259213
Fax.: 886 2 7556123
(Insurance)
Patrick Poon, General Manager
Aetna Life & Casualty

American Express Bank
Nanking E. Rd., Sec. 2
P.O. Box 1753
Taipei, Taiwan
Republic of China
Tel.: 886 2 5633182
(Banking, finance)
James M. Kaul, Vice President
American Express Bank

Bank of America
205 Tun Hwa Rd., P.O. Box 127
Taipei, Taiwan
Republic of China
Tel.: 886 2 7154111
Fax.: 886 2 2532850
(Banking)
Warren Prostello, Vice President
Bank of America

Bankers Trust Co.
BT Shin Yi Plaza 3F, 51, Sec. 2
Chung Ching South Rd., P.O. Box 5-44
Taipei, Taiwan
Republic of China
Tel.: 886 2 3225555
(Banking)
Peter Kwok, Managing Director
Bankers Trust Co.

Bankers Trust New York Corp.
Bankers Tower, 8th Floor, 205 Tun Hwa N. Rd.
P.O. Box 81-231
Taipei, Taiwan
Republic of China
Tel.: 886 2 715 2888
(Bank holding co.)
James D. Seymour, General Manager
Bankers Trust New York Corp.

Chase Manhattan Bank
72 Nanking E. Rd., Sec. 2 (104)
P.O. Box 3396
Taipei, Taiwan
Republic of China
Tel.: 886 2 5313262
(Banking)
Carter Booth, Vice President
Chase Manhattan Corp.

Citibank NA
Citicorp Center Bldg.
742 Min Sheng E. Rd.
Taipei, Taiwan
Republic of China
Tel.: 886 2 7315931
(Banking)
Citibank NA

First Interstate Bank
675 Min Sheng E. Rd.
Taipei 10446, Taiwan
Republic of China
Tel.: 886 2 7153572
(Banking)
H. Scott Stevenson, Vice President
First Interstate Bank of California

General Motors Taiwan Credit Sales Office
No. 658 Tun Hua S. Rd. 4-1F
Taipei, Taiwan
Republic of China
(Automobile financing)
General Motors Acceptance Corp.

Manufacturers Hanover Trust Co.
Taipei Financial Center, 10th Floor
62 Tun Hwa N. Rd.
Taipei 10567, Taiwan
Republic of China
Tel.: 886 2 7213150
Fax.: 886 2 7515808
(Banking)
Gisa Wagner, Vice President

Metropolitan Insurance and Annuity Co.
11th Floor, 85 Jen Ai Rd., Sec. 4,
Taipei 10649, Taiwan
Republic of China
Tel.: 886 2 7417810
(Insurance)
Harry C. Hsiang, General Manger
Metropolitan Life Insurance Co.

INDUSTRIAL MANUFACTURING

Bausch & Lomb Taiwan
998 Minsheng E. Rd., 2F-3
Taipei 10583, Taiwan
Republic of China
(Optics products)
Bausch & Lomb

Bristol-Myers (Taiwan)
P.O. Box 22659
Taipei, Taiwan
Republic of China
(Household products, toiletries)
Bristol-Myers Squibb Co.

Digital Equipment Taiwan
255 Jen Ho Rd. Sec. 2 Nan
Hsing Li Tashi Chen
Tahsi, Tao Yuan, Taiwan
Republic of China
(Computers)
Kenneth H. Olsen, Chairman
Digital Equipment Corp.

Eaton Aerospace & Commercial Controls
2nd Floor, 51 Park Ave.
2 Hsin Chu Science-Based Industrial Park
Hsin Chu, Taiwan
Republic of China
Tel.: 886 35 772147
Fax.: 886 35 779602
(Aerospace systems)
Eaton Corp.

Eli Lilly & Co. (Taiwan)
683-685 Min Sheng E. Rd.
World-Wide House, 5th Floor
Taipei 104, Taiwan
Republic of China
Tel.: 886 2 716 3301
(Pharmaceuticals, medical instruments)
Eli Lilly and Co.

General Electric USA Solid Taiwan
2nd Floor No. 1, Mei Long St.,
Long Kang Lee
Taoyuan, Tao Yuan, Taiwan
Republic of China
(Electronic resistors)
Carl Joner, Chairman
General Electric Co.

Goodyear Taiwan
71 Nanking E. Rd., Sec.3
Taipei, Taiwan
Republic of China
(Tires)
Goodyear Tire & Rubber Co.

Grace Taiwan
#84-1, Kwah Yeh West Rd., Hsin Fu Village
Ping Tsing Hsiang, Taoyuag County 32417
Taiwan
Republic of China
Tel.: 886 3 4586554
Fax.: 886 3 4573006
(Chemicals, sealants)
W.R. Grace & Co.

Johnson & Johnson Taiwan
6th Floor, 2, Tun Hwa S. Rd.
Taipei, Taiwan
Republic of China
Tel.: 886 02 7214311
(Health care products)
Johnson & Johnson

Mattel (Taiwan)
Rm. 505, No. 3 Tun Hwa S. Rd.
Taipei, Taiwan
Republic of China
(Toys)
Chao Ting Chen, Chairman
Mattel Inc.

Motorola Electronics Taiwan
516 Chung-Hwa Road Sec. 1
Chungli, Taiwan
Republic of China
Tel.: 886 34 527121
(Electronics)
Motorola Inc.

President Frito-Lay Corp.
181 Ching-Shan Rd., Shin Shih Hsiang
Tainan, Taiwan
Republic of China
Tel.: 886 6 5993565
Fax.: 886 6 5994815
(Food products)
Ten Napel, CEO

Singer Industries (Taiwan)
Tai Yang Hsin Yi Bldg., 208
Sec. 2, Hsin Yi Rd.
Taichung, Taipei
Republic of China
(Sewing machines)
SSMC Inc.

Taiwan Fuji Xerox Corp.
8th Floor No. 122, Tun Hua N. Rd.
Taipei, Taiwan
Republic of China
(Photo equipment)
Cheng Fu Woo, President

Taiwan Scott Paper Corp.
Bank Tower, 4th Floor
205 Tun Hwa N. Rd.
Taipei 10592, Taiwan
Republic of China
Tel.: 886 2 7134669
Fax.: 886 2 7150326
(Paper products)
Scott Paper Co.

Unisys (Taiwan)
Overseas Trust Bldg., 5th Floor
477 Tun Hua S. Rd.
Taipei, Taiwan
Republic of China
Tel.: 886 2 7411151
(Computer systems)
John Wen, General Manager
Unisys Corp.

Wrigley Taiwan
No. 288 Kung Fu S. Rd., 2nd Floor, Rm. 4
Taipei, Taiwan
Republic of China
(Chewing gum)
Wm. Wrigley Jr. Co.

Zenith Taiwan Corp.
No. 16 Chung Kung First Rd.,
Chung-Li Industrial District,
Chung-Li Shih
Taoyuan, Hsien, Taiwan
Republic of China
Tel.: 886 034 522801
(Electronic components)
Thomas Landgraf, Manager
Zenith Electronics

RETAILING AND WHOLESALING

Amway Taiwan
Cathay Minsheng, Chien Kuo Bldg., 12th Floor
350 Min Sheng E. Rd.
Taipei, Taiwan
Republic of China
Tel.: 886 2 5015400
Fax.: 886 2 5019572
(Personal care products)
Roger J. C. Chen, General Manager

Avon Cosmetics (Taiwan)
127 Chung Hsing N. St.
San Chung City, Taipei, Taiwan
Republic of China
(Cosmetics, toiletries)
Avon Products

Wang Industrial Co.
62 Tun Hwa N. Rd.
Taipei Financial Center, 5th Floor
Taipei, Taiwan
Republic of China
Tel.: 886 2 27216121
(Data processing sales)
Jackson Lin, Manager
Wang Laboratories

SERVICE INDUSTRIES

American President Lines
Harng Lien Bldg., 8th Floor, Rm. 1
533 Chung Shan 2nd Rd.
Kaohsiung, Taiwan
Republic of China
Tel.: 886 7 8310581
Fax.: 886 7 603203141
(Shipping)
American President Companies

Westinghouse Taiwan Corp. Technology Center
Bank Tower,12th Floor, No. 205
Tun Hwa N. Rd.
Taipei, Taiwan
Republic of China
Tel.: 886 2 7126982
Fax.: 886 2 7169069
(Research & development)
Westinghouse Electric Corp.

MAJOR DOMESTIC COMPANIES IN TAIWAN

The following is a listing of the major domestic companies of Taiwan. They are classified by business area: Banking and Finance; Industrial Manufacturing; Retailing and Wholesaling; Service Industries. Company information includes type of business and contact name. These companies will generally hire their own nationals first but may employ Americans.

BANKING AND FINANCE

Bank of Communications
No. 91 Heng Yang Rd.
P.O. Box 621
Taipei 10003, Taiwan
Republic of China
Tel.: 886 2 3613000
Fax.: 886 2 3612046
(Banking)
Jong-Tian Ren, Personnel Manager

Bankers Association of the Republic of China
46 Kuanchien Rd., 8th Floor
Taipei, Taiwan
Republic of China
Tel.: 886 2 3616019
(Banking)
Y. D. Sheu, Chairman

Bank of Taiwan
No. 120 Sec. 1 Chungking S. Rd.
P.O. Box 5
Taipei 10036, Taiwan
Republic of China
Tel.: 886 2 3147377
(State bank)
S. C. Liu, Managing Director

Central Bank of China
2 Roosevelt Rd., Sec. 1
Taipei 10757, Taiwan
Republic of China
Tel.: 886 2 3936161
(Banking)
Patrick C. J. Liang, General Manager

Central Trust of China
No. 49 Sec. 1 Wu Chang St.
Taipei 10006, Taiwan
Republic of China
Tel.: 886 2 3111511
Fax.: 886 2 3118107
(Banking)
Wei-Hsin King, Chairman

Export-Import Bank of the Republic of China
8th Floor, 3, Nan Hai Rd.
Taipei 10728, Taiwan
Republic of China
Tel.: 886 2 3210511
Fax.: 886 2 3940830
(Banking)
J. C. Wu, Manager

International Commercial Bank of China
100 Chi Lin Rd.
Taipei 10424, Taiwan
Republic of China
Tel.: 886 2 5633156
Fax.: 886 2 5632614
(Banking)
Vicky Hsieh, Personnel Manager

Overseas Chinese Commercial Banking Corp.
8 Hsiang Yang Rd.
P.O. Box 1636
Taipei, Taiwan
Republic of China
Tel.: 886 2 3715181
Fax.: 886 2 3814056
(Banking)
L. S. Lin, President

Shanghai Commercial & Savings Bank
16 Jen Ai Rd., Sec. 2
P.O. Box 1648
Taipei 10019, Taiwan
Republic of China
Tel.: 886 2 3933111
Fax.: 886 2 3928391
(Banking)
Richard J. R. Yen, President

Taipei Bank (City Bank of Taipei)
50 Chung Shan N. Rd., Sec. 2
P.O. Box 1646
Taipei 10419, Taiwan
Republic of China
Tel.: 886 2 5425656
Fax.: 886 2 5231235
(Banking)
Shao-King Wang, President

INDUSTRIAL MANUFACTURING

Acer Inc.
602 Min Sheng E. Rd.
Taipei, Taiwan
Republic of China
Tel.: 886 2 7132252
Fax.: 886 2 7151950
(Computers)
Shih Chen-Jung, Chairman

Chinese Automobile Co.
No. 169 Nanking E Rd. Sec. 2
Taipei, Taiwan
Republic of China
(Motor vehicles)
T. K. Chang, Chairman

Chinese Petroleum Corp.
83 Chung Hwa Rd., Sec. 1
Taipei 10031, Taiwan
Republic of China
Tel.: 886 2 3717121
Fax.: 886 2 3319645
(Petrochemicals)
Y. S. Chen, President

Fortune Motors Co.
5th Floor, No. 270 Nanking E. Rd., Sec. 3
Taipei, Taiwan
Republic of China
(Motor vehicles)
Lu Liang Pi, General Manager

SERVICE INDUSTRIES

Central Daily News Co.
260 Pah Teh Rd. Sec. 2
Taipei 10401, Taiwan
Republic of China
(Publishing)
Tsu Shung Chiu, Chairman

China Airlines
131 Nanking E. Rd. Sec. 3
Taipei 104, Taiwan
Republic of China
Tel.: 886 2 7152626
(Airline)
Gen. Jung-Chung Chi, President

China Times
132 Ta Li St.
Taipei, Taiwan
Republic of China
(Publishing)
Yu Chi Chung, Chairman

Far Eastern Air Transport Corp.
No. 5 Alley, 123 Lane 405, Tun Hua N. Rd.
Taipei, Taiwan
Republic of China
(Air transportation)
K. L. Hsiao, President

Formosan Magazine Press
6th Floor, No. 189, Yen Ping S. Rd.
Taipei, Taiwan
Republic of China
(Publishing)
Charles Chen, President

MAJOR INTERNATIONAL COMPANIES IN TAIWAN

There are many international firms operating in Taiwan. These companies will be classified by business area: Banking and Finance; Industrial Manufacturing; Retailing and Wholesaling; and Service Industries. The company information includes type of business, international parent company, and contact name where possible. Your chances of achieving employment are substantially greater if you contact the subsidiary company in Taiwan rather than the parent company in the home country.

BANKING AND FINANCE

Algemene Bank Nederland, Taipei
481-483 Min Sheng E. Rd., 3rd Floor
Taipei, Taiwan
Republic of China
Tel.: 886 2 5037888
Fax.: 886 2 5065805
(Banking)
Thomas R. Stevens, Manager
Algemene Bank Nederland, Netherlands

Australia and New Zealand Banking Group
Shin Kong Bldg., 2nd Floor
Section 2, 123 Nanking E. Rd.
Taipei, Taiwan
Republic of China
Fax.: 886 2 5083035
Australia and New Zealand Banking Group Limited, U.K.

Banque Indosuez
483 Min Sheng E. Rd., 11th Floor
P.O. Box 22969
Taipei, Taiwan
Republic of China
Tel.: 886 2 5029670
Fax.: 886 2 5061929
(Banking)
Bertrand Lepissier, Manager
Banque Indosuez, France

Barclays Bank
Bank Tower, 10th Floor
205 Tun Hwa N. Rd.
Taipei, Taiwan
Republic of China
Tel.: 886 2 7132040
Fax.: 886 2 7132405
(Banking)
S. A.Wood, Representative
Barclays Bank, England

Credit Lyonnais
Nanking E. Rd., Sec. 2, Asia Tr. Bldg.
15th Floor, Rm. 116, P.O. Box 46204
Taipei, Taiwan
Republic of China
Tel.: 886 2 5629475
Credit Lyonnais, France

Credit Suisse
Rm. 905, Worldwide House
685 Min Sheng East Rd.
Taipei, Taiwan
Republic of China
Tel.: 886 2 7170174
Fax.: 886 2 7126509
(Banking)
M. Piquerez, Representative
Credit Suisse, Switzerland

Deutsche Bank
Cathay Life Insurance Bldg, 10th Floor
296 Jen Ai Rd., Sec. 4
P.O. Box 87-340
Taipei 10650, Taiwan
Republic of China
(Banking)
Ernst-August Borchert, General Manager
Deutsche Bank, Germany

International Bank of Singapore
178 Nanking E. Rd., Sec. 2
Taipei, Taiwan
Republic of China
Tel.: 886 2 5810533
(Banking)
Na Wu Beng, Manager

Midland Bank
30 Chung King S. Rd., 19th Floor, Sec. 1
Taipei, Taiwan
Republic of China
Tel.: 886 2 3618333
(Banking)
L. Y. F. Fu, Representative
Midland Bank, U.K.

National Australia Bank
First Commercial Bank Bldg., 18th Floor
30 Chung King S. Rd., Sec. 1
Taipei, Taiwan
Republic of China
Tel.: 886 2 3822027
Fax.: 886 2 3822033
(Banking)
G. K. P. Lam, Representative

Royal Bank of Canada
8th Floor, Tun Hwa Finl Bldg.
214 Tun Hwa N. Rd.
P.O. Box 81-775
Taipei 10484, Taiwan
Republic of China
Tel.: 886 2 7130911
Fax.: 886 2 7132884
(Banking)
Mark J. Bielarczyk, General Manager

Societe Generale
629 Ming Shen E. Rd., P.O. Box 81-577
Taipei 10446, Taiwan
Republic of China
Tel.: 886 2 7155050
Fax.: 886 2 7152781
(Banking)
Guy Pasturand, General Manager

Westpac Banking Corp.
World Financial Center, 15th Floor
99 Fu Hsing North Rd.
Taipei 10559, Taiwan
Republic of China
Tel.: 886 2 7129133
Fax.: 886 2 7154207
(Banking)
Laurie George, Chief Manager
Westpac Banking Corp., Australia

RETAILING AND WHOLESALING

NEC Computers Taiwan
Asia Trust Bldg. 8th Floor, No. 116 Sec. 2
Nanking E. Rd.
Taipei, Taiwan
Republic of China
Tel.: 886 2 5517171
Fax.: 886 2 5432109
(Computers)
NEC Corp., Japan

INDUSTRIAL MANUFACTURING

BASF Taiwan
Empire Bldg., 16th Floor
87 Sung Chiang Rd.
P.O. Box 3134
Taipei, Taiwan
Republic of China
Tel.: 886 2 5068131
Fax.: 886 2 5061554
(Chemicals, electronics)
BASF Group, Germany

Mitsui & Co.
11th Floor, Chang Hwa Commercial Bank
Tai, Taipei, Taiwan
Republic of China
Tel.: 886 2 5614171/80
(Metals, machinery)
Mitsui & Co., Japan

Philips Electronics Industries
10th-11th Floor No. 150 Tun Hua N. Rd.
Taipei, Taiwan
Republic of China
(Electron tubes)
J. Bergvelt, Chairman
Philips Goleilampenfabrieken N V, Netherlands

Sanyo Electric Taiwan Co.
266 Sung Chiang Rd.
Taipei, Taiwan
Republic of China
(Refrigerators, freezers)
Chang Chuan Liu, Chairman
Sanyo, Japan

SERVICE INDUSTRIES

Ogilvy & Mather Direct Response
Min Sheng Commercial Bldg., 8th Floor
483 Min Sheng E. Rd.
Taipei 10477, Taiwan
Republic of China
Tel.: 886 2 5055789
Fax.: 886 2 5024491
(Advertising)
Mark Bainbridge, Managing Director
WPP Group, U.K.

Saatchi & Saatchi Advertising
311 Nanking E. Rd., Sec. 3, 10th Floor
Taipei, Taiwan
Republic of China
Tel.: 886 2 7135201
Fax.: 886 2 7150548
(Advertising)
Graeme Robinson, Chairman
Saatchi & Saatchi Advertising International, U.K.

INTERNATIONAL NON-PROFIT ORGANIZATIONS IN TAIWAN

Asian-Pacific Society of Cardiology
c/o National Taiwan University Hospital
1 Chang Te St.
Taipei, Taiwan
Republic of China
Tel.: 886 2 3123456

Asian Vegetable Research and Development Center
P.O. Box 42, Shanhua
Tainan, Taiwan
Republic of China
Tel.: 886 6 5837801

Association of Christian Universities and Colleges in Asia
P.O. Box 5-927
Taichung, Taiwan
Republic of China
Tel.: 886 4 2515824

MAJOR HOTEL EMPLOYERS IN TAIWAN

Ambassador Hotel
63 Chung Shan North Rd., Sec. 2
Taipei, Taiwan
Republic of China
Tel.: 886 2 551 111

Grand Hotel
Chung Shan N. Rd.
Taipei 10452, Taiwan
Republic of China
Tel.: 886 2 5965565

Hilton International
38 Chung Hsiao W. Rd., Sec. 1
Taipei, Taiwan
Republic of China
Tel.: 886 2 3115151

Howard Plaza Hotel
160 Jen Aird Sec. 3
Taipei, Taiwan
Republic of China
Tel.: 886 2 7002323

Lai Lai Sheraton Hotel Taipei
38 Chung Hsiao Rd.
Taipei, Taiwan
Republic of China
Tel.: 886 2 3215511

President Hotel
9 Teh Hwei St., 10469
Taipei, Taiwan
Republic of China
Tel.: 886 2 5951251

Royal Taipei
Chung Shan North Rd.
Taipei, Taiwan
Republic of China

Sheraton Lai Lai
12 Chung Shan North Rd.
Taipei, Taiwan
Republic of China
Tel.: 886 2 3215511

INTERNATIONAL SCHOOLS IN TAIWAN

International Schools Services
P.O. Box 5910
Princeton, NJ 08543
American teachers seeking employment abroad may contact this recruitment service.

Dominican School
76 Tah Chih
Taipei, Taiwan
Republic of China
Tel.: 886 2 5028456
(U.S. school, pre-K-9)

Morrison Academy
136-1 Shui Nan Rd.
Taichung, Taiwan 40098
Republic of China
Tel.: 886 4 2921171
(U.S. school, K-12)

Taipei American School
731 Wen Lin Rd., Section 1, Shihlin
Taipei, Taiwan 11141
Republic of China
Tel.: 886 2 712111
(U.S., International Baccalaureate school, K-9)

HONG KONG

Hong Kong is a Crown Colony of Great Britain located on the southeastern coast of China, about 90 miles from Guangzhou. The entire colony consists of slightly over 400 square miles and 236 islands. China, Macau, and Taiwan are the nearest neighbors. Hong Kong is divided into three principal regions: Hong Kong Island, containing nearly 3 million people and 29 square miles; Kowloon Peninsula, with another 2.5 million inhabitants but measuring only 4 square miles; and the mainland New Territories, with probably less than 1 million people and most of the colony's territory, with 370 square miles.

Over 98% of Hong Kong's people are Chinese. Most of them are Cantonese, but many refugees from Shanghai also came to the colony. The Tanka and Hoklo from Fukien province and the Hakka are also represented in the Chinese population. The remaining 2% consists of Europeans, Americans, Japanese, Australians, and Southeast Asians. English is the official language although the Chinese Cantonese dialect is the first language of most of Hong Kong's people. The government's policy is to use Chinese as widely as possible in its officical documents and communications.

Hong Kong was a sparsely inhabited set of agricultural villages until the nineteenth century. In 1839, the Chinese government expelled foreigners from Guangzhou, the primary trading center, in order to curb the growth of the opium trade. The British fled to Macau, a Portuguese colony near Guangzhou, but could not be guaranteed safety by the local authorities. Consequently, the British settled in Hong Kong Harbor, across the Pearl River estuary from Macau. In 1841, Britain negotiated a treaty with China, ceding Hong Kong, which was proclaimed a colony. The Kowloon Peninsula was added in 1860 and the New Territories were leased in 1898. The New Territories' 99-year lease expires in 1997, when the entire colony will return to China.

Hong Kong is presently governed by a Governor, appointed by Britain, and the Executive, Legislative, and Urban councils. Only the Urban Council currently has elected members. Most of the Executive and Legislative councils are appointed by the Governor. The government is responsible for virtually all legal and financial matters concerning the colony. An independent judicial system also operates in Hong Kong and attempts to apply English common law to the greatest extent possible. Democratic reforms enabling direct popular election of government officials is planned but not likely to occur.

Hong Kong was occupied by the Japanese during World War II when over 1 million residents were relocated to the mainland. After the war, however, over 1 million refugees flooded into Hong Kong. The population today is probably over 6 million people. The colony has one of Asia's lowest birth rates and increases its population largely through immigration. Hong Kong Island contains Victoria, the capital city and commerical center. Most of the major industrial areas and the wharves are located on Kowloon Peninsula. The New Territories have had a predominantly rural character but are now being rapidly developed.

The most significant event in Hong Kong's near future is the reversion to China in 1997. The megalopolis of Hong Kong has never actually lived under Chinese rule, having grown as a British colony. Many local residents are apprehensive about the return to China. The older generation includes thousands of people who fled from China. Moreover, the Tiananmen massacre in 1989 alarmed most people in Hong Kong. The Chinese government announced that it will allow Hong Kong to maintain its capitalist system for 50 years under a "one country-two systems" formula.

The Basic Law negotiated between Britain and China in 1989, guaranteeing fundamental liberties, is supposed to become Hong Kong's constitution in 1997. Nonetheless, a large-scale brain drain is now underway, as many Hong Kong inhabitants acquire foreign, particularly British, passports. Emmigration levels increased by 50% between 1988 and 1990. Over 60,000 people are leaving each year.

Likewise, companies based in Hong Kong have also sought to protect their assets before 1997. Jardine Matheson Holdings, a powerful trading company, incorporated abroad in 1984. The Hongkong & Shanghai Banking Corp., one of the world's largest banks, is reorganizing under a British holding company. Hundreds of companies have incorporated in Britain, the U.S., Canada, Australia, and elsewhere.

China declared in January, 1991, that only it could speak for the people of Hong Kong, raising even more concern in the colony. Specifically, the planned new Hong Kong airport has created significant tension between China and Britain. The colonial government estimates that construction and access cost will be $16 billion, although the actual costs are expected to be much higher. By mid-1991, China refused to approve the project unless Britain granted more control over Hong Kong's affairs. Without Chinese approval, most foreign banks and investors would balk at financing the airport.

Some Chinese enterprises, however, have begun investing in Hong Kong to learn about capitalism. China has over 750 companies in Hong Kong, with over $10 billion invested there, more than either Japan or the U.S. The China International Trust and Investment Corporation, for example, has purchased 12% of Cathay Pacific Airlines, the third most profitable Hong Kong company, and 30% of Hong Kong Telecommunications, the second most profitable. Additionally, the state-owned Bank of China controls the second largest banking group in the colony and occupies the world's fifth tallest building, costing over $250 million.

HONG KONG'S LARGEST TRADING PARTNERS

Imports:	Japan	24%
	China	20%
	Southeast Asia	12%
	United States	10%
	Taiwan	8%
	European Community	7%
Exports:	United States	32%
	European Community	20%
	Japan	5%
	China	4%

Current Economic Climate

Hong Kong has enjoyed one of the world's highest growth rates. The gross national product of $60 billion has been growing at an average of 2.5% in recent years, although from 1986 to 1988 the economy averaged over 10% annual growth. In the last ten years, average real income after inflation rose by over 30%. The per capita income of $14,000, higher than Britain and Japan, is expected to rise by 2% in 1991. Unemployment is extremely low at 1.5%, thereby generally tending to drive up wages. Inflation increased from 3% in 1986 to 11% in 1990.

The largest industries are textiles, tourism, electronics, and plastics. Exports are the base of the economy, valued at over $85 billion in 1990. A wide variety of products, ranging from watches to toys, are manufactured or assembled in Hong Kong. Over 300 banking and finance firms are located in the colony. Many semi-processed goods are also exported to China, primarily to Guangdong province, to be finished and then reexported. Over 2 million people are employed in China by Hong Kong investors, more than twice the size of the colony's workforce.

After Japan, Hong Kong is the second largest investor in Asian countries. In 1990, Hong Kong companies invested nearly $3 billion in China, $1 billion in Thailand, and over $500 million in Singapore, Taiwan, and Indonesia. Companies are investing abroad because of rising costs. Inflation, wages, and real estate prices have all been increasing since the mid-1980s, when the economy grew at a phenomenal rate.

Foreign investment in Hong Kong is quite significant as well. Japanese investment in the colony is expected to continue even after 1997. The Japanese view Hong Kong as the gateway to China, with its huge market and cheap labor. Most of the foreign investment in the southern part of China is financed through private Hong Kong companies. Currently, over 60 Japanese banks operate in Hong Kong, also focusing on southern China.

The United States maintains a very visible presence in Hong Kong, too. American companies own about 160 factories in the colony, making the U.S. the largest foreign investor in the industrial manufacturing sector. Over $1.5 billion has been invested by American manufacturers. The U.S. and Hong Kong also maintain active trade relations. Hong Kong ranks as America's twelfth largest export market.

Hong Kong has been able to prosper by maximizing the benefits of its natural harbor and industrious people through regulations favoring economic growth. Taxes are minimal and no rules exist limiting the repatriation or movement of capital. Regulations also treat domestic and foreign companies equally, welcoming all investors.

Regular business hours are from 9:00 am to 5:00 pm, Monday to Friday. Most businesses also open from 9:00 am to 12:30 pm on Saturday. Government offices and retail stores generally are open six days a week, too, with stores typically staying open until the evening.

HONG KONG'S 10 MOST PROFITABLE COMPANIES (1990)
(figures are rounded in millions of U.S. dollars)

1.	Hong Kong & Shangahai Banking	$620
2.	Hong Kong Telecommunications	$550
3.	Cathay Pacific Airways	$430
4.	Swire Pacific	$410
5.	Hutchison-Whampoa	$390
6.	Cheung Kong Holdings	$360
7.	Sun Hung Kai Properties	$270
8.	China Light & Power	$260
9.	Hang Seng Bank	$250
10.	Hong Kong Electric Holdings	$230

Getting Around in Hong Kong

International flights into Hong Kong arrive at Kai Tak airport, only a few miles from Kowloon and Victoria. A rail line operates in the New Territories and ultimately links the colony to Guangzhou. A huge subway system serves nearly 1 million passengers daily on the island and the peninsula. The road system is excellent and constantly being improved. The colony has over 700 miles of good roads. Taxis are plentiful at all hours in Victoria and on Kowloon. Rental cars are also available.

Making a good first impression

It is a good idea to carry business cards in Hong Kong. Cards can be printed overnight. The cards should contain one's name, full title or position, employer or organization, phone number, and address. You should have this information in Chinese on one side and in English on the other. Presenting business cards is a common custom in East Asia and will help potential employers, customers, clients, or anyone else you may meet remember you. Chinese society is much more formal than ours, and full titles and positions are important things to know about people.■

Employment Regulations for Americans

Americans staying for 30 days or less and presenting proof of onward transportation do not need a visa, unless planning to work. Americans planning to work also require a work permit, which must be obtained by the employer. Visitors' visas may be obtained at any British consulate or at the British embassy. An entry visa is valid for six months and allows the holder to work within guidelines. The Immigration Department provides regularly updated information on visa and employment requirements.

Because of the labor shortage and ongoing brain drain prior to 1997, employment may be found for foreigners. A wide array of American companies operate in the colony, as well as firms from throughout Europe, especially Britain. Qualified, skilled Americans should find themselves on a relatively equal footing with nationals of other countries in applying for employment.

Tourism is a major industry and offers seasonal employment. About 7% of Hong Kong's gross domestic product and over 140,000 jobs are produced by the tourist industry. In 1990, over 500,000 Americans visited the colony as tourists. The Japanese made over 1 million trips, and about 4 million other visitors came, too.

Immigration Department
International Bldg.
141 Des Voeux Rd.
Central, Hong Kong

Teaching English in Hong Kong

After Japan, Hong Kong is probably the largest market for teaching English in East Asia. Hundreds of language schools, varying widely in quality and clientele, can be found throughout the colony. Jobs tutoring private individuals are also easily available by simply posting notices on bulletin boards in apartment buildings. Americans will find that British citizens have an easier time gaining employment, especially since they do not need work visas.

Wages in Hong Kong are also generally quite low, so you may find yourself working long hours. Nonetheless, jobs teaching English can be found by anyone willing to inquire. The Hong Kong English Club is one of the most respected language institutes in the colony and has several branches.

Hong Kong English Club
190 Nathan Rd.
Kowloon, Hong Kong
Tel.: 852 3 666961

Organizations for Further Information

The following organizations, both in the U.S. and Hong Kong, may be helpful in the job search. American embassies and consulates have commercial and/or economic sections that can provide you with business information and explain aspects of the local economy. World Trade Centers usually include many foreign companies operating in the country. Foreign government missions in the U.S. such as National Tourist Offices and embassies and consulates can furnish visas and information on work permits and other important regulations. They may also offer economic and business information about the country.

CHAMBERS OF COMMERCE

American Chamber of Commerce in Hong Kong
1030 Swire House, P.O. Box 355
Central, Hong Kong
Tel.: 852 5 260165

Hong Kong Chamber of Commerce
Union House, 9th Floor, P.O. Box 852
Hong Kong, Hong Kong
Tel.: 852 5 237177

CONSULAR OFFICE IN HONG KONG

American Consulate General, Hong Kong
26 Garden Rd., Box 30
Hong Kong
Tel.: 852 5 239011
Ying Price, Commercial Officer

WORLD TRADE CENTER IN HONG KONG

World Trade Centre Hong Kong
c/o World Trade Centre Club Hong Kong
2/M and 3/F World Trade Centre
Causeway Bay, Hong Kong
Tel.: 852 5 779528

OTHER INFORMATIONAL ORGANIZATIONS

Hong Kong Tourist Association, Chicago
333 N. Michigan Ave., Suite 218
Chicago, IL 60601
Tel.: (312) 782-3872

Hong Kong Tourist Association Headquarters
Connaught Place, Jardin House, 35th Floor
Central, Hong Kong
Tel.: 852 8017111

Hong Kong Tourist Association, Los Angeles
10940 Wilshire Blvd., Suite 1220
Los Angeles, CA 90024
Tel.: (213) 208-4582

Hong Kong Tourist Association, New York
590 5th Ave., 5th Floor
New York, NY 10036
Tel.: (212) 869-5008

Hong Kong Tourist Association, San Francisco
160 Sansome St., Suite 1102

San Francisco, CA 94104
Tel.: (415) 781-4582

Business Directories

Although not always easy to find, business directories can prove invaluable in the international job search. Most directories list company names, addresses, products, and phone numbers. Some directories include executive names and titles and financial information about the company. These sources provide you with the names of the people to contact for employment information as well as financial data.

American Chamber of Commerce Directory. Annual publication of the American Chamber of Commerce, 1030 Swire House, Central, Hong Kong. Lists basic information on comapnies engaged in bilateral trade and investment.

Business Directory of Hong Kong. Published annually by Current Publications, 504 Enterprise Bldg., 238 Queen's Road, Central, Hong Kong. Provides basic information on over 12,000 companies in various fields.

Directory of the China Commercial Relations Committee. Annual publication of the American Chamber of Commerce, 1030 Swire House, Central, Hong Kong. Includes basic information on 150 companies investing in the People's Republic of China.

Directory of Hong Kong Industries. Published annually by the Hong Kong Productivity Council, TST Box 99027, Hong Kong. Includes basic information on about 4,000 manufacturing companies.

Federation of Hong Kong Industries Directory. Biennial publication of the Federation of Hong Kong Industries, 21 Ma Tau Wei Rd., Hung Kom, Kowloon, Hong Kong. Lists basic information on over 1,000 manufacturers.

Guide to Hong Kong Products. Annual publication of International Publications, 2 King's Rd., 11th Floor, Causeway Bay, Hong Kong. Provides basic information on companies engaged in international trade.

Hong Kong Exporters Association Directory. Published annually by the Hong Kong Exporters Association, Star House, Rm. 825, 3 Salisbury Rd., Kowloon, Hong Kong. Provides basic information on nearly 200 firms engaged in international trade.

Hong Kong Stock Exchange Yearbook. Annual publication of the Hong Kong Stock Exchange, Hutchison House, Hong Kong. Lists detailed financial data on almost 200 companies quoted on the stock exchange.

MAJOR AMERICAN COMPANIES IN HONG KONG

Some American firms operate in Hong Kong. The following companies are classified by business area: Banking and Finance; Industrial Manufacturing; Retailing and Wholesaling; and Service Industries. The company information includes type of business, American parent company, and contact name where possible. Your chances of achieving employment are substantially greater if you contact the subsidiary company in Hong Kong rather than the parent company in the U.S.

BANKING AND FINANCE

Allied Bank International
St. George's Bldg., 10th Floor
2 Ice House St.
Hong Kong, Hong Kong
(Banking)
Allied Bank International

American Express Leasing Corp.
Alexandria House, 8th Floor
16/20 Charter Rd.
P.O. Box 3
Hong Kong, Hong Kong
(Financial and travel-related services)
American Express Co.

BA Asia
Bank of America Tower, 20th Floor
#12 Harcourt
P.O. Box 472
Hong Kong, Hong Kong
Tel.: 852 5 8476666
(Investment)
Robert Slaymaker, Managing Director
Bankamerica Corp.

Bankers Trust Asia
Admiralty Centre Tower 1, 30th Floor
18 Harcourt Rd.
GPO Box 10098
Hong Kong, Hong Kong
Tel.: 852 5 281211
(Banking)
Michael Grogan, Vice President
Bankers Trust New York Corp.

Chase Manhattan Asia
1 Exchange Square
Central, Hong Kong
Tel.: 852 5 8431234
(Banking)
Chase Manhattan Corp.

Chemical Bank Hong Kong
Gloucester Tower, 42nd Floor
The Landmark
11 Pedder St.
Central, Hong Kong
Tel.: 852 5 2673333
(Banking)
Cary W. Jackson
Chemical Banking Corp.

Citibank
Citibank Tower
8 Queen's Rd., P.O. Box 14
Central, Hong Kong
(International banking)
Citibank NA

Continental Illinois National Bank & Trust Co. of Chicago
Edinburg Tower, 32nd Floor
15 Queen's Rd.
Central, Hong Kong
(Banking)
Continental Illinois National Bank & Trust Co. of Chicago

CS First Boston
One Exchange Square, 9th Floor
Central, Hong Kong
Tel.: 852 5 8470388
(Banking)
Allen D. Wheat, Chairman
CS First Boston

Goldman Sachs
Edinburg Tower, The Landmark, 35th Floor
15 Queen's Rd.
Central, Hong Kong
Tel.: 852 5 255078
Fax.: 852 5 8681435
(Investment banking)
Goldman, Sachs & Co.

Kidder, Peabody & Co.
1707-0 Connaught Centre
Connaught Rd.
Central, Hong Kong
(Investment bankers)
Kidder, Peabody & Co.

Manufacturers Hanover Asia
Edinburgh Tower, 43rd Floor
The Landmark
Hong Kong, Hong Kong
Tel.: 852 5 8416900
(Banking)
Manufacturers Hanover Corp.

Marine Midland Bank NY
Hang Chong Bldg.
5 Queen's Rd.
Central, Hong Kong
(Banking)
Marine Midland Bank NA

Mellon Bank
1728-30 Prince's Bldg.
Des Voeux Rd.
Central, Hong Kong
(Banking)
Mellon Bank NA

Merrill Lynch, Pierce, Fenner & Smith International
St. George's Bldg., 15th Floor
2 Ice House St.
Hong Kong, Hong Kong
(Brokers)
Merrill Lynch, Pierce, Fenner & Smith

J.P. Morgan Investment Management
3506 Gloucester Tower
11 Peddar St.
Hong Kong, Hong Kong
(Investment services)
J.P. Morgan & Co.

Paine Webber Mitchell
Hutchins International Hong Kong
St. George's Bldg.
2 Ice House St.
Hong Kong, Hong Kong
(Brokerage firm)
Paine Webber Mitchell Hutchins International

Prudential-Bache Securities
Central Bldg., 16th Floor
Peddar St.
Hong Kong, Hong Kong
(Investment banking)
William Custard, Director
Prudential-Bache Securities

Salomon Bros.
2907 Alexandra House
15-20 Chater Rd.
Hong Kong, Hong Kong
(Securities, underwriters)
Salomon Bros.

Security Pacific National Bank
2101 Bank of Canton Bldg.
6 Des Voeux Rd.
Central, Hong Kong
(Banking)
Security Pacific National Bank

Shearson Loeb Rhoades
St. George's Bldg., 7th Floor
2 Ice House St.
Hong Kong, Hong Kong
(Investment banking)
American Express Co.

Texas Commerce Bank
Alexandra House - 1810
16-20 Chater Rd.
Hong Kong, Hong Kong
(Banking)
Texas Commerce Bank

United California Bank
3101 Connaught Centre
Connaught Rd.
Central, Hong Kong
(Banking)
United California Bank

Country-by-Country Listings

INDUSTRIAL MANUFACTURING

Amoco Chemicals Far East
Far East Finance Centre, 11th Floor
16 Harcourt Rd.
Hong Kong, Hong Kong
Tel.: 852 5 290370
(Petrochemicals)
G.A. Nersesian, President
Amoco Corp.

Apple Computer International
Exchange Tower II, 14th Floor
8 Connaught Rd.
Hong Kong, Hong Kong
Tel.: 852 5 8442400
Fax.: 852 5 8100073
(Personal computers)
Apple Computer

Baxter Healthcare
Shui On Centre, Rm. 2009-11
6-8 Harbour Rd.
Wanchai, Hong Kong
Tel.: 852 5 8654535
Fax.: 852 5 8654096
(Medical supplies)
Baxter International

Bristol-Myers
29 Wong Chuk Hang Rd.
Aberdeen, Hong Kong
(Cosmetics)
Bristol-Myers Squibb Co.

Ciba-Corning Diag
Units B&D, 20th Floor
65 Wong Chuk Hang Rd.
Hong Kong, Hong Kong
(Medical instruments)
Ciba-Corning Diag. Corp.

Coca-Cola Central Pacific
GPO Box 916
Hong Kong, Hong Kong
Tel.: 852 5 7903323
(Beverages)
The Coca-Cola Co.

Colgate-Palmolive Hong Kong
1423-9 Prince's Bldg.
10 Chater Rd.
P.O. Box 1324
Hong Kong, Hong Kong
(Pharmaceuticals, cosmetics, detergents, toiletries)
Colgate-Palmolive Co.

Dow Chemical Hong Kong
Gammon House
12 Harbour Rd.
P.O. Box 711
Hong Kong, Hong Kong
(Chemicals, plastics, fibers, pharmaceuticals)
Dow Chemical Co.

DuPont Far East
915 Prince's Bldg.
10 Charter Rd.
Hong Kong, Hong Kong
(Chemicals, plastics, fibers)
E.I. Du Pont De Nemours & Co.

Eastern Energy
St. George's Bldg., 10th Floor
2 Ice House St.
Hong Kong, Hong Kong
(Petrochemicals)
Exxon Corp.

Exxon Energy
St. George's Bldg.
Hong Kong, Hong Kong
Tel.: 852 5246041
(Electric power generation)
Exxon Corp.

General Electric China Co.
1301 Two Exchange Square, 13th Floor
GPO Box 705
Hong Kong, Hong Kong
(Technology, services)
General Electric Company

General Foods
Connaught Center, Stes. 1509-13
1 Connaught Pl
Central, Hong Kong
(Foods)
General Foods Corp.

General Mills Hong Kong
Star House, Rm. 1608-1610
Salisbury Rd.
Kowloon, Hong Kong
(Breakfast cereals, flour, cake mixes)
General Mills

B.F. Goodrich Chemical
AIA Bldg. No. 1, Suite 1406
Stubbs Rd.
Hong Kong, Hong Kong
Tel.: 852 5 7432246
Fax.: 852 5 8345529
(Vinyl)
H. Higgenbotham, Manager
B.F. Goodrich Co.

W.R. Grace
Wilson House 12-13th Floors
19-27 Wyndham
Central, Hong Kong
Tel.: 852 5 243192
Fax.: 852 5 8104324
(Construction, chemicals)
R. Bryan Lloyd, Managing Director
W.R. Grace & Co.

Hewlett-Packard Asia
GPO Box 863
Hong Kong, Hong Kong
(Computational equipment)
Hewlett-Packard Co.

IBM World Trade Corp.
Two Exchange Square, 47th Floor
Central District, Hong Kong 1003
Hong Kong
(Office equipment)
Robert Savage, Managing Director
International Business Machines

ITT Far East & Pacific
P & O Bldg., 5th Floor
23 Des Voeux Rd.
Central, Hong Kong
(Telecommunications)
International Telephone & Telegraph Corp.

Johnson & Johnson Hong Kong
Sun Hung Kia Center
Hong Kong, Hong Kong
Tel.: 852 5 8912022
(Surgical, medical, baby products)
Johnson & Johnson

Kodak Far East
Watson's Estate, Block C, 6th Floor
Watson Rd.
P.O. Box 48
North Point, Hong Kong
(Photo products, chemicals, information management)
Eastman Kodak Co.

Levi Strauss
Hong Kong Spinners Industrial Bldg., 9th Floor
603 Tai Nan West St.
Kowloon, Hong Kong
(Clothing)
Levi Strauss & Co.

Merck, Sharp & Dohme
1401 Guardian House
3201 Kwan Rd.
Hong Kong, Hong Kong
(Pharmaceuticals, chemicals, biologicals)
Merck, Sharp & Dohme International

Monsanto Far East
Hng Lung Bank Bldg., 7th Floor
6-8 Hyson Ave.
Hong Kong, Hong Kong
(Chemicals, plastics)
Monsanto Co.

Motorola Asia
Citicorp Centre, Rm. 1402-4
18 Whitfield Rd.
Causeway Bay, Hong Kong
Tel.: 852 5 66706
(Digital watch displays)
Motorola, Inc.

National Cash Register Co. Hong Kong
Nacareco House, 6th Floor
99 King's Rd.
North Point, Hong Kong
(Data processing systems)
NCR Corp.

Philip Morris Asia-Pacific
2807 Realty Bldg.
71-72 Des Voeux Rd.
Central, Hong Kong
(Cigarettes, beverages)
Philip Morris

Phillips Petroleum Co. Asia
Citibank Tower, 9th Floor
8 Queen's Rd.
Central, Hong Kong
(Petrochemicals)
Phillips Petroleum Co.

Raytheon Worldwide Co.
Swire House, Rm. 813, 8th Floor
Central District, Hong Kong
(Industustrial tubes, radar/sonar systems, appliances, construction)
Raytheon Co.

Revlon Hong Kong
64-66 To Kwa Wan Rd.
Kowloon, Hong Kong
(Cosmetics, health care products)
Revlon Inc.

SmithKline Corp.
c/o American Chamber of Commerce
1030 Swire House
Hong Kong, Hong Kong
(Pharmaceuticals, instruments)
SmithKline Corp.

Squibb Far East
1 Hysan Ave.
Hong Kong, Hong Kong
(Pharmaceuticals)
E.R. Squibb & Sons

Standard Brands Hong Kong
P.O. Box 20415
Hennessy Rd.
Hong Kong, Hong Kong
(Food products, toys, cosmetics)
Nabisco Brands

Sterling International Hong Kong
Sterling International Bldg.
132 Wai Yip St.
Kwun Tong, Kowloon
(Paper products)
Sterling International

Texaco Hong Kong
American International Tower, Rm. 2005
16-18 Queen's Rd.
Central, Hong Kong
(Petrochemicals)
Texaco Inc.

3M Far East
GPO Box 270
S. China Morning Post Bldg., 6th Floor
Tong Chong St.
Quarry Bay, Hong Kong
(Abrasives, adhesives, chemicals, diversified industries)
3M Co.

UC Asia
Windsor House, 38th Floor
Causeway Bay, Hong Kong
(Chemicals, plastics)
Union Carbide Corp.

Uniroyal International
1008 Shell House
26 Queen's Rd.
Central, Hong Kong
(Tires, rubber products)
Uniroyal Inc.

Wang Pacific
Lap Hong House, 9th Floor
47-50 Gloucester Rd.
Hong Kong, Hong Kong
(Computers, peripheral devices)
Wang Laboratories

Warner-Lambert Hong Kong
GPO Box 567
Hong Kong, Hong Kong
(Pharmaceuticals)
Warner-Lambert Co.

Weyerhaeuser Co.
GPO Box 3818
Hong Kong, Hong Kong
(Wood products)
Weyerhaeuser Co.

Wrigley Company
14 Wongchukhang Rd.
Hong Kong, Hong Kong
Tel.: 852 5 21070
(Chewing gum)
Wm. Wrigley Jr. Co.

RETAILING AND WHOLESALING

Alcoa International
St. George's Bldg., 17th Floor
3 Ice House
Hong Kong, Hong Kong
Tel.: 852 5 228077
(Aluminum products)
Aluminum Co. of America

Alpha Merchandising Service
Hecny Tower, 9th-10th Floors
9 Chatham Rd.
Kowloon, Hong Kong
(Department stores)
May Department Stores Co.

Amway
Citicorp Centre, 30th Floor
18 Whitfield Rd.
Causeway Bay
Hong Kong, Hong Kong
Tel.: 852 5 662239
Fax.: 852 5 8073920
(Appliances)
Eva Cheng, Managing Director
Amway Corp.

Castle & Cooke Worldwide
409 Melbourne Plaza
33 Queen's Rd.
Central, Hong Kong
Tel.: 852 5 5245187
(Sales)
Castle & Cooke

Circle K Convenience Store
Witty Comml. Bldg., 3rd Floor
1A-1L Tung Choi St.
Mongkok, Kowloon, Hong Kong
Tel.: 852 3880883
Fax.: 852 3857843
(Convenience stores)
Butt Lau, Managing Director
Circle K Corp.

Coca-Cola Central Pacific
GPO Box 916
Hong Kong, Hong Kong
Tel.: 852 5 7903323
(Beverages)
Coca-Cola Co.

Cyanamid
Watson's Estate, Block C, 14th Floor
Watson Rd.
North Point, Hong Kong
Tel.: 852 5 7192815
(Chemicals)
American Cyanamid Co.

Fox-Columbia Film Distributors
Loong San Bldg.
140-142 Connaught Rd.
Central, Hong Kong
(Motion pictures producers/distributers)
Columbia Pictures Industries

General Foods
Connaught Center, Suites 1509-13
1 Connaught Pl
Central, Hong Kong
(Foods)
General Foods Corp.

Hewlett-Packard Asia
West Tower, 22nd Floor
Bond Centre, 89 Queensway
GPO Box 863
Hong Kong, Hong Kong
Tel.: 852 5 8487777
(Computer products)
Hewlett-Packard Co.

Honeywell Asia Pacific
One Exchange Square, Suite 3408
Hong Kong, Hong Kong
Tel.: 852 5 8445566
(Automatic control instruments)
L.W. Knoblauch, President
Honeywell

International Paper
1207 Alexandra House
16-20 Chater Rd.
Hong Kong, Hong Kong
(Paper products)
International Paper Co.

K Mart Far East
18 B United Center, 18th Floor
95 Queensway
Hong Kong, Hong Kong
(Goods)
D.M. Starling, Managing Director
K Mart Corporation

R.H. Macy & Co.
922-924 Ocean Centre
Canton Rd.
Kowloon, Hong Kong
(Department stores, importers)
R.H. Macy & Co.

Metro-Goldwyn-Mayer Hong Kong
225-6 J. Hotung House
5-15 Hankow Rd.
Kowloon, Hong Kong
(Motion pictures)
Metro-Goldwyn-Mayer Film Co.

Montgomery Ward & Co.
605 Star House
3 Salisbury Rd.
Kowloon, Hong Kong
(Department stores)
Montgomery Ward & Co.

Polaroid Far East
Windsor House
311 Gloucester Rd.
Causeway Bay, Hong Kong
Tel.: 852 5 8940333
Fax.: 852 5 8951382
(Photographic equipment)
Polaroid Corp.

Revlon Hong Kong
64-66 To Kwa Wan Rd., 7th Floor
Kowloon, Hong Kong
(Cosmetics, health care products)
Revlon

RJR Nabisco Holdings
401 Asian House
1 Hennessy Rd.
Hong Kong, Hong Kong
(Tobacco products)
R.J. Reynolds Tobacco Co.

Shell Company of Hong Kong
Shell House
24-28 Queen's Rd.
Hong Kong, Hong Kong
Tel.: 852 5 8478000
Fax.: 852 5 8612847
(Petrochemicals)
Royal Dutch/Shell Group of Companies

Sunkist Promotion
Swire House, 12th Floor
11 Chater Rd.
Hong Kong, Hong Kong
Tel.: 852 5 249219
(Citrus products)
Sunkist Growers

SERVICE INDUSTRIES

Air Express International Hong Kong
KAFAT Bldg., Rm. 306
70-78 Sung Wong Toi Rd.
Kowloon, Hong Kong
(Air freight forwarder)
Air Express International Corp.

Airborne Freight Corp.
G1 Kowloon Air Freight Agent Terminal
70-77 Sung Wong Toi Rd.
Kowloon, Hong Kong
(Total air transportation service)
Airborne Express

American Airlines
Caxton House
1 Duddell St.
Hong Kong, Hong Kong
(Air transportation)
American Airlines

American Express Leasing Corp.
8th Floor, Alexandria House
16/20 Charter Rd.
P.O. Box 3
Hong Kong, Hong Kong
(Financial and travel related services)
American Express Co.

American Industrial Report
Guardian House, Suite 905
32 Oi Kwan St.
Happy Valley, Hong Kong
(Publishing, broadcasting)
McGraw-Hill

Asian Wall Street Journal
1 Stubbs Rd.
P.O. Box 9825
Wanchai, Hong Kong
Tel.: 852 5 737121
(Publication)
Michael Wilson, Publisher
Dow Jones & Co.

AT&T International
9 Floor, Hong Kong Club Bldg.
3A Chater Rd.
Central District, Hong Kong
(Telecommunications)
AT&T International

Avis Hong Kong
2 Watson Rd.
North Point, Hong Kong
(Car rentals)
Avis

Burson-Marstellar
Sincere Insurance Bldg., 3rd Floor
4 Hannessy Rd.
Hong Kong, Hong Kong
(Public relations consultants)
Burson-Marstellar International

Carte Blanche International Hong Kong
c/o Far East Bank
Far East Bank Central Bldg.
M/F 116-118 Des Voeux Rd.
Central, Hong Kong
(Credit card system)
Carte Blanche Corp.

CBS Publishing
2-11 Floor
3 Hinden Row
Hong Kong, Hong Kong
(Publishing)
CBS Educational & Professional Publishing

Coopers & Lybrand
7th Floor, Sheel House
26 Queen's Rd.
P.O. Box 417
Central, Hong Kong
(Accountants, auditors)
Coopers & Lybrand International

Deloitte Haskins & Sells International
Wing On Centre, 26th Floor
111 Connaught Rd.
GPO Box 3348
Central, Hong Kong
(Accountants, advisors)
Deloitte Haskins & Sells International

Diner's Club Hong Kong
304 Chartered Bank Bldg., 11th Floor
4-4A Des Voeux Rd.
Central, Hong Kong
(Credit card service)
Diner's Club International

Dun & Bradstreet
Sun Hung Kai Centre, 20th Floor
30 Harbour Rd.
Wanchai, Hong Kong
Tel.: 852 8 284333
Fax.: 852 8 345301
(Credit services)
Dun & Bradstreet Corp.

Flying Tiger Line
New Cargo Complex Office Block, Rm. 223
International Airport
Hong Kong, Hong Kong
(Air freight carrier)
Flying Tiger Line

Gray Line Tours of Hong Kong
501 Cheong Hing Bldg.
72 Nathan Rd.
P.O. Box 6710
Kowloon, Hong Kong
(Sightseeing tours)
Gray Line Association

Hill & Knowlton Asia
Windsor House, 35th Floor
311 Gloucester Rd.
Hong Kong, Hong Kong
(Public relations, communicaton counseling)
Hill & Knowlton

Holt, Rinehart & Winston Publishing Asia
Alexandria House, 11th Floor
16-20 Chater Rd.
Hong Kong, Hong Kong
(Publishers)
Barry John Dingley, Managing Director
Harcourt Brace Jovanich

McCann-Erickson
Sunning Plaza, 1st Floor
10 Hysan Ave.
Hong Kong, Hong Kong
Tel.: 852 5 772821
Fax.: 852 5 769136
(Advertising)
Kinsley John Smith, Chairman
McCann-Erickson Worldwide

Ogilvy & Mather Hong Kong
Centre Point
181-185 Gloucester Rd.
Wanchai, Hong Kong
(Advertising agency)
Ogilvy & Mather

Peat Marwick Mitchell & Co.
Prince's Bldg.
GPO Box 50
Hong Kong, Hong Kong
(Accountants, consultants)
Peat Marwick Mitchell & Co.

Price Waterhouse & Co.
Princes Bldg., 22nd Floor
P.O. Box 690
Hong Kong, Hong Kong
(Accountants, auditors)
Price Waterhouse & Co.

Reader's Digest Asia
Toppan Bldg., 6-7th Floors
22 Westland Rd.
GPO Box 497
Quarry Bay, Hong Kong
(Publishing)
Reader's Digest Association

Texaco Hong Kong
New World Tower
16-18 Queen's Rd.
Hong Kong, Hong Kong
(Service company)
W.S. Barrack, Jr., Chairman
Texaco

J. Walter Thompson Co.
Great Eagle Centre
23 Harbour Rd.
Wanchai, Hong Kong
(Consultants)
J. Walter Thompson Co.

Time-Life News Service
205 Prince's Bldg.
Des Voeux Rd.
Central, Hong Kong
(Publishers)
Time

Touche Ross & Co.
1505 Prince's Bldg.
Hong Kong, Hong Kong
(Accounting, auditing)
Touche Ross & Co.

Towers, Perrin, Forster, & Crosby
1302 Admiralty Centre
Tower 11, Harcourt Rd.
Hong Kong, Hong Kong
(Consultants)
Towers, Perrin, Forster, & Crosby

Westinghouse Broadcasting Co.
1-A Gardena Court
2 Kennedy Terrace
Hong Kong, Hong Kong
(Radio/television broadcasting)
Westinghouse Co.

Arthur Young & Co.
Hopewell Centre, 53rd Floor
813 Queen's Rd., East
P.O. Box 5044
Hong Kong, Hong Kong
(Accountants)
Arthur Young & Co.

MAJOR HONG KONG DOMESTIC COMPANIES

The following is a listing of the major domestic companies of Hong Kong. They are classified by business area: Banking and Finance; Industrial Manufacturing; Retailing and Wholesaling; Service Industries. Company information includes type of business and contact name. Such companies will generally hire their own nationals first but may employ Americans.

BANKING AND FINANCE

First Pacific Company
2 Exchange Square, 24th Floor
8 Connaught Place
Central, Hong Kong
Tel.: 852 5 8424388
Fax.: 852 5 8459243
(Banking, securities brokerage)
Maisie Lam, Assistant Vice President, Human Resources

Hongkong & Shanghai Banking Corp. (Hongkong Bank)
1 Queen's Rd.
Central, Hong Kong
Tel.: 853 5 8221111
Fax.: 852 5 8101112
(Banking)
W. Purves, Chairman

Overseas Trust Bank
Otb Bldg.
Wan Chai, Hong Kong 1015
(Commercial banking)
David F. Turner, Managing Director

Shanghai Commercial Bank
12 Queen's Rd. C
Central District, Hong Kong 1003
(Commerical banking)
Ju Tang Chu, Chairman

INDUSTRIAL MANUFACTURING

Gold Peak Industries
FML Bldg., 8th Floor
30-34 Kwai Wing Rd.
Kwai Chung N.T., Hong Kong
Tel.: 852 0271133
(Batteries, electronics)
Kevin Lo, Chairman

RETAILING AND WHOLESALING

Swire Pacific
Swire House, 4th Floor
9 Connaught Rd.
Central, Hong Kong
Tel.: 852 5 8408888
Fax.: 852 5 8454876
(Beverages, beverage cans, packaging of sugar)
D.A. Gledhill, Chairman

SERVICE INDUSTRIES

Cathay Pacific Airways
Swire House, 4th Floor
Central District, Hong Kong
1003
Hong Kong
(Air transportation)
David A. Gledhill, Chairman

China Travel Service
Cts House, 21st Floor
Central District, Hong Kong
1003
(Travel agencies)
Chi Man Ma, General Manager

First Pacific Company
2 Exchange Square, 24th Floor
8 Connaught Place
Central, Hong Kong
Tel.: 852 5 8424388
Fax.: 852 5 8459243
(Telecommunications)
Maisie Lam, Assistant Vice President, Human Resources

Furama Hotel Enterprises
Whole Bldg.
Central District, Hong Kong
1003
(Hotels)
Han Cha Fu, Executive Officer

Hong Kong Land Co.
1 Exchange Square, 8th Floor
Central, Hong Kong
Tel.: 852 5 8458428
Fax.: 852 5 8459226
(Property leasing and development)
Nigel M.S. Rich, Chairman and Managing Director

Hong Kong Telecommunications
Three Exchange Square, 15th Floor
Hong Kong, Hong Kong
Tel.: 852 8 488718
Fax.: 852 8 685187
(Telecommunications)
B.A. Pemberton, Deputy Chairman

Hongkong & Shanghai Hotels
George's Bldg., 8th Floor
Central District, Hong Kong
1003
(Hotels)
H.G. Webb-Peploe, Managing Director

Kowloon Motor Bus Co.
51-53 Kwai Cheong Rd.
Kwai Chung
New Territories, Hong Kong
Tel.: 852 0296161
Fax.: 852 04898602
(Public passenger carrier)
The Honorable Pak Cheun Woo, Chairman

New World Development Company
New World Tower
30th Floor
18th QueenÆs Rd.
Central, Hong Kong
Tel.: 852 5 231056
Fax.: 852 5 8104673
(Real estate, hotel investment, engineering)
Andrew Fook-Ming Choi

Wing On Department Store
Wing On Center, 7th Floor
Central District, Hong Kong
1003
(Department stores)
Chi Yan Kwok, General Manager

MAJOR INTERNATIONAL COMPANIES IN HONG KONG

There are many international firms operating in Hong Kong. These companies will be classified by business area: Banking and Finance; Industrial Manufacturing; Retailing and Wholesaling; and Service Industries. The company information includes type of business, international parent company, and contact name where possible. Your chances of achieving employment are substantially greater if you contact the subsidiary company in Hong Kong rather than the parent company in the home country.

BANKING AND FINANCE

Allianz Cornhill Insurance
Ruttonjee House, 20th Floor
11 Duddell St.
Hong Kong, Hong Kong
Tel.: 852 5216651
Fax.: 852 8106191
(Insurance)
Martin F. Quigley, Managing Director
Allianz, Germany

Australia & New Zealand Banking Group
1 Exchange Square, 27th Floor
8 Connaught Place
Central, Hong Kong
Tel.: 852 8437111
Fax.: 852 5279084
(Banking)
Australia & New Zealand Bank Group, Australia

Bank of China
Bank of China Bldg.
Central District, Hong Kong 1003
(Commercial banking)
Xue Yao Zhang, General Manager
Bank of China, PRC

Banque Indosuez
Alexandra House
11 Des Voeux Rd.
Hong Kong, Hong Kong
Tel.: 852 5 265411
(Banking)
Raymond-Philippe Martin, Manager
Compagne Financiere de Suez, France

Credit Agricole Hong Kong
1 Exchange Square, 50th Floor
Hong Kong, Hong Kong
Tel.: 852 5 255231
Fax.: 852 5 8611427
(Banking)
Marc Mayer, Chief Executive Officer
Caisse Nationale de Credit Agricole, France

Deutsche Bank
New World Tower, 40th Floor
16-18 Queen's Rd. C
GPO Box 3193
Hong Kong, Hong Kong
(Banking)
Reiner Rusch, General Manager
Deutsche Bank, Germany

Dresdner Bank
World Wide House
19 Des Voeux Rd. C.
Hong Kong, Hong Kong
Tel.: 852 5 210427
(Banking)
Dr. Erich Brogl, Chief Operations Officer
Dresdner Bank, Germany

Morgan Grenfell (Hong Kong)
9th Floor, Hutchison House, 10 Harcourt Rd.
Hong Kong, Hong Kong
Tel.: 852 8 108686
Fax.: 852 8 459172
(Financial services)
A. F. Hohler, Managing Director
Deutsche Bank, Germany

National Australia Bank
Floor 46, 1 Garden Rd. Central
Hong Kong, Hong Kong
Tel.: 852 5 8268111
Fax.: 852 5 8459251
(Banking)
E. J. McLedd, Managing Director
Natl. Australia Bank, Australia

Paribas Asia
11 Pedder St.
GPO Box 11681
Central, Hong Kong
Tel.: 852 5 25396
(Financial services)
Compagnie Finaciere de Paribas, France

Standard Chartered Bank
Edinburgh Tower
Central District, Hong Kong 1003
(Banking)
Standard Chartered, England

Westpac Banking Corp.
Exchange Square 111, Level 19
8 Connaught Place
Hong Kong, Hong Kong
Tel.: 852 5 8429888
Fax.: 852 5 8400591
(Banking)
Darcy Ford, General Manager, Asian Operations
Westpac Banking Corp., Australia

INDUSTRIAL MANUFACTURING

British American Tobacco Co.
3 Heung Yip Rd.
Aberdeen, Hong Kong
Tel.: 852 5 520283
(Tobacco products)
B.A.T. Industries, England

Nestle China
Wing On Centre
Hong Kong, Hong Kong
Tel.: 852 5 434161
(Chocolate and dairy products)
Nestle S.A., Switzerland

RETAILING AND WHOLESALING

Daihatsu Motor
64-66 Gloucester Rd.
Hong Kong, Hong Kong
Tel.: 852 5 283038
Fax.: 852 5 273368
(Automobiles)
Masayuki Ikehashi, President
Daihatsu Motors Co., Japan

NEC Electronics Hong Kong
Chaun Hing Industrial Bldg., 6-7th Floors
14 Wang Tai Rd.
Kowloon, Hong Kong
Tel.: 852 3 7559008
Fax.: 852 3 7962404
(Electronic devices)
H. Chiyoda, Managing Director
NEC Corp., Japan

Sanyo Electric
Chuan Kei Factory Bldg., 14th Floor
15-23 Kin Hong St.
Kwai Chung New Territories, Hong Kong
Tel.: 852 0269321
(Electronics)
Sanyo Electric Co., Japan

Sony Corp. of Hong Kong
St. George's Bldg., 22nd Floor
2 Ice House St.
Hong Kong, Hong Kong
Tel.: 852 5 228061
(Electronics)
Sony Corporation, Japan

Ssangyong Co.
Wing On Centre, Rm. 1209
111 Connaught Rd.
Hong Kong, Hong Kong
Tel.: 852 5 423151
Fax.: 852 5 8100480
(Paper products, computer software, electronics)
Ssangyong Group of Companies, South Korea

SERVICE INDUSTRIES

Reuters Hong Kong
P.O. Box 25
Hong Kong, Hong Kong
Tel.: 852 8415888
(News information service)
Reuters Holdings, England

Saatchi & Saatchi Advertising
Shui On Centre, 22nd Floor
6-8 Harbour Rd.
Hong Kong, Hong Kong
Tel.: 852 5 8643333
Fax.: 852 5 8651213
(Advertising)
Michael Cooper, Managing Director
Saatchi & Saatchi Advertising International, England

Thorn EMI Rentals
Watson''s Estate, Block C, 1st Floor
North Point, Hong Kong
Tel.: 852 5 789318
(Video rentals)
C.T. Lam, Managing Director
Thorn EMI, England

MAJOR HOTEL EMPLOYERS IN HONG KONG

Holiday Inn Golden Mile
50 Nathan Rd.,Tsimshatsui
Kowloon, Hong Kong
Tel.: 852 3 693111

Holiday Inn Harbour View
70 Mody Rd., Tsimshatsui
Kowloon, Hong Kong
Tel.: 852 3 7215161

Hong Kong Hotel
Harbour City
Kowloon, Hong Kong
Tel.: 852 3 676011

Hong Kong Marriott
88 Queensway, Pacific Place, Central
Hong Kong, Hong Kong
Tel.: 852 5 8108366

Hotel Furama Intercontinental
1 Connaught Rd. Central
Hong Kong, Hong Kong
Tel.: 852 5 255111

Hyatt Regency Hong Kong
67 Nathan Rd.
Kowloon, Hong Kong
Tel.: 852 3 3111234

Park Lane Radisson
310 Gloucester Rd.
Hong Kong, Hong Kong
Tel.: 852 5 8903355

Peninsula, Hong Kong
Salisbury Rd.
Kowloon, Hong Kong
Tel.: 852 3 666251

Ramada Inn Hong Kong
61-73 Lockhart Rd.
Hong Kong, Hong Kong
Tel.: 852 5 8611000

Ramada Inn Kowloon
73-75 Chatham Rd. S.
Kowloon, Hong Kong
Tel.: 852 3 3111100

Ramada Renaissance
8 Peking Rd.
Kowloon, Hong Kong
Tel.: 852 3 3113311

Regal Airport Hotel
Hong Kong International Airport
Kowloon, Hong Kong
Tel.: 852 3 7180333

Regal Meridien Hotel
71 Mody Rd.
Kowloon, Hong Kong
Tel.: 852 3 7221818

Regal Riverside Hotel
Tai Chung Kiu Rd.
Shatin, Hong Kong
Tel.: 852 0 6497878

Royal Park Hotel
8 Pak Hok Ting St.
Shatin, New Territories,
Hong Kong
Tel.: 852 6013666

Shamrock Hotel
223 Nathan Rd, Yau Ma Tei
Kowloon, Hong Kong
Tel.: 852 7352271

Sheraton Hong Kong Hotel
20 Nathan Rd.
Kowloon, Hong Kong
Tel.: 852 3 691111

Windsor Hotel
39-43A Kimberley Rd,
Tsimshatsui
Kowloon, Hong Kong
Tel.: 852 7395665

INTERNATIONAL SCHOOLS IN HONG KONG

International Schools Services
P.O. Box 5910
Princeton, NJ 08543
American teachers seeking employment abroad may contact this recruitment service.

Chinese International School
7 Eastern Hospital Road
Causeway Bay, Hong Kong
Tel.: 852 5 770557
(U.S.-U.K. school, pre-K-6)

Hong Kong International School
6 South Bay Close
Repulse Bay, Hong Kong
Tel.: 852 5 8122305
(U.S. school, K-12)

Island School
20 Borrett Road
Hong Kong, Hong Kong
Tel.: 852 5 247135
(U.K. school, grades 7-13)

MACAU

Macau measures only 6 square miles and is located on China's southeastern coast, only 40 miles from Hong Kong. China, Hong Kong, and Taiwan are the nearest neighbors. The colony consists of a peninsula and two small islands, Taipa and Coloane. The peninsula, on which the city of Macau is located, is connected to China by a narrow isthmus.

Over 95% of the people are Chinese, primarily Cantonese. The remaining 5% are mostly Europeans, especially Portuguese. The Portuguese influence is readily seen in the local cuisine, monuments, architecture, and place names. Official business is conducted in Portuguese, but Chinese is the language spoken by most people. English is also widely known in the business and tourist communities.

Jorge Alvares, a Portuguese navigator, explored the southeastern coast of China in 1513. By 1515, Portuguese traders began settling in Macau, and in 1557 the area was recognized as under Portuguese sovereignty. Macau served as a communication and trading center between China and Japan and later between China and Europe. In the eighteenth century, foreign merchants engaging in trade at Guangzhou lived most of the year in Macau.

By the late nineteenth century, the harbor had lost much of its previous utility due to sediment buildup. As the British moved to Hong Kong, Macau gradually lost its importance as a major international trading center. Macau's economy is now based on tourism and light manufacturing of products for export. The government and business community intend to capture much of Hong Kong's tourist business through a new development plan.

The colony was granted autonomy in 1976, with its own financial and legislative administration. Portugal and China agreed in 1987 that Macau would revert to China in 1999. China has promised that Macau's capitalist system will remain unhindered for an additional 50 years. The Bank of China building now dwarfs the rest of Macau's skyline.

Current Economic Climate

Total population is slightly less than 500,000, and the vast majority lives on the peninsula, although the tourist industry is bringing increasing numbers of people to Taipa and Coloane, too. Large resort facilities are being built on the outer islands, taking advantage of the availability of land. The new airport, costing $450 million, is also spurring movement toward Taipa. The container port is being expanded by 29 acres.

Despite the colony's impending reversion to China in 1999, the attitude in Macau is confident and optimistic. New offices and apartment complexes are being built. Most of the hotels are expanding their facilities, too. The Hotel Lisboa, for instance, is adding an additional 300 rooms. Tourism is a major part of the local economy and will very likely benefit from the new airport. The colony is famous for its casinos and is a favorite weekend or holiday destination for Hong Kong residents. Both the Macau pataca and the Hong Kong dollar are freely traded.

Getting Around in Macau

Air transportation is currently through the airport in Hong Kong. Hydrofoils, ferries, jetfoils, jumbocats, and helicopters depart from Hong Kong to Macau regularly every day. The new airport being built on Taipa will provide international service directly to Macau. The government predicts that the facility will provide an alternative to the crowded Hong Kong airport. It should open in 1994 and will be capable of serving nearly 5 million passengers annually.

The bus system provides stops near most points of interest. "Mokes" are jeeps with canvas roofs that can be rented from agencies in Macau. They are extremely convenient for driving on some of the more hilly and rugged terrain on the islands. Taxis provide transportation throughout Macau and the islands. Pedicabs are still available on Macau, although the hilly parts of the colony cannot be accessed by them. Rental car agencies are available as well.

Employment Regulations for Americans

Americans do not need a visa to enter Macau for stays of less than 90 days. Visas can be obtained at a Portuguese consulate in the U.S. or upon arrival. The government maintains very tight restrictions on immigration and foreign workers, but a tightening labor market may loosen these policies. Employment can most likely be found in the tourist industry.

Making a good first impression

It is a good idea to carry business cards in Macau. Cards can be printed overnight in Hong Kong. The cards should contain one's name, full title or position, employer or organization, phone number, and address. You should have this information in Chinese on one side and in English on the other. Presenting business cards is a common custom in East Asia and will help potential employers, customers, clients, or anyone else you may meet remember you. Chinese society is much more formal than ours, and full titles and positions are important things to know about people.■

Organizations for Further Information

The following organizations, both in the U.S. and Macau, may be helpful in the job search. American embassies and consulates have commercial and/or economic sections that can provide you with business information and explain aspects of the local economy. World Trade Centers usually include many foreign companies operating in the country. Foreign government missions in the U.S. such as National Tourist Offices and embassies and consulates can furnish visas and information on work permits and other important regulations. They may also offer economic and business information about the country.

CONSULAR OFFICE IN U.S.

Embassy of Portugal
2125 Kalorama Rd. N.W.
Washington, DC 20009
Tel.: (202) 328-8610

OTHER INFORMATIONAL ORGANIZATIONS

Department of Tourism
Travessa do Paiva, No. 1
Macau
Tel.: 853 77218

Macau Association of Building and Property Development Companies
Rua do Campo, 11-15th Floors
Macau
Tel.: 853 573226

Macau Commercial Association
Largo do Senado, 20
Macau
Tel.: 853 572042

Macau Exporters Association
Tai Fung Bldg., Rms. 1001-1002
Avenida Almeida Ribeiro, 2-10th Floors
Macau
Tel.: 853 75859/553187

Macau Industrial Association
Travessa da Praia Grande, 1st Floor
Macau
Tel.: 853 71021/574125

Macau Tourist Information Bureau, Chicago
P.O. Box 3501
Kenilworth, IL 60043
Tel.: (708) 251-6421

Macau Tourist Information Bureau, Hong Kong
Shun Tak Centre, Rm. 305
200 Connaught Rd.
Central, Hong Kong
Tel.: 852 5 408180

Macau Tourist Information Bureau, Honolulu
999 Wilder Ave., Suite 1103
Honolulu, HI 96822
Tel.: (808) 538-7613

Macau Tourist Information Bureau, Los Angeles
3133 Lake Hollywood Dr.
Los Angeles, CA 90078
Tel.: (213) 851-3402

Macau Tourist Information Bureau, New York
608 5th Ave., Suite 309
New York, NY 10020
Tel.: (212) 581-7465

Portuguese National Tourist and Information Office
570 5th Ave.
New York, NY 10036
Tel.: (212) 354-4403

Travel Agencies Association
c/o Pedro Hyndman Lobo
Hotel Lisboa, Macau

MAJOR INTERNATIONAL COMPANIES IN MACAU

The following companies operate in Macau, although the local economy is tourism-oriented. To find employment in Macau, focus upon the hotels and other tourist industry employers. Contacting business associations listed in the "Organizations for Further Information" section above may also turn up employers hiring to meet new construction demands.

Deutsche Bank
97-97a Rua da Praia Grande
Macau
(Banking)
Ingolf Grabs, Manager
Deutsche Bank, Germany

Standard Chartered Bank
99 Rua da Praia Grande
Box 3014
Macau
(Banking)
Standard Chartered, England

MAJOR HOTEL EMPLOYERS IN MACAU

Beverly Plaza
Avenida do Dr. Rodrigo Rodrigues
Macau
Tel.: 853 88345
Fax.: 853 308878

Central
26-28, Avenida Almeida Ribeiro
Macau
Tel.: 853 77700
Fax.: 853 332275

Estoril
Avenida Sidonio Pais
Macau
Tel.: 853 572081 3
Fax.: 853 571215

Guia
Estrada do Engenheiro Trigo, No. 1-5
Macau
Tel.: 853 513888
Fax.: 853 559822

Hyatt Regency
2 Estrada Almirante Marques Esparteiro
Taipa Island, Macau
Tel.: 853 27000

Lisboa
Avenida de Amizade
Macau
Tel.: 853 577666
Fax.: 853 567193

Mandarin Oriental
Avenida da Amizade
Macau
Tel.: 853 567888

Matsuya
5 Estrada de Sao Francisco
Macau
Tel.: 853 575466, 575467

Metropole
63 Rua da Praia Grande
Macau
Tel.: 853 388166
Fax.: 853 330890

Mondial
Rua de Antonio Basto
Macau
Tel.: 853 566866
Fax.: 853 514083

Oriental Hotel
Avenida da Amizade
Macau
Tel.: 853 567888

Pousada De Coloane
Praia de Cheoc Van
Macau
Tel.: 853 328251
Fax.: 853 328251

Pousada De Sao Tiago
Avenida da Republica
Macau
Tel.: 853 78111
Fax.: 853 552170

President
Avenida de Amizade
Macau
Tel.: 853 553888
Fax.: 853 552735

Royal
Estrada da Vitoria
Macau
Tel.: 853 552222
Fax.: 853 563008

Sintra
Avenida D. Joao IV
Macau
Tel.: 853 385111
Fax.: 853 552735

The Koreas: South and North

SOUTH KOREA

South Korea is known as the Republic of Korea. The country measures 38,000 square miles along the southern portion of the Korean Peninsula in northeast Asia. South Korea is about the size of Indiana. North Korea borders along the north and Japan lies 150 miles to the east across the Sea of Japan, known in Korea as the East Sea. China and the Soviet Union are the next closest neighbors.

Most of the territory is mountainous. The western and southern coastal plains contain most of the cities. Nearly all of the people are Korean. Over 40% of the population is Buddhist. Christianity claims another 25%, with nearly 80% of those being Protestant. Confucianism is also popular among the older generation in South Korea.

Historical records of Korea date from the first century B.C.E., although Paleolithic sites at least 600,000 years old have been found. The Silla dynasty united the peninsula into a single kingdom in 688 by defeating two rival Korean principalities. In 918, the Silla dynasty was overthrown by another group, the Koryo, from which the country derives its name. Mongols invaded in 1213 and ruled until 1392, when the Yi dynasty came to power.

Korea fought off Japanese invaders from 1592 to 1598 and Manchurians in the 1620s. China eventually succeeded in establishing a protectorate over Korea. The country reacted by withdrawing from any international affairs, earning the title of the Hermit Kingdom. By 1876, Japan forced Korea to open its ports. The U.S. and several European powers then received trade agreements. In 1910, Japan formally annexed Korea under the name of Chosen and ruled there until 1945. Following Japan's defeat in World War II, the 38th parallel was chosen as the dividing line between American and Soviet zones of occupation.

The Republic of Korea was formed in 1948 in the U.S. zone. North Korea, known as the Democratic People's Republic of Korea, attempted to conquer the south in 1950, initiating the Korean War. The war escalated into a superpower confrontation as the U.S. and other U.N. nations militarily supported South Korea, while China militarily supported North Korea. The war ended in 1953 when a cease fire established the present boundary along the Demilitarized Zone between the two countries. U.S. troops are still stationed in South Korea.

Border raids continued until 1972, when the two republics agreed to pursue peaceful unification. In 1985, the republics began discussing economic issues and in 1990 the prime ministers of North and South Korea met for high-level unification talks. As of mid-1991, the talks have failed to reach any significant conclusion. Student protests in South Korea continuously pressure the government for unification.

In other foreign affairs, South Korea is actively improving relations with the Soviet Union, China, and Eastern Europe. Presidents Gorbachev and Roh met in San Francisco in 1990. South Korea and the Soviet Union now have full diplomatic relations. Formal trade offices are being opened in Beijing as well.

SOUTH KOREA'S 10 LARGEST CHAEBOL
(figures for sales rounded in billions of U.S. dollars)

1.	Samsung	$37
2.	Hyunda	$32
3.	Lucky Goldstar	$24
4.	Daewoo	$16
5.	Sunkyong	$12

6.	Ssangyong	$ 7.5
7.	Kia	$ 6.3
8.	Lotte	$ 5.1
9.	Hyosung	$ 4.8
10.	Hanjin	$ 4.1

Current Economic Climate in South Korea

South Korea has experienced one of the world's fastest growth rates, mainly fueled by exports, and now enjoys a gross national product of $230 billion. Exports grew from $33 million in 1960 to $33 billion in 1986. From 1960 to 1985, the economy grew by an average rate of 9%. Then from 1985 to 1988, the average growth rate was over 12%. The economy slowed to 7% in 1989, grew by 9% in 1990, and should grow by 8% in 1991.

Much of the problem with the Korean economy's slowdown today lies with the chaebol, huge conglomerates that virtually control the entire economy. The top 40 chaebol had sales of nearly $190 billion in 1990. The government pursued policies in the 1970s designed to allow the chaebol to grow and thereby concentrate the country's limited capital resources. The result has been tremendous economic development.

Today, however, the chaebol are rich enough to invest in areas other than those targeted by the government. Many of these areas produce high profit margins but not necessarily economic growth. As privately owned enterprises, the chaebol are controlled by families. Thus less than 1% of the population controls over 65% of Korea's land and the vast majority of its private production. The companies owned by the chaebol are notoriously filled with nepotism and often experience very low morale. Workers are consequently more willing to strike and intensify their demands in labor negotiations.

Likewise, the chaebol have generally failed to improve product quality and productivity. The Korean Chamber of Commerce concedes that hundreds of its members receive complaints regarding the quality of their products. In the past this has not been a significant problem because Korean products sold as a result of their internationally low prices. Korean inefficiency also posed less of a problem a few years ago. It takes an average of 200% more time for Korean industry to manufacture a consumer durable than for the Japanese. At one time Korean wages were a fraction of the Japanese but are now only half and climbing. Southeast Asian wages are even lower than Korean.

Inflation in 1990 officially reached 10% but was actually closer to 20% in real terms. Rapidly rising domestic demand is primarily responsible for increasing prices. Koreans are taking advantage of their new wealth by spending it on consumer and luxury goods. Wages have also been rising significantly, although wage increases were limited to 17% in 1990, down from 24% in 1989. Wages are expected to rise by 15% in 1991, slower than 1990 but still inflationary. The chaebol are contributing to inflation as well by focusing upon real estate and land investment. As a result, rents and land prices are spiraling, driving up the cost of living.

Exports have decreased in recent years. The result has been a trade deficit of $1.9 billion in 1990. In large part, increasing production costs have hurt the international competitiveness of Korean companies. Many foreign companies operating in Korea are relocating to Southeast Asia where labor costs are much lower. In addition, Korea has restricted foreign investors to producing for the export market in order to protect domestic manufacturers. Consequently, foreign firms are now willing to relocate to the U.S. or Europe, where they can produce for the local domestic markets.

South Korea and the U.S. are currently experiencing very tense trade relations. American officials believe that Korean companies and the government are deliberately attempting to reduce U.S. imports. The Korean government admits that it has launched a campaign to reduce consumer spending on products labeled "luxury items" but denies that it has specifically targeted American products. About 50% of U.S. goods imported into Korea are labeled "luxury items."

American imports into South Korea have grown by 20% in recent years but slowed to 5% in 1990. Korean exports to the U.S. have decreased to 30% of total exports in 1990 from 35% in 1988. Korean firms are therefore seeking to diversify their export markets. Samsung, for instance, has reduced its dependence on the U.S. to only 27% of its exports, down from 45% in 1988. Nonetheless, Korea still enjoys a $3.2 billion trade surplus with the U.S.

Eastern Europe and the Soviet Union are providing new markets for Korean products. Exports to Eastern Europe increased by 40%, to nearly $3 billion in 1990. Hyundai exported over 9,000 cars in 1990 to Yugoslavia and expects to send 10,000 more in 1991. Korean television manufacturers accounted for half of Yugoslavia's color television market in 1990. Plans are now underway to open trade and diplomatic offices in the Soviet Union. The South Koreans are also actively improving trade relations with China.

The country's leading industries are electronic equipment, steel, shipbuilding, textiles, and automobiles. The *won* is the national currency and fluctuates regularly. It currently trades at about 700 won to the U.S. dollar, but it has been steadily depreciating. Over 50% of the workforce is engaged in the service sector, 30% in manufacturing, and 20% in agriculture.

Korea's 43 million people are 70% urban. Over 40% of South Koreans live in the four largest cities. Almost a quarter of the population lives in Seoul, the capital and largest city with 10 million inhabitants. Other large cities are Pusan with 4.2

million people, Taegu with 2.3 million, Inchon with 1.6 million, Kwangju with 1.2 million, and Taejon with 1 million.

Regular business hours are from 9:00 am to 6:00 pm, Monday through Friday, and from 9:00 am to 1:00 pm on Saturday. Banks open at the same time but close at 4:00 pm on weekdays. Stores usually stay open until 7:00 pm and all day Saturday. Manual and industrial workers are expected to work about 48 hours per week, but this has been decreasing.

SOUTH KOREA'S 10 MOST PROFITABLE COMPANIES
(figures are rounded in millions of U.S. dollars)

1.	Korea Electric Power	$900
2.	Daewoo Trading	$320
3.	Samsung Electronics	$250
4.	Pohang Iron & Steel	$220
5.	Yukong Chemicals	$110
6.	Lucky Chemicals	$100
7.	Hyundai Motor	$ 70
8.	Cheil Sugar	$ 62
9.	Korea Air	$ 47
10.	Kia Motor	$ 40

Getting Around in South Korea

Korean Air Lines (KAL) provides international service into Seoul and also links most of the major cities. Asiana Airlines is a new private carrier that provides both domestic and international service. The Korean National Railway is fairly comprehensive and covers most of the major cities. Express and luxury trains are available. Seoul and Pusan also have excellent, cheap subway systems, with signs marked in both Korean and English.

Bus lines run throughout the country and are often the most efficient means of getting around. Different luxury levels can also be found in the bus system. In the cities, buses are the cheapest and most convenient means of transportation, although local buses are extremely crowded. Almost all cities and most towns are connected by a good highway system. Rental cars are available, but road signs are, of course, in Korean. Taxis are a very effective way of getting around in the big cities.

Using the language

Korean is the country's single language. It is similar to Chinese in some vocabulary and to Japanese in some of the grammar, but it is a distinct language of the Altaic group. The script, called Han Gul, is one of the world's most efficient, with phonetic consistency and few characters. English is probably the most common second language. Many young people are fairly conversant in English. It is always appropriate to begin a conversation in Korean and then shift into English if possible.■

Employment Regulations for Americans

Americans do not need a visa to enter the country for 15 days or less. Tourist visas are valid for 90 days and transit visas are valid for 15 days. A work permit is necessary in order to obtain legal employment. You must show proof of employment before entering the country in order to acquire a work permit.

Unemployment is relatively low in South Korea. An average of about 3% of the workforce of 30 million is unemployed. Very high rates of education also make jobs in the service sector scarce for foreigners. Many Koreans have degrees from American universities.

Teaching English in South Korea is a definite possibility for Americans. Wages are somewhat lower than in Japan, but there is less competition for jobs. Seoul and Pusan have many English language schools. Private tutoring or translation for individuals is also available.

Making a good first impression

It is a good idea to carry business cards in Korea. The cards should contain one's name, full title or position, employer or organization, phone number, and address. You should have this information in Korean on one side and in English on the other. Presenting business cards is a common custom in East Asia and will help potential employers, customers, clients, or anyone else you may meet remember you.■

Organizations for Further Information

The following organizations, both in the U.S. and South Korea, may be helpful in the job search. American embassies and consulates have commercial and/or economic sections that can provide you with business information and explain aspects of the local economy. World Trade Centers usually include many foreign companies operating in the country. Foreign government missions in the U.S., such as National Tourist Offices and embassies and consulates, can furnish visas and information on work permits and other important regulations. They may also offer economic and business information about the country.

Country-by-Country Listings

CHAMBERS OF COMMERCE

American Chambers of Commerce in Korea
Chosun Hotel, Rm. 307
87 Sohong-dong
Seoul 100, South Korea
Tel.: 82 02 7536471

Andong Chamber of Commerce
Doug Hwi Cho, 139-5
Wunheung-dong
Kyungbuk, Andong
South Korea
Tel.: 82 2 57122643

Cheongju Chamber of Commerce
Jae Chul Park, 116-84, 2-ka,
Bugmun-ro
Gangwon, Cheongju
South Korea
Tel.: 82 042 31320021/6

Inchon Chamber of Commerce
163 Changjeon-ri, Inchon-eup,
Incheon-kun
Kyunggi, Inchon
South Korea
Tel.: 82 032 625725

Korean Chamber of Commerce
981 S. Western Ave., Rm. 201,
Los Angeles, CA 90006
Tel.: (213) 733-4410

Korea Chamber of Commerce & Industry
45, 4-ka, Namdaemun-ro, CPO
Box 25
Chung-ku, Seoul
South Korea
Tel.: 82 02 7570757
Fax.: 82 02 7579475

Pusan Chamber of Commerce & Industry
36, 6-ka, Chungang-Dong
Chung-ku, Pusan
South Korea
Tel.: 82 051 4637801/9

Seoul Chamber of Commerce
45, 4-ka, Namdaemun-ro
Chung-ku, Seoul
South Korea
Tel.: 82 02 7570757

Suncheon Chamber of Commerce
Yung Gi O, 58-2
Jangcheon-dong, Suncheon
South Korea
Tel.: 82 0661 7415511

U.S.-Korea Society
725 Park Ave.
New York, NY 10021
Tel.: (212) 517-7730

CONSULAR OFFICES

American Embassy, Commercial Section
82 Sejong-Ro
Chongro-ku, Seoul
South Korea
Tel.: 82 02 7322601
Peter Frederick, Commercial Officer

Embassy of Korea
2320 Massachusetts Ave. N.W.
Washington, DC 20008
Tel.: (202) 939-5600

WORLD TRADE CENTER IN SOUTH KOREA

World Trade Center Korea
Korean Traders Association
10-1, 2-Ka Hoehyon-dong

CPO Box 1117
Chung-Ku, Seoul
South Korea
Tel.: 82 02 77141

OTHER INFORMATIONAL ORGANIZATIONS

Korean National Tourism Corporation, Chicago
230 N. Michigan Ave.
Chicago, IL 60601
Tel.: (312) 819-2560

Korean National Tourism Corporation, Hawaii
1188 Bishop St., Century Sq.
Honolulu, HI 96813
Tel.: (808) 521-8066

Korean National Tourism Corporation, Headquarters
Kukdong Bldg., 3rd Floor
60-1, 3-ka Chungmuro
Chung-ku, Seoul
South Korea
Tel.: 82 02 7576030

Korean National Tourism Corporation, Los Angeles
510 W. 6th St.
Los Angeles 90014
Tel.: (213) 382-3435

Korean National Tourism Corporation, New York
460 Park Ave., Suite 400
New York, NY 10022
Tel.: (201) 585-0909

Korean National Tourism Corporation, Seattle
c/o Ehrig and Association
Vine Bldg., 4th Floor
Seattle, WA 98121
Tel.: (206) 441-6666

SOUTH KOREA'S MAJOR TRADING PARTNERS

Export partners:	United States	40%
	Japan	18%
	European Community	8%
	Southeast Asia	6%
	Hong Kong	3%
Import partners:	Japan	26%
	United States	22%
	European Community	9%
	Southeast Asia	4%
	Hong Kong	3%

Business Directories

Although not always easy to find, business directories can prove invaluable in the international job search. Most directories list company names, addresses, products, and phone numbers. Some directories include executive names and titles and financial information about the company. These sources provide you with the names of the people to contact for employment information as well as financial data.

Korea Directory. Annual publication of the Korea Directory Co., Box 242, Kwanghwamoon, Seoul 1, South Korea. Lists basic information on 5,000 companies and associations involved in international trade.

Korean Business Directory. Published annually by the Korean Chamber of Commerce, 45 4-ka, Namdaemunro, Chung, Seoul, South Korea. Provides detailed financial information on several thousand companies in a variety of industries.

Korean Trade Directory. Annual publication of the Korean Traders Association, CPO Box 1117, Seoul, South Korea. Provides basic information on nearly 5,000 companies engaged in international trade.

Korean Trade Directory of New York. Biennial publication of the Korean Traders Representative Club of New York, 460 Park Ave., Suite 402, New York, NY 10022. Provides basic information on almost 300 Korean firms with offices in the New York area.

MAJOR AMERICAN COMPANIES IN SOUTH KOREA

Many American firms operate in South Korea. The following companies are classified by business area: Banking and Finance; Industrial Manufacturing; Retailing and Wholesaling; Service Industries. The company information includes type of business, American parent company, and contact name where possible. Your chances of achieving employment are substantially greater if you contact the subsidiary company in South Korea rather than the parent company in the U.S.

BANKING AND FINANCE

Bankers Trust New York Corp.
Center Bldg., 10th Floor
91-1 Sokong Dong
CPO Box 7480
Chung-Ku, Seoul, South Korea
Tel.: 82 27789010
(Banking)
Keun-Sam Lee, General Manager
Bankers Trust Corp.

Citibank
1-1 1-ga Jong-ro
CPO Box 749
Jongro-gu, Seoul, South Korea
Tel.: 82 02 7332625
(Banking)
Citicorp

First Citicorp Leasing
21-9 Cho-Dong
Seoul, Seoul, South Korea
(Banking)
Citicorp

INDUSTRIAL MANUFACTURING

Acheson Korea Ltd.
1305-6 Seocho-Dong
Kangnan-ku, Seoul, South Korea
(Chemicals)
Acheson Industries

Allied-Signal International
Kyobo Bldg., Suite 1603
1-Ka Chongro
Chongro-ku, Seoul, South Korea
Tel.: 82 02 7346052
Fax: 82 02 7346055
(Automotive products)
Allied-Signal

AMP Korea
451-9 Yanggi-Ri Gongolo-Myeon
Ansung-Gun, Gyunggi-Do
18022
South Korea
Tel.: 82 27448181
(Electronics)
C.B. Lee, Manager
AMP Inc.

Best Foods-Miwon
Miwon Bldg., 14th Floor
43 Yoido-Dong
Yeongdeungpo-ku, Seoul 150,
South Korea
Tel.: 82 02 7848131
Fax: 82 02 7853780
(Food products)
Cheon S. Park, President
CPC International

Control Data Korea
148 Ahnkook-Dong
Chong-ku, Seoul 110, South
Korea
(Computer components)
Control Data Far East

Cyanamid Korea
CPO Box 1452
Seoul, Seoul, South Korea
Tel.: 82 02 5523541
(Chemicals)
American Cyanamid Co.

Dong Suh Foods Corp.
316-11 Hyosung-Dong Buk-Ku
Inchon City, Inchon, South
Korea
(Roasted coffee)
Phillip Morris Cos.

Exxon Chemical Eastern
Chosun Hotel
87-1 Sokong-Dong
Choong-Ku, Seoul, South Korea
Tel.: 82 02 7764769
(Chemicals)
Exxon Corp.

Fullbright Industrial
1049-695 Myunmok-Dong
Dongdaeman-Ka
Seoul, Seoul, South Korea
(Knit tops)
Mankyu Park, President
Fullbright Industrial Co.

IBM Korea
25-11 Youido-dong
Yongdungpo-gu, Seoul, South
Korea
Tel.: 82 02 7816114
Fax: 82 02 7840889
(Computers)
John H. Bishop, President
IBM World Trade Americas/Far
East

Janssen Korea
11 Floor Seowoo Bldg.
837-12 Yuksam-Dong
Seoul, Seoul , South Korea
Tel.: 82 02 5672041
(Pharmaceuticals)
Jung Hoon Chang, President
Johnson & Johnson

Johnson & Johnson Korea
Kukje Center Bldg., 19th Floor
191 Hangangno 2-ga
P.O. Box 175
Yongsan-gu, Seoul, South Korea
Tel.: 82 02 7988081
(Pharmaceuticals)
A.J. Andrews, President
Johnson & Johnson

Korea Vickers Systems Company,
Hyunam Bldg., 4th Floor
1 Changkyo-Dong
Chung-ku, Seoul, South Korea
Tel.: 82 02 729346199
Fax: 82 02 7293500
(Hydraulic equipment)
Cheool Soo Park, President
Trinova Corp.

Pfizer Ltd.
136-46 Yonji-Dong Chongro-Ku
Seoul, Seoul, South Korea
(Pharmaceuticals)
Pfizer Corp.

Purina Korea
120 Namdaemon-Ro
S Ka Chung-Ku
Seoul, Seoul, South Korea
(Livestock feed)
Ralston Purina Co.

Rockwell-Collins International
Rm. 902 Shinwha Bldg.
14-33 Yeouido Don
Yeongdeungpo-Ku, Seoul, South Korea
Tel.: 82 02 7831431
(Navigation equipment, telecommunication systems)
Rockwell International Corp.

Rohm & Haas Asia
65-228 Hangang Ro 3-Ka
Seoul, Seoul, South Korea
(Chemicals)
Rohm & Haas Co.

Seoul Heinz
191 Hangang-Ro 2-Ga
Yongsan-Ku, Seoul, South Korea
Tel.: 82 02 79363315
(Food Products)
Dietmar Kluth, President

Squibb Korea
Rm. 1006 Samkoo Bldg.
70 Sokong-Dong
Chung-ku, Seoul 100, South Korea
(Pharmaceuticals)
Linson Investment

Yuhan-Cyanamid
832-2 4th Floor Wooduk Bldg.
Yoksam-Dong
Kangnam-Ku, Seoul, South Korea
(Pharmaceuticals, chemicals)
American Cyanamid

Yuhan-Kimberly
823 Yeok Sam-Dong
Kangnam-Ku, Seoul, South Korea
(Sanitary paper products)
J.D. Lee, President
Kimerly-Clark Corp.

RETAILING AND WHOLESALING

Fuqua World Trade Corporation
CPO Box 3110
Seoul, Seoul, South Korea
Tel.: 82 02 223345
(Sporting goods)
Fuqua Industries,

SERVICE INDUSTRIES

Air Express International
3rd Floor Lotte Hotel Iibunka Bldg.
1 Sokong-Dang
Chung-Ku, Seoul 100, South Korea
Tel.: 82 02 75655009
(Air freight forwarder)
Air Express International Corp.

MAJOR DOMESTIC COMPANIES IN SOUTH KOREA

The following is a listing of the major domestic companies of South Korea. They are classified by business area: Banking and Finance; Industrial Manufacturing; Retailing and Wholesaling; Service Industries. Company information includes type of business and contact name. These companies will generally hire their own nationals first but may employ Americans.

BANKING AND FINANCE

Bank of Pusan
830-38 Beomil-Dong Dong-Gu
Pusan City, Pusan, South Korea
(Banking)
Hwang Yong Woon, President

Bank of Seoul
10-1 Namdaemun-ro, 2-ka
Chung-ku, Seoul 100, South Korea
Tel.: 82 02 77160
Fax: 82 02 7566389
(Commercial banking)
Kwang Soo Lee, Chairman and President

Cho Hung Bank
14 1-ka Namdaemun-ro
CPO Box 2997
Chung-ku, Seoul 100, South Korea
Tel.: 82 02 7332000
Fax: 82 02 7320835
(Banking)
Young Suk Kim, Chairman

Commercial Bank of Korea
111-1 2 Ka Namdaemun-Ro
Chung-Ku, Seoul, South Korea
(Commercial banking)
Kin Sang Chan, President

Daegu Bank
118 2-Ga Susong-Dong Susong-Gu
Taegu City, Taegu, South Korea
(Banking)
Kwon Tae-Hak, President

Hanil Bank
130 Namdaemun-No
2-Ga Chung-Gu
Seoul, Seoul 100
South Korea
Tel.: 82 02 277120
(Bank holding company)
Kwai Byeong Yoon, Chairman

Hanjin Group
Kai Bldg., 118 Namdaemun-ro 2-kg
Choong-ku, Seoul 100, South Korea
(Federal reserve banks, insurance)
Cho Choong-Hoon, Chairman

Korea Development Bank
140-1 2-GA Namdaemoon-Ro
Joong-Gu, Seoul 100, South Korea
Tel.: 82 02 7768344
(Banking)
Yeung Ki Hah,Chairman

Korea Exhange Bank
181 2-KA Eulchi-Ro
Chung-Ku, Seoul, South Korea
(Banking)
In Young Chung, Chairman

Korea First Bank
53-1 1-Ka Choongmu-Ro
Choong-Ku, Seoul, South Korea
(Banking)
Lee Pil-Sun, President

INDUSTRIAL MANUFACTURING

Asia Motors Co.
Kia Bldg., 5th Floor
15-1 Youido Dong Yong Dungpo Gu
Seoul, Seoul, South Korea
(Auto bodies)
Park Shi Yoon, President

Daelim Industrial Company
146-12 Soonsong-dong
Chongro-ku, Seoul 110-140, South Korea
Tel.: 82 02 7308221
Fax: 82 02 733664
(Construction, petrochemicals, electrical works)
In Jik Chung, Vice President, Personnel

Dae Woo Motor Co.
199 Cheong Cheon-Dong
Dong Buk-Ku
Inchon City, Inchon, South Korea
(Auto bodies)
Choi Myung Gul, President

Daewoo Corp.
541 5-Ga Namdaemoon-Ro
Jung-ku
Seoul, Seoul, South Korea
Tel.: 82 02 277191
(Construction machinery, engines)
Woo Choong Kim, President

Daewoo Corp.
470-1 Garibong-Dong
Guro-ku, Seoul 150, South Korea
(Auto parts)
Shin Kang Ho Eung-Soon Lee, Chairman

Daewoo Electronic Components Co.
543 Tangchung-Ri Kunpo-Eup
Sihung Gun, Kyonggi Do, South Korea
(Electric capacitators)
Yong Won Kim, President

Daewoo Heavy Industries
6 Manseog-dong
Dong-gu, Inchon 401-010, South Korea
Tel.: 82 032 7621011
Fax: 82 032 7627901
(Engines, construction equipment, defense products)
Woo-Choong Kim, Chairman

Goldstar Co.
P.O. Box 335
Seoul, Seoul, South Korea
Tel.: 82 02 7873502
Fax: 82 02 7073400
(Electronics, appliances)
Keun-sun Choi, President

Honam Oil Refinery Co.
Lucky Goldstar Twin West Bldg.
20 Yoido Dong
Youngdungpo-Gu, Seoul 100, South Korea
(Petrochemicals)
Koo Pyung Hoi, President

Hyosung Heavy Industries
27-2 Youido Dong Yeong
Deuyngpo-Gu, Seoul, South Korea
(Power distribution equipment)
Sang Mo Soihn, President

Hyundai Corp.
140-2 Kye-dong
Chongro-ku, Seoul, South Korea
Tel.: 82 02 7414141
Fax: 82 02 7412341
(Oil, gas, contracting)
Choon Lim Lee, Chairman

Hyundai Heavy Industries Co.
1 Junha-Dong
Ulsan, Kyongsang, South Korea
(Steel works)
Ju Young Chung, President

Hyundai Motor Co.
140-2 Kye-dong
Chongro-ku, Seoul, South Korea
Tel.: 82 02 7630211
(Motor vehicles)
Se Yung Chung, President

Inchon Iron and Steel Co.
1 Songhyun-dong
Dong-ku, Inchon, South Korea
Tel.: 82 032 7635000
Fax: 82 032 7635046
(Iron and steel products)
Mong-koo Chung, Chairman

Kia Motors Corp.
15 Yoido-dong
Youngdeungpo-ku, Seoul, South Korea
Tel.: 82 02 7841501
Fax: 82 02 7840746
(Motor vehicles)
Min Kyung Jung, Chairman

Kolon Industries
Kolon Bldg.
45 Mukyo Dong
Chung-Gu, Seoul, South Korea
(Textiles, synthetic fabrics)
Dong-Chan Lee, President

Korean Electronics Co.
Chamber Bldg., 9th Floor
45 4-Ga Namdaemun-Ro
Jung-Ku, Seoul 100, South Korea
(Semiconductors)
Yoo Won Young, President

Lucky Ltd.
20 Yoido-dong
Youngdeungpo-ku, Seoul 150, South Korea
Tel.: 82 02 7871114
Fax: 82 02 7877038
(Petrochemicals, chemicals, cosmetics)
Kwan-Yong Choi, Senior Managing Director, Personnel

Lucky-Goldstar Group
Lucky-Goldstar Bldg.
537 5-ka Naedaemoon-ru
Chung-ku, Seoul 100, South Korea
Tel.: 82 02 77132
(Petrochemicals, construction, electronics, foods, insurance)
Koo Cha-kyung, Chief Executive Officer

Pohang Iron & Steel Co.
Kum Se Ki Building
16 Ulchiro 1-Ga
Chung-ku, Seoul, South Korea
(Steel products)
Tae-Joon Park, Chairman

Samsung Co.
CPO Box 1144
Seoul, Seoul, South Korea
Tel.: 82 02 277133
(Metals, minerals, chemicals)
P.G. Rhee, President

Samsung Electronics Co.
Joong-Ang Daily News Building
7 Soonwha-dong
Seoul, Seoul, South Korea
Tel.: 82 02 7516114
Fax: 82 02 7516363
(Electronics, computers, televisions, home appliances)
Joon-Sung Kim, Chairman

Ssangyong Cement Industrial Corporation
Ssangyong Building
24-1 Jeo-dong, 2-ka
Chung-ku, Seoul 100, South Korea
Tel.: 82 02 2665151
Fax: 82 02 2757040
(Building materials, cement)
Chae Kyum Kim, President

Ssangyong Motor Co.
Ssanyong Bldg. 24-1
2-Ga Cho-Dong
Chung-Gu, Seoul, South Korea
(Auto bodies)
Son Myung-Won, President

Yukong
Yukong Building
26-4 Yoido-dong
Youngdeungpo-gu, Seoul, South Korea
Tel.: 82 02 7885114
Fax: 82 02 7887001
(Petrochemicals)
Jong-Hyon Chey, Chairman

RETAILING AND WHOLESALING

Dae Woo Electronics Co.
541 5-Ga Namdaemun-Ro 5-Ga
Chung-Gu, Seoul 150, South Korea
(Audio/video equipment)
Kim Woo Choong, President

Gold Star Co. Ltd.
537 5-Ga Namdaemun No
Chung-Gu, Seoul, South Korea
(Audio/video equipment)
Hun Shin Koo, President

Lucky-Goldstar International Corp.
20 Yoiko-dong
Youngdeungpo-ku, Seoul 150, South Korea
Tel.: 82 02 7871114
Fax: 82 02 7857762
(Clothing, foods, electronics, machinery)
Cha-Hak Koo, Vice Chairman

SERVICE INDUSTRIES

Daewoo Corp.
P.O. Box 2810
Seoul, Seoul 8269, South Korea
Tel.: 82 02 7592114
Fax: 82 02 233414
(Development, construction)
Hyung-Suk Suh, President

Korea Heavy Industries & Construction Co.
555 Guigok-dong
P.O. Box 77
Changwon, Kyongsangnam-do 615, South Korea
Tel.: 82 55 861515
Fax: 82 55 862551
(Engineering, construction)
Nack-chung Sung, President

Korean Air Lines Co.
41-3 Seosomoon-dong
Chung-ku, Seoul, South Korea
Tel.: 82 02 7517114
(Air transportation)
Ha Ryong Chung, Vice President, Personnel

Ssangyong Corp.
CPO Box 409
Seoul, Seoul, South Korea
Tel.: 82 02 2708114
Fax: 82 02 2730981
(General trade)
Ki-Ho Kim, President

Sunkyong Ltd.
Sunkyong Bldg.
36-1 Eulji-Ro 2-Ga
Jung-Gu, Seoul, South Korea
Tel.: 82 02 7582114
Fax: 82 02 7549414
(Trading)
Young Bum Yoon, Director, Personnel Management Office

MAJOR INTERNATIONAL COMPANIES IN SOUTH KOREA

There are many international firms operating in South Korea. These companies will be classified by business area: Banking and Finance; Industrial Manufacturing; Retailing and Wholesaling; and Service Industries. The company information includes type of business, international parent company, and contact name where possible. Your chances of achieving employment are substantially greater if you contact the subsidiary company in South Korea rather than the parent company in the home country.

BANKING AND FINANCE

Algemene Bank Nederland-Seoul
ABN, Rheema Bldg.
Rms. 1405/1406
146-1 Ku, Susong-Dong
Chongro-ku, Seoul, South Korea
Tel.: 82 02 7332301
Fax: 82 02 7379803
(Banking)
W.A.E.J. Lemstra, General Manager
Algemene Bank Nederland, Netherlands

Australia & New Zealand Banking Group
Kyobo Bldg., 18th Floor
KPO 1065
Chongro-ku, Seoul, South Korea
Tel.: 82 02 7303151
Fax: 82 02 7376325
(Banking)
Australia & New Zealand Bank Group, Australia

Credit Lyonnais
Daewoo Center, Rm. 171
541-KA, P.O. Box 5506
Chung-ku, Seoul, South Korea
Tel.: 82 02 7545161
Fax: 82 02 7555379
(Banking)
Credit Lyonnais, France

Deutsche Bank
Korea Development Bank Bldg.
44 2-ka Chungang-Dong
P.O. Box 789
Chung-Ku, Pusan 600, South Korea
(Banking)
Deutsche Bank, Germany

Standard Chartered Bank
Nae Wei Bldg.,13th Floor
9-1 2-Ka Ulchi-ro
Kwangwhamun 259
Seoul, Seoul, South Korea
Tel.: 82 02 7575131
Fax: 82 02 7577444
(Banking)
Standard Chartered, England

INDUSTRIAL MANUFACTURING

BASF Korea
Korea Chamber of Commerce & Industry Bldg., 11th Floor
45 4-Ka Namdaemun-Ro
CPO Box 1151
Chung-ku, Seoul, South Korea
Tel.: 82 02 7784661
Fax: 82 02 7569650
(Chemicals, electronics)
BASF Group, Germany

Fujitsu Korea
Korean Reinsurance Bldg., 9th Floor
80 Susong-Dong
Chongro-Gu, Seoul, South Korea
Tel.: 82 02 7393281
(Electronics, communications systems)
Fujitsu

Gold Star Telecommunications Co.
Kukdong Bldg., 8th Floor
60-1 3-Ga Chungmu-Ru
Seoul, Seoul, South Korea
(Telecommunications equipment)
Siemens, Germany

Korea Sanyo Electric Co.
Chang Won Industrial Complex
Mok Dong Area, 2nd Block
Changwon, Kyungsangnam-Do, South Korea
Tel.: 82 551 842742
(Electronics, appliances)
Sanyo Electric Co., Japan

SERVICE INDUSTRIES

Mitsui & Co.
Kwangyang Bldg., 2nd Floor
Control Office
615 Gumho-ri
Taegeummyon, Kwangsan-kun
Kwangsan, Chollanam-do, South Korea
Tel.: 82 667 44371
(Trading, chemicals, machinery)
Mitsui & Co., Tokyo

MAJOR HOTEL EMPLOYERS IN SOUTH KOREA

Astoria Hotel
13-2 Namhak-dong
Chongno-gu, Seoul, South Korea
Tel.: 82 02 2677111

Boolim Tourist Hotel
620-27 Chonnong 2-dong
Tongdaemun-gu, Seoul, South Korea
Tel.: 82 02 9620061

Clover Tourist Hotel
129-7 Chongdam-dong
Kangnam-gu, Seoul, South Korea
Tel.: 82 02 5461411

Hilton International
395 Namdaemum Ro 5-ka
Chung-Ku, Seoul, South Korea
Tel.: 82 02 7537788

Hotel Intercontinental Seoul
159-1 Samsung-Dong
Kangnam-Ku, Seoul 135-090, South Korea
Tel.: 82 02 5538181

Hotel Lotte World
40-1, Chamsil-Dong
Songpa-Ku, Seoul, South Korea
Tel.: 82 02 4197000

Hotel Shilla
202 2GA Jangchung Dong
Chung Ku, Seoul, South Korea
Tel.: 82 02 2333131

Hyatt Regency
747-7 Hannam-Dong
Yongsan-Ku, Seoul, South Korea
Tel.: 82 02 7980061

Hyatt Regency Cheju
3039-1, Saekdal-Dong
Seogwipo-Si
Cheju-Do, Cheju 697-130, South Korea
Tel.: 82 64 331234

Hyatt Regency Pusan
1405-16 Jung Dong
Haeundae Beach, Pusan 612-010, South Korea
Tel.: 82 051 7431234

Hyatt Regency Seoul
747-7 Hannam-dong
Yongsan-gu, Seoul, South Korea
Tel.: 82 02 7971234

Plaza Hotel
23 2-Ka, Taipyung-Ro
Seoul, Seoul, South Korea
Tel.: 82 02 77122

Ramada Olympia
108-2 Pyung Chang Dong
Seoul 110-00, Seoul, South Korea
Tel.: 82 02 3535121

Ramada Renaissance Hotel Seoul
76 Yuksam-Dong,
Kangnam-Ku, Seoul 135-080, South Korea
Tel.: 82 02 5550501

Seoul Hilton International
395 5-KA Namdaemun-Ro
Chungku, Seoul, South Korea
Tel.: 82 02 7537788

Sheraton Walker Hill
CPO Box 714
Seoul 133-210, Seoul, South Korea
Tel.: 82 02 4530121

Westin Chosun Beach
Woo 1-dong
Haeundae-Ku, Pusan 60704, South Korea
Tel.: 82 51 7427411

INTERNATIONAL SCHOOLS IN SOUTH KOREA

International Schools Services
P.O. Box 5910
Princeton, NJ 08543
American teachers seeking employment abroad may contact this recruitment service.

Korean Christian Academy
210-3 O Jung Dong
Taejon 300, South Korea
Tel.: 82 42 6223663/6233140
(U.S. school, K-12)

Seoul Academy
Kang Nam
Daichi Dong, Seoul, South Korea
Tel.: 82 02 5541690
(U.S. school, pre-K-8)

Seoul Foreign School
55 Yunhi Dong
Seoul, South Korea
Tel.: 82 02 3234784
(U.S., International Baccalaureate school, pre-K-9)

Seoul International School
Bokjung-dong
Song Nam City, Seoul, South Korea
Tel.: 82 342 2334551/2334552
(U.S. school, pre-K-9)

NORTH KOREA

North Korea is officialy called the Democratic People's Republic of Korea. The country measures about 47,000 square miles, about the size of Mississippi. North Korea occupies the northern portion of the Korean Peninsula in northeast Asia. China and the Soviet Union border along the north, and South Korea is its southern neighbor.

The entire country is mountainous or hilly, with a few small valleys and plains areas. Almost all of the people are Korean and speak only Korean. Buddhism and Confucianism are the largest traditional religious groupings, although very little religious activity occurs today.

North Korea was proclaimed the Democratic People's Republic of Korea in 1948. Prior to that, it was in the Soviet zone of occupation following World War II. In 1950 North Korea attempted to conquer the south, initiating the Korean War. Chinese troops fought with North Korea, and the U.S. fought with South Korea. The war ended in 1953, with only minor border adjustments.

Kim Il Sung, referred to as the Great Leader, has led North Korea throughout its existence. His Stalinist policies have led to significant industrial growth. The Korean Workers Party is the ruling communist party, although the military is considered to be the source of real power. Kim Il Sung's son, the Dear Leader Kim Jong Il, is expected to assume power in 1992. His authority, however, is likely to be challenged by rivals in the military after his father dies.

One-seventh of the population belongs to the ruling party and has been well-schooled in juche doctrine, Kim Il Sung's ideology of national self-reliance. The Korean Workers Party has over 3 million members, including most of the 1 million people in the armed forces. Defense spending consumes one-quarter of North Korea's gross national product.

North Korea is presently striving to improve relations with South Korea and Japan. Its former patrons, the Soviet Union and China, are now undergoing their own economic transformations and are weakening their links to North Korea. While aid from South Korea and Japan should help prop up the regime, infusions of capitalist investment have a record of promoting change as well. Some observers believe that the younger members of the military are more reformist and pragmatic than the present rulers.

Current Economic Climate

North Korea has a gross national product of about $20 billion, which is only growing at the rate of 2% annually and is about 10% of South Korea's GNP. The leading industries include textiles, chemicals, and food processing. The country has extensive, but mostly undeveloped, mineral and hydroelectric resources. North Korea's leading trade partners are the Soviet Union, China, and Japan.

In 1991, the Soviet Union and China announced that North Korea will have to pay for imports in hard currency rather than on credit or barter. Bilateral trade with the Soviet Union had already dropped from $3 billion in 1988 to $2.3 billion in 1990. The balance is in the Soviets' favor. Over 80% of North Korean products are raw materials or unfinished goods.

The Soviet Union and China are now pressuring North Korea to reform economically in order to decrease the amount of aid they send. The Soviets particularly want North Korea to improve its international image as a terrorist sponsor and enhance relations with South Korea. The Soviets predict that these steps would facilitate investment from South Korea and the republics of the Soviet Union.

North Korea is attempting to secure South Korean, Japanese, and Western loans, investment, and aid to offset the decrease in Soviet and Chinese support. The two state-owned banks, the Foreign Trade Bank and Korea Daesong Bank, are responsible for arranging new aid. North Korea owes over $800 million to Western banks on loans it has defaulted on and must begin repayment before new aid can be approved. The country's total foreign debt is $5 billion.

Japan has expressed a significant interest in aid for and investment in North Korea, which demands reparation payments from Japan at least equivalent to the $500 million that South Korea received in 1965, worth about $5 billion today. Japan sent a delegation to Pyongyang in 1990 to negotiate the establishment of diplomatic relations. The Japanese delegation was shocked when Kim Il Sung dismissed the idea of establishing quasi-diplomatic offices in favor of fully normalizing diplomatic relations.

South Korea expressed outrage at the Japanese-North Korean dialog, forcing Japan to take a more cautious approach. Japanese motives are very suspect in Seoul, where it is widely believed that the Japanese aim to undermine South Korea's efforts to isolate North Korea. Southern leaders argue that they will eventually force North Korea into a weak position as the Soviets and Chinese pursue South Korean capital, but that Japanese aid would undermine their strategy.

Taiwan is also being courted for foreign investment. Despite its long relationship with China, North Korea began issuing visas to Taiwanese business people in 1991. The move is seen as a response to China's establishment of diplomatic relations with South Korea. North Korea opened a tourist office capable of processing visa applications in Macau in 1991 as well. North Korea has a total population of 21 million people. The capital, Pyongyang, is home to 1.3 million North Koreans. About half of the population still lives in rural areas.

Employment in North Korea

At the present time, employment in North Korea for Americans is not really an option. As the country becomes involved in the international economy through foreign aid and investment, opportunities may appear. In the long term, your best strategy is to work in South Korea or Japan and then transfer to North Korea when relations improve and your company opens operations there. Japanese or South Korean firms may be allowed to invest in the country in the next five years.

Employment for Americans in North Korea is clearly a long way off. Meanwhile, if you happen to be in East Asia, you may be able to visit the country by obtaining a visa at the North Korean tourist office planned for Macau. You may also be able to get a visa from a consulate or embassy in China, Eastern Europe, or other socialist or formerly communist countries that maintain relations with North Korea.

You may also want to try to contact the Chamber of Commerce in Pyongyang. Although its precise street address and telephone number are difficult to acquire, they may potentially provide some information to those skillful enough to locate it or one of its representatives. Good luck.

Indochina: Thailand, Vietnam, Cambodia, Laos

THAILAND

The Kingdom of Thailand measures almost 200,000 square miles, about the size of Texas. The country is located in Southeast Asia, bordering Malaysia to the south, Burma to the west, Laos to the north, and Cambodia to the east. Thai topography is extremely varied, ranging from mountains and plateaus in the north to forested areas in the south.

Over 75% of the population consists of Thais. Chinese are the next largest ethnic group, comprising almost 15%. Historically, Chinese business people have dominated the Thai economy, occasionally resulting in ethnic tensions. Thai is the national langauge, but various regional dialects are also spoken by many people. Most Thais, approximately 95%, are Buddhist. Muslims are the largest religious minority.

The Thais began migrating from southern China in the eleventh century and settled in the area now known as Thailand but previously referred to as Siam. The Thai monarchy was able to avoid colonization by signing trade agreements with the major European powers. The regime also pursued a policy of modernization in the late nineteenth century. In 1932, the monarchy accepted constitutional limitations.

During World War II, Japan occupied Thailand but maintained only minimal control over the country. Thailand has followed a pro-Western foreign policy designed to promote economic development. The government has essentially allowed business and foreign investment to grow unhindered. Consequently, while the economy has grown tremendously, most of the benefits have flown into Bangkok and not reached the majority of the population.

The military ousted a civilian government in 1976 but gradually returned power to democratically elected leaders in the 1980s. In 1991, the military charged the elected government of prime minister Chatichai Choonhavan with massive corruption and inefficency and staged a coup. A new assembly appointed by the military consists of an armed forces majority and other supporters. The military promises that civilians will return to power by 1992. This was the seventeenth coup attempt since 1932.

THAILAND'S LARGEST TRADING PARTNERS

Imports:	Japan	25%
	United States	14%
	Singapore	7%
Exports:	United States	17%
	Japan	15%
	Singapore	14%

Current Economic Climate

Thailand's gross national product of $82 billion and per capita income of $2,000 have been growing rapidly in recent years. Thailand's economy has been the world's fastest growing since 1987, expanding by an average of 11% annually. The economy grew by 12% in 1989 and by 10% in 1990 and is expected to grow by 9% in 1991. The inflation rate was 5.5% in 1989 and 6% in 1990. Inflation for 1991 is expected to remain at 6%.

The largest industries include textiles, lumber products, manufacturing, and mining. Thailand is a leading producer of tin and teak. Construction is the fastest growing sector of the economy, expanding by 21% in 1989 and 23% in 1990. The industrial manufacturing sector grew by 15% in 1989 and 14%

in 1990. Manufacturing is expected to overtake agriculture in production of GNP in 1991.

Thailand has been able to fuel the world's fastest growing economy by promoting exports. Exports grew by 28% in 1989 and by 16% in 1990, and they are expected to grow by 16% again in 1991. Imports have also been increasing due to capital upgrading and consumer demand for luxury items. Imports grew by 30% in 1989 and 25% in 1990, and they are expected to grow by 15% in 1991. Thai economic expansion has been largely fueled by foreign investment. Japanese companies, for example, have invested over $5 billion in Thailand since 1988.

Foreign investors have pumped an average of $1.3 billion into the economy since 1988, but they are now cautious about the economy due to the recent coup. The military junta appointed a cabinet of business people and technocrats, but the real power still rests with the armed forces. In addition, Thailand's communication and transportation infrastructure is inadequate to meet present growth levels. Traffic congestion in Bangkok, for example, is estimated to reduce GNP by 10%.

Nonetheless, large infrastructure projects are still underway. British Telecom, in a joint venture with the Charoen Pokhpand group, has been awarded a $6 billion contract to triple the country's telephone capacity. Hopewell Holdings of Hong Kong received a $3 billion contract to build a new rail and road system to alleviate Bangkok's congestion problems. Lavalin Group of Canada is also building a $2 billion rail transport system.

Thailand's population of nearly 55 million is less than one-third urban. Bangkok is the nation's major urban center, with a rapidly growing population of over 8 million people. The Bangkok metropolitan area produces almost half of Thailand's GNP. About 60% of the workforce is still engaged in agriculture.

Getting Around in Thailand

Thai Airways International provides international service into Bangkok and services other important cities. The State Railways of Thailand provides efficient and comprehensive service to most of the country. The intercity bus system is cheap but very crowded. Passenger boat service is also available along the Chao Phya River between Bangkok and other points.

Getting around Bangkok is a problem. The buses are extremely overcrowded and no rail system serves the city effectively as mass transit. Bangkok also lacks adequate roads, leading to some of the world's worst traffic jams and multi-hour commutes. New infrastructure projects are planned, but getting around the city now is inconvenient and often frustrating.

Employment Regulations for Americans

Americans do not need a visa for stays of 15 days or less. Transit visas are valid for 30 days, tourist visas for 60 days, and business visas for 90 days. A work permit must be obtained in order to work legally in Thailand. You must provide proof of employment to acquire a work permit.

English-language teaching jobs can be found in Thailand, but wages are lower than in other parts of Southeast Asia. Immigration authorities tend to be more lenient about enforcing work permit regulations in Thailand than elsewhere.

Making a good first impression

It is a good idea to carry business cards in Thailand. The cards should contain one's name, full title or position, employer or organization, phone number, and address. You should have this information in Thai on one side and in English on the other. Presenting business cards is a common custom in East Asia and will help potential employers, customers, clients, or anyone else you may meet remember you. Also avoid touching people on the head, which is considered offensive by many Thais.■

Organizations for Further Information

The following organizations, both in the U.S. and Thailand, may be helpful in the job search. American embassies and consulates have commercial and/or economic sections that can provide you with business information and explain aspects of the local economy. World Trade Centers usually include many foreign companies operating in the country. Foreign government missions in the U.S. such as National Tourist Offices and embassies and consulates can furnish visas and information on work permits and other important regulations. They may also offer economic and business information about the country.

CHAMBERS OF COMMERCE

American Chamber of Commerce
Nana P.O. Box 1095, 10112
Bangkok, Thailand
Tel.: 66 2 2519266
Fax.: 66 2 2537388

Board of Trade of Thailand
150 Rajbopit Rd., 10200

Bangkok, Thailand
Tel.: 66 2 2210555

Thai Chamber of Commerce
150 Rajbopit Rd., 10200
Bangkok, Thailand
Tel.: 66 2 2213351

CONSULAR OFFICES

American Embassy, Commercial Section
95 Wireless Rd.
Bangkok, Thailand
Tel.: 66 2 2525040
Herbert A Cochran, Commercial Officer

Embassy of Thailand
2300 Kalorama Rd. N.W.
Washington, DC 20008
Tel.: (202) 483-7200

WORLD TRADE CENTER IN THAILAND

World Trade Center Bangkok Co.
8th Floor Sinthon Bldg.
132 Wireless Rd., Patumwam
Bangkok 10500, Thailand
Tel.: 66 2501801 7

OTHER INFORMATIONAL ORGANIZATIONS

Tourism Authority of Thailand, Headquarters
Ratchadamnoen Nok Ave.
Bangkok 10100, Thailand
Tel.: 66 28211437

Tourism Authority of Thailand, Los Angeles
3440 Wilshire Blvd. No. 1101
Los Angeles, CA 90010
Tel.: (213) 382-2353

Tourism Authority of Thailand, New York
5 World Trade Center, No. 2449
New York, NY 10048
Tel.: (212) 432-0433

Business Directories

Although not always easy to find, business directories can prove invaluable in the international job search. Most directories list company names, addresses, products and phone numbers. Some directories include executive names and titles and financial information about the company. These sources provide you with the names of the people to contact for employment information as well as financial data.

American Chamber of Commerce in Thailand Directory. Biennial publication of the American Chamber of Commerce, 140 Wireless Rd., Bangkok, Thailand. Lists several hundred American companies operating in Thailand.

Million Bhat Business Information. Annual publication of Pan Siam Communication, 138-1 Pensak Bldg., Petchburi Rd., Phyathai, Bangkok 4, Thailand. Lists over 2,000 companies with 1 million or more bhat in capital.

Thailand Business Buyer's Guide. Published annually by Business Publications, 9-42 Soi Kingpetch, Petchburi Rd., Bangkok 10400, Thailand. Provides basic information on over 5,000 companies.

MAJOR AMERICAN COMPANIES IN THAILAND

Many American firms operate in Thailand. They are classified here by business area: Banking and Finance; Industrial Manufacturing; Retailing and Wholesaling; and Service Industries. Company information includes type of business, American parent company, and contact name where possible. Your chances of achieving employment are substantially greater if you contact the subsidiary company in Thailand rather than the parent company in the U.S.

BANKING AND FINANCE

American International Assurance Co.
American International Bldg.,
181 Surawong Rd.
Bangkok 10500, Thailand
Tel.: 66 2 2349130
(Insurance)
S. Dhararag, Regional Vice President
American International Assurance Co.

BA Finance and Securities
c/o Bank of America
2/2 Wireless Rd.
Bangkok 10500, Thailand
Tel.: 66 2 2517181
Fax.: 66 2 2531905
(Securities)
Jimmy Chien-Kwang Han, Managing Director
BankAmerica Corp.

Bankers Trust New York Corp.
Boon-Mit Bldg., 12th Floor
138 Silom Rd.
Bangkok, Thailand
Tel.: 66 2 2355591
(Banking)
Suthai Unenanond, Vice President
Bankers Trust New York Corp.

Chase Manhattan Bank
Siam Center, 965 Rama 1 Rd.
Bangkok 10500, Thailand
(Banking)
Chase Manhattan Corp.

INDUSTRIAL MANUFACTURING

Bristol-Myers
294/8 Soi Somprasong 3
Petchburi Rd.
Bangkok, Thailand
(Pharmaceuticals)
Bristol-Myers Squibb Co.

Crown Cork & Seal Co.
Kasemkji Bldg., 6th Floor, Rm. 602
120 Silom Rd.
Bangkok 10500, Thailand
(Packaging equipment)
Terrance D. Moore, Director
Crown Cork & Seal Co.

Data General Thailand
c/o Cybernetics Co.
62/17-18 Thami Silom
Bangkok, Thailand
(Computers and equipment)
Data General Corp.

Dole Thailand
1037 Ploenchit Rd.
Bangkok, Thailand
(Produce)
Castle & Cooke

W.R. Grace
2 Bangpoo Industrial Estate
252 Sukhumvit Rd., Km. 34
Samutpraken 10280, Thailand
Tel.: 66 2 3239660
Fax.: 66 2 3239807
(Chemicals, construction, automobiles products)
Surachate Na-Thaland, General Manager
W.R. Grace & Co.

Kodak
197 Vipavadi Rangsit Rd.
Bangkok 10400, Thailand
Tel.: 66 2 2799570
(Photographic equipment)
Eastman Kodak Co.

Mobil Oil Thailand
37 Soi SomPrasong 3
P.O. Box 1698
Bangkok, Thailand
Tel.: 66 2 2520435
(Petrochemicals)
B.H.S. Fraser, Managing Director
Mobil Corp.

Monsanto Thailand
Silom Center Bldg., 17th Floor
P.O. Box 2316
Bangkok 10500, Thailand
(Chemicals, pharmaceuticals)
S. Chanprapavut, Managing Director
Monsanto

Richardson-Vicks
White Group Bldg.,
75 SOI Rubia, Sukhumvit 42
Phrakanong, Bangkok 10110, Thailand
Tel.: 66 2 3901059
(Pharmaceuticals)
D.A. McKay, Chief Operations Officer
Procter & Gamble Co.

3M Thailand
GPO Box 1650
Bangkok, Thailand
Tel.: 66 2 2519191
(Business equipment)
D.T. Gibbons, Managing Director
3M

Upjohn Co.
P.O. Box 11-245
Bangkok 10110, Thailand
(Pharmaceuticals)
Upjohn Co.

RETAILING AND WHOLESALING

Amway
2479 New Petchburi Rd.
Bangkok 10310, Thailand
Tel.: 66 2 3183015
Fax.: 66 2 3182045
(Household products)
Jim Payne, General Manager
Amway Corp.

Avon Cosmetics
1765 Ramkamhaeng Rd.
Hua Mark, Bangkapi
P.O. Box 1331
Bankgkok 10240, Thailand
Tel.: 66 2 3141415
Fax.: 66 2 3144944
(Cosmetics)
Kriengask Sanghong, General Manager
Avon Products

SERVICE INDUSTRIES

Amex & Grey Advertising
Regent House, 10th Floor
183 Rajdamri Rd.
Bangkok 10500, Thailand
Tel.: 66 2 2544355
Fax.: 66 2 2544360
(Advertising)
Kitti Issariyapracha, Managing Director
Grey Advertising

Chemco Leasing
297 Wang Lee Bldg., 5th Floor
Surawongse Rd.
Kwong Suriya Wongse, Khet Bangrak
Bangkok, Thailand
Tel.: 66 2 2511752
(Leasing)
Parichart Svebsantiqongse, Director
Chemical Banking Corp.

Circle Airfreight International
1126/1 New Petchburi Rd., Rm. 1206
Bangkok 10400, Thailand
Tel.: 66 2 2534173
(Cargo shipment)
John Muller, Branch Manager
Harper Group

D'Arcy Masius Benton & Bowles
A.I. Tower, 14th Floor
181 Suriwongse Rd.
Bangkok 10500, Thailand
Tel.: 66 2 2351940-8
(Advertising)
Michael Ryan, Managing Director
D'Arcy Masius Benton & Bowles

MAJOR DOMESTIC COMPANIES IN THAILAND

The following is a listing of the major domestic companies of Thailand. They are classified by business area: Banking and Finance; Industrial Manufacturing; Retailing and Wholesaling; and Service Industries. Company information includes type of business and contact name where possible. These companies will generally hire their own nationals first but may employ Americans.

BANKING AND FINANCE

Asia Credit
320 Rama IV Rd.
Bangkok 10500, Thailand
Tel.: 66 2 2351477
Fax.: 66 2 2361556
(Financial services)
Chanchai Leetavorn, Chairman

Bangkok Bank
333 Silom Rd.
Bangkok 10500, Thailand
(Banking)
Prasit Kanchanawat. Chairman

Bangkok Insurance Co.
302 Silom Rd.
Bangkok 10500, Thailand
Tel.: 66 2 2341155
Fax.: 66 2 2366541
(Insurance)
C. Sophonpanich, Chairman

Bangkok Metropolitan Bank
2 Chalermkhet 4 St.
Bangkok 10100, Thailand
Tel.: 66 2 2230561
(Banking)
Udane Tejapaibul, Chairman

INDUSTRIAL MANUFACTURING

Asia Fiber Co.
123-131 Rajprasong Rd.
Bangkok 10500, Thailand
Tel.: 66 2 2517754
Fax.: 66 2 2543934
(Fabrics)
S. Viravan, Chairman

Bangkok Iron & Steel Works Co.
627-633 Jawaraj Rd.
Bangkok 10100, Thailand
Tel.: 66 2 2225611
(Steel products)
A. Phijitphongchai, Managing Director

Bangkok Rice Co.
Bangkok Rice Bldg.
211/3 Rajawongse Rd.
Bangkok 10100, Thailand
Tel.: 66 2 2221737
(Agricultural products)
Pichai Korapinttanont, Managing Director

Bangkok Steel Industry Co.
UFM Bldg., 5th Floor
205 Rajawong Rd.
Bangkok 10100, Thailand
Tel.: 66 2 2229154
(Steel products)
P. Nithivasin, Managing Director

Capital Rice Co.
1400-1404 Songwad Rd.
Bangkok 10100, Thailand
Tel.: 66 2 2232412
(Agricultural products)
Paisal Vanichchakvong, Chairman

Chao Phya Co.
56/1 Poochaosamingprai Rd.
Samrong Thai, Samutprakarn, Thailand
Tel.: 66 2 3946819
(Food products)

Laemthong Corp.
Vanit Bldg.
1126/1 New Petchburi Rd.
Bangkok 10400, Thailand
Tel.: 66 2 2523777
Fax.: 66 2 2539922
(Agricultural products)
Yongsak Kanathanavanich, Chairman

Siam Cement Company
1 Siam Cement Rd.
Bangsue, Dusit
Bangkok 10800, Thailand
Tel.: 66 2 5863333
Fax.: 66 2 5872199
(Cement, bricks)
Paron Israsena, President

Unicord Co.
606-608 Luang Rd.
Phomprab, Bangkok 10100,
Thailand
Tel.: 66 2 2250025
Fax.: 66 2 2249308
(Canned foods)
K. Evmsakulrat, Managing
Director

RETAILING AND WHOLESALING

Hong Yiah Seng Co.
196/8 Rajawongse Rd.
Bangkok 10100, Thailand
Tel.: 66 2 2210121
(Agricultural products)
Porn Liewphairatana, Managing
Director

Huay Chuan Co.
816-818 Songwad Rd.
Bangkok 10100, Thailand
(Rubber goods)
Chin Sophonpanich, Chairman

Metro Co.
Metro Bldg., 180-184
Rajawongse Rd.
Bangkok 10100, Thailand
Tel.: 66 2 2229154-60
(Chemicals)
Sawang Laohathai, Chairman

SERVICE INDUSTRIES

SCT Co.
1 Saim Cement Rd.
Bangsue, Bangkok 10800,
Thailand
Tel.: 66 2 5870222
Fax.: 66 2 5872145
(Trading)
Sanya Dharmasakati, Chairman

MAJOR INTERNATIONAL COMPANIES IN THAILAND

There are many international firms operating in Thailand. These companies will be classified by business area: Banking and Finance; Industrial Manufacturing; Retailing and Wholesaling; and Service Industries. The company information includes type of business, international parent company, and contact name where possible. Your chances of achieving employment are substantially greater if you contact the subsidiary company in Thailand rather than the parent company in the home country.

BANKING AND FINANCE

AGC Finance & Securities Co.
Asoke Tower, 219 Sukhumvit 21
Bamgkok 10110, Thailand
(Financing)
Westpac Banking Corp.,
Australia

Credit Agricole
Kian Gwan House, 8th Floor
140 Wireless Rd.
Bangkok 10500, Thailand
Tel.: 66 2 2520609
(Banking)
Bernard Lefort, Manager
Caisse Nationale de Credit
Agricole, France

National Australia Bank
Sathorn Thani Bldg., 16th Floor
Bangkok 10500, Thailand
Tel.: 66 2 2366016
Fax.: 66 2 2366018
(Banking)
P.J. Murray, Representative
National Australia Bank,
Australia

Standard Chartered Bank
Dusit Thani Office Bldg.
946 Rama IV Rd.
Bangkok 10501, Thailand
Tel.: 66 2 2340821
Fax.: 66 2 2365427
(Banking)
Standard Chartered, England

International Commercial Bank of China
95 Suapa Rd.
Bangkok, Thailand
Tel.: 66 2 2218121
Fax.: 66 2 2252439
(Banking)
Shu-Shen Wang, Vice President
International Commercial Bank
of China, Taiwan

INDUSTRIAL MANUFACTURING

BASF
Asoke Towers, 17th Floor
219/56-59 Sukhumvit 21 Rd.
Bangkok 10110, Thailand
(Electronics)
BASF Group, Germany

BDF Intanin Co.
437 Soi Sirijulsawak Silom Rd.
Bangkok 10500, Thailand
Tel.: 66 2 2356624
Fax.: 66 2 2356626
(Silicone products)
Apichat Piyaavidhaijakarn,
Managing Director
Beiersdorf AG, Germany

Electrolux Thailand Co.
Electrolux Bldg.
Bangkok 10110, Thailand
Tel.: 66 2 3929313
(Household appliances)
Ulf Persson, Chief Operations
Officer
Electrolux AB, Sweden

EMI Ltd./Audiovision
78 Kiat Nakin Bldg.
Captain Bush Lane, New Rd.
Bangrak, Bangkok 10500,
Thailand
Tel.: 66 2 2336462
(Audio/visual equipment)
P. Boodsakorn, General
Manager
Thorn EMI, England

Hagemeyer
719 Siphrya Rd.
GPO Box 46
Bangkok 10501, Thailand
Tel.: 66 2 2340994
(Electronics, chemicals, foods,
cosmetics)
Hagemeyer NV, Netherlands

Lever Brothers
1037 Pleonchit Arcade, 5th Floor
Pleonchit Rd.
Bangkok, Thailand
(Foods)
Viroj Phtrakul, Chairman
Unilever, U.K.

Mitsui & Co.
Boonmitr Bldg., 6th Floor
138 Silom Rd.
Bangkok, Thailand
Tel.: 66 2 2345940
(Trading, industrial goods)
Mitsui & Co., Japan

NEC
Asoke Tower, 19th Floor
219/63-65 Sukhumuit 21 Rd.
Bangkok 10110, Thailand
Tel.: 66 2 2591192
Fax.: 66 2 2591199
(Electronics, computers)
M. Jimpu, Managing Director
NEC Corp., Japan

Sanyo Co.
Sanyo Bldg. No. 19
Asoke-Dindaeng Rd..
Phyathai, Bangkok, Thailand
Tel.: 66 2 2450620
Fax.: 66 2 2454408
(Electronics)
Sanyo Electronics Co., Japan

Toshiba Thailand Co.
201 Viphavadi Rangsit Rd.
Bangkhem, Bangkok 10900, Thailand
Tel.: 66 2 5111873
(Electronics)
K. Suriyasat, President
Toshiba Corp., Japan

Toyota Motor Thailand Co.
180 Suriwongse Rd.
P.O. Box 520
Bangkok, Thailand
Tel.: 66 2 2370079
Fax.: 66 2 2367141
(Automobiles)
Koichi Nambu, Chief Operations Officer
Toyota Motor Corp., Japan

RETAILING AND WHOLESALING

Daiei Inc.
Dusit Thani Bldg., 9th Floor
946 Rama, 4 Rd.
Bangkok 10500, Thailand
Tel.: 66 2 2339054
Fax.: 66 2 2368036
(Purchasing)
Nobuomi Shirahashi, Chief Operations Officer
Daiei Inc., Japan

Asian Honda Motor Co.
Bangkok Investment Bldg.
102 Sukhumvit 26 (Soi Aree)
Phrakanong, Bangkok 10110, Thailand
Tel.: 66 2 2580130
(Automobiles, appliances)
Michio Kitamura, CEO
Honda Motor Co., Japan

SERVICE INDUSTRIES

NKK Engineering
Dusit Thani Office Bldg., 8th Floor
946 Rama IV Rd.
Bangkok 10500, Thailand
Tel.: 66 2 2334261
Fax.: 66 2 2365614
(Engineering)
NKK Corp., Japan

Ogilvy & Mather
Silom Center, 10th Floor
2 Silom Rd.
Bangkok 10500, Thailand
Tel.: 66 2 2348723
Fax.: 66 2 2371546
(Advertising)
Sunandha Tulayadhan, Managing Director
WPP Group, England

MAJOR NON-PROFIT ORGANIZATIONS IN THAILAND

Asia and the Pacific Commission on Agricultural Statistics
39 Phra Atit Rd.
Bangkok 10200, Thailand
Tel.: 66 2 2817844

Asia and Pacific Plant Protection Commission
c/o Prof. Zhu Wanli
Phra Atit Rd.
Bangkok 10200, Thailand
Tel.: 66 2 2817844

Asian and Pacific Regional Agricultural Credit Association
Maliwan Mansion
Phra Atit Rd.
Bangkok 10200, Thailand
Tel.: 66 2 2817844

Association of Food Marketing Institutions in Asia and the Pacific
c/o FAO Regional Office for Asia and the Pacific
Phra Atit Rd.
Bangkok 10200, Thailand
Tel.: 66 2 2817844

Association of Geoscientists for International Development
c/o Asian Institute of Technology
P.O. Box 2754
Bangkok 10501, Thailand
Tel.: 66 2 5239300

Association of Southeast Asian Institutions of Higher Learning
Chulalongkorn University
Ratasastra Building 2
Bangkok 10500, Thailand
Tel.: 66 2 516966

Ecumenical Coalition on Third World Tourism
P.O. Box 9-25, Bangkhen
Bangkok 10900, Thailand
Tel.: 66 2 5796879

Pan Pacific Public Relations Federation
G.P.O. Box 1651
Bangkok, Thailand
Tel.: 66 2 234 0310

Seameo Project in Archaeology and Fine Arts
Darakarn Bldg.
920 Sukumuit Rd.
Bangkok 10110, Thailand
Tel.: 66 2 3811310

Southeast Asian Ministers of Education Organization
Darakarn Building
920 Sukumuit Road
Bangkok 10110, Thailand
Tel.: 66 2 3910144

U.N. Economic and Social Commission for Asia and the Pacific
United Nations Bldg.
Rajadamnern Ave.
Bangkok 10200, Thailand
Tel.: 66 2 829161

MAJOR HOTEL EMPLOYERS IN THAILAND

Cape Panwa Sheraton Hotel
27/8 Sakdidej Rd.
Phuket, Thailand
Tel.: 66 76 391123

Central Plaza Hotel
1695 Phaholyothin Rd.
Bangkok 10310, Thailand
Tel.: 66 2 541 1234

Dusit Inn
112 Changklan Rd.
Chiangmai 50000, Thailand
Tel.: 66 53 251033

Dusit Thani
Rama IV Rd.
Bangkok, Thailand
Tel.: 66 2360450

Holiday Inn Phuket
86/11 Thaweewong Rd.
Phuket 83121, Thailand
Tel.: 66 76 3210205

Hotel Siam Intercontinental
967 Rama 1 Rd.
Bangkok 10500, Thailand
Tel.: 66 2 2 53035557

Hotel Sofitel Central Hua-Hin
1 Damnernkasem Rd.
Hua-Hin 77110, Thailand
Tel.: 66 32 512021

Landmark Hotel & Plaza
138 Sukhumvit Rd.
Bangkok 10100, Thailand
Tel.: 66 2 2540404

Le Meridien Phuket
P.O. Box 277
Phuket 83000, Thailand
Tel.: 66 76 321480/5

Le Meridien President
135/26 Gaysorn Rd.
Bangkok 10500, Thailand
Tel.: 66 2 2530444

Regent of Bangkok
155 Rajadamri Rd.
Bangkok 10500, Thailand
Tel.: 66 2 2516127

Shangri-La Hotel
89 Soi Wat Suan Plu
Bangkok 10500, Thailand
Tel.: 66 2 2367777

Tawana Ramada Hotel
80 Surawongse Rd.
Bangkok 10500, Thailand
Tel.: 66 2 2360351

INTERNATIONAL SCHOOLS IN THAILAND

International Schools Services
P.O. Box 5910
Princeton, NJ 08543
American teachers seeking employment abroad may contact this recruitment service.

Chiang Mai International School
13 Chetupon Rd.
Chiang Mai, Thailand
Tel.: 66 53 242027
(U.S. school, K-8)

International School Bangkok
36 Soi Ruamchai (15),
Sukhumvit Rd.
Bangkok, Thailand 10110
Tel.: 66 2 2528141-4
(U.S., International Baccalaureate school, K-12)

Ruamrudee International School
123/15 Ruamrudee Lane,
Wireless Rd.
Bangkok, Thailand 10500
Tel.: 66 2 2530308
(U.S., International Baccalaureate school, grades 1-12)

VIETNAM

The Socialist Republic of Vietnam is located on the eastern coast of Indochina, bordering Laos and Cambodia to the west, China to the north, and the South China Sea to the east. The country measures nearly 130,000 miles, about the size of New Mexico. The territory is long and narrow, with plains near the coasts and mountains in the interior.

Vietnamese provide 85% of the country's population. Chinese, Thais, Khmers, and several other groups comprise the remaining 15%. The national language is Vietnamese, although English is still spoken by many business people, especially in the south. French is also known by many older people.

The area was settled by the Viet people from central China over 2,000 years ago and was a part of China for over 1,000 years, until 939. Although Vietnam was able to defeat the Mongols in 1288, the French were able to begin establishing protectorates in 1858. Japan occupied the country in 1940. The Vietminh, led by Ho Chi Minh, were formed to fight for independence.

In 1954, the Vietminh defeated the French, but a pro-French State of Vietnam had already been established in the south. The Republic of Vietnam was proclaimed in the south in 1955, followed by proclamation of the Democratic Republic of Vietnam in the north in 1959. Communist Vietcong guerillas sought to overthrow the regime in the south and unite the country with the north.

Several military coups occurred in the south in 1963. North Vietnamese troops began intervening directly in the civil war in the south in 1964, with Soviet and Chinese aid. In 1964, the U.S. began bombing raids on North Vietnam, and American troops entered the conflict in 1965. American troop withdrawals began in 1969, but air bombings intensified in 1972. Despite a cease fire agreement signed by the U.S., North Vietnam, South Vietnam, and the Vietcong in 1973, intense fighting continued until 1975.

North Vietnamese and Vietcong forces defeated the remaining forces in South Vietnam in 1975 and began reorganizing the country along communist lines. The Socialist Republic of Vietnam was proclaimed in 1976 under northern leadership. Vietnam invaded Cambodia in 1977, defeated the communist Khmer Rouge regime, and established a new government. China briefly attacked Vietnam in 1979 in retaliation for the invasion of Cambodia. Vietnamese troops largely withdrew from Cambodia in 1989.

In 1987, a new reform program, called *doi moi,* was initiated to bolster economic growth and end the country's chronic food shortages. Several state enterprises have been privatized, and agriculture is almost entirely private. The economy has improved, but significant economic growth is hampered by the U.S. embargo against Vietnam, preventing American companies from doing business with the country. Japan also follows the U.S. lead.

Several countries maintain investments in Vietnam, but no large-scale foreign involvement is likely until the U.S. lifts the embargo, allowing American and Japanese firms into Vietnam and reopening trade relations. The U.S. claims that relations will be reevaluated if the entire Cambodian conflict is settled and if all remains of American prisoners of war are returned.

Current Economic Climate

The country has a gross national product over $12 billion and a per capita income of about $200. Vietnam's largest industries are textiles and food processing. Inflation in 1988 ran over 700% but has decreased to 50% in 1990 due to the government's economic reform policies.

The Soviet Union, Japan, Hong Kong, and Taiwan are Vietnam's principal trading partners. Exports totalled over $1 billion in 1990. Rice, of which Vietnam is the world's third largest exporter, is the most important agricultural product. Over 70% of the workforce is involved in agriculture.

The U.S. embargo means that no American firms can operate in Vietnam and that no trade occurs between the two countries. Japan also follows the U.S. policy in regard to investment. Consequently, the U.S. and Japan combine their votes to stop loans and aid from sources such as the International Monetary Fund, the World Bank, and the Asian Development Bank.

Without such assistance, the country cannot repair its poor transportation and communications infrastructure, thereby limiting large investments. The American chambers of commerce in Hong Kong and Bangkok both advocate scrapping the embargo. The U.S. government claims that Vietnam must first pay the $140 million it owes the IMF before any multilateral loans or aid can be approved.

Additionally, the Soviet Union, which has previously subsidized the Vietnamese economy, is dramatically reducing its foreign aid. The U.S.S.R. provided Vietnam with 90% of its fuel and steel and 80% of its fertilizer. The lack of Soviet fertilizer is expected to affect Vietnamese rice production adversely in 1991.

Sweden and Finland are now the only countries that provide Vietnam with significant foreign aid. Japan trades with Vietnam, although it is often disguised through Indonesian or Hong Kong companies. In 1990, Japanese exports to Vietnam totaled over $300 million. In 1991, Japan is expected to surpass the Soviet Union as Vietnam's leading trade partner.

Other foreign investors have also been attracted by Vietnam's efforts to liberalize its economy and foreign investment regulations. Over 200 joint ventures, valued at $2 billion, have been established since 1988. Over $400 million was invested in 1990. French companies are the largest foreign investors in Vietnam, with over 20% of the total. Taiwanese firms, however, are probably the fastest growing. Private enterprises now account for 40% of Vietnam's national output.

Only 20% of Vietnam's 68 million people live in urban areas. Ho Chi Minh City (Saigon) is the largest city with 4 million inhabitants. Hundreds of thousands of refugees have fled the country, especially in recent years. The capital, Hanoi, has over 3 million people. Haiphong and Da Nang are also important ports. Air Vietnam is the national airline.

Employment in Vietnam

Americans seeking employment in Vietnam have very few options. The U.S. and Vietnam do not maintain diplomatic relations. Americans can not be prohibited from traveling to Vietnam, but companies are severely restricted by the U.S. boycott. Companies from other countries, however, do invest in Vietnam, although they are much more likely to hire their own nationals first.

Japanese companies investing in the country include Mitsubishi, Mitsui, Sanyo, Victor, and Kanematsu. Other foreign firms that either operate in Vietnam now or intend to are Heineken of Holland, Sunforth of Taiwan, Hanesco-Fiston of Hong Kong, and South East Asia Timber of Australia. The petroleum industry is expected to grow rapidly once foreign funds begin to finance drilling and refining.

Organizations for Further Information

The following organizations may be helpful in the job search. Because the U.S. and Vietnam do not maintain diplomatic relations, no consular offices or national tourist organizations exist between the two countries. These chamber of commerce organizations, however, may offer economic and business information about Vietnam.

Danang Chamber of Commerce
32, Thong-Nhut
Danang, Vietnam

Saigon Chamber of Commerce
69, Tu-Do-St., P.O. Box F2

Saigon, Vietnam
Tel.: 20 102 20102

CAMBODIA

The Republic of Cambodia measures approximately 70,000 square miles, about the size of Missouri, and is adjacent to Thailand on the west and north, Laos on the north, Vietnam on the east, and the Gulf of Thailand on the south. Over 75% of the country is forested. Khmers comprise 90% of Cambodia's people, with Vietnamese and Chinese providing another 5% each. Khmer is the official language. Over 95% of the people are Therevada Buddhists.

The great Khmer empire of the thirteenth century included most of present-day Indochina and Thailand, but it eventually eroded under pressure from invaders. By 1863, France was able to establish a protectorate that lasted until 1953. Prince Norodom Sihanouk served as king from 1941 to 1955 and then as head of state from 1960 until 1970, when he was overthrown by a pro-American faction. Sihaouk formed a government in exile in Beijing.

Cambodia became increasingly involved with the conflict in Vietnam. Thousands of Vietcong forces occupied parts of Cambodia and ultimately led to the birth of the Khmer Rouge. The U.S. heavily bombed parts of Cambodia during the Vietnam War. In 1975, the Khmer Rouge captured Phnom Penh and initiated a policy of emptying the cities and towns in order to return the people to the land. Approximately 1 million Cambodians died from executions and extreme living conditions.

Border clashes with Vietnam in 1978 led to a full Vietnamese invasion and the occupation of Phnom Penh by the Vietnamese-backed Kampuchean National United Front. Vietnamese forces continued to wage war against the Khmer Rouge. In 1989-90, Vietnam began withdrawing its troops, although most observers estimate that some Vietnamese forces are still in the country. The civil war, however, continues to send thousands of refugees into Thailand.

The government, led by Premier Hun Sen, is fighting an opposition consisting of two groups. The Khmer Rouge, supported by China, provides most of the armed resistance. Another opposition group, led by Prince Sihanouk and the Khmer People's Liberation Front, is supported by the U.S. but does little actual fighting.

Peace negotiations are being led by France and Indonesia. As of mid-1991, a power-sharing plan negotiated by the U.S., the U.S.S.R., China, France, and Britain has been encountering resistance in Vietnam, which fears the return of the Khmer Rouge. Recently, the Cambodian government has been fighting the Khmer Rouge more effectively, but the rebels benefit from sanctuaries inside Thai borders.

Current Economic Climate

With a gross national product around $2 billion and per capita income of approximately $200, Cambodia is currently suffering economically. Major economic activities include rice milling, lumber, and rubber gathering. The country possesses a few deposits of iron and copper. Cambodian trade primarliy occurs with Vietnam and Thailand. At least 75% of the workforce is involved in agriculture. Cambodia's population is around 6 million. Phnom Penh, the capital, contains 300,000 people. The main port is Kompong Som while Siem Reap is the nearest town to Angkor Wat, the ancient archaeological site.

Employment in Cambodia

Employment, due to the continuous civil war, is extremely difficult to find in Cambodia. Foreigners should not expect to find a job. The United States and Cambodia do not maintain diplomatic relations. Japan has promised massive economic development aid once the war ends. Japanese business investment tends to accompany Japanese aid, but no end to the war can presently be seen.

Several private English language schools are opening in Phnom Penh, where teaching positions may be available. Cambodia officially claims that a chamber of commerce exists in Phnom Penh, but it may not actually provide any services and its precise location is unknown.

Your best bet of getting into the country is probably through Thailand. Thai lumber interests in Cambodia are hoping to expand production after a peace settlement. Thailand also maintains a tour route to the ancient temples of Angkor Wat. Likewise, Thais are building a new hotel in the border town of Aranyaprathet in order to accommodate tourists who may want to take side trips to the temples.

LAOS

The Lao People's Democratic Republic measures over 91,000 miles, about the size of Utah. Laos is located in Indochina, bordering China to the north, Thailand to the west, Cambodia to the south, and Vietnam to the east. The entire country is landlocked and mostly forested. The Mekong River forms much of the western border.

Only 15% of Laos's 4 million people live in urban areas. The capital, Vientiane, is the largest city, with 120,000 inhabitants. The country is very ethnically diverse. The Lao comprise about half of the population, Khmers about one-quarter, and various other groups form the remainder. Nearly half of the people are Buddhist, with a large number of traditional religions as well. Lao is the official language, but French is still spoken by many people.

Laos has historically been a battlefield for Thais, Vietnamese, Chinese, Khmers, and others. France eventually established a protectorate over the country in 1893. Japan invaded during World War II, and Laos became an independent constitutional monarchy in 1949. Civil war commenced in 1960 among various political factions, but a coalition government was formed in 1962.

In 1964, the communists, called the Pathet Lao, withdrew from the coalition and renewed the revolution. During the Vietnam War, the U.S. bombed Vietcong supply and communication lines running through Laos. Despite intensified U.S. aid, the Pathet Lao assumed control of the government in 1975. Vietnam has provided significant aid since then.

The governing Lao People's Revolutionary Party began an economic reform movement in 1986, the New Economic Mechanism. The project aims at gradually liberalizing the Laotian economy but has been proceeding at an extremely slow pace. No plans exist to reform the political system.

Current Economic Climate

Laos claims a gross national product of less than $1 billion and a per capita income of about $300. Major Laotian products include wood and lumber goods, rice, tobacco, and corn. Over 85% of the workforce is engaged in agriculture. Thailand, China, and Japan are the major trading partners.

The country is economically weak but is attempting some reforms. Privatization efforts are allowing state-owned enterprises to be sold off. Foreign donors have responded with nearly $160 million in aid annually. Additionally, the government relaxed its foreign investment laws in 1988. Thai businesses are now very active in the opening Laotian economy. Thailand and Laos recently agreed to build a new bridge across the Mekong River. Thai banks and lumber companies are beginning to penetrate Laos for business.

Employment in Laos

Lao's poor economy makes obtaining employment there quite difficult. Your best chance may be to contact a Thai company hoping to expand into Laos and move in as a part of their operations. Japanese firms have also been exploring opportunities in Laos but are unlikely to hire Americans.

Americans traveling to Laos must possess a visa. Business and visit visas are valid for up to 30 days and can be extended for another 30 days. Tourist visas are valid for 15 days and can be extended. Tourist visas are much easier to obtain but must generally be part of a tour package. Applying to the tourist office a few months ahead of time is advisable. Only people who look decently dressed and groomed are allowed into Laos.

Organizations for Further Information

The following organizations may be helpful in the job search. American embassies and consulates have commercial and/or economic sections that can provide you with business information and explain aspects of the local economy. Foreign government missions in the U.S. can furnish visas and information on work permits and other important regulations. They may also offer economic and business information about the country.

CHAMBERS OF COMMERCE

Luang Prabang Chamber of Commerce
Luang Probang, Laos

CONSULAR OFFICE IN LAOS

American Embassy, Commercial Section
Rue Bartholonie B.P. 114
Vientiane, Laos
Tel.: 2220, 2357, 2384, or 3570
E. James Steele, Commercial Officer

Embassy of the Lao People's Democratic Republic
2222 S St. N.W.
Washington, DC 20008
Tel.: (202) 332-6416

OTHER INFORMATIONAL ORGANIZATIONS

Lao Tourism
P.O. Box 2912
Vientiane, Laos
Tel.: 2998, 3627

Lao-American, Inc.
(National Tourist Office)
338 S. Hancock Ave.
South Elgin, IL 60177
Tel.: (708) 742-2159
Fax: (708) 742-4320

Southeast Asia: Malaysia, Indonesia, The Philippines, Brunei

MALAYSIA

The Federation of Malaysia is located in Southeast Asia, comprising the Malay Peninsula and the northern coast of Borneo. The country measures 127,000 square miles, a little larger than New Mexico. The Malay Peninsula contains a mountainous forested area with coastal plains. Sarawak and Sabah on Borneo are very forested, with a wide coastal plain. Thailand borders the peninsula to the north, Indonesia borders Sarawak and Sabah, Singapore lies at the tip of the peninsula, and Brunei is located on the coast of Sarawak.

Malays comprise about 55% of the population. The government encourages large families in order to create a large domestic market. Chinese provide another 33% of the population, and Indians 10%. The population is divided into indigenous people, Malays and others, and non-indigenous people, Chinese, Indians, and others. Government policies recognize this distinction and favor the indigenous races.

Bahasa Malaysia is the official language, but English, Chinese, Tamil, and Hindi are all widely spoken as well. Bahasa Malaysia is romanized Malay. English is widespread in the business community and is known by most young people. The largest religious groupings include Muslims, Hindus, Buddhists, and Confucians. Sabah's population is mainly Christian.

The peninsula, called Malaya, has been known as one of the world's most strategic trade areas for centuries, attracting traders from throughout the world. The Malacca Malay kingdom reached the apex of its power by 1400. European traders arrived in the sixteenth century, and in 1511 Portugal conquered Malacca. The Dutch took over in 1641 but gradually lost influence to the British.

Britain established control over most of the area by 1867. In 1914, Malaya became a British protectorate. The territories on the peninsula became independent in 1957 as the Federation of Malaya. Malaysia was formed in 1963 as a federation comprising Malaya plus the British colonies of Sabah, Sarawak, and Singapore. In 1965 Singapore became independent. Malaysia is a member of ASEAN, the Association of Southeast Asian Nations.

The government is a federal parliamentary democracy. A monarch is elected every five years by the hereditary rulers of the states. The United Malay National Organization, or UMNO, is the governing party. Its leader, Dr. Datuk Seri Mahathir bin Mohamad, has been prime minister since 1981. His policies favor foreign investment and economic growth. In 1990, Dr. Matahir suggested the creation of an East Asian Economic Grouping as a regional trading bloc. Only Singapore has endorsed the proposal.

MALAYSIA'S LARGEST TRADING PARTNERS

Imports:	Japan	22%
	United States	18%
	Singapore	14%
	European Community	8%
Exports:	Singapore	20%
	Japan	20%
	United States	18%
	European Community	10%

Current Economic Climate

Malaysia has a gross national product of over $40 billion and a per capita income of about $3,000. The economy grew by 9.4% in 1990 and by 8.6% in 1989. Malaysia posted the highest growth rate in the ASEAN in 1990. The economy is expected to grow by 8% in 1991. Inflation has averaged 2% in recent years, but it climbed to 3% in 1990 and should rise to 5% in 1991. Unemployment is about 8%. In 1990 imports increased by 30% while exports rose by 18%.

A few Malaysian firms have begun investing in China in search of cheaper production costs. Malaysia's largest company is Sime Darby, a diversified manufacturer with profits over $100 million and a market value of $2 billion. Most of the private sector in Malaysia is controlled by firms owned by Chinese. The economic disparity between Chinese and Malays has created ethnic tensions in the past. The government attempts to remedy the situation by promoting Malay business investment.

Malaysia has historically been dependent upon commodity exports, but diversification into manufacturing has helped maintain strong levels of economic growth. The largest industries include agriculture, rubber goods, steel, and electronics. Malaysia produces 35% of the world's rubber and possesses 35% of the world's tin reserves. Other important commodities include palm oil, cocoa, and petroleum. Manufacturing is now the largest economic sector, growing by 12% in 1990 and 8% in 1989. Manufacturing exports grew by 25% in 1990.

The government actively encourages foreign investment, especially in manufacturing. Japan is the largest overall foreign investor in Malaysia. Over 500 Japanese companies operate in Malaysia, having invested over $700 million since 1986 and over $3 billion since 1970. Japanese companies invested $1.5 billion in 1990. Companies from Taiwan, however, invested nearly $1.7 billion in Malaysia in 1990.

A Japanese joint-venture in Malaysia is producing an automobile, the Proton. Over 100,000 Protons were sold in Malaysia in 1990. An additional 10,000 of the Mitsubishi-designed vehicles were exported to Europe in 1990. Mitsubishi owns 30% of the car company and provides most of the upper level management. Other Japanese companies are heavily involved in the Malaysian economy. Mitsui is one of the country's largest construction contractors. In addition, Sony, Canon, and Toyota all have significant interests.

Japanese investment, however, also causes problems. While large companies have been able to absorb local staff, most of the smaller companies only employ Japanese managers and thereby alienate the Malays. Japanese investors have been implicated in supporting UMNO by allocating business to companies supporting the government party and by denying aid to states supporting the opposition parties. The Japanese have also been accused of cooperating to limit the wages offered to skilled workers, who are currently in short supply.

Consequently, American and European firms have taken advantage of these deficiencies by hiring skilled workers away from Japanese companies by offering higher wages and by advancing Malays further in the company. The largest foreign company in Malaysia is Thompson Electronics, a French firm. American companies are most active on the west coast of the Malay Peninsula and in Johor state, near Singapore.

Kuala Lumpur, the capital, is the largest city with over 1 million inhabitants. Although only 40% of Malaysia's over 18 million people live in urban areas, urbanization is growing by 4% annually. Most of the population, 15 million people, live on the peninsula, 1.7 million live in Sarawak, and 1.5 million in Sabah. Port Kelang is the country's largest port. Other large cities are Penang, Melaka, Kuantan, and Johor Bahru on the peninsula; and Kuching, Labuan, and Kota Kinabalu in East Malaysia.

Regular business hours are from 8:30 am to 5:30 pm, Monday through Friday, and from 8:30 am to 1:00 pm on Saturday. Banking hours are usually from 10:00 am to 3:00 pm on weekdays and from 9:30 am to 11:30 am on Saturday. Stores are open from 10:00 am to 10:00 pm in the major cities. Some businesses are now pursuing a 40-hour, 5-day work week. In some states, most offices and businesses close on Friday and for the last half of the day on Thursday for Muslim prayers, staying open on Saturday and Sunday.

Getting Around in Malaysia

Malaysia Airlines provides international service as well as domestic flights to most of the major cities. The bus system is also very good on the west coast of the peninsula but poorer in East Malaysia. Buses are the most popular means of transporation in the cities, and air-conditioned buses link the major towns. The roads in the western part of the peninsula are generally good, and rental cars are available.

Rail transportation is well developed on the west coast of the peninsula, with lines extending to most of the major cities along a north-south route. The Railpass offers special discount rates for travel throughout the country. Rail lines in East Malaysia and on the east coast of the peninsula are not as comprehensive. Ferries also provide transportation between the islands and the peninsula.

Employment Regulations for Americans

Americans do not need a visa to enter Malaysia for a period of 90 days or less. Visas are required for employment or other long-term visits. To obtain legal employment, foreigners must also acquire a work permit and demonstrate that a Malaysian is not available to fill the position.

Shortages of qualified personnel in many skilled occupations mean that jobs are available for individuals who market themselves effectively. Nonetheless, domestic Malaysian companies are likely to only hire Malays while Japanese companies tend to hire their own nationals for management positions and local people for the less-skilled jobs. Consequently, Americans do not have favorable employment opportunities. Your best chance is to look for work with an American firm. Most of the Kuala Lumpur foreign language schools recruit qualified English teachers abroad rather than hire casual teachers.

Organizations for Further Information

The following organizations, both in the U.S. and Singapore, may be helpful in the job search. American embassies and consulates have commercial and/or economic sections that can provide you with business information and explain aspects of the local economy. World Trade Centers usually include many foreign companies operating in the country. Foreign government missions in the U.S. such as National Tourist Offices and embassies and consulates can furnish visas and information on work permits and other important regulations. They may also offer economic and business information about the country.

CHAMBERS OF COMMERCE

American Business Council of Malaysia
Amoda, 15th Floor
Jalan Imbi 55100, Malaysia
Tel.: 60 01 281223

Associated Chinese Chamber of Commerce and Industry
Chinese Assembly Hall, Ground Floor
1 Jalan Maharajalela
Kuala Lumpur 50150, Malaysia
Tel.: 60 03 2320474

Associated Indian Chamber of Commerce
c/o Wisma UDA
36 Jalan Ampang
Kuala Lumpur 50450, Malaysia
Tel.: 60 03 2387919

Malay Chamber of Commerce & Industry of Malaysia
Tingkat 17, Plaza Pekeliling
No. 3 Jalan Tun Razak
Kuala Lumur 50400, Malaysia
Tel.: 60 03 2928522

Malaysian Association of Malay Exporters
Sdn. Bhd., YM Raja Rosdin, c/o Rosdin Corp.
Kuala Lumpur Hilton, 35 Mezz. Floor
Jalan Sultan Ismail, 50250
Kuala Lumpur 50250, Malaysia
Tel.: 60 03 2480255

Malaysia International Chamber of Commerce & Industry
Tingkat 10 Wisma Damansara
Jalan Semantan, P.O. Box 10192
Kuala Lumpur 10192, Malaysia
Tel.: 60 03 2542117

National Chamber of Commerce & Industry of Malaysia
Plaza Pekeliling, 17th Floor
Jalan Tun Razak
Kuala Lumpur 50400, Malaysia
Tel.: 60 03 2989873

Sabah Chamber of Commerce
Bangunan Central
Jalan Saqunting
Kota Kinabalu 88300, Malaysia

Sabah United Chinese Chamber of Commerce
P.O. Box 2176
Kota Kinabalu 88824, Malaysia

Sarawak Chamber of Commerce
c/o Room 301, 3rd Floor
Wisma Bukit Mata
Jalan Tuanku Abdul Rahman
Kuching 93100, Malaysia

CONSULAR OFFICES

American Embassy, Commercial Section
376 Jalan Tun Razak
Kuala Lumpur 50400, Malaysia
Tel.: 60 03 2489011
Jonathan Bensky, Commercial Officer

Consulate General of Malaysia, Hawaii
1st Hawaiian Bank
P.O. Box 3200
Honolulu, HI 96847
Tel.: (808) 525-8144

Consulate General of Malaysia, New York
140 East 45th St., 43 Floor
New York, NY 10017
Tel.: (212) 490-2722

Consulate General of Malaysia, Portland
6144 S.W. 37th Street
Portland, OR 97221
Tel.: (503) 246-0707

Consulate of Malaysia, Los Angeles
350 S. Figueroa Street
Los Angeles, CA 90071
Tel.: (213) 617-1000

Consulate of Malaysia, New York
630 Third Ave., 11th Floor
New York, NY 10017
Tel.: (212) 682-0232

Embassy of Malaysia
2401 Massachusettes Ave. N.W.
Washington, DC 20008
Tel.: (202) 328-2700

Permanent Mission of Malaysia to the United Nations
140 E. 45th St., 43 Floor
New York, NY 10017
Tel.: (212) 986-6310

WORLD TRADE CENTER IN MALAYSIA

Putra World Trade Centre
Rahim and Co., Chartered Surveyors Sdn. Bhd.
64 Jalan Raja Muda
P.O. Box 11215
Kuala Lumpur, Malaysia
Tel.: 60 03 919922

OTHER INFORMATIONAL ORGANIZATIONS

Malaysian Airlines
933 W. Century Blvd., #506
Los Angeles, CA 90045
Tel.: (213) 642-0849

Malaysian Industrial Development Authority, Chicago
John Hancock Center, Suite 3350
875 N. Michigan Ave.
Chicago, IL 60611
Tel.: (312) 787-4769

Malaysian Industrial Development Authority, Los Angeles
World Trade Center, Suite 400
350 S. Figueroa Street
Los Angeles, CA 90071
Tel.: (213) 621-2661

Malaysian Industrial Development Authority, New York
630 3rd Ave., 11th Floor
New York, NY 10017
Tel.: (212) 687-2491

Malaysia Tourist Information Center, Los Angeles
818 W. 7th Street
Los Angeles, CA 90017-3432
Tel.: (213) 689-9702

Malaysia Tourist Information Center, New York
420 Lexington Ave.
New York, NY 10170

Tourist Development Corp.
Putra World Trade Centre, 24th-27th Floors, Menara Dato Onn
Jalan Tun Ismail
Kuala Lumpur 50480, Malaysia

Business Directories

Although not always easy to find, business directories can prove invaluable in the international job search. Most directories list company names, addresses, products, and phone numbers. Some directories include executive names and titles and financial information about the company. These sources provide you with the names of the people to contact for employment information as well as financial data.

Kompass Buku Merah Malaysia. Biennial publication of Berita Kompass, Balai Berita, 31 Jalang Riong, 59100 Kuala Lumpur, Malaysia. Provides information on 15,000 manufacturers and services firms.

Kuala Lumpur Stock Exchange Annual Companies Handbook. Published annually by the Kuala Lumpur Stock Exchange, Block C, Damansara Centre, Kuala Lumpur 50490, Malaysia. Privides financial information on several hundred firms listed on the stock exchange.

Making a good first impression

It is a good idea to carry business cards in Malaysia. The cards should contain one's name, full title or position, employer or organization, phone number, and address. You should have this information on Malay on one side and in English on the other. You will find it convenient to also print cards in Chinese. Even though many business people in Malaysia speak English, presenting business cards is a common custom in East Asia and will help people remember you. It is also important when sitting not to cross your legs or point your toes or the soles of your feet in someone's direction. These are considered to be offensive gestures.■

MAJOR AMERICAN COMPANIES IN MALAYSIA

The following is a listing of the major American companies in Malaysia. They are classified by business area: Banking and Finance; Industrial Manufacturing; Retailing and Wholesaling; and Service Industries. Company information includes type of business, American parent company, and contact name where possible. Such companies will generally hire their own nationals first but may employ Americans.

BANKING AND FINANCE

Alexander Stenhouse (Malaysia)
Bangunan Ming Jalan Bukit Nanas, 9th Floor
Kuala Lumpur, Selangor 0401, Malaysia
Tel.: 60 03 3202166
(Insurance)
Alexander & Alexander Services

Bank of Commerce
Wisma Stephens, 88 Jalan Raja Chulan, Kuala Lumpur, Malaysia
(Commercial bank)
J. P. Morgan & Co.

Chase Manhattan Bank
Pernas International, Jalan Sultan Ismail
50250 Kuala Lumpur, Malaysia
(Commercial bank)
Chase Manhattan Corp.

Citicorp International Trading Co.
28 Medan Pasar, Kuala Lumpur
Selangor, Malaysia
(Trading)
Citicorp

INDUSTRIAL MANUFACTURING

Beatrice Foods
70 Jalon University, Petaling Jaya
Selangor, Malaysia
Tel.: 60 03 565600
(Food products)
J. D. H. Neill, Manager
KKR Associates

Bristol-Myers (Malaysia)
P.O. Box 1044 Jalan Semahgat
Petaling Jaya, Selangor, Malaysia
(Pharmaceuticals)
Bristol-Myers Squibb Co.

Colgate-Palmolive
P.O. Box 11076
50734 Kuala Lumpur, Malaysia
Tel.: 60 03 7566544
Fax.: 60 03 7576914
(Household detergents)
G. B. Murray, Managing Director
Colgate-Palmolive Co.

Esso Malaysia
Kompleks Antarabangsa, Jalan Sultan Ismail
50250 Kuala Lumpur, Malaysia
Tel.: 60 03 2422322
Fax.: 60 03 2428760
(Petroleum products and ammonia)
C. M. Bateman, Managing Director
Esso Eastern

Eveready Battery Co. (Malaysia)
Pudu P.O. Box 6066
3021 Regent Hotel, JI Sultan Ismail
50250 Kuala Lumpur, Malaysia
Tel.: 60 03 2425233
Fax.: 60 03 2434916
(Batteries)
Robert Wiles, Managing Director
Eveready Battery Co.

Goodyear Malaysia
P.O. Box 49, 40700 Shah Alam
Selangor, Malaysia
Tel.: 60 03 5592411
Fax.: 60 03 5594106
(Tires)
H. J. Wilson, Managing Director
Goodyear Tire & Rubber Co.

W.R. Grace (Malaysia)
Bangunan Cho-Tek, Rm. 601
Jalan Tuanku Abdul Rahman
50100 Kuala Lumpur, Malaysia
Tel.: 60 03 2928918
Fax.: 60 03 2912940
(Construction products)
A. H. Tee, Manager
W. R. Grace & Co.

Hewlett-Packard Malaysia
Bayan Lepas Free Trade Zone
Penang, Malaysia
Tel.: 60 04 831611
(Semiconductor materials)
S. Cooper, Managing Director
Hewlett-Packard

Johnson & Johnson
P.O. Box 17, Jin Tandang
Petaling Jaya, Malaysia
Tel.: 60 03 574166
(Hospital products)
Johnson & Johnson

Kimberly-Clark Malaysia
46700 Petaling Jaya, P.O. Box 77
Selangor Malaysia
Tel.: 60 3 7552322
(Facial tissue, feminine products)
B. C. Cheah, Managing Director
Kimberly-Clark Corp.

Levi Strauss (Malaysia)
78/78A Lorong Selamat
Penang, Malaysia
Tel.: 60 04 28545
(Apparel)
Len Bennett, General Manager
Levi Strauss & Co.

Mobil Oil Malaysia
3rd Floor, Wisma Damansara, Julian Semantan
P.O. Box 2225
Kuala Lumpur, 01-02 Malaysia
Tel.: 60 03 945622
(Petroleum products)
M. Tanaka, Managing Director
Mobil Corp.

Motorola Malaysia
Bayan Lepas Free Trade Zone
Penang, 11900 Malaysia
Tel.: 60 4 832511
(Electronic equipment)
Jerome Anthony Mysliwiec, Director
Motorola

Nabisco Brands (Malaysia)
126A Batu 4-3/4 Jalan Skudai, Tampoi
Johor Bahru, Johor 81200, Malaysia
Tel.: 60 07 375545
Fax.: 60 03 367094
(Biscuits, sweets)
Giam Kar Kheng, Managing Director
RJR-Nabisco

Procter & Gamble (Malaysia)
Lot 16B Jalan 225 Petaling Jaya
Selangor, Malaysia
Tel.: 60 03 746933
(Soaps and detergents)
W. Kastner, Chief Operating Officer
Procter & Gamble Co.

Quaker Products (Malaysia)
No. 54 Jalan SS 15/4 Subang
Jaya Selangor Malaysia
(Food products)
Michael Tay, Director
Quaker Oats Co.

R.J. Reynolds Tobacco Co.
Jalan Perbadanan 3/5 Syah A
P.O. Box 37, Keland Selangor, Malaysia
(Tobacco products)
RJR Nabisco Holdings

Scott Paper (Malaysia)
4 1/2 Miles Jalan Mersing, Kluang
Johor 86007, Malaysia
Tel.: 60 07 789226
(Paper products)
H. J. Tang, Manager
Scott Paper Co.

Texas Instruments Malaysia
1 Lorong Enggang 33, Ampang/Ulu Kelang
54200 Kuala Lumpur, Malaysia
Tel.: 60 03 4567077
Fax.: 60 03 4579966
(Integrated circuits, thermostats)
Effendi A. Rahman, Personnel Director
Texas Instruments

Union Carbide Malaysia
Suites 3020/3022, Regent Hotel
Kuala Lumpur 0610, Malaysia
Tel.: 60 03 425233
(Latex)
Union Carbide Corp.

Warner-Lambert (Manufacturing)
P.O. Box 87, 46710 Petaling Jaya
Selangor, Malaysia
Tel.: 60 03 7565011
Fax.: 60 03 7557602
(Pharmaceuticals, toiletries)
John Chan, Director
Warner-Lambert Co.

RETAILING AND WHOLESALING

Amway (Malaysia)
P.O. Box 84, Jalan Sultan
46710 Petaling Jaya
Selangor, Malaysia
Tel.: 60 03 7758477
Fax.: 60 03 7743261
(Home and personal care products)
L. H. Choong, Managing Director
Amway Corp.

SERVICE INDUSTRIES

Air Express International
Kompleks Kargo Udara Subang
Kuala Lumpur Intl. Airport
Subang, Selangor 47200,
Malaysia
Tel.: 60 03 7764411
(Airline)
Air Express International Corp.

Korn/Ferry International
6th Floor UBN Tower, Kuala
Lumpur
Selangor 50250, Malaysia
Tel.: 60 03 2381655
(Management consultants)
A. David Marchington,
Managing Director
Korn/Ferry International

Price Waterhouse
11th Floor, Wisma Sime Darby
Jalan Raja Laut
Kuala Lumpur 50350, Malaysia
Tel.: 60 03 2931077
Fax.: 60 03 2930997
(Accounting)
Price Waterhouse

MAJOR DOMESTIC COMPANIES IN MALAYSIA

The following is a listing of the major domestic companies of Malaysia. They are classified by business area: Banking and Finance; Industrial Manufacturing; Retailing and Wholesaling; and Service Industries. Company information includes type of business and contact name. These companies will generally hire their own nationals first but may employ Americans.

BANKING AND FINANCE

Arab-Malaysian Merchant Bank
22/F Bangunan Arab-Malaysian
55 Jl Raha Chulan
Kuala Lumpur 50200, Malaysia
Tel.: 60 03 238 2633
Fax.: 60 03 238 2842
(Merchant bank)
YB Dato Malek Merican,
Managing Director

Bank Bumipatra Malaysia
51 Jalan Selat Tebrau
Johor Bahru, Malaysia
Tel.: 60 07 224833
(Banking)

Bank Islam Malaysia
9/F Menar Tun Razak, Jalan Raja
Laut
P.O. Box 11080
Kuala Lumpur 50734, Malaysia
Tel.: 60 03 2935566
(Banking)
Dr. Andul Halim bin Haji Ismail,
Managing Director

Bank of Commerce
G/F Wisma Stephens, 88 Jalan
Raja Chulan
P.O. Box 10566
Kuala Lumpur 50718, Malaysia
Tel.: 60 03 2429177
(Commercial bank)
Mohd Nor bin Mohd Yusof,
Director

Bank Pembangunan Malaysia
19th Floor Complex, Tun Abdul Razak
Jalan Wong Ah Fook
Malaysia, Johor Bahru
Tel.: 60 07 224465
(Banking)

Bank Pusat Kerjasama
34, Jalan A, Off Jalan Tun Abdul Razak
Johor Bahru, Malaysia
Tel.: 60 07 234191
(Banking)

Bank Utama Malaysia
18B Jalan Haji Taha, P.O. Box 2049
93740 Kuching, Sarawak, Malaysia
Tel.: 60 249257
Fax.: 60 424954
(Commercial bank)
Haji Ali Sheikh Salim, Director

Development & Commercial Bank
Wisma On Tai, 161B Jalan Ampang
50450 Kuala Lumpur, Malaysia
Tel.: 60 03 2617177
Fax.: 60 03 2619541
(Banking and finance)
Mohd Alkaf bin Mohd Kahar, Divisional Manager

Hock Hua Bank (Sabah)
22 Jalan Pantai, 5th Floor, Kota Kinabalu
Sabah, Malaysia
Tel.: 60 0218922
(Banking and finance)
Datuk Temenggong Ting Lik Hung, Vice Chairman

Kwong Lee Bank
82 Jalan Wong Ah Fook
Johor Bahru, Malaysia
Tel.: 60 07 222633
(Banking)

Malayan Banking
Menera Maybank, 100 Jalan Tun Perak
Kuala Lumpur 50050, Malaysia
Tel.: 60 03 2308833
Fax.: 60 03 2304027
(Banking)
Salleh Amran Mohd Jamian, General Manager

Oriental Bank
14th Floor, Menara Promet, Jalan Sultan Ismail
Kuala Lumpur 50250, Malaysia
Tel.: 60 03 2437088
Fax.: 60 03 2430906
(Commercial bank)
Rosman Bandu, Sr. Personnel Manager

Paramount Corp.
15th Floor, Wisma Hangsam, No. 1 Jalan Hang Lekir
Kuala Lumpur, Malaysia
Tel.: 60 03 2329827
Fax.: 60 03 2305186
(Property development, insurance, investment holding)
Y. B. Dato Teo Soo Cheng, Managing Director

Perwira Habib Bank Malaysia
Wisma SPK, Jalan Sultan Ismail
P.O. Box 10469, Kuala Lumpur, Malaysia
Tel.: 60 03 2432000
Fax.: 60 03 2437642
(Banking)
Tuan Haji Mohd Alam Abdul Rahman, General Manager

Public Bank
Bangunan Public Bank, 6 Jalan Sultan Sulaiman
50000 Kuala Lumpur, Malaysia
Tel.: 60 03 2741766
Fax.: 60 03 2742179
(Commercial bank)
Harry K. Menon, General Manager

Sime Darby
21st Floor, Wisma Sime Darby,
Jalan Raja Laut
Kuala Lumpur 50350, Malaysia
Tel.: 60 03 2914122
Fax.: 60 03 2987398
(Holding co.)
Anthony Yoon Hoon Wah,
Group Manager, Personnel

United Asian Bank
2 Jalan Bukit Timbalan
Johor Bahru, Malaysia
Tel.: 60 07 221028
(Banking)

United Malayan Banking Corp.
Kompleks Tun Abdul Razak,
Jalan Wong Ah Fook
Johor Bahru, Malaysia
Tel.: 60 07 222305
(Banking)

INDUSTRIAL MANUFACTURING

Asia Automobile Industries
11 Jalan 219, Federal Highway,
Petaling Jaya
Selangor 46100, Malaysia
Tel.: 60 03 7575349
Fax.: 60 03 7561453
(Automobile assembly)
P. H. Seng, Managing Director

Asiatic Development
12/F Wisma Genting, Jalan
Sultan Ismail
Kuala Lumpur 50250, Malaysia
Tel.: 60 03 2613733
Fax.: 60 03 2615304
(Agriculture)
Tan Sri Abdul Kadir bin Yusof,
Director

Associated Motor Industries Malaysia
Jalan Sesiku, 40000 Shah Alam
Selangor Darul Ehsan, Malaysia
Tel.: 60 03 5591601
Fax.: 60 03 5596962
(Motor vehicle assembly)
M. Arumugam, Personnel
Manager

Austral Amalgamated Tin
32nd Floor, Menara PNB, 201-A
Jalan Tun Razak
Kuala Lumpur, Malaysia
Tel.: 60 03 2616000
(Mining and dredging)
Dato Dr. Yahya Bin Ismail,
Director

Cement Industries of Malaysia
Bukit Ketri, Mukim of Chuping
Perlis, Malaysia
Tel.: 60 03 982006
Fax.: 60 04 982722
(Cement)
Mohd Saadullah Suhaimi,
Managing Director

Federal Aluminium
2025, Lorong Perusahaan 8, Prai
Industrial Complex
Prai 13600, Malaysia
Tel.: 60 04 307477
Fax.: 60 04 394142
(Aluminium products)
Chong Tet Phin, General
Manager

Kemayan Oil Palm
5E Foh Chong Bldg., 66 Jalan
Ibrahim
Johor Baru, Malaysia
Tel.: 60 07 3221946
(Oil, palm and cocoa products)
Dr. Siow Kon Sang, Chairman

RETAILING AND WHOLESALING

Arab-Malaysian Development
9th Floor, Bangunan Arab Malaysian, Jalan Raja Chulan
Kuala Lumpur 50200, Malaysia
Tel.: 60 03 2382322
Fax.: 60 03 2383112
(Textiles, fabrics, investment holding, property development)
Mdm Azian Hashim, Personnel Manager

SERVICE INDUSTRIES

Malaysian Airline System
33rd Floor, Bangunan MAS, Jalan Sultan Ismail
50250 Kuala Lumpur, Malaysia
Tel.: 60 03 2610555
Fax.: 60 03 2613472
(Airline)
Abdullah Mat Zaid, Personnel Director

Shin Min Daily News
87-88 Jalan Bangsar
Kuala Lumpur 59200, Malaysia
Tel.: 60 03 2748622
Fax.: 60 03 2748812
(Newspaper publisher)
Cheng Song Huat, General Manager

Tourist Development Corp. Malaysia
24-27 Floor, Menara Dato Onn
Putra World 50480 Trade Center
Kuala Lumpur, Malaysia
Tel.: 60 03 2935188
Fax.: 60 03 2935884
(Tourist promotion)
Y. M. Raja Tan Sri Mohar, Chairman of the Board

MAJOR INTERNATIONAL COMPANIES IN MALAYSIA

There are many international firms operating in Malaysia. They are classified by business area: Banking and Finance; Industrial Manufacturing; Retailing and Wholesaling; and Service Industries. Company information includes type of business and international parent company. Your chances of achieving employment are substantially greater if you contact the subsidiary company in Malaysia rather than the parent company in the home country.

BANKING AND FINANCE

Algemene Bank Nederland-Kuala Lumpur
71 Jalan Raja Chulan, P.O. Box 10094
Wisma Boustead, Kuala Lumpur, Malaysia
Tel.: 60 03 2416800
(Banking)
R. G. Nieuwenhujis, General Manager
Algemene Bank Nederland, Netherlands

Commerce International Merchant Bankers
20th Floor, Pernas International
Jalan Sultan Ismail
Kuala Lumpur 50250, Malaysia
Tel.: 60 03 2613411
(Merchant bank)
Sanwa Bank, Japan

Deutsche Bank
Apera-ULG Center, 84, Jalan Raja Chulan
Kuala Lumpur 50200, Malaysia
(Banking)
Heinz Pohlsen, General Manager
Deutsche Bank, Germany

Hongkong and Shanghai Banking Corp.
1 Jalan Bukit Timbalan
Johor Bahru, Malaysia
Tel.: 60 07 223355
(Banking)
Hongkong and Shanghai Banking Corp., Hong Kong

Morgan Grenfell
P.O. Box 112, UBN Tower, 10th Floor
10 Jalan P. Ramlee
Kuala Lumpur 50250, Malaysia
Tel.: 60 03 2326959
Fax.: 60 03 2327026
(Representative bank)
Sieh Kok Jiun, Representative
Deutsche Bank, Germany

National Australia Bank
23rd Floor, Bangunan Kuwasa, No. 5
Jalan Raja Laut
Kuala Lumpur 50350, Malaysia
Tel.: 60 03 2936111
Fax.: 60 03 29329722
(Banking)
B. Rowe, Representative
National Australia Bank, Australia

Rothmans of Pall Mall (Malaysia)
Virginia Park, Jalan Universiti, 46200 Petaling Jaya
Selangor Darul Ehsan, Malaysia
Tel.: 60 03 7566899
Fax.: 60 03 7558416
(Holding company)
Dato G. Vessey, Managing Director
Member of the Rothmans International Group, U.K.

Westpac Banking Corp.-Malaysia
Chung Khiaw Bank Bldg., 13th Floor
Jalan Raja Laut
Kuala Lumpur 50350, Malaysia
Tel.: 60 03 2920611
Fax.: 60 03 2980016
(Banking)
A. L. Ch'ng, Representative
Westpac Banking Corp., Australia

INDUSTRIAL MANUFACTURING

BASF Chemdyes
Lot 254 Lorong Perusahaan 10
Kawasan Perindustrian Perai
Perai Penang 13600, Malaysia
Tel.: 60 04 308488
Fax.: 60 04 307898
(Chemicals)
BASF Group, Germany

East Asiatic Company (Malaysia)
1 Jalan 205, 46050 Petaling Jaya
Selangor, Malaysia
Tel.: 60 03 7914233
Fax.: 60 03 7919416
(Rubber, pharmaceuticals, printing machinery, beer)
John Madsen, Managing Director
East Asiatic Co., Denmark

Ericsson Telecommunications
Jalan Sepana 15/3
P.O. Box 28, 40000 Shah Alam
Selangor, Malaysia
Tel.: 60 03 5591821
Fax.: 60 03 5593084
(Telecommunications equipment)
Aslan Mohamed, Divisional Manager
Telefonaktiebolaget Ericsson, Sweden

Fujitsu Component (Malaysia)
No. 1 Lorong Satu Kawasam
Perindustriam Parit Raja 86400
Batu, Pahat, Johore Bahru, Malaysia
Tel.: 60 7 481392
(Electronic components)
Fujitsu, Japan

General Electric Co. of Malaysia
Wisma GEC, Jalan 215-Templer
46050 Petaling Jaya, Selangor, Malaysia
Tel.: 60 03 7911388
Fax.: 60 03 7921350
(Communications equipment)
J. P. Hoare, Chief Operating Officer
General Electric Co., U.K.

Guinness Malaysia
Sungei Way Brewery
P.O. Box 144, Petaling Jaya
Selangor 46710, Malaysia
Tel.: 60 03 7763022
Fax.: 60 03 7740986
(Beer)
P. T. J. Banner, Managing Director
Guiness Overseas, U.K.

Malaysian Tobacco Co.
178/3 Jalan Sungai Besi, Peti Surat 10187
Kuala Lumpur 50910, Malaysia
Tel.: 60 03 2213066
Fax.: 60 03 2213130
(Cigarettes)
B. E. Wilkinson, Director
BAT Industries, U.K.

Matsushita Industrial Corp.
P.L.O. No. 1, Kawasan Perdaag Anga
81400 Bebas, KS No. 104, Senai
Johore, Malaysia
Tel.: 60 07 592668
(Electronic products, appliances)
Matsushita Electric Industrial Co., Japan

Nestle (Malaysia)
Resource Plaza, 4 Lorong Pesearan Barat
Petaling Jaya, Malaysia
Tel.: 60 03 7554466
(Food products)
Mohd Yusof Talif, Group Personnel Manager
Nestle, Switzerland

PERNAS NEC Telecommunications
Kawasan Perindustrian Ampang/Ulu Kelang Peti Surat 11
Kuala Lumpur, Malaysia
Tel.: 60 03 460188
Fax.: 60 03 4577659
(Telecommunications equipment)
A. A. Derwish, Executive Director
NEC Corp., Japan

Sanyo Industries (Malaysia)
73 Jalan SS22/23, Damansara Jaya
47400 Petaling Jaya
Selangor, Malaysia
Tel.: 60 03 7193164
Fax.: 60 05 830727
(Electronics, appliances)
Hajime Yoshida, Managing Director
Sanyo Electric Co., Japan

Shell Malaysia
Bangunan Shell off Jalan Semantan
Damansara Heights
Malaysia, Kuala Lumpur
Tel.: 60 03 2559144
(Oil and gas production)
Royal Dutch/Shell Group, Netherlands

Toshiba Electronics Malaysia
42507 Telok Panglima Garang
Kuala Langat Selangor, Malaysia
Tel.: 60 03 3526001
(Electronic products)
Y. Morimoto, Managing Director
Toshiba Corp., Japan

UMW Toyota Motor
Jalan 219, Federal Highway,
Petaling Jaya
Selangor 46100, Malaysia
Tel.: 60 03 7575666
Fax.: 60 03 7562745
(Motor vehicles)
Michael Lim Heenpok, Chief Operating Officer
Toyota Motor Corp., Japan

RETAILING AND WHOLESALING

BP Malaysia
9/F Wisma Damansara, Jalan Semantan
50490 Kuala Lumpur, Malaysia
Tel.: 60 03 2554322
Fax.: 60 03 2550387
(Petroleum products)
Stephen Pettit, Managing Director
British Petroleum Co., U.K.

NEC Sales (Malaysia)
13th Floor, Bangnana Arab-Malaysian
55, Jalan Raja Chulan, Letter Box No. 13c
Kuala Lumpur 50200, Malaysia
Tel.: 60 03 2387788
Fax.: 60 03 2387312
(Electronics, computers, communications equipment)
Noborn Sato, Managing Director
NEC Corp., Japan

Sanyo Sales & Service
No. 73 Jalan SS22/23,
Damansara Jaya, Petaling Jaya
Selangor 47400, Malaysia
Tel.: 60 03 7197001
Fax.: 60 03 7195946
(Televisions, VCRs, appliances)
Sanyo Electric Co., Japan

SERVICE INDUSTRIES

Ogilvy & Mather (Malaysia)
8th Floor, Wisma MCIS, Jalan Barat
46200 Petaling Jaya, Selangor, Malaysia
Tel.: 60 03 7569066
Fax.: 60 03 7554572
(Advertising)
Mike Murphy, Managing Director
WPP Group, U.K.

Saatchi & Saatchi Advertising
10th Floor, Wisma Damansara, Jalan Sri Semantan Dua
50490 Damansara Heights
Kuala Lumpur, Malaysia
Tel.: 60 03 2554333
Fax.: 60 03 2558105
(Advertising)
Pat Brett, CEO
Saatchi & Saatchi, U.K.

MAJOR NON-PROFIT ORGANIZATIONS IN MALAYSIA

Asia Pacific Broadcasting Union
P.O. Box 1164
Pejabat Pos
Jalan Pantai Baru
Kuala Lumpur 22-07, Malaysia
Tel.: 60 3 2743592

Asia-Pacific Institute for Broadcasting Development
P.O. Box 1137
Pejabat Pos
Jalan Pantai Baru
Kuala Lumpur 59700, Malaysia
Tel.: 60 3 444618

Association of Natural Rubber Producing Countries
148 Jalan Ampang
Kuala Lumpur 04-06, Malaysia
Tel.: 60 3 481735

CIOS-World Council of Management
c/o Malaysian Institute of Management
227 Jalan Ampang
Kuala Lumpur 16-03, Malaysia
Tel.: 60 3 425255

Consumer Interpol
IOCU Regional Office for Asia and the Pacific
P.O. Box 1045
Penang 10830, Malaysia
Tel.: 60 4 20391

International Natural Rubber Organization
MUI Plaza, 12th Floor
Jalan P. Ramiee
Kuala Lumpur 50250, Malaysia
Tel.: 60 3 2486466

International Rubber Association
Malaysian Rubber Exchange and Licensing Board
P.O. Box 10531
Kuala Lumpur 50716, Malaysia
Tel.: 60 2615566

International Society for the Developement of Organizations
No. 7, Jalan 16/3
Petaling Jaya
Selangor 46350, Malaysia
Tel.: 60 3 7571130

WHO Western Pacific Regional Centre for the Promotion of Environmental Planning and Applied Studies
P.O. Box 12550
Kuala Lumpur 50782, Malaysia
Tel.: 60 3 9480311

MAJOR HOTEL EMPLOYERS IN MALAYSIA

Holiday Inn
P.O. Box 2870
Damai Beach 93756, Malaysia
Tel.: 60 082 411777

Holiday Inn Johor Bahru
Jalan Dato Sulaiman,
Century Garden
Johor Bahru 80990, Malaysia
Tel.: 60 07 323800

Holiday Inn City Centre
Jalan Raja Luat
Kuala Lumpur 11586, Malaysia
Tel.: 60 03 2939233

Holiday Inn Damai Beach
P.O. Box 2870
Kuching 93756, Malaysia
Tel.: 60 082 411777

Holiday Inn Kuching
Jln Tunku Abdul Rahman
Kuching 93100, Malaysia
Tel.: 60 082 423111

Holiday Inn on the Park
Julan Pinang
Kuala Lumpur 10983, Malaysia
Tel.: 60 03 2481066

Holiday Inn Penang
Batu Ferringhi
Penang 111000, Malaysia
Tel.: 60 4 811601

Hyatt Saujana
Subang Int'l. Airport
Petaling Jaya 46710, Malaysia
Tel.: 60 3 746188

Palm Beach Hotel
Batu Ferringi Beach
Penang 111000, Malaysia
Tel.: 60 4 811621

Pan Pacific Kuala Lumpur Hotel
Jalan Putra
Kuala Lumpur 50746, Malaysia
Tel.: 60 03 4425555

Pan Pacific Resort Pangkor
Teluk Belanga (Golden Sands)
Pangkor Island 32300,
Perak, Malaysia
Tel.: 60 05 951091

Ramada Beach Resort
152 Sungai Karanj
Kuantan 26100, Malaysia
Tel.: 60 609 587544

Shangri-La Hotel
Magazine Rd.
Penang 10300, Malaysia
Tel.: 60 4 622622

Shangri-La Hotel
11 Jalan Sultan Ismail
Kuala Lumpur 50250, Malaysia
Tel.: 60 3 232 2388

INTERNATIONAL SCHOOLS IN MALAYSIA

International Schools Services
P.O. Box 5910
Princeton, NJ 08543

Dalat School
Tanjong Bungah Rd.
Penang, Malaysia
Tel.: 60 4 894369
(U.S. school, grades 1-12)

Kinabalu International School
Likas Bay Rd., Kota Kinabalu
Sabah, Malaysia
Tel.: 60 88 31871
(U.K.-Australian school)

International School of Kuala Lumpur
Jalan Kerja Ayer Lama,
Kuala Lumpur 68000, Malaysia
Tel.: 60 3 4560522
(U.S. school, K-12)

INDONESIA

The Republic of Indonesia consists of the largest archipelago in the world, with over 13,000 islands. About 6,000 of the islands are inhabited. The main islands are Java, Sumatra, Kalimtan (formerly Borneo), Sulawesi (formerly Celebes), and Irian Jaya. Most of the islands are mountainous and forested. The country stretches along the equator for a total of 735,000 square miles. Malaysia and Singapore are neighbors to the north, Papua New Guinea borders on the east, and Australia lies to the south.

Most Indonesians are ethnic Malays, with Chinese and Indian minorities in the cities. The population of Irian Jaya is Papuan, and people in the eastern islands are of mixed race. Bahasa Indonesian, a form of Malay, is the official language. Javanese and over 300 other regional dialects are spoken throughout the country. Chinese, English, and Dutch are all found in the business and academic communities. Nearly 90% of the population is Muslim, 5% is Christian, 2% Buddhist, and 2% Hindu.

Hindu culture reached Java about 2,000 years ago as small Hindu kingdoms were established along the Indian trading routes. Indian Buddhists arrived about 1,000 years ago and significantly influenced Indonesian culture. Islam arrived along the trading routes in the fifteenth century and rapidly became the majority religion. Hindus who rejected Islam fled to Bali, which remains today as the only island where a majority of the people are Hindu.

In the sixteenth century, traders from Portugal and Holland reached Indonesia. Dutch traders established their dominance over most of the region in the seventeenth century and the region was known as the Dutch East Indies. By 1750, Java was fully under Dutch control, but the outer islands were not subdued until the twentieth century.

Japan occupied Indonesia from 1942 to 1945 during World War II. Nationalists were allowed influence in the administration during the Japanese occupation. Following the Japanese withdrawal, nationalists proclaimed an independent republic. After 4 years of fighting, the Dutch retreated in 1949. Indonesian troops raided Malaysia until 1965, protesting the formation of the new republic. Malaysian and Indonesia ended hostilities in 1966. Indonesia annexed West Irian in 1969.

The leader of Indonesian independence, Sukarno, suspended the parliament in 1960 and became president for life in 1963. Sukarno followed nationalist economic and foreign policies. The Indonesian Communist Party attempted to seize power in 1965 but was crushed by the army. Over 300,000 communists and others were executed by the armed forces. Sukarno, suspected of favoring the communists, was gradually eased out of power. China cut off aid in 1967, igniting riots against the country's ethnic Chinese population. Indonesia and China began reestablishing diplomatic relations in 1990.

In 1967, General Suharto, the army chief, was named president. He has been reelected continuously since then and the government party, GOLKAR, dominates elections to the legislature. Opposition parties are allowed to contest elections but are generally restricted. Military leaders run most of the country's affairs. Indonesia has followed a policy favoring economic growth through development of the manufacturing sector and foreign investment.

INDONESIA'S LARGEST TRADING PARTNERS

Imports:	Japan	25%
	United States	12%
	Singapore	9%
Exports:	Japan	40%
	United States	18%
	Singapore	10%

Current Economic Climate

Indonesia is still primarily an agricultural country of small landholders. Enclaves of industrial manufacturing can be found in the large cities. The most prominent industries are petroleum, food processing, textiles, industrial manufacturing, mining, forestry, and agriculture. The government's economic policies favor investment in the manufacturing sector in order to lessen the country's dependence upon oil exports. Protective tariffs exist to allow local industry to grow and create a strong domestic market.

Indonesia's gross national product of $75 billion has grown steadily in recent years. GNP grew by 6% in 1990 and by 7% in 1989. Exports grew by 15% in 1990, but non-oil exports grew by only 10%. Imports grew by 20% in 1990, as a result of increased capital imports to equip new facilities. Rising consumer demand for luxury goods is also increasing imports.

Inflation topped 9% in 1990, up from 6% in 1989, and is expected to reach 7% in 1991. The government is attempting to hold down prices by keeping spending low and tightening monetary policy. Consequently, the country's private banks, which were deregulated in 1988, are now suffering from the government's anti-inflationary policies. Private lending by Indonesia's banks is credited with the tremendous growth rates enjoyed in recent years.

Indonesia has a huge population of nearly 170 million people, with an annual growth rate over 2%. About half of the population is under 20 years of age. Jakarta is the largest city, with 8 million inhabitants. Other large cities include Surabaja with 3 million, Medan with 1.7 million, and Bangdung with 1.5 million. Only a third of the population lives in urban areas, although that percentage is increasing. About two-thirds of the population lives on Java, making its population density one of the highest in the world. Some of the other islands are barely populated at all.

Regular business hours are from 8:00 am to 3:00 pm, Monday through Thursday. On Friday, most businesses close at 11:30 am for Muslim prayers. Saturday business hours are from 8:00 am to 2:00 pm. Labor laws limit the work week to 40 hours. Many foreign companies have been able to maintain a Monday through Friday, 8-hour schedule, with the weekends off.

Getting Around in Indonesia

Buses are probably the most convenient means of transportation in Indonesia, both within cities and between them. Taxis are widely available in the cities. Getting from island to island may best be accomplished by ferry. The government runs numerous sailing lines between most of the major islands. Rental cars are only occasionally found. The rail system connects the major cities of Java but is generally inadequate elsewhere.

Employment Regulations for Americans

Americans do not need a visa for stays of 60 days or less. A work permit is necessary to obtain legal employment. The employer must demonstrate that an Indonesian is not available for the job. Work permits are not granted for casual employment.

Americans will generally find getting a job in Indonesia quite difficult. The largest foreign investors, the Japanese, tend to hire their own nationals. Domestic companies in Indonesia are unlikely to hire foreigners at all. The banking industry, however, is rapidly expanding and lacks qualified personnel. Individuals with banking backgrounds may have a better chance than other foreigners of finding employment in Indonesia. Most of the Jakarta language schools recruit qualified English teachers abroad rather than hire casual teachers.

Organizations for Further Information

The following organizations, both in the U.S. and Indonesia, may be helpful in the job search. American embassies and consulates have commercial and/or economic sections that can provide you with business information and explain aspects of the local economy. World Trade Centers usually include many foreign companies operating in the country. Foreign government missions in the U.S. such as National Tourist Offices and embassies and consulates can furnish visas and information on work permits and other important regulations. They may also offer economic and business information about the country.

CHAMBERS OF COMMERCE

American Chamber of Commerce in Indonesia
Citibank Bldg., 8th Floor, J1 M.H. Thamrin 55
Jakarta, Indonesia
Tel.: 62 332602

American-Indonesian Chamber of Commerce
12 E. 41st St., Suite 701
New York, NY 10017
Tel.: (212) 637-4505

Indonesian Chamber of Commerce & Industry
Jalan Merdeka Timur No. 11
Jakarta Pusat, Indonesia
Tel.: 62 3670196

CONSULAR OFFICES

American Embassy-Commercial Section
Medan Merdeka Selatan 5
Jakarta, Indonesia
Tel.: 62 21 360360
Paul T. Walters, Commercial Officer

Embassy of the Republic of Indonesia
2020 Massachusetts Ave. N.W.
Washington, DC 20036
Tel.: (202) 775-5200

WORLD TRADE CENTER IN INDONESIA

World Trade Center of Indonesia
P.T. Jakarta Land, P.O. Box 3164/JKT
Level 10, Wisma Metropolitan
Jalan, Sudiman, Jakarta, Indonesia
Tel.: 62 584801

OTHER INFORMATIONAL ORGANIZATIONS

Indonesian Tourist Promotion Office
3457 Wilshire Blvd.
Los Angeles, CA 90010
Tel.: (213) 387-2078

Business Directories

Although not always easy to find, business directories can prove invaluable in the international job search. Most directories list company names, addresses, products and phone numbers. Some directories include executive names and titles and financial information about the company. These sources provide you with the names of the people to contact for employment information as well as financial data.

Kompass Indonesia. Annual publication of Kompass Division, P.T. Gramedia, 22 Jalan Palmera Selatan, Jakarta, Indonesia. Lists basic information on over 8,000 companies.

Standard Trade and Industry Directory of Indonesia. Biennial publication of P.T. Indira, 37 Jalan Dr., Samratulangi, Jakarta, Indonesia. Provides detailed information on 25,000 companies engaged in international trade.

MAJOR AMERICAN COMPANIES IN INDONESIA

Many American firms operate in Indonesia. The following companies are classified by business area: Banking and Finance; Industrial Manufacturing; Retailing and Wholesaling; and Service Industries. The company information includes type of business, contact name, and American parent company. Your chances of achieving employment are substantially greater if you contact the subsidiary company in Indonesia rather than the parent company in the U.S.

BANKING AND FINANCE

American Express Bank
Arthaloka Bldg.
2 Jalan Jenderal Sudirman
Jakarta, Indonesia
Tel.: 62 587401
(Banking, financial services)
James Kaul, Sr. Executive
American Express Co.

Asian & Euro-American Capital Corp.
JI Kebon Sirih 66-70
P.O. Box, 3259/JKT
Jakarta, Indonesia
(Investment banking, brokers)
Goldman Sachs & Co.

Bank of America
17 JI Medan Merdeka Selatan
P.O. Box 195
Jakarta, Indonesia
(International banking)
Bank of America

Bankers Trust Co.
JI M.H. Thamrin 59
Wisma Nusantara Bldg., 26th Floor
Jakarta, Indonesia
(Banking)
Bankers Trust Co.

Chase Manhattan
Jalan Medan Merdeka Barat 6
GPO Box 311
Jakarta, Indonesia
(International banking)
Chase Manhattan Bank

Chemical Bank
Level 10, Wisma Metropolitan
Kav 29
JI Jen
Sudirman, Jakarta, Indonesia
(Banking)
Chemical Bank

Citicorp Leasing Indonesia
Ji Jend Sudiram Kav 70A
Jakarta, Indonesia
(Banking)
Citicorp

First National City Bank
Jl M.H. Thamrin 55
P.O. Box 2463
Jakarta, Indonesia
(International banking)
Citibank

Manufacturers Hanover Trust Co.
Jl Thamrin 59
Jakarta, Indonesia
(Banking)
Manufacturers Hanover Trust Co.

Marine Midland Bank
M.H. Thamrin 59
P.O. Box 2680/JKT
Nusantara Bldg.
Jakarta Pusat, Indonesia
(Banking)
Marine Midland Bank

J.P. Morgan
Wisma Stephens
88 Jalan Raja Chulan (05-12)
Jakarta, Indonesia
(Banking)
J.P. Morgan

INDUSTRIAL MANUFACTURING

Abbott Indonesia
Jl Raya Jakarta-Bogor
Km 37-Cimanggis
Desa Sukamaju B
Bogor, West Java, Indonesia
Tel.: 62 21870436
(Pharmaceuticals)
R.H. Morhead, President
Abbott Labs.

Bristol-Myers Indonesia
Jalan Wahid Hasyim 19
Jakarta, Indonesia
(Pharmaceuticals, food)
Bristol-Myers Squibb Co.

Caltex Pacific Indonesia
Jl Thamrin
P.O. Box 158
Jakarta, Indonesia
(Petrochemicals)
Standard Oil of California

Georgia-Pacific Indonesia
Jl Prof. Kasuma Atmadja 83
Jakarta, Indonesia
(Lumber, paper, metals, chemicals, plastics)
Georgia-Pacific Corp.

Goodyear Indonesia
P.O. Box 5
Jalan Pemuda 27
Bogor, West Java, Indonesia
Tel.: 62 0251 22071
Fax.: 62 0251 28088
(Tires, tubes)
W.E. Koenig, President
Goodyear Tire and Rubber Co.

Goodyear Sumatra Plantations Co.
Merangir Estate
Padang, West Sumatra, Indonesia
(Tires)
Richard Lee, Chairman
Goodyear Tire & Rubber Co.

Johnson & Johnson Indonesia
17 Jalan Merdeka Selatan Pusat
Jakarta, Indonesia
Tel.: 62 21346095
(Hospital products)
M.S. Grewal, President
Johnson & Johnson

I.T.T. Far East & Pacific
Jl Gondangdia Lama No. 26
Mentang
P.O. Box 2401
Jakarta, Indonesia
(Electronics)
International Telephone & Telegraph Corp.

Marathon Oil Indonesia
P.O. Box 3293
Five Pillars Office Park
J.L. Leklem
M.T. Haryono No. 58
Jakarta, Indonesia
(Petroleum exploration)
Marathon Oil Co.

Mobil Oil Indonesia
Ratu Plaza
JI Jenderal Sudirman
Senayan, Jakarta, Indonesia
Tel.: 62 711211
(Oil exploration)
Abas Kartadinata, Sr. Vice President, Support Services
Mobil Oil Corp.

Monsanto Co.
11th Floor, Wisma Kosgoro Bldg.
Jakarta, Indonesia
(Chemicals, plastics, petrochemicals, fibers)
Monsanto Co.

Nabisco Brands
Tembakau B.V., PT
Taru Martani Baru, 2A
JI Arguiobang
Yogyakarta, Indonesia
(Foods, toys, cosmetics)
Nabisco Brands

Pacific Chemicals Indonesia
Jalan M H Thamrin 53
Jakarta, Indonesia
(Plastics)
Dow Chemical Co.

Phillips Petroleum Co. Indonesia
JI Melawai Raya No. 16
Keb. Baru, Jakarta, Indonesia
(Petrochemicals)
Phillips Petroleum Co.

R.J. Reynolds Indonesia
Rajawali Selatan 1
P.O. Box 3248
Jakarta, Indonesia
(Tobacco products)
R.J. Reynolds Tobacco

Richardson-Vicks Indonesia
Tifa Bldg. 8th Floor
JI Kuningan Barat 26
Jakarta 12710, Indonesia
Tel.: 62 5780333
Fax.: 62 5780093
(Pharmaceuticals)
E.A. Zaragoza, President
Richardson-Vicks

Rohm & Haas Asia
Summitmas Tower 4th Floor
JI Jend Sudirman Kav 61-62
Jakarta, Indonesia
(Plastics, paints)
Rohm & Haas Co.

Squibb Indonesia
Jalan Cimandiri 24
Cikini, Jakarta Pusat, Indonesia
(Pharmaceuticals)
M.A. Kitchen, President
Linson Investment

3M
P.O. Box 12/KBYT
Kebayoran Timur
Jakarta Selatan, Indonesia
(Abrasives, adhesives, chemicals)
3M Co.

Warner Lambert Indonesia
9th Floor, Arthaloka Bldg.
2 Jalan Jenderal Sudirman
Jakart, Indonesia
Tel.: 62 21 583172
Fax.: 62 21 587615
(Confectionary, pharmaceuticals)
Bobba Venkatadri, President Director
Warner Lambert Corp.

SERVICE INDUSTRIES

Avis Rent A Car System
JI DiPonegoro 25
Jakarta, Indonesia
(Car rentals)
Avis

Bechtel
JI Thamrin
P.O. Box 460
Jakarta, Indonesia
(Engineering, construction)
Bechtel Group

Coopers & Lybrand International
Wisma Metropolitan
P.O. Box 3376/JKT
Jalan Jenderal Sudirman
Kav 29, Jakarta, Indonesia
(Accountants, auditors)
Coopers & Lybrand International

Deloitte Haskins Sells International
P.O. Box 2134
Jakart, Indonesia
(Accountants)
Deloitte Haskins & Sells International

Diner's Jaya Indonesia International
Deeta Merlin Shopping Complex, 3rd. Floor
JI Galah Mada 3-5
P.O. Box 3128
Jakarta Pusa, Indonesia
(Credit card services)
Diner's Club International

Pan American World Airways
JI Thamrin
P.O. Box 2376
Jakarta, Indonesia
(Air transportation)
Pan American World Airways

Peat Marwick Mitchell Co.
3 JI Prof. Supomo SH
Jakarta, Selatan, Indonesia
(International accountants, consultants)
Peat Marwick Mitchell & Co.

Price Waterhouse
P.O. Box 2169/2473 JKT
Jakarta, Indonesia
(Accountants, auditors)
Price Waterhouse

MAJOR DOMESTIC COMPANIES IN INDONESIA

The following is a listing of the major domestic companies of Indonesia. They are classified by business area: Banking and Finance; Industrial Manufacturing; Retailing and Wholesaling; Service Industries. Company information includes type of business and contact name. These companies will generally hire their own nationals first but may employ Americans.

BANKING AND FINANCE

Bank Buana Indonesia
32-35 Jalan Asemka
Jakarta Barat 11110, Indonesia
Tel.: 62 672901
Fax.: 62 676916
(Banking, financial services)
Hendra Suryadi, President

Bank Bumi Arta Indonesia
12-14 Jalan Roa Malaka
Selatan, Jakarta 11230, Indonesia
(Banking, financial services)
Hadi Budiman, Chairman

Bank Bumi Daya
Bank Bumi Daya Plaza, 16/F
Jalan Imam Bonjol 61
Jakarta 10002, Indonesia
Tel.: 62 333721
Fax.: 62 330153
(Banking)
M. Safiudin, Managing Director

Bank Central Asia
27/30 Jalan Asemka
Jakarta 11110, Indonesia
Tel.: 62 021 671771
Fax.: 62 021 674336
(Banking, financial services)
Soedono Salim, Chairman

Bank Dagang Nasional Indonesia
Wisma Hayam Wuruk
JI Hayam Wuruk 8
Jakarta 10120, Indonesia
Tel.: 62 3803530
(Banking)
Syamsul Nursalim, President

Bank Dagang Negara
JI Mohammad Husni Thamrin 5
Jakarta Pusat, Indonesia
Tel.: 62 321707
(Banking)
Samadikun Hardjodarsono, President

Bank Duta
JI Kebon Sirih 12
Jakarta 10110, Indonesia
Tel.: 62 021 3800900
Fax.: 62 021 3801005
(Banking)
Drs Abdulgani, President

Bank Niaga
JI JI Muhammad Husni Thamrin 55
Jakarta Pusat, Indonesia
Tel.: 62 373672
(Banking)
Soedarpo Sastrosatomo, Chairman

Bank Pembangunan Indonesia
JI R.P. Soeroso 2-4
Jakarta 10002, Indonesia
Tel.: 62 021 321908
Fax.: 62 021 333644
(Banking)
Subekti Ismaun, President

Bank Rakyat Indonesia
P.O. Box 94
Jalan Jendral Sudirman 44-46
Jakarta 10210, Indonesia
Tel.: 62 588828
Fax.: 62 581363
(Banking)
Widodo Budidarmo, Chairman

Pan Indonesia Bank
Panin Bank Centre
JI Jendral Sudirman
Senayan, Jakarta, Indonesia
Tel.: 62 7394545
Fax.: 62 7200340
(Commercial banking)
Prijatna Atmadja, President

INDUSTRIAL MANUFACTURING

ASEAN Aceh Fertilizer
P.O. Box 09
Lhok Seumawe, Aceh, Indonesia
Tel.: 62 064522433
Fax.: 62 064522121
(Fertilizer)
Rahman Subandi, President

Federal Motor
JI Yos Sudarso
P.O. Box 3009
Jakarta, Indonesia
Tel.: 62 490709
(Automobile bodybuilders, assemblers)
Budi Setiadharma SH, Managing Director

Modern Photo Film Co.
JI Matraman Raya 12
Jakarta, Indonesia
Tel.: 62 883782
(Photographic equipment, home appliances)
Linda Sihaja, Chairman

Pertamina
P.O. Box 12
JI Merdeka Timur 1
Jakarta, Indonesia
Tel.: 62 3031
(Oil and gas exploration)
Abdul Rachman Ramly, President

Prospect Motor
Jalan Yos Sudarso (Sunter)
P.O. Box 31/JKU
Jakarta, Indonesia
Tel.: 62 490478
(Motorcar assembling)
Hadi Budiman, Chairman

RETAILING AND WHOLESALING

Kompas Morning Daily
26-28 Jalan Palmerah Selatan
Jakarta 10270, Indonesia
Tel.: 62 5483008
Fax.: 62 5486085
(Publisher)
Jakob Oetama, CEO

SERVICE INDUSTRIES

Garuda Indonesian Airways
15 Jalan Ir H. Juanda
Jakarta Pusat 01, Indonesia
Tel.: 62 370709
(Airline)
R.A.J. Lumenta, President

Tunas Indonesia Tour & Travel
Jl Abdul Muis 70A
Jakarta Pusat, Indonesia
Tel.: 62 355167
(Travel/tour services)
Endang Sulbi Suska

MAJOR INTERNATIONAL COMPANIES IN INDONESIA

There are many international firms operating in Indonesia. These companies will be classified by business area: Banking and Finance; Industrial Manufacturing; and Retailing and Wholesaling. The company information includes type of business, contact name, and international parent company. Your chances of achieving employment are substantially greater if you contact the subsidiary company in Indonesia rather than the parent company in the home country.

BANKING AND FINANCE

Banque Indosuez
17/F Wisma Bumiputera
Jl Jend Sudirman Kav 75
Jakarta 12910, Indonesia
Tel.: 62 5782949
(International banking)
M. Courjaret, Sr. Executive
Banque Indosuez, France

Deutsche Bank
Eurasbank Bldg.
Jalan Imam Bonjol 80
Jakarta, Indonesia
Tel.: 62 21 331092
Fax.: 62 21 335252
(Banking)
G.F. Strauch, General Manager
Deutsche Bank, Germany

Societe Generale
9th Floor, Wisma Kosgoro
53 Jl M.H. Thamrin
Jakarta 10350, Indonesia
Tel.: 62 320097
Fax.: 62 326573
(Banking, financial services)
B. Duboè, Chief Representative
Societe Generale, France

INDUSTRIAL MANUFACTURING

BAT Indonesia
Wisma Dharmala Sakti 17-18/F
Jalan Jend Sudirman 32
Jakarta 10220, Indonesia
Tel.: 62 5781825
Fax.: 62 021 5701128
(Cigarettes)
BAT Industries, U.K.

Bridgestone Tire Indonesia
18th Floor, Wisma Nusantara Bldg.
59 Jalan M.H. Thamrin
Jakarta, Indonesia
Tel.: 62 330871
(Rubber products, tires)
Sukanta Tanudjaja, Director
Bridgestone Corp., Japan

Unilever Indonesia
P.O. Box 1162
Jl HR Rasuna Said Kav B-9
Jakarta 12920, Indonesia
Tel.: 62 21 516190
Fax.: 62 21 516341
(Detergents, foods, cosmetics, chemicals)
A. Burgmans, Chairman
Unilever Group, Netherlands

RETAILING AND WHOLESALING

Astra-Graphia
Jl Kramat Raya 43
Jakarta, Indonesia
Tel.: 62 358634
Fax.: 62 359306
T.P. Rachmat, Chairman
(Copying machines, computers)
Astra International , Sweden

MAJOR NON-PROFIT ORGANIZATIONS IN INDONESIA

Association of South East Asian Nations
70 A, Jalan Sisingamangaraja
Jakarta, Indonesia
Tel.: 62 21 712272

International Federation for Family Health
Jalan Pasirkaliki 186
P.O. Box 504
Bandung, Indonesia
Tel.: 62 22 52902

MAJOR HOTEL EMPLOYERS IN INDONESIA

Bali Hyatt
P.O. Box 392
Szanur
Bali, Indonesia
Tel.: 62 361 88271

Hilton International
Jln. Jend. Gatot Subroto
Senayan
Jakarta, Indonesia
Tel.: 62 21 587981

Hotel Borobudur Intercontinental
P.O. Box 329 Jin Lapangan
Banteng Selaton
Jakarta, Indonesia
Tel.: 62 21 270108

Hotel Indonesia
JI. M.H. Thamrin
Jakarta, Indonesia
Tel.: 62 21 322008

Hyatt Aryaduta Jakarta
Jl Prapatan 44-48
Jakarta, Indonesia 10110
Tel.: 62 21 376008

Jakarta Hilton Intercontinental
Jalan Gatot Subroto
Senayan
Jakarta, Indonesia 10002
Tel.: 62 583051

Sari Pacific Jakarta
Jalan M H Thamrin
Jakarta, Indonesia 10340
Tel.: 62 323 707

INTERNATIONAL SCHOOLS IN INDONESIA

International Schools Services
P.O. Box 5910
Princeton, NJ 08543

Bamboo River International School
Serukam
Samalantan, Kalimantan Barat
Indonesia
(U.S. school, K-8)

BAMCO International School
Bukit Asam Mine Construction, Box 1
Tanjung Enim, South Sumatra
Indonesia
(U.S. school, pre-K-9)

Bandung Alliance School
Jalan Gunung Agung 14
Bandung, Java 40142
Indonesia
Tel.: 62 22 81844
(U.S. school, 1-6)

Bandung International School
JI. Drg. Suria Sumantri
Bandung, West Java
Indonesia
Tel.: 62 22 85615
(U.S.-U.K. school, pre-K-8)

Bogor Expatriate School
JI Papandayan 9
Bogor, West Java
Indonesia
Tel.: 62 251 24360
(U.K-U.S. school, K-7)

Bontang International School
Bontang, Kalimantan
Indonesia
Tel.: 62 21 375323
(U.S. school, K-8)

British International School
Kebon Nanas II
Kebayoran Lama, Jakarta
Indonesia
Tel.: 62 21 5484376
(U.K. school, pre-K-9)

Caltex American School
CPI Rumbai and Duri
Pekanbaru, Riao Sumatra
Indonesia
Tel.: 62 761 21377
(U.S. school, K-8)

Central Intermission School
Cabean Rt 5 RK I Mangunsari
Salatiga, Jawa Tengah
Indonesia
(U.S. school,1-12)

International School Of Lhokseumawe
Pioneer Camp
Summatra, Lhokseumawe
Indonesia
(U.S. school, pre-K-8)

ISS School at Tembagapura
Tembagapura, Irian Jaya
Indonesia
(U.S. school, K-8)

Jakarta International School
Jalan Terogong Raya 33, Jakarta
Indonesia
Tel.: 62 21 762555
(U.S., IB school, K-12)

Medan International School
Jln. Brastagi Km. 10
Medan, Sumatra
Indonesia
Tel.: 62 61 27099
(U.S. school, pre-K-9)

Semarang International School
Jalan Guntur 23, Candi Baru
Semarang, Central Java
Indonesia
Tel.: 62 24 315923
(U.S.-U.K. school)

Sentani International School
Sentani, Irian Jaya
Indonesia
Tel.: 62 967 21264
(U.S. school, 1-8)

Surabaya International School
Jl Kupang Indah IX/17,
Surabaya
Indonesia
Tel.: 62 31 69324
(U.S. school, 1-10)

PHILIPPINES

The Republic of the Philippines is an archipelago measuring over 115,000 square miles, about the size of Arizona. The country is located about 500 miles off of the southeastern coast of East Asia. The nearest neighbors are Taiwan to the north, Indonesia and Malaysia to the south, and China to the west. The Philippines includes over 7,000 islands, but most of the people and territory are on the 10 largest islands. Except for a few coastal plains, most of the land is mountainous.

Most Filipinos are descendents of Malays who migrated from Southeast Asia. Chinese form the next largest ethnic group. Large numbers of people of European descent are also present. The national language is Philippino, essentially a form of Tagalog. English is spoken by everyone and is an official language as well. About 85 other languages are also spoken. Over 80% of the population is Roman Catholic; Protestants comprise another 10% and Muslims 5%.

The Malays lived throughout the archipelago before the Europeans arrived, having traded with China and other parts of Asia for centuries. Magellan was the first European to visit the islands in 1521. By 1571, the Spanish had founded Manila and named the islands after King Philip II. Following the Spanish-American War, the Philippines were ceded by Spain to the United States in 1898.

A bloody, but unsuccessful, guerilla war against the U.S. was then fought by Filipino nationalists from 1899 to 1905. In 1934, the U.S. promised independence for the Philippines in 1946. Filipinos consequently note that their country spent "300 years in a convent and 50 years in Hollywood."

Japan attacked the Philippines in 1941 and occupied the islands during World War II. After the Japanese withdrawal, the Philippines became an independent republic on July 4, 1946. A communist rebellion was suppressed in 1954, but the country has continued to suffer from periodic political violence. The New People's Army is the current communist guerilla movement, and a Muslim separatist army is fighting on the island of Mindanao.

The Philippines maintained a democratic form of government until 1972, when President Ferdinand Marcos declared martial law and ruled by decree. In 1973, Marcos proclaimed a new constitution. His wife, Emelda, began supervising the country's economic development in 1978. Corruption and nepotism were widespread in the government, which also repressed civil liberties. As a result of population pressures, poverty and unemployment also rose during the Marcos era.

Opposition intensified after Marcos opponent Benigno Aquino was assassinated in 1983. Marcos called for snap elections in 1986, expecting to easily defeat the opposition. Aquino's widow, Corazon Aquino ran as the opposition candidate. Marcos was declared the winner, but massive vote fraud denied the legitimacy of his claim. On Feb. 26, 1986, Marcos fled the country after his supporters in the military deserted him and the U.S. urged him to resign. Aquino was immediately recognized as president, and a new constitution was adopted in 1987.

The Aquino government has attempted land reforms but has been unable to revive economic growth or to alleviate poverty. The military only partially backs her government and coup attempts have been frequent. The U.S. maintains two military bases in the Philippines whose leases are presently being renegotiated.

Current Economic Climate

The country has a gross national product of $38 billion and a per capita income slightly less than $700. GNP grew by 2.5% in 1990, down from 6% in 1989. Inflation is currently running at 15% and unemployment has averaged 8% in recent years. The government succeeded in securing a new loan of $375 million from the International Monetary Fund in 1991. Japan also promised $226 million in development aid. The country presently owes $30 billion in foreign debts.

Foreign investment in the Philippines is significant due to the country's cheap labor, weak currency, use of English, and preferential trading agreements with the United States. South Korea's Kia Motors is involved in a $34 million joint-venture with local investors to produce automobiles, called Columbian Autocar. Japanese companies are also quite active. Uniden is moving its manufacturing operations to the Philippines. In addition, Mitsubishi, Nissan, and Toyota have large investments.

The largest industries are textiles, food processing, pharmaceuticals, lumber and pulp, and consumer electronics. Important agricultural products include sugar, rice, pineapples, palm oil, and coconuts. About half or the workforce is engaged in agriculture or forestry.

The Philippines has a total population of 67 million people. Manila is the largest city, with nearly 4 million inhabitants and produces about one-third of the GNP. Quezon City is the next largest urban center, with nearly 2 million people. Cebu has about 1 million people and is growing at four times the national average. Almost half of the population lives in urban areas.

THE PHILIPPINES'S LARGEST TRADING PARTNERS

Imports:	Japan	20%
	United States	19%
	Southeast Asia	14%
	European Community	12%
Exports:	United States	38%
	Japan	20%
	European Community	17%
	Southeast Asia	10%

Getting Around in the Philippines

Philippine Air Lines flies into Manila and services most of the major cities. Air travel is the best way to get around the islands because they are divided by sea and mountains. Ferries can also provide transportation between the islands. The bus system is extremely comprehensive and cheap. Buses are probably the best way to get around, both within cities and between cities on an island. The rail system is rather poor and basically only services Manila. A Light Rail Transit system services the metropolitan Manila area. Rental cars are available.

Employment Regulations for Americans

Americans do not need a visa for stays of 21 days or less. Visitor visas can be obtained for longer stays. Work permits are necessary to gain legal employment. The employer must apply for the permit and demonstrate that a local worker can not fill the position.

Unemployment has been fairly high in the Philippines, making it difficult to find casual labor. In fact, thousands of unskilled Filipino workers typically go abroad seeking employment. Americans with particular skill, however, may find employment opportunities in the Philippines better than elsewhere in the Asia-Pacific region. English is the primary language, and the heritage of U.S. administration for 50 years makes the Philippines an easier adjustment for Americans than many other Pacific Rim countries.

Organizations for Further Information

The following organizations, both in the U.S. and the Philippines, may be helpful in the job search. American embassies and consulates have commercial and/or economic sections that can provide you with business information and explain aspects of the local economy. World Trade Centers usually include many foreign companies operating in the country. Foreign government missions in the U.S. such as National Tourist Offices and embassies and consulates can furnish visas and information on work permits and other important regulations. They may also offer economic and business information about the country.

CHAMBERS OF COMMERCE ORGANIZATIONS

American Chamber of Commerce of the Philippines
Corinthian Plaza, 2nd Floor
Paseo de Roxas, Legaspi Village
Makati, Metro Manila, Philippines
Tel.: 63 818 7911

European Chamber of Commerce of the Philippines
Electra House, 3rd Floor
115-117 Esteban St., Legaspi
Makati, Metro Manila, Philippines
Tel.: 63 854747

Federation of Filipino-Chinese Chamber of Commerce and Industry
Federation Center Bldg.
Muelle de Binondo Street

Manila, Philippines
Tel.: 63 474921

Philippine-American Chamber of Commerce, Los Angeles
c/o Philippine Consulate
447 Sutter Street
San Francisco, CA 94108
Tel.: (415) 433-6666

Philippine-American Chamber of Commerce, New York
711 3rd Ave., 17th Floor
New York, NY 10017
Tel.: (212) 972-9326

Philippine Chamber of Commerce & Industry
CCPF Bldg., Magallanes Dr..
Intramuros, Manilla, Philippines
Tel.: 63 481641

CONSULAR OFFICES

American Consulate, Cebu
PCI Bank, 3rd Floor, Gorordo Avenue, Lahug
Cebu, Philippines
Tel.: 63 2 5217116
Kathleen H. Manalo, Consular Officer

American Embassy, Commercial Section
1201 Roxas Blvd.
Manila, Philippines
Tel.: 63 2 5217116
Theodore J. Villinski, Commercial Officer

Embassy of the Philippines
1617 Massachusetts Ave. N.W.
Washington, DC 20036
Tel.: (202) 483-1414

OTHER INFORMATIONAL ORGANIZATIONS

Asian Development Bank, Manilla
2330 Roxas Blvd.
P.O. Box 789
Manilla, Philippines
Tel.: 63 2 807251

Department of Tourism
Department of Tourism Bldg.
Agrifina Circle, Manila, Philippines
Tel.: 63 2 599031

Philippine Convention & Visitors Corporation
Legaspi Towers 300, 4th Floor, Roxas Blvd.
Metro Manila, Philippines

Business Directories

Although not always easy to find, business directories can prove invaluable in the international job search. Most directories list company names, addresses, products, and phone numbers. Some directories include executive names and titles and financial information about the company. These sources provide you with the names of the people to contact for employment information as well as financial data.

American Chamber of Commerce Directory. Annual publication of the American Chamber of Commerce, Box 1578 MCC, Makati, Manila, Philippines. Contains basic information on several hundred American and Filipino companies engaged in bilateral trade.

Business Day's Top 1,000 Corporations in the Philippines. Published annually by Businessday Corp., 113 West Ave., Quezon City, Philippines. Lists basic information on over 3,000 companies.

Philippine Chamber of Commerce Directory. Biennial publication of the Philippine Chamber of Commerce, Chamber of Commerce Bldg., Magallanes Dr., Intramuros, Metro Manila 2801, Philippines. Lists financial data on member firms.

MAJOR AMERICAN COMPANIES IN THE PHILIPPINES

The following is a listing of the major American companies in the Philippines. They are classified by business area: Banking and Finance; Industrial Manufacturing; Retailing and Wholesaling; and Service Industries. Company information includes type of business, American parent company, and contact name where possible.

BANKING AND FINANCE

BA Finance Corp.
BAFC Bldg., Gamboa St., Legaspi Village
Makati, Metro Manila, Philippines
Tel.: 63 2 8161870
(Finance company)
Jose P. Mendoza, President
BankAmerica International

Bank of America
Dona Narcisa Bldg., 108 Paseo de Roxas
Makati, Metro Manila, Philippines
Tel.: 63 2 8158046
(Banking)
David Stahl, Country Manager
Bank America Corp.

Bank of Boston of the Philippines
Boston Bank Center, 6764 Ayala Ave.
Makati, Metro Manila, Philippines
Tel.: 63 2 8174906
(Banking)
Elena S. Lim, Chairman
Bank of Boston Corp.

Bankers Trust Co.
3/F Corinthian Plaza, Paseo de Roxas, Makati
Metro Manila, Philippines
Tel.: 63 2 8190231
(Banking)
Jose Camacho, Vice President
Bankers Trust New York Corp.

Chase Manhattan Bank
Filinvest Financial Center Bldg., 18th Floor, Paseo de Roxas
Makati, Metro Manila, Philippines
Tel.: 63 2 8189851
(Banking)
Douglas Asper, Vice President
Chase Manhattan Bank

Chemical Bank
Filinvest Bldg., 8758 Paseo de Roxas, Makati
Metro Manila, Philippines
Tel.: 63 2 8181011
(Banking)
Kai Jhin, General Manager
Chemical Bank

Citibank NA
Citibank Centre, 8741 Paseo de Roxas, Makati
Metro Manila, Philippines
Tel.: 63 2 8152000
(Banking)
N. Pamnani, Sr. Executive
Citibank NA

Manufacturers Hanover Trust Co.
P.O. Box 2674
Manila D-406 Philippines
(Banking)
Manufacturers Hanover Trust Co.

Merrill Lynch & Co.
Pacific Bank Bldg., 15th Floor, 6776 Ayala Ave.
Makati, Metro Manila, Philippines
(Securities, commodities)
Merrill Lynch Pierce Fenner & Smith

Security Pacific National Bank
11/F Metrobank Plaza, Sen. Gil Puyat Ave. Ext.
Makati, Metro Manila, Philippines
(Banking)
Security Pacific Corp.

Wells Fargo Bank
P.O. Box 5146, Makati
Metro Manila, Philippines
(Banking)
Wells Fargo Bank NA

INDUSTRIAL MANUFACTURING

3M Philippines
MCC P.O. Box 840, Makati, Rizal D-708
Metro Manila, Philippines
Tel.: 63 2 8177061
R. T. Rawa, CEO
(Chemicals, adhesives, consumer products)
3M Co.

Abbott Laboratories
102 EDSA, Mandaluyong
Metro Manila, Philippines
Tel.: 63 2 780041
(Pharmaceuticals)
Abbott Laboratories

Avon Cosmetics
150 East Rodriguez Jr. Ave., Libis
Quezon City, Metro Manila, Philippines
Tel.: 63 2 7222431
(Cosmetics)
David D. Guttierez, President
Avon Cosmetics

Borden International Philippines
Filipinas Life Bldg., 6786 Ayala Ave.
Makati, Metro Manila, Philippines
Tel.: 63 2 8161720
Fax.: 63 2 8176485
(Synthetic resins)
Romeo Garcia, Personnel Manager
Borden

Del Monte Philippines
Bugo, Cagayan de Oro City
Tel.: 63 3200
Fax.: 63 8174717
(Produce processing)
Michael J. Clark, Vice President-Personnel
Del Monte Fresh Fruit Co.

Exxon Chemical Eastern
New BPI Bldg., Ayala Ave., Makati
Metro Manila, Philippines
Tel.: 63 2 885356
(Petrochemicals)
Exxon Corp.

Ford Philippines
Bo Sucat, South Superhighway, Muntinlupa
Metro Manila, Philippines
Tel.: 63 2 8289851
(Assembly of motor vehicles)
J. Sagovac, Managing Director
Ford Group

General Electric Philippines
2291 Pasong Tamo Extention, Makati
Metro Manila, Philippines
Tel.: 63 2 8158761
Fax.: 63 2 8160423
(Electrical products)
Renato O. Romero, Vice President-Staffing
General Electrical Co.

General Motors Filipinas
Bo Almanza, Las Pinas
Metro Manila, Philippines
Tel.: 63 2 8011701
(Motor vehicles)
General Motors

Gillette (Philippines)
2318 Pasong Tamo Ext., Makati
Metro Manila, Philippines
Tel.: 63 2 8423154
(Razor blades, pens)
Brian Matthews, Manager
Gillette Co.

Goodyear Tire & Rubber Co. of the Philippines
790 Pasay Rd., Corner Pasong Tamo, Makati
Metro Manila, Philippines
Tel.: 63 2 892041
(Tires)
J. Polhemus, President
Goodyear Tire & Rubber Co.

W.R. Grace (Philippines)
Silangang, Canlubang Industrial Park
Canlubang, Laguna, Philippines
Tel.: 63 894 927343
Fax.: 63 894 927383
(Chemicals, packaging materials)
Manuel E. Ramos, General Manager
W. R. Grace & Co.

Johnson & Johnson (Philippines)
Fortune Bldg., Legaspi St., Legaspi Village
Makati, Metro Manila, Philippines
Tel.: 63 2 897031
(Pharmaceuticals, health care products)
Silver C. Queano, Director
Johnson & Johnson

Kimberly-Clark Philippines
Goodwill Bldg. 2nd Floor, 393
Sen. Gil J. Puyat Ave.
Makati, Metro Manila,
Philippines
Tel.: 63 2 886656
(Paper products)
C. T. Peralta, President
Kimberly-Clark Corp.

Kodak Philippines
2247 Pasong Tamo, Makati
Metro Manila, Philippines
Tel.: 63 2 8158851
Fax.: 63 2 8166718
(Photographic equipment and supplies)
R. Skow, President
Eastman Kokak Co.

Kraft Foods (Philippines)
Dr.. A. Santos Ave., Paranaque
Metro Manila, Philippines
Tel.: 63 2 8285546
(Foods)
Kraft Group

Levi Strauss (Philippines)
2264 Pasong Tamo Ext., Makati
Metro Manila, Philippines
Tel.: 63 2 862991
(Textiles)
Mike Lam, General Manager
Levi Strauss Group

Mobil Philippines
PITC Bldg., Tordesillas St.,
Salcedo Village
Makati, Metro Manila,
Philippines
Tel.: 63 2 8108501
(Chemicals, fuels)
M. V. Luna, Vice President
Mobil Group

Motorola Philippines
MCC P.O. Box 2231
Makati, Metro Manila,
Philippines
Tel.: 63 2 827911
(Electronics)
Motorola

Procter & Gamble Philippine Manufacturing Corp.
Solid Bank Bldg., 777 Paseo de Roxas
Makati, Metro Manila,
Philippines
Tel.: 63 2 8172921
(Soap, detergents)
Proctor & Gamble Co.

Reynolds Philippine Corp.
Combank Bldg., 11th Floor,
Ayala Ave.
Makati, Metro Manila,
Philippines
Tel.: 63 2 8100341
Fax.: 63 2 8170377
Henry W. Pinkey, General Manager
Reynolds International

Rohm & Haas Philippines
Metrobank Plaza 19th Floor,
G.J. Puyat Ave.
Makati, Metro Manila,
Philippines
Tel.: 63 2 855091
(Chemicals)
V. G. Floresca, CEO
Rohm and Haas Co.

Texas Instruments (Philippines)
Baguio Export Processing Zone,
33 Yangco Street
Baguio City, Philippines
(Wiring devices)
Texas Instruments

Wrigley Philippines
Pasigi, Rizal
Metro Manila, Philippines
Tel.: 63 2 6311745
(Gum)
Wm. Wrigley Jr. Co.

Warner-Lambert Philippines
National Life Insurance Bldg,
Ortigas Ave., San Juan
Metro Manila, Philippines
(Pharmaceuticals, gum, chemicals)
Warner-Lambert Co.

Country-by-Country Listings

RETAILING AND WHOLESALING

Bristol-Meyers
Mead Johnson Bldg., 2309
Pasong Tamo Ext.
Makati, Metro Manila,
Philippines
(Pharmaceuticals, toiletries,
household products)
Bristol-Meyers Squibb Co.

Coca Cola Export Corp.
807 EDSA, Quezon City
Metro Manila, Philippines
Tel.: 63 2 998701
(Beverages)
Coca Cola Group

Colgate-Palmolive Philippines
1049 J. P. Rizal St., Makati
Metro Manila, Philippines
Tel.: 63 2 8163711
Fax.: 63 2 8164455
(Household products, toiletries)
A. John Salter, Chairman
Colgate-Palmolive Co.

IBM Philippines
IBM Bldg., 8757 Paseo de Roxas,
Makati
Metro Manila, Philippines
Tel.: 63 2 8192000
(Information systems and
services)
Roberto R. Romulo, General
Manager
International Business
Machines

Monsanto Philippines
Commercial Center, P.O. Box
599
Makati, Metro Manila,
Philippines
Tel.: 63 2 8183966
Fax.: 63 2 8181202
(Agricultural chemicals)
Monsanto Co.

Pepsi-Cola Botting Co. of the Philippines
Rico Finance Bldg., 113 Aguirre
St., Legaspi Village
Makati, Metro Manila,
Philippines
Tel.: 63 2 8189826
(Beverages)
Peter K. Warren, Director
PepsiCo

Pfizer
Araza Bldg., 6th Floor, Paseo de
Roxas
Makati, Metro Manila,
Philippines
Tel.: 63 2 882621
(Pharmaceuticals, chemicals)
C. L. Sarris, Director
Pfizer

Upjohn
MCC P.O. Box 57, Makati
Manila, Philippines
(Pharmaceuticals, agricultural
products)
Upjohn Co.

SERVICE INDUSTRIES

American Airlines
P.O. Box 4297
Metro Manila, Philippines
(Airline)
American Airlines

Avis Rental Office
311 P. Casal Street
Metro Manila, Philippines
(Car rental)
Avis

Aero Asia
Manila Hilton, United Nations
Ave.
Manila, Philippines
(Airline)
Eastern Air Lines

ITT World Communications
P.O. Box 770, 669 United
Nations Ave.
Manila, Philippines 2801
(Telecommunications)
ITT World Communications

Price Waterhouse Philippines
BA-Lepanto Bldg., 7th, 8th and 15th Floor
8747 Paseo de Roxas, Makati
Metro Manila, Philippines
Tel.: 63 2 8187622
Fax.: 63 2 8153514
(Accountants)
Price Waterhouse & Co.

Trans World Airlines Inc
Ground Floor, Manila Hilton,
United Nations Ave.
Ermita, Manila, Philippines
(Airlines, hotels)
Trans World Airlines

MAJOR DOMESTIC COMPANIES IN THE PHILIPPINES

The following is a listing of the major domestic companies of the Philippines. They are classified by business area: Banking and Finance; Industrial Manufacturing; Retailing and Wholesaling; and Service Industries. Company information includes type of business and contact name. These companies will generally hire their own nationals first but may employ Americans.

BANKING AND FINANCE

Associated Bank
6793 Ayala Ave., Makati
Metro Manila, Philippines
Tel.: 63 2 8159017
(Banking)
Ramon T. Garcia, President

China Banking Corp.
China Bank Bldg., Dasmarinas,
Cor Juan Luna St., Binondo
Metro Manila, Philippines
Tel.: 63 2 482041
(Banking)
Gilbert Dee, Chairman

Development Bank of the Philippines
Corner Gil J. Puyat & Makati Avenues, Makati
Metro Manila, Philippines
Tel.: 63 2 8189511
(Financing)
Roberto F. de Ocampo, Director

Land Bank of the Philippines
LBP Bldg. I, 319 Senator Gil Puyat Ave, Makati
Metro Manila, Philippines
Tel.: 63 2 8189411
(Banking)
Deogracias N. Vistan, President

Philippine Banking Corp. (Philbank)
Philbank Bldg., Ayala Ave., Makati
Metro Manila, Philippines
Tel.: 63 2 8170901
(Banking)
John S. Gaisano, President

Philippine National Bank
P.O. Box 1844, Manila, Philippines
Tel.: 63 2 402051
Fax.: 63 2 496091
(Banking)
Edgardo B. Espiritu, President

Security Bank & Trust Co.
6778 Ayala Ave., Makati
Metro Manila, Philippines
Tel.: 63 2 8187677
(Banking)
Philip T. Ang, Director

United Coconut Planters Bank
UCPB Bldg., Makati Ave.,
Makati
Metro Manila, Philippines
Tel.: 63 2 8188361
Fax.: 63 2 8178131
(Banking)
Enrique M. Herbosa, President

INDUSTRIAL MANUFACTURING

Asia Brewery
Allied Bank Center,4th Floor,
Ayala Ave., Makati
Metro Manila, Philippines
Tel.: 63 2 8163421 to 40
Fax.: 63 2 8102386
(Brewery)
Roberto B. Tan, President

Atlas Consolidated Mining & Development
A. Soriano Bldg., 3rd Floor, 8776
Paseo de Roxas
Makati, Metro Manila,
Philippines
Tel.: 63 2 8190251
Fax.: 63 2 8153089
(Mining)
Rogelio C. Salazar, President

Benguet Corp.
Benguet Centre, 12 San Miguel
Ave.
Mandaluyong, Metro Manila,
Philippines 1501
Tel.: 63 2 7216801
Fax.: 63 2 7211291
(Mining, construction,
shipping)
Amado S. Lagdameo, Vice
President, Personnel

Fortune Cement Corp.
5/F ENZO Bldg., 399 Sen. Gil
Puyat Ave., Makati
Metro Manila, Philippines
Tel.: 63 2 8159436
(Cement)
Enrique Zobel, Director

Francisco Motors Corp.
2235 Pasong Tamo, Makati
Metro Manila, Philippines
Tel.: 63 2 8100131
(Motor vehicle assembly and
distribution)
F. T. Franscisco, President

Petron Corp.
Petron Bldg., 7901 Makati Ave.,
Makati
Metro Manila, Philippines
Tel.: 63 2 859061
Fax.: 63 2 8153094
(Petroleum and automobile
products)
Paul Limgenco, Vice President,
Human Resources

Philippine National Oil Co.
Petron Bldg., 7901 Makati Ave.,
Makati
Metro Manila, Philippines
Tel.: 63 2 8159061
Fax.: 63 2 8153094
(Petroleum products)
Paul Limgenco, Vice President,
Human Resources

Planters Products
Planters Products Bldg., Esteban
St., Legaspi Village
Makati, Metro Manila,
Philippines
Tel.: 63 2 858861
(Agricultural products)
A. Montelibano, President

San Miguel Corp.
40 San Miguel Ave.,
Mandaluyong
Metro Manila, Philippines
Tel.: 63 2 7223000
(Foods and beverages)
Jose B. Lugay, Division Manager
Human Resources

RETAILING AND WHOLESALING

National Book Store
701 Rizal Ave., Metro Manila,
Philippines
Tel.: 63 2 494306
Fax.: 63 2 9212411
(Books, school supplies)
Alfredo C. Ramos, President

SERVICE INDUSTRIES

Manila, Philippines Electric Co. (Meralco)
Ortigas Ave., Pasig
Metro Manila, Philippines
Tel.: 63 2 7219777
Fax.: 63 2 7224686
(Electric power co.)
Roberto M. Paterno, Vice President, Manpower Services

Philippine Airlines
PAL Administration Bldg.,
Legaspi St., Legaspi Village
Makati, Metro Manila,
Philippines
Tel.: 63 2 8180111
Fax.: 63 2 8109214
(Airline)
Dante G. Santos, President

Philippine Long Distance Telephone Co
Makati HQ, Makati Ave., Makati
Metro Manila, Philippines
Tel.: 63 2 8178865
(Telephone service)
Antonio O. Cojuangco,
President

MAJOR INTERNATIONAL COMPANIES IN THE PHILIPPINES

The following is a listing of the major international companies in the Philippines. They are classified by business area: Banking and Finance; Industrial Manufacturing; Retailing and Wholesaling; and Service Industries. Company information includes type of business, contact name where possible, and international parent company. Your chances of achieving employment are substantially greater if you contact the subsidiary compny in the Philippines rather than the parent company in the home country.

Country-by-Country Listings

BANKING AND FINANCE

Bank of Nova Scotia
Pioneer House Bldg., 108 Paseo de Roxas, Makati
Metro Manila, Philippines
Tel.: 63 2 8172021
(Banking)
Agnes B. Santos, General Manager
Bank of Nova Scotia, Canada

Banque Nationale de Paris
PCIB Tower II, Makati Ave.
Corner H V dela Costa Street
1200 Makati, Metro Manila, Philippines
Tel.: 63 2 8158821
Fax.: 63 2 8179237
(Banking)
J. Desmond Ormsby, Country Manger
Banque Nationale de Paris, France

Barclays Bank
Dolmar Gold Tower, 107 Alvarado St., Legaspi Village
Makati, Metro Manila, Philippines
Tel.: 63 2 8159291
(Banking)
Alan Anderson, Sr. Vice President
Barclays Bank , England

Credit Lyonnais
China Bank Bldg., Paseo de Roxas, Makati
Metro Manila, Philippines
Tel.: 63 2 8171616
Fax.: 63 2 8177145
(Banking)
J. M. Giovanetti, Chief Manager
Credit Lyonnais, France

Deutsche Bank
BPI Paseo de Roxas Condominium, 17th Floor
8753 Paseo de Roxas, 1200 Makati
Metro Manila, Philippines
(Banking)
Angelica Yap-Azurin, Manager
Deutsche Bank, Germany

Far East Bank & Trust Co.
Far East Bank Complex, Muralla St., Intramuros
Manila, Philippines
Tel.: 63 2 401021/30
(Banking and finance)
Octavio V. Espiritu, Vice President
Mitsui Bank, Japan; Chemical Bank, USA

Hongkong & Shanghai Banking Corp.
6780 Ayala Ave., Makati
Metro Manila, Philippines
Tel.: 63 2 8101661
(Banking)
B. Landells, Director
Hong Kong & Shanghai Banking Corp., Hong Kong

Societe Generale
Corinthian Plaza, Paseo de Roxas, Makati
Metro Manila, Philippines
Tel.: 63 2 856061
(Banking)
M. Sevin-Allouet, General Manager
Societe Generale de Belgique, Belgium

INDUSTRIAL MANUFACTURING

BASF Philippines
Emerald Bldg., 5th Floor
14 Emerald Ave., Ortigas Office Bldg.
Complex Pasig, Makati
Metro Manila 1299, Philippines
Tel.: 63 2 6731446
Fax.: 63 2 6733625
(Electronics, chemicals)
BASF Group, Germany

Bayer Philippines
Equitable Bank Bldg., Ortigas Ave, Greenhills, San Juan
Metro Manila, Philippines
Tel.: 63 2 7216011/21
(Pharmaceuticals)
Raimund Geyer, President
Bayer, Germany

NEC Technologies Philippines
Mectan Export Processing Zone
Standard Factory, Bldg. 2F
Lapu-Lapu, Cebu. Philippines
Tel.: 63 32 86669
Fax.: 63 32 86691
(Communications and computer equipment)
NEC Corp., Japan

Nestle Philippines Inc
Cabuyao, Laguna
Metro Manila, Philippines
Tel.: 63 2 8188706
(Beverages)
A. G. D. Gilmour, President
Nestle S.A., Switzerland

Pilipinas Shell Petroleum Corp.
Shell House, 156 Valero St.,
Salcedo Village
Makati, Metro Manila,
Philippines
Tel.: 63 2 8166501
(Petroleum products)
E. T. Francisco, Vice President, Personnel
Royal Dutch/Shell Group,
Netherlands

Pillsbury-Mindanao Flour Milling Co.
110 Legaspi St., Makati
Metro Manila, Philippines
Tel.: 63 2 8188082
(Flour milling)
Grand Metropolitan , England

Rohm Electronics Philippines
People's Technology Complex
Carmona, Cavite, Philippines
(Electronics)
Rohm Co. Ltd., Japan

Sanyo (Philippines)
Bagumbayan, Taguig
Manila, Philippines
Tel.: 63 2 8220201
(Electronics)
Sanyo Electric Co., Japan

Shell Chemical Co. (Philippines)
Shell House, 156 Valero St.,
Salcedo Village
Makati, Metro Manila,
Philippines
Tel.: 63 2 8166501
(Chemical Products)
Jaime Zobel de Ayala, President
Royal Dutch/Shell Group,
Netherlands

Smith Kline & French Overseas Co.
P.O. Box 229 MCC, Makati
Metro Manila 3117, Philippines
Tel.: 63 2 854223
(Pharmaceuticals)
Smith Kline Beecham, England

RETAILING AND WHOLESALING

Compania General de Tabacos de Filipinas
900 Romualdez St., Paco
Metro Manila, Philippines
Tel.: 63 2 508026/39
Fax.: 63 2 5219014
(Tobacco products)
D. Manuel Meler Urchaga, President
Compania General de Tabacos de Filipinas, Spain

Mitsui & Co.
17th Floor, Citibank Center Bldg.
8741 Pa Makati, Metro Manila
Philippines
Tel.: 63 2 892461
(Trading)
Mitsui & Co. Ltd., Japan

SERVICE INDUSTRIES

Jardine Davies
222 Sen. Gil Puyat Ave., Makati
Metro Manila, Philippines
Tel.: 63 2 45170
Fax.: 63 2 8160281
(Insurance, management services, trading)
Percy Weatherall, President
Jardine Pacific Holdings Ltd., Hong Kong

MAJOR NON-PROFIT ORGANIZATIONS IN THE PHILIPPINES

Asian Alliance of Appropriate Technology Practitioners
Yutivo Bldg.
270 Dasmarinas
Binondo, Manila, Philippines

Asian Association of Convention and Visitor Bureaus
Asian Institute of Tourism
University of the Philippines
Don Mariano Marcos Avenue
Dilman, Quezon City
Metro Manila, Philippines
Tel.: 63 2 995542

Asian-Pacific Postal Union
Post Office Bldg.
Plaza Bonifacio, Manila 2801, Philippines
Tel.: 63 2 470760

Association of Development Financing Institutions in Asia and the Pacific
PDCP Bldg., 2nd Floor
6758 Ayala Ave.
Makati, Metro Manila, Philippines
Tel.: 63 2 8161672

Association of Pediatric Societies of the Southeast Asian Region
1122 Gral. Luna Street
Ermita, Metro Manila, Philippines
Tel.: 63 2 507874

Center for the Development of Human Resources in Rural Asia
P.O. Box 458
Greenhills, Metro Manila 3113. Philippines
Tel.: 63 2 8274562

International Center for Living Aquatic Resources Management
MCC P.O. Box 1501
Makati, Metro Manila, Philippines
Tel.: 63 2 8180466

International Federation of Asian and Western Pacific Contractors' Associations
Padilla Bldg.
Emerald Ave.
Ortigas Commercial Complex
Pasig, Metro Manila, Philippines
Tel.: 63 6732097

Orient Airlines Association
Standard Bldg., 5th Floor
151 Paseo de Roxas
Makati, Metro Manila, Philippines
Tel.: 63 2 872525

South East Asia Iron and Steel Institute
507 Ortigas Bldg.
Ortigas Ave.
Pasig, Metro Manila, Philippines
Tel.: 63 2 6732161

MAJOR HOTEL EMPLOYERS IN THE PHILIPPINES

Century Park Sheraton Manila
Vito Cruz Corner, M
Adriatico Street
Manila, Philippines
Tel.: 63 596041

Hilton International
United Nations Ave.
Manila, Philippines
Tel.: 63 573711

Holiday Inn Manila
3001 Roxas Blvd.
Manila 3129, Philippines
Tel.: 63 597961

Hotel Intercontinental Manila
1 Ayala Ave.
Makati, Manila, Philippines
Tel.: 63 8159711

Hyatt Regency
2702 Roxas Blvd Pasay City
Manila 3129, Philippines
Tel.: 63 8312611

Hyatt Terraces
South Drive
Baguio City 0201, Philippines
Tel.: 63 5670

Inter-Continental
Ayala Ave Makati
Manila, Philippines
Tel.: 63 815 9711

Inter-Continental Punta Baluarte
Calatagan 4001, Philippines
Tel.: 63 81 59 711

Manila Peninsula
Ayala & Makati Aves.
Manila 3116, Philippines
Tel.: 63 8193456

Sheraton Century Park
Vito Cruz & M Adriatico
Manila, Philippines
Tel.: 63 501 201

Westin Philippine Plaza
Roxas Blvd
Manila 1000, Philippines
Tel.: 63 832 0701

INTERNATIONAL SCHOOLS IN THE PHILIPPINES

International Schools Services
P.O. Box 5910
Princeton, NJ 08543

Brent School
Brent Rd.
Baguio City, Philippines
Tel.: 63 4424050
(U.S., IB school, pre-K-12)

Brent School-Manila
University of Life Complex,
Mercalco Ave.
Pasig, Metro Manila, Philippines
(U.S., IB school, K-12)

Cebu International School
Banilad, Cebu City 6401,
Philippines
Tel.: 63 32 97268/70193
(U.S.-Filipino school)

Faith Academy
Victoria Valley Subdivision,
Valley Golf Rd.
Cainta, Rizal, Philippines
Tel.: 63 2 6950640
(U.S.-U.K. school, K-12)

International School
Gen Luna St. and Imelda Ave.
Bel Air
Makati, Metro-Manila,
Philippines
Tel.: 63 2 889891-95
(U.S., IB school, K-12)

BRUNEI

The State of Brunei Darussalam consists of a 2,200-square-mile encalve on the northern coast of Borneo in the Indonesian archipelago. Brunei is surrounded by the Malaysian state of Sarawak and the South China Sea. Brunei's 370,000 people are 65% Malay, 20% Chinese, with an ethnically diverse remainder. Malay, English, and Chinese are the principal languages. Muslims comprise 60% of the population, Buddhists 15%, and Christians 10%. Brunei's largest town is Bandar Seri Begawan, with 50,000 inhabitants.

The sixteenth century Brunei sultanate controlled all of Borneo and parts of the Philippines. In 1888 Britain established a protectorate that lasted until 1984. The Sultan of Brunei, Sir Muda Hassanal Bolkiah Mu'izzadin Waddaulah, is one of the world's richest individuals, personally owning much of the country and its resources. He contributed $10 million to the Nicaraguan contras in 1987. Brunei is extremely stable, although authoritarian.

Economic and Employment Climate

Brunei is almost completely dependent upon oil exports, which provide over 90% of the country's revenues. Bananas and rice are also grown. The Brunei dollar trades at the rate of 2 per U.S. dollar. The country has a gross national product over $3 billion, and a per capita income of about $20,000, although the distribution of wealth is extremely skewed. Manual labor may be found in the petroleum industry, although workers from neighboring countries already fill that role.

CONSULAR OFFICES

American Embassy, Commercial Section
P.O. Box 2991
Bandar Seri Begawan, Brunei
Tel.: 673 2 29670
James P. Wojtasiewicz, Commercial Officer

Embassy of the State of Brunei Darussalam
Watergate, #300, 3rd. Floor., 2600 Virgina Ave. N.W.
Washington, DC 20037
Tel.: (202) 342-0159

MAJOR AMERICAN COMPANIES IN BRUNEI

The following is a listing of the major American companies in Brunei. They are classified by business area: Banking and Finance; Industrial Manufacturing; and Service Industries. Company information includes type of business, American parent company, and contact name where possible.

BANKING AND FINANCE

American International Assurance
P.O. Box 2064, 2nd Floor
Wisma Hajjah Fatimah
Bandar Seri Begawan, Brunei
Tel.: 673 2 22007
(Insurance)
American International Assurance Co.

Bank of America
147 Jalan Pemancha
Bendar Seri Begawan, Brunei
Tel.: 673 2 23983
(Banking)
D.L. Hardy, Sr. Executive
Citibank

INDUSTRIAL MANUFACTURING

Christiansen Drilling Systems Sdnn.
Lot 4091 Jalan Kerma Negara
Kuala Belait, Negara Brunei Darussalam, Brunei
Tel.: 673 3 32686
(Petrochemicals)
Norton Co.

SERVICE INDUSTRIES

Weatherford Products & Services
Lot 4085
P.O. Box 910, Jalan Jaya Negara
Kuala Belait, Brunei
(Oilfield equipment and services)
Weatherford International

MAJOR DOMESTIC COMPANIES IN BRUNEI

The following is a listing of the major domestic companies in Brunei. They are classified by business area: Banking and Finance; Industrial Manufacturing; and Service Industries. Company information includes type of business and contact name. These companies will generally hire their own nationals first but may employ Americans.

BANKING AND FINANCE

Borneo Insurance
Bangunan Kambang Pasang, Unit 103
Jalan Gadong Mile 2
Bandar Seri Begawan, Brunei
Tel.: 673 2 20550
(Insurance)

International Bank of Brunei
Bangunan IBB, Lot 155-Jalan Roberts
P.O. Box 2725
Bandar Seri Begawan, Brunei
Tel.: 673 2 20676
Fax.: 673 2 21470
(Banking)

INDUSTRIAL MANUFACTURING

Hiap Hing Aluminum Works Co.
Seri Shopping Complex, Rm. 403
P.O. Box 2439
Bandar Seri Begawan, Brunei
Tel.: 673 2 25325
(Aluminum products)
Peter Ling, Managing Director

Hiap Lee Aluminum Works Co.
P.O. Box 1405
686 Jalan Gadong, Mile 6.5
Bandar Seri Begawan, Brunei
Tel.: 673 2 21569
Fax.: 673 2 60188
(Aluminum products)
Chong Vun Chiang, Chairman

SERVICE INDUSTRIES

Aryaduta
P.O. Box 2987, BR-1929
Bandar Seri Begawan
Tel.: 673 2 20202
(Contracting)
Kamaruddin Dato Hj Talib, Managing Director

L & L Engineering Corp.
409 Seri Shopping Complex, 1st Floor
Jalan Tutong
Bandar Seri Begawan, Brunei
Tel.: 673 2 21991
(Engineering, construction)
Pee Wong Kho, Chairman

MAJOR INTERNATIONAL COMPANIES IN BRUNEI

There are many international firms operating in Brunei. They are classified by business area: Banking and Finance; Industrial Manufacturing; Retailing and Wholesaling; and Service Industries. Company information includes type of business, contact name where possible, and international parent company. Your chances of achieving employment are substantially greater if you contact the subsidiary company in Brunei rather than the parent company in the home country.

BANKING AND FINANCE

Credit Corp.
Tang Ching Ying Bldg.,
Lot No. 1624, Ground Floor
Mile 2 Jalan Gadong, Bandar
Seri Begawan
Begawan 3180 Brunei
Tel.: 02 28245
(Financial services)
Standard Chartered, U.K.

Hongkong & Shanghai Banking Corp.
P.O. Box 59
Corner Jalan Sultan, Jalan
Pemancha
Bandar Seri Begawan, Brunei
Tel.: 673 2 42305
(Banking)
Hongkong & Shanghai Banking
Corp., Hong Kong

Malayan Banking
148 Jalan Pemancha
Bandar Seri Begawan, Brunei
Tel.: 673 2 42494
(Banking)
Wan Mohd Den, Branch
Manager
Malayan Banking ., Malaysia

Mortgage and Finance
Goodwood Bldg., Shops 3-4
P.O. Box 59, Bandar Begawan
Darussalam 3180, Brunei
Tel.: 673 2 27969
Fax.: 673 2 41316
(Financial services)
Chong Teng Fook, General
Manager
Hongkong & Shanghai Banking
Corp., Hong Kong

Standard Chartered Bank
51-55 Jalan Sultan
P.O. Box 186
Bandar Seri Bagawan, Brunei
Tel.: 673 2 42386
Fax.: 673 2 42390
(Banking)
M.G. Palin, Manager
Standard Chartered Bank,
England

INDUSTRIAL MANUFACTURING

Brunei Shell Petroleum
Seria Brunei
Tel.: 6733 73999
Fax.: 6733 72040
(Petrochemicals)
Royal Dutch/Shell Group of Co.,
Netherlands

RETAILING AND WHOLESALING

East Asiatic Co.
6 Bangunan Haji Tahir
Kampong Pengkalan Gadong
Bandar Seri Begawan, Brunei
Tel.: 673 2 22050
Fax.: 673 2 27526
(Printing equipment)
East Asiatic Co., Denmark

SERVICE INDUSTRIES

British Airways
Jalan Kianggeh
Bandar Seri Begawan, Brunei
Tel.: 673 2 43911
(Air transportation)
British Airways, U.K.

Cathay Pacific Airways
1101 Jalan Jawatan Dalam
Bandar Seri Begawan, Brunei
Tel.: 673 2 28642
(Air transportation)
Cathay Pacific Airways, Hong Kong

MAJOR HOTEL EMPLOYERS IN BRUNEI

Brunei Hotel
95 Jalan Pemancha
P.O. Box 50
Bandar Seri Begawan, Brunei
Tel.: 673 2 22372

National Inn
P.O. Box 1090, Batu 1-1/4 Jalan Tutong
Bandar Seri Begawan, Brunei
Tel.: 673 2 21128

Sheraton Utama Hotel
Jalan Bendahara
Bandar Seri Begawan 2087, Brunei
Tel.: 673 2 44272

Australia and New Zealand

AUSTRALIA

The Commonwealth of Australia forms an island continent southeast of Asia, lying between the Pacific and Indian oceans. Almost as large as the continental U.S., nearly 3 million square miles, the country has a varied geography, with a mountain range along the east coast and a large plateau in the west. The western parts of the country contain deserts while the northeastern portion of Australia enjoys a tropical climate.

As a result of immigration policies that favored Europeans until 1973, over 95% of Australians are of European descent, primarily from Great Britain. Asians comprise another 4%, and during the 1989-90 fiscal year, 40% of all immigrants came from Asia. In religious composition, Catholics, Anglicans, and other Protestant denominations each claim approximately 25% of the population.

The continent's original inhabitants, the Aborigines, number slightly over 200,000 people, including mixed-race individuals. Australia's aboriginal peoples lived on the continent for over 40,000 years before the Europeans arrived.

Willem Jansz of the Dutch East India Company was the first European to discover the continent, but he established no settlements. In 1770, James Cook reached the eastern coast at Botany Bay, then inhabited by a variety of peoples organized into tribes, which have since dissipated. The first European settlers arrived in 1788, primarily convicts, as well as military and administrative personnel. Free European settlers only began to arrive after 1830, when Britain successfully claimed the entire continent.

Australia became a commonwealth in 1901 and was granted self-rule in 1978. The country is organized as a federal commonwealth, recognizing Queen Elizabeth II as the titular head of state, with a national parliament based in Canberra. Although the Japanese bombed Darwin during World War II, no foreign troops have ever reached Australian soil. Australia participated in the Korean and Vietnam wars as well. Prime Minister Bob Hawke and his Labour Party have governed since 1983. Both Labour and the opposition Liberal and National parties accept a free-enterprise economic system with a welfare state.

In 1990, the Hawke government imposed tight monetary policies in order to curb inflation. Unfortunately, the lower-growth monetary policy coincided with the global recession, severely hurting the nation's economy. In December, 1990, the government cut interest rates to 12% in order to revive economic growth. While Bob Hawke's opinion poll ratings have declined during the recession, his opposition has failed to mobilize effectively as of mid-1991.

AUSTRALIA'S LARGEST TRADING PARTNERS
(figures rounded in billions of U.S. dollars)

Exports:	Japan	$12
	European Community	$ 6.2
	United States	$ 4.5
	Southeast Asia	$ 3.9
Imports:	European Community	$11
	United States	$10.2
	Japan	$9.8
	Southeast Asia	$2.9

Current Economic Climate

Australia is a highly industrialized state with iron, steel, machinery, textiles, automobiles, chemicals, ships, and aircraft ranking as the leading industries. Australia further benefits from large deposits of gold, coal, copper, iron, uranium, and zinc. In fact, mineral exports rose by 15% in 1990, leading the Australian export sector. The Australian dollar generally trades at a rate of 1.3 to the U.S. dollar.

The country is one of the world's leading agricultural exporters, particularly of beef, wheat, wool, and lamb. Yet, agricultural exports fell by 5% in 1990 due to the global recession. Wool exports actually fell by 40% in 1990. A lack of adequate rainfall during the 1990-91 planting season is expected to reduce the 1992 wheat harvest by up to 35%. Farmers are consequently shifting to other grains and crops.

The Hawke government is attempting to reduce the country's tariff barriers, currently averaging over 10% on most products and as high as 15% on some. The government plans to reduce all tariffs to 5% by 1993. Nonetheless, many industries such as automobiles and textiles will remain exempt from the reforms.

With a gross national product over $230 billion, Australians enjoy an extremely high per capita income of $14,500, the 15th highest in the world. About 40% of the workforce engages in manufacturing, 45% in services, and less than 10% in agriculture.

Inflation was 8% in 1989, then slowed to 6% in 1990, and is expected to continue falling to 5% in 1991. Over the same three-year period, unemployment increased from 6% to 9%, making it more difficult for foreigners to find work. Overall growth has also decreased from 3.4% in 1989 to recession levels in 1990. The economy actually shrank 1.6% in the last quarter of 1990. Australia's largest bank, Westpac, predicts that the economy will grow by less than 1% in 1991 but will recover to 3% in 1992.

Most of Australia's 17 million people live in the eastern states, particularly New South Wales, with nearly 6 million people and Victoria with over 4 million. The other Australian states include: Queensland, Western Australia, South Australia, and Tasmania, as well as the Northern Territory and the Australian Capital Territory. Despite the country's vast expanses of plateaus and arid areas, 85% of Australians live in urban areas. Almost one-third of Australia's people live in the two largest cities, Sydney, with over 3.5 million inhabitants, and Melbourne with over 3 million. Additionally, Brisbane, Adelaide, and Perth each contain over 1 million people.

Newspapers and Periodicals in Australia

Australia and New Zealand Banking Group
Australia and New Zealand Banking Group
55 Collins St.
Melbourne, Victoria 3000, Australia
Fax.: 61 03 6581276
(Business bank indicators)

Australian American Dialog
American Chamber of Commerce in Australia
50 Pitt St., 3rd Floor
Sydney, New South Wales 2000, Australia

Australian Banker
Australian Institute of Bankers
385 Bourke St.
Melbourne, Victoria 3000, Australia
Fax.: 61 03 6023923

Australasian Post
Southdown Press
32 Walsh St.
Melbourne, Victoria 3003, Australia

Bulletin
Australian Consolidated Press
Box 4088
Sydney, New South Wales 2001, Australia
(Incorporates The Australian Financial Times)

Overland
P.O. Box 249
Mount Eliza, Victoria 3930, Australia
Tel.: 61 03 7871545
(Literary/cultural interests, Australian affairs)

Quadrant
Australian Association of Cultural Freedom
404 Kent St., 5th Floor
Sydney, New South Wales 2000, Australia
Tel.: 61 02 2648152

The South Sea Digest
Pacific Publications
GPO Box 3408
Sydney, New South Wales 2001, Australia

The Sydney Morning Herald
John Fairfax & Sons
Box 506, Government Printing Office
Sydney, New South Wales 2001, Australia

Getting Around in Australia

The Australian rail system is generally slow but inexpensive. Special passes offering discounted or unlimited travel must be purchased before entering the country. The more popular routes also require advance reservations. Most lines run along the southern and eastern coasts, but suburban lines are also available in the major cities. The Austrailpass offers unlimited travel on virtually all lines for particular periods of time and can be purchased in Australia as well as in advance.

Australia's major airlines, Trans-Australia and Ansett, are the easiest means to travel between the major cities. Each of these carriers also offers special discounts and multi-use passes, which usually must be purchased prior to arrival in Australia.

Regional carriers include East West Airlines, Air New South Wales, Airlines of Northern Australia, Air Queensland, and Airlines of Western Australia. Quantas provides service to Australia from North America.

Bus travel is probably the cheapest and fastest way to get around. Both national bus services, Greyhound Australia and Pioneer Express, offer a wide array of discounted and unlimited travel passes. Bus reservations can be made with the line in Australia. Rental cars are also available and usually cost as much as in the U.S. Major highways are generally in good condition, but the smaller roads will vary in quality. The Australian Automobile Association provides services similar to the American Automobile Association.

Fruit picking dates in Australia

Temporary work can often be found in agricultural or fruit picking areas:

New South Wales: grapes (Feb.-Apr.), apples (Feb.-May), oranges (Sep.-Feb.), peaches (Feb.-Mar.), pears (Feb.-May).

Victoria: grapes (Feb.-Mar.), apples (Mar.-May), peaches (Jan.-Mar.), tomatoes (Jan.-Apr.), pears (Jan.-Mar.).

South Australia: grapes (Feb.-Apr.), oranges (May-July), peaches (Jan.-Feb.), apricots (Dec.-Jan.).

Western Australia: grapes (Feb.-Apr.), apples (Mar.-May), peaches (Dec.-Mar.), apricots (Dec.-Jan.).

Queensland: apples (Feb.-Mar.), peaches (Dec.-Mar.), tomatoes (Aug.-Nov.), pineapples (Jan.-Apr.).■

Employment Regulations for Americans

Americans must provide a visa to enter Australia. Proof of return or forward transportation will also be required for each visit. To work in Australia, apply to a consulate for a resident visa. This may take up to six months for processing. Unless you have relatives in the country, you must also demonstrate proof of employment. A tourist visa is easier to get, valid for six months, and renewable for another six months. However, tourist visas state that the bearer is ineligible to work. When applying for a job in Australia, it is highly recommended that you emphasize your experience in a particular line of work.

With its diversified and thriving economy, a wide variety of seasonal and temporary employment may be found in Australia. Employers have traditionally maintained a comparatively relaxed attitude toward employment regulations, but government agencies are now enforcing the rules more stringently than in the past. The authorities particularly focus upon large agricultural enterprises, where illegal foreign workers often find employment. Moreover, all employees are now required to apply for an official tax number, complicating undocumented employment; these can be applied for at Postal Service offices.

Some teaching jobs may be found in Western Australia, where temporary positions are occasionally available. You can contact the education office for Western Australia at:

Education Dept. of Western Australia
151 Royal St.
East Perth, Western Australia 6000
Australia

Festive employment

Temporary work, sometimes for only a day, can often be found at wine festivals, agricultural shows, major sporting events, and other festivities:

Festival of Sydney (Jan.): month-long arts and cultural festival

Royal Easter Show (Mar.): held in Sydney, the country's largest agricultural show

Barossa Valley Vintage Festival (Apr): biennial wine festival in South Australia

Melbourne Royal Show (Sep.): large agricultural show in Victoria

Royal Hobart Show (Oct.): agricultural show in Tasmania

Jacaranda Festival (Oct.): major festival in Grafton, New South Wales■

Workcamps for Volunteers

Volunteers can find work in various workcamps and other nature conservation projects. The Australian Trust for Conservation Volunteers (ATCV) is the country's best known workcamp program and can place foreigners throughout the country in projects primarily involving conservation, such as planting, path maintenance, seed collection, soil erosion work, and protection of flora and fauna. Ecumenical Work Camps is involved in building projects in New South Wales and in central Australia. The Involvement Volunteers organization sponsors projects concerning conservation work, archaeology, and environmental research throughout the country. Willing Workers on Organic Farms covers over 100 organic farms, which hire agricultural help throughout the year.

Australian Trust for Conservation Volunteers
National Head Office
Box 423
Ballarat, Victoria 3350, Australia

Ecumenical Work Camps
Australian Council of Churches
P.O. Box C199, Clarence St. Post Office
Sydney, New South Wales 2000, Australia

Involvement Volunteers
P.O. Box 218
Port Melbourne, Victoria 3207, Australia

Willing Workers on Organic Farms
Mt. Murrindal Reserve, West Tree
Via Buchan, Victoria 3885, Australia

You can also find a place to stay, which may or may not involve some kind of labor, on farms throughout Australia or with a local family. The exact location and type of accommodation will vary widely. The following organizations provide information on farm or family accommodations.

Bed and Breakfast International--Australia
18 Oxford St., P.O. Box 442
Woollahra, New South Wales 2025, Australia

Farm Holidays
9 Fletcher St.
Woollahra, New South Wales 2025, Australia

Host Farms Association
7 Abbott St.
North Balwyn, Victoria 3104, Australia

Organizations for Further Information

The following organizations, both in the U.S. and Australia, may be helpful in the job search. American embassies and consulates have commercial and/or economic sections that can provide you with business information and explain aspects of the local economy. World Trade Centers usually include many foreign companies operating in the country. Foreign government missions in the U.S. such as National Tourist Offices and embassies and consulates can furnish visas and information on work permits and other important regulations. They may also offer economic and business information about the country.

Country-by-Country Listings

CHAMBERS OF COMMERCE

American Chambers of Commerce in Australia, Adelaide
68 Grenfell St., 1st Floor
Adelaide, South Australia 5000, Australia
Tel.: 61 07 2240761

American Chambers of Commerce in Australia, Brisbane
66 Queensland St.. 23 Floor
Brisbane, Queensland 4000, Australia
Tel.: 61 07 2218542

American Chambers of Commerce in Australia, Melbourne
80 Collins St., Level 41
Melbourne, Victoria 3000, Australia
Tel.: 61 03 5415100

American Chambers of Commerce in Australia, Perth
231 Adelaide Terrace, 6th Floor
Perth, Western Australia 6000, Australia
Tel.: 61 09 3259540

American Chambers of Commerce in Australia, Sydney
50 Pitt St., 3rd Floor
Sydney, New South Wales 2000, Australia
Tel.: 61 02 2411907

Australian Chamber of Commerce
Commerce House, P.O. Box E139
Queen Victoria, Australian Capital Territory 2600, Australia
Tel.: 61 062 732381
Fax.: 61 062 733646

Canberra Chamber of Commerce
33 Ainslie Ave., Civic Sq., P.O. Box 190
Canberra City, Australian Capital Territory 2601, Australia
Tel.: 61 062 486344
Fax.: 61 062 476682

Chamber of Commerce & Industry of South Australia
136 Greenhill Rd., Unley
Adelaide, South Australia 5061, Australia
Tel.: 61 07 2211766
Fax.: 61 07 2216872

Hobart Chamber of Commerce
65 Murray St., GPO Box 969K
Hobart, Tasmania 7000, Australia
Tel.: 61 02 344325

State Chamber of Commerce & Industry, New South Wales
93 York St., P.O. Box 4280
Sydney, New South Wales 2001, Australia
Tel.: 61 02 2997888
Fax.: 61 02 2903278

State Chamber of Commerce & Industry, Queensland
243 Edward St., 8th Floor
GPO Box 1390
Brisbane, Queensland 4000, Australia
Tel.: 61 07 2211766
Fax.: 61 07 2216872

State Chamber of Commerce & Industry, Victoria
World Trade Centre, Level 1, Commerce House
Melbourne, Victoria 3005, Australia
Tel.: 61 03 6112233
Fax.: 61 03 6112266

Western Australian Chamber of Commerce & Industry
14 Parliment Pl., GPO Box D170
Perth, Western Australia 6005, Australia
Tel.: 61 09 3222688
Fax.: 61 09 4810980

CONSULAR OFFICES

American Consulate, Brisbane
383 Wickham Terr.
Brisbane, Queensland 4000, Australia
Tel.: 61 07 8398955

American Consulate General, Melbourne
24 Albert Rd.,
South Melbourne, Victoria 3205, Australia
Tel.: 61 03 6977900
Fax.: 61 03 6992608
Sandra A. Stevens, Consular Officer

American Consulate General, Perth
16 St., Georges Terr., 13th Floor
P.O. Box 6044
East Perth, Western Australia 6004, Australia
Tel.: 61 09 2211177
Fax.: 61 09 3253569
Charles M. Reese, Commercial Officer

American Consulate General, Sydney
Electricity House Cnr. Park and Elizabeth Sts., 36th Floor
Sydney, New South Wales 2000, Australia
Tel.: 61 02 2619200
Fax.: 61 02 2649908
Robert Taft, Commercial Officer

American Embassy, Economic/Commercial Section
Moonah
Canberra, ACT 2600, Australia
Tel.: 61 062 705000

Australian Consulate General, Chicago
One Illinois Center, Suite 2212
111 E. Wacker Dr.
Chicago, IL 60601
Tel.: (312) 645-9440

Australian Consulate General, Los Angeles
3550 Wilshire Blvd., Suite 912
Los Angeles, CA 90010
Tel.: (213) 469-4300

Australian Consulate General, New York
636 5th Ave.
New York, NY 10020
Tel.: (212) 245-4000

Australian Consulate General, San Fransisco
360 Post St.
San Francisco, CA 94108
(213) 469-4300

Embassy of Australia
1601 Massachusetts Ave. N.W.
Washington, DC 20036
Tel.: (202) 797-3000

WORLD TRADE CENTER IN AUSTRALIA

World Trade Center Melbourne
Cnr Flinoers and Spencer Sts.
P.O. Box 4721
Melbourne, Victoria 3001, Australia
Tel.: 61 03 6111999

OTHER INFORMATIONAL ORGANIZATIONS

Australian Development Assistance Bureau
P.O. Box 887
Canberra City, ACT 2601, Australia

Australian Home Accommodation
9 Westbourne Rd.
Kensington, Victoria 3031, Australia

Australian Institute of Travel & Tourism
309 Pitt St., 3rd Floor
Sydney, New South Wales 2000, Australia
Tel.: 61 02 2649616

Australian Tourist Commission, Head Office
324 St. Kilda Rd.
Melbourne, Victoria 3004, Australia

Australian Tourist Commission, Los Angeles
3550 Wilshire Blvd., Suite 1740
Los Angeles, CA 90010

Australian Tourist Commission, New York
636 Fifth Ave., Suite 467
New York, NY 10111

Australian Travel Industry Association
GPO Box 461
Canberra City, Australian Capital Territory 2601, Australia
Tel.: 61 062 571170

New South Wales Tourist Commission
2049 Century Park East, Suite 1736
Los Angeles, CA 90067

Northern Territory Government Tourist Bureau
31 Smith St.
Darwin, Northern Territory 5790, Australia

Northern Territory Tourist Commission
3550 Wilshire Blvd., Suite 1610
Los Angeles, CA 90010

Queensland Government Tourist Centre
Adelaide and Edward Sts.
Brisbane, Queensland 4000, Australia

Queensland Tourist and Travel Corporation
3550 Wilshire Blvd., Suite 1738
Los Angeles, CA 90010

South Australian Department of Tourism
3550 Wilshire Blvd., Suite 1740
Los Angeles, CA 90010

South Australian Government Travel Centre
18 King William St.
Adelaide, South Australia 5000, Australia

Student Travel Australia, Melbourne
220 Faraday St.
Carlton
Melbourne, Victoria 3053, Australia

Student Travel Australia, Sydney
1A Lee St.
Railway Square
Sydney, New South Wales 2000, Australia

Tasmanian Department of Tourism
3550 Wilshire Blvd., Suite 1740
Los Angeles, CA 90010

Tasmanian Government Tourist Bureau
80 Elizabeth St.
Hobart, Tasmania 7000, Australia

Travel Centre of New South Wales
16 Spring St.
Sydney, New South Wales 2000, Australia

Victorian Tourism Commission, Head Office
230 Collins St.
Melbourne, Victoria 3000,
Australia

Victorian Tourism Commission, Los Angeles
3550 Wilshire Blvd., Suite 1736
Los Angeles, CA 90016

Western Australian Tourist Commission
3550 Wilshire Blvd., Suite 1610
Los Angeles, CA 90010

10 MOST PROFITABLE AUSTRALIAN COMPANIES
(figures are rounded in millions of U.S. dollars for 1989 fiscal year)

	Company	Profit
1.	Broken Hill (Metals, petroleum, consumer products)	$800
2.	Westpac Banking (Banking)	$600
3.	National Australia Bank (Banking)	$580
4.	CRA (Mining and processing)	$450
5.	News Corp. (Broadcasting and publishing)	$380
6.	Elders IXL (Food wholesaling)	$360
7.	BTR Nylex (Manufacturing)	$400
8.	ANZ Group Holdings (Banking and finance)	$390
9.	Western Mining (Mining and processing)	$350
10.	Coles Meyer (Retailing)	$300

Business Directories

Although not always easy to find, business directories can prove invaluable in the international job search. Most directories list company names, addresses, products, and phone numbers. Some directories include executive names and titles and financial information about the company. These sources provide you with the names of the people to contact for employment information as well as financial data.

Australian-American Business Review/Directory. Published annually by Motivational Communications, Inc., 207 W. 21st St., New York, NY 10011. Contains 900 listings of trade and manufacturing firms engaged in both countries.

Australian Buying Reference. Annual publication of R.G. Riddell, 100 Alexander St., 1st Floor, Crows Nest, New South Wales 2065, Australia. Lists over 12,000 manufacturers and wholesalers.

Australian Exports. Published annually by Peter Isaacson Publications, 46-49 Porter St., Prahan, Victoria 3181, Australia. Covers over 1,000 firms involved in the export sector.

Australian Imports. Published annually by Peter Isaacson Publications, 46-49 Porter St., Prahan, Victoria 3181, Australia. Covers over 1,200 firms involved in the import sector.

Australian Key Business Directory. Annual publication of Dun & Bradstreet Australia, 24 Albert St., South Melbourne, Victoria 3205, Australia. Includes detailed financial information on nearly 18,000 firms.

Business Who's Who of Australia. Annual publication of R.G. Riddell, 100 Alexander St., 1st Floor, Crows Nest, New South Wales 2065, Australia. Lists about 9,000 firms, primarily mining companies and industrial manufacturers.

Kompass Australia. Published annually by Peter Isaacson Publications, 46-49 Porter St., Prahan, Victoria 3181, Australia. Covers over 20,000 firms in industrial manufacturing, wholesaling, and the service sector.

Trade Names of Australia. Published irregularly by Margaret Gee Media Group, 384 Flinders Lane, Melbourne, Victoria 3000, Australia. Contains basic information on industrial manufacturers and over 40,000 product trade names.

UBD Business to Business Directory. Published annually by Universal Press, 64 Talavera Rd., North Ryde, New South Wales 2113, Australia. Lists basic information on firms by region.

Who's Who in U.S. Business in Australia. Annual publication of the American Chamber of Commerce in Australia, 50 Pitt St., 3rd Floor, Sydney, New South Wales 200, Australia. Lists over 1,400 businesses involved in trade between Australia and the United States.

MAJOR AMERICAN COMPANIES IN AUSTRALIA

Many American firms operate in Australia. The following companies are classified by business area: Banking and Finance; Industrial Manufacturing; Retailing and Wholesaling; and Service Industries. The company information includes type of business, American parent company, and contact name where possible. Your chances of achieving employment are substantially greater if you contact the subsidiary company in Australia rather than the parent company in the U.S.

BANKING AND FINANCE

Alexander Stenhouse Australia Holdings
Exchange Center, 20 Bond St.
Sydney, New South Wales 2001, Australia
Tel.: 61 02 2310099
(Insurance brokers)
Noel Walters, Managing Director
Alexander & Alexander Services

American Express International
380 George St.
Sydney, New South Wales 2000, Australia
(Financial and travel related services)
American Express Co.

Bank of America
167 Macquarie St.
Sydney, New South Wales
2000, Australia
(International banking)
Bank of America

Bank of Boston
BHP House, 140 Williams St.
GPO Box 2273U
Melbourne, Victoria 3000,
Australia
(Commercial banking)
First National Bank of Boston

Bankers Trust Australia
Australia Square, Level 40
Sydney, New South Wales
2000, Australia
(Banking)
Bankers Trust Co.

BFC Finance
58-64 McQuarie St., P.O. Box
247
Parramatta, New South Wales
2223
Australia
(Holding company)
Beneficial Corp

Chase Manhattan Regional Office
AMP Tower, 535 Bourke St.
P.O. Box 5469 CC
Melbourne, Victoria 3001,
Australia
(International banking)
Chase Manhattan Bank North
America

Chemical Bank
CBA Center, 29 Level
60 Margaret St.
Sydney, New South Wales
2000, Australia
(Banking)
Chemical Bank

Cigna Insurance Australia
Cigna Building, 28-34 O'Connell
St.
Sydney, New South Wales
2000, Australia
Tel.: 61 02 2315166
(Insurance)
H.E. Hanway, Chairman
Cigna Corporation

Citibank N.A.
14th Floor, 257 Collins St.
Melbourne, Victoria 3000,
Australia
(International banking)
Citibank N.A.

First Boston Corporation
535 Bourke St.
Melbourne, Victoria 3000,
Australia
(Underwriter, distributor of
securities, financial services)
First Boston Corp.

First Chicago Australia
AMP Center, Level 12
50 Bridge St., GPO Box 4293
Sydney, New South Wales
2000, Australia
(Banking)
Ronald Enestrom, Managing
Director
First National Bank of Chicago

GMAC Australia
499 St. Kilda Rd.
P.O. Box 622E
Melbourne,Victoria 3001,
Australia
(Automobile financing)
General Motors Asseptance
Corp.

Hartford Fire Insurance
53-61 Walker St., P.O. Box 806
North Sydney, New South
Wales 2060, Australia
(Insurance)
AFIA

Marsh & McLennan
80 Alfred St.
Milson's Point, New South
Wales 1061, Australia
(Insurance)
Marsh & McLennan Cos.

Mellon Australia
525 Collins St.
Melbourne, Victoria 3000,
Australia
(Commercial & trade banking)
Mellon Bank North America

Merrill Lynch & Co.
Collins Wales House,
360 Collins St.
Melbourne, Victoria 3000,
Australia
(Brokers, securities,
commodities)
Merrill Lynch Pierce Fenner &
Smith

NCNB Australia Holdings
Level 55, MLC Centre
Sydney, New South Wales
2000, Australia
Tel.: 61 02 2350377
(Banking)
NCNB Corp.

Oxy Metal Industries
Canterbury Rd.
Kilsyth, Victoria 3137, Australia
(Insurance)
Occidental Life Insurance Co. of
California

Price Waterhouse & Co.
GPO Box 4177
Sydney, New South Wales
2001, Australia
(Accountants and auditors)
Price Waterhouse and Co.

**Security Pacific National
Bank**
20 Bond St.
Sydney, New South Wales
2000, Australia
Tel.: 61 02 2590759
(Banking)
Fred Kempson, Managing
Director
Security Pacific National Bank

Vigilant Insurance Co.
P.O. Box 427
Melbourne, Victoria 3000,
Australia
(Insurance underwriter)
Chubb & Son Inc

INDUSTRIAL MANUFACTURING

Abbott Australasia
P.O. Box 101
Cronulla, New South Wales
2230, Australia
(Pharmaceuticals, laboratory
products)
Abbott Laboratories

Aladdin Industries
43 Bridge Rd.
Stanmore, New South Wales
2048, Australia
(Vacuum bottles)
Aladdin Industries

Alberto-Culver Co.
14 Loyalty Rd.
North Rocks, New South Wales
2151, Australia
(Hair care products)
Graham Fish, Managing Director
Alberto-Culver Co.

Alcoa of Australia
535 Bourke St.
Melbourne, Victoria 3000,
Australia
(Bauxite, alumina, aluminum
products)
N.F. Stephen, Managing
Director
Aluminum Co. of America
(ALCOA)

Allen-Bradley
188 Whitehorse Rd.
Balwyn, Victoria 3103, Australia
(Electric motors, components)
Rockwell International Corp.

Allied Chemical
71 Queens Rd.
Melbourne, Victoria 3004,
Australia
(Chemicals, plastics, fibers)
Allied Corp.

Anaconda Australia
9th Floor, 130 Philip St.
GPO Box 2521
Sydney, New South Wales
2001, Australia
(Copper mining)
Anaconda Co.

Armco Australia
127-141 Bath Rd., P.O. Box 2
Sutherland, New South Wales
2232, Australia
(Steel products, construction, oil field equipment, insurance, finance leasing)
Armco International

Armstrong World Industries
P.O.Box 240
North Ryde, New South Wales
2113, Australia
(Interior furnishings, building products, auto and textile industries)
Armstrong World Industries

Australian General Electric
86-90 Bay St.
Ultimo, New South Wales 2007, Australia
(Diversified manufacturer of high-technology, electrical, and related products)
General Electric Co.

Australian Gulf Oil
Royal Exchange Building, 56
Pitt St., 16th Floor
Sydney, New South Wales
2000, Australia
(Petroleum and petroleum products)
Gulf Oil Corp

Bailey Controls Australia
26 Auburn Rd.
Regents Park, New South Wales
2143, Australia
Tel.: 61 02 6453322
(Analog and digital instrument controls and control systems)
Joseph Callus, Managing Director
Bailey Controls Co.

Beloit International
Village Gate, Suite 3
145-147 Canterbury Rd.
Melbourne, Victoria 3142 , Australia
(Paper making machinery and equipment)
Beloit Corp.

Bendix International Service Corp.
66 Dudley St.
West Melbourne, Victoria 3003, Australia
(Aircraft, electrical, communication, defense and environmental systems)
Bendix Aerospace

Borden Chemical Co.
46 Wellington Rd.
P.O. Box 57
Granville, New South Wales
2142, Australia
Tel.: 61 02 6814011
(Milk processing, dairy foods, specialty foods, chemicals, plastics)
R.W. Haigh, Managing Director
Borden

Borg-Warner
52 Lisbon St.
Fairfield, New South Wales
2165, Australia
(Air conditioning equipment, chemical and plastic products)
Borg-Warner Corp.

Bristol Babcock Controls
258 Rocky Point Rd.
P.O. Box 49
Ramsgate, New South Wales
2217, Australia
(Electronic and digital process control and instrument computer systems)
Bristol Babcock

Bristol-Myers Co.
345 Pacific Hwy.
Crows Nest, New South Wales
2065, Australia
(Cosmetics)
Bristol-Myers Squibb Co.

Buckman Laboratories
P.O. Box 672
Parramata, New South Wales
2150, Australia
(Chemicals and barite mining, industrial chemicals)
Buckman Laboratories

Country-by-Country Listings

Campbell Soups
Fawkner Center
499 St. Kilda Rd.
Melbourne, Victoria 3004,
Australia
(Food products)
Paul G. Bourke, CEO
Campbell Soup Co.

Carrier International Corporation
84 Pitt St.
Sydney, New South Wales 2000,
Australia
(Air conditioning, heating, refrigeration and power equipment)
Carrier International Corp.

Carter-Wallace
4 Powells Rd., P.O. Box 216
Brookvale, New South Wales
2100, Australia
(Pharmaceuticals and toiletries)
Carter-Wallace

Caterpillar of Australia
1 Sharps Rd., Private Mail Bag 4
Tullamarine, Victoria 3042,
Australia
(Earth/material handling and construction machinery, engines, generators)
Caterpillar Tractor Co.

Champion Spark Plug Co.
83 Bourke Rd.
Alexandria, New South Wales
2015, Australia
(Surgical supplies, hardware)
Kevin Maybury, Managing Director
Champion Spark Plug Co.

Clark Equipment Australia
30 Salesbury Rd.
Hornsby, New South Wales
2077, Australia
(Construction machinery, industrial trucks, heavy-duty drive line components)
Clark Equipment Co.

Colgate-Palmolive
109-113 Pitt St.
Sydney, New South Wales
2000, Australia
(Pharmaceuticals, cosmetics, toiletries, detergents)
Colgate-Palmolive Co.

Conoco Australia
Hays St., P.O. Box 6008
East Perth, WA 6000, Australia
(Oil, gas, coal, chemicals, minerals)
Conoco

Cooper Laboratories
1 Domic Place
Dee Way, New South Wales
2099, Australia
(Pharmaceutical products, dental products)
Cooper Laboratories

Cyanamid Australia
5 Gibbon Rd.
Baulkham Hills, New South Wales 2153, Australia
(Pharmaceuticals)
A.R. Bates

Data General Australia
30-32 Ellingworth Parade
Melbourne, Victoria 3123,
Australia
(Computers)
Data General Corporation

Davis & Geck Australia
59 Halstead St.
Hurtsville, New South Wales
2220, Australia
(Pharmaceuticals, chemicals, agricultural, and consumer products)
American Cyanamid Co.

Diamond Shamrock
Campbelfield, P.O. Box 66
Broadmeadows, Victoria 4061,
Australia
Tel.: 61 26355822
(Organic and inorganic chemicals and specialties; agricultural chemicals)
Diamond Shamrock Corp.

Dow Chemical
1000 Miller St.
North Sydney, New South Wales 2060, Australia
(Chemicals, plastics, fibers, pharmaceuticals)
G.S. Norris, Managing Director
Dow Chemical Co.

Dow Corning Australia
21 Tattersall Rd.
Blacktown, New South Wales 2148, Australia
(Silicones, silicon chemicals, solid lubricants)
Dow Corning Corp.

DuPont
P.O. Box 930
North Sydney, New South Wales 2060, Australia
(Chemicals, plastics, specialty products and fibers)
E. I. DuPont de Nemours & Co.

Duracell
P.O. Box 146
North Ryde, New South Wales 2113, Australia
(Batteries)
Duracell International

Eagle Signal Company of Australia
599-601 Victoria. St.
Abbotsford, Victoria 3067, Australia
(Widely diversified consumer products)
Gulf & Western Industries

Elizabeth Arden
GPO Box 4005
Sydney, New South Wales 2001, Australia
(Cosmetics, fragrances, toiletries)
Elizabeth Arden

Essex Laboratories
11 Gibbon Rd.
Baulkham Hills, New South Wales 2153, Australia
(Pharmaceuticals)
Shering Overseas

Exxon Chemical
160 Row St.
Eastwood 2122
Sydney, New South Wales 2000; Australia
(Petroleum and petroleum products)
Exxon Corp.

Faberge Australia
5 Woodcock Pl
Lane Cove, New South Wales, 2066, Australia
(Cosmetics, toilettries)
McGregor Corp.

Ford Motor Company of Australia
1735 Sydney Rd.
Campbellfield, Victoria 3061, Australia
(Motor vehicles, parts)
William Dix, Chairman
Ford Motor Co.

Garrett International
P.O. Box 142
Niddrie, Victoria 3042, Australia
(Aerospace research and systems, engines, electrical systems)
Garrett Aerospace

General Dynamics
P.O. Box 856
Canberra City, A.C.T. 2601, Australia
(Aircraft and marine systems, missiles and space vehicles, electronic systems)
General Dynamics Corp.

B F Goodrich Chemical
14 Queens Rd.
Melbourne, Victoria 3004, Australia
Tel.: 61 03 2676488
(Polyvinyl chloride resins)
John Herbig, Manager
B F Goodrich Co.

Goodyear Tire & Rubber Company of Australia
4-16 Yorong St. , Darlinghurst
Sydney, New South Wales 2010, Australia
(Tire, rubber products)
E.R. Culler, Chairman
Goodyear Tire & Rubber Co.

W.R. Grace Australia
1126 Sydney Rd.
Fawkner, Victoria 3060,
Australia
Tel.: 61 03 3592244
(Specialty chemicals, consumer services)
W.R. Grace & Co.

Heinemann Electric
81382 Springvale Rd., Box 241
Springvale, N. Victoria. 3171,
Australia
(Circuit breakers, relays, etc.)
Heinemann Electric Co.

Hughes Tool Company of Australia
420 George St.
Brisbane, Queensland 4000,
Australia
(Oil field equipment)
Hughes Tool Co.

Intel Australia
200 Pacific Hwy., 6th Floor
Spectrum 200
Crows Nest, New South Wales
2065, Australia
Intel Corp.

Kimberly-Clark of Australia
20 Alfred St.
Milsons Point, New South Wales
2061, Australia
(Fiber-based, pulp and forest products)
Kimberly-Clark Corp.

Kraft Foods
GPO Box 1673N
Melbourne, Victoria 3001,
Australia
(Dairy products, processed food, chemicals)
E.L. Smeds, Chairman
Kraft

Lilly Industries
Wharf Rd.
West Ryde, New South Wales
2114, Australia
(Pharmaceuticals, agricultural and cosmetic products)
Douglas Vawter, Managing Director
Eli Lilly & Co.

Lockheed Aircraft
P.O. Box 359
London Circuit
Canberra, A.C.T. 2601, Australia
(Aircraft, missiles)
Lockheed Corp.

Lubrizol Australia
28 River St.
Silverwater, New South Wales
2141, Australia
Tel.: 61 06 485122
(Industrial chemicals)
Lubrizol Corp.

Marathon Petroleum Australia
Hay St. E., P.O. Box 6192
Perth, Western Australia 6000,
Australia
Tel.: 61 09 3251988
(Minerals)
J.H. Brannigan, President
USX Corp.

Mary Kay Cosmetics
511 Burwood Hwy
Knoxfield, Victoria 3180,
Australia
Tel.: 61 03 2216144
(Cosmetics and toiletries)
John Watt, Managing Director
Mary Kay Cosmetics

Merck, Sharp, & Dohme
54-68 Ferndell St.
Granville, New South Wales
2142, Australia
(Pharmaceuticals, chemicals, and biologicals)
P.R. Bell, Managing Director
Merck, Sharp, & Dohme International

Monsanto Australia
Box 4077 Mail Exchange
Melbourne, Victoria 3001,
Australia
(Chemicals, plastics, petroleum products, man-made fibers)
Monsanto Co.

Motorola Australia
666 Wellington Rd., Mulgrave
Melbourne, Victoria
3170,Australia
(Televisions, radios, communciation equipment, semiconductors)
Christopher Barter, Secretary
Motorola

Olin Australia
1-3 Atchison St., P.O. Box 141
St. Leonards, New South Wales
3004, Australia
Tel.: 61 05 2221822
(Chemicals, metals, applied physics in electronics, defense, aerospace)
Neil W.S. Suggitt, Managing Director
Olin Corp.

Parke Davis
32-40 Cawarra Rd., Caringbah
Sydney, New South Wales
2229, Australia
(Pharmaceuticals, biologicals)
Parke Davis & Co.

Passiona Bottling Co.
363-369 Scaborough Beach Rd.
Osborne Park, Western Australia, Australia
(Carbonated beverages, soft drinks extract)
Canada Dry International Corp.

Pepsi Cola Co. of Australia
275 Alfred St.
North Sydney, New South Wales 2060, Australia
(Beverages, food products and services, sporting goods)
Pepsico

Pfizer
38-32 Wharf Rd.
Ryde West, New South Wales
2114, Australia
Tel.: 61 08 582666
(Pharmaceuticals, cosmetics, chemicals)
J.S. Baker, Manager
Pfizer Corp.

Phillips Petroleum International Australia
Captain Cook Dr.
Kurnell, New South Wales 2231, Australia
(Petrochemicals)
C.L. Wyndham, Chairman
Phillips Petroleum International Corp.

Playtex
104 Briens Rd.
Northmead, New South Wales
2145, Australia
(Intimate apparel, personal products, cosmetics, and fragrances)
International Playtex

Plough Australia
P.O. Box 130
North Ryde, New South Wales
2113, Australia
(Drugs and cosmetic products)
Plough

Polaroid Australia
Enden Park Estate 31, Waterloo Rd.
North Ryde, New South Wales
2113, Australia
(Photographic and optical products)
Frank Murphy, Manager
Poloroid Corp.

Purex Australia
76 Bonar St.
Arncliffe, New South Wales
2205, Australia
(Cleaning, household, and food products, chemicals)
Purex Industries

Quaker Products Australia
Sunshine Rd.
West Footscray, Victoria 3012, Australia
(Foods, pet foods, toys, chemicals)
Quaker Oats Co.

Raytheon Worldwide Co.
International Data Systems Division
50 Margaret St., GPO Box 4988
Sydney, New South Wales 2000, Australia
(Industrial tubes, radar and sonar systems, appliances, aviation, construction)
Raytheon Worldwide Co.

Revlon
122 Arthur St.
Sydney North, New South Wales 2060, Australia
(Cosmetics)
Revlon Manufacturing

R J Reynolds Tobacco, Australia
Northpoint Suite 2401
100 Miller St., Level 42
Sydney North, New South Wales 2060, Australia
(Cigarettes)
J.C. Vermeijden, Director
R.J. Reynolds Tobacco Co.

Richardson-Vicks
10-28 Biloela St.
Villawood, New South Wales 2163, Australia
Tel.: 61 02 7277888
(Pharmaceuticals)
G.C. Leonard, Managing Director
Richardson-Vicks

Rohm & Haas Australia
969 Burke Rd.
Camberwell, Victoria 3124, Australia
(Chemicals)
R.W. Watts, Manager
Rohm & Haas Co.

SmithKline & French Labs Australia
P.O. Box 89-90
Brookvale, New South Wales 2100, Australia
(Pharmaceuticals, diagnostic instruments, laboratory service)
SmithKline Corp.

E R Squibb & Sons
556 Prince's Hwy
Noble Park, Victoria 3174, Australia
(Pharmaceuticals)
E R Squibb & Sons

Standard Telephones & Cables
552-280 Botany Rd.
Alexandria, New South Wales 2015, Australia
(Electronic equipment)
International Telephone & Telegraph Corp.

Texaco Overseas Petroleum Co.
GPO Box 4991
Sydney, New South Wales 2001, Australia
(Exploration, petrochemicals)
Texaco

Texas Instruments Australia
P.O. Box 63
Elizabeth 5112, Australia
(Semiconductors, electrical controls)
Texas Instruments

3M Australia
P.O. Box 99
Pymble, New South Wales 2073, Australia
(Abrasives, adhesives, chemicals, diversified industrial and consumer products)
3M Co.

TRW Australia
Carrington Rd., P.O. Box 43
Marrickville, New South Wales 2204, Australia
(Electronics, computer services, automotive and aerospace products)
M. Gilles, Director
TRW

Union Carbide Australia
GPO Box 5322
Sydney, New South Wales 2001, Australia
(Carbon products, chemicals, plastics, gases)
Union Carbide Corp.

Uniroyal
1028-1042 South Rd.
Edwardstown, South Australia
5039, Australia
(Tires, tubes, and other rubber products, chemicals, plastics, textiles)
Uniroyal

Upjohn
P.O. Box 138
Parramatta, New South Wales
2150, Australia
(Pharmaceuticals, agricultural products, industrial chemicals)
Upjohn Co.

Valvoline
Wetherill Pk.
Smithfield, New South Wales
2164, Australia
(Petrochemicals, lubricants)
E.J. Lacey, Director
Valvoline

Vickers
Private Bag 15
Ascot Vale, Victoria 3032,
Australia
(Fluid power systems, compressors)
Vickers

Weyerhaeuser
Bennelong Rd.
Homebush Bay, New South
Wales 2140, Australia
(Wood, wood fiber products)
Weyerhaeuser Co.

RETAILING AND WHOLESALING

Abbott Australian Holdings Pty.
Captain Cook Dr.
Kurnell, New South Wales
2230, Australia
Tel.: 61 02 6689711
(Pharmaceuticals, professional equipment)
Brian Ritter, Managing Director
Abbott Labs

Addison-Wesley Publishing Company
6 Byfield St.
North Ryde, New South Wales
2113, Australia
Tel.: 61 02 8882733
(Scholastic books)
Derek Hall, General Manager
International Publishing Group

Amco Wrangler
213-219 Miller St.
North Sydney, New South
Wales, Australia
(Western wear jeans)
Wrangler

Amway of Australia
46 Carrington Rd., P.O. Box 202
Castle Hill, New South Wales
2145, Australia
(Household cleaning, nutrition, and diet commercial products)
Amway Corp.

Apple Computer Australia
37 Waterloo Rd., P.O. Box 371
North Ryde, New South Wales
2113, Australia
(Personal computers, peripherals, and software)
Apple Computer,

Avon Products
P.O. Box 180
Dee Way, New South Wales
2099, Australia
(Cosmetics, perfumes)
John Woods, Manager
Avon Products

Baldwin Australia
126 Bombany St.
Licombe, New South Wales
2141, Australia
(Pianos, organs)
Baldwin Piano & Organ Co.

Country-by-Country Listings

Beatrice Australia
71 Queens Rd., 6th Floor
Melbourne, Victoria 3004, Australia
(Food and consumer products, luggage, cosmetics)
Beatrice Companies

Bell & Howell Australia
47 Hartham Pl, P.O. Box 312
Artarmon, New South Wales 2064, Australia
(Audio/visual systems, communication, and information storage systems)
Bell & Howell Co.

Black & Decker
Maroondah Hwy.
Croydon, Victoria 3136, Australia
(Portable electric and pneumatic power tools, household products)
Black & Decker Co.

Borden Chemical Co.
46 Wellington Rd., P.O. Box 57
Granville, New South Wales 2142, Australia
(Dairy foods, specialty foods, chemicals, plastics)
Borden

Carnation Co.
130 Little Collins St., GPO Box 2631
Melbourne, Victoria 3001, Australia
(Milk products)
Carnation Co.

Carrier Air Conditioning
Seven Hills Rd.
Seven Hills, New South Wales 2147, Australia
Tel.: 61 02 8189700
(Air conditioning, heating, refrigeration, and power equipment)
David Daffey, Managing Director
Carrier International Corp.

CBS Records Australia
15 Blue St.
North Sydney, New South Wales 2060, Australia
(Recorded music, music publishing)
CBS Records Group Division

CIC International Corporation
P.O. Box 4040
Sydney, New South Wales 2001, Australia
(Film production and distribution)
Paramount International Films

Continental Carbon Australia
Private Bag
Cronulla, New South Wales 2230, Australia
(Carbon black manufacturing and sales)
Continental Carbon Co.

Digital Equipment Corporation
Northern Tower Chatswood Piz
Railway St.
Chatswood, New South Wales 2067, Australia
(Computers)
Maxwell Burnett, Manager
Digital Equipment Corp.

E.M.I.
P.O. Box 352
Haymarket, New South Wales 2000, Australia
(Phonograph records and albums, prerecorded tapes)
Capitol Records

Esso Australia
Esso House, 127 Kent St.
Sydney, New South Wales 2001, Australia
(Petrochemicals)
James F. Kirk, Chairman
Exxon Corp.

Fox Columbia Film Distributors
404-523 George St.
Sydney, New South Wales
2001, Australia
(Producer and distributer of motion pictures)
Columbia Pictures Industries

Franklin Mint
742 Springdale Rd.
Mulgrave, Victoria 3170,
Australia
(Creation and marketing of collectibles)
Franklin Mint Corp.

General Mills Creative Products
104 Bourke Rd.
Alexandria, New South Wales
2015, Australia
(Breakfast cereals, flour, cake mixes)
General Mills

General Motors-Holden's
GPO Box 1714
Melbourne, Victoria 3001,
Australia
(Automotive products and electronics)
John Bagshaw, President
General Motors Corp

Gillette
504-520 Princes Hwy.
Noble Park, Victoria 3174,
Australia
Tel.: 61 03 7904500
(Razors, blades, toiletries, small electrical appliances)
Kerry Gleeson, Manager
Gillette Co.

H.J. Heinz Co., Australia
P.O. Box 57
Dandenong, Victoria 3175,
Australia
(Food products)
Terrence Ward, Managing Director
H. J. Heinz Co.

Hewlett-Packard Australia
P.O. Box 221
Blackburn, Victoria 3130,
Australia
(Measurement and computation products and systems)
Hewlett-Packard Co.

Hoover Australia
P.O. Box 101
West Ryde, New South Wales
2114, Australia
(Floor care products, laundry appliances)
Hoover Worldwide Corp.

Kellogg
41-57 Wentworth Ave.
Pagewood, New South Wales
2019, Australia
Tel.: 61 02 6669541
(Food products)
M. John Cook, Manager
Kellogg Co.

Kentucky Fried Chicken
Yeo St., P.O. Box 333
Neutral Bay Junction, New South Wales, Australia
(Food marketing)
Kentucky Fried Chicken Corp.

Kinney Shoes
578-584 Swanston St.
Carlton, Victoria 3053, Australia
Tel.: 61 03 342133
(Footwear)
J.B. Williams, Managing Director
Kinney Shoe Corp.

Kodak
173-199 Elizabeth St.
Coburg, Victoria 3058, Australia
(Photo products, chemicals, information management)
Donald F. Hogarth, Chairman
Eastman Kodak Co.

Levi Strauss
41 McLaren St.
North Sydney, New South Wales 2060, Australia
(Wearing apparel)
Levi Strauss & Co.

Mattel
55 Queensbridge St.
South Melbourne, Victoria
3205, Australia
Tel.: 61 03 6452422
(Toys)
Donald Howell, Managing
Director
Mattel

McCormick Foods Australia
P.O. Box 342
Clayton, Victoria 3168,
Australia
(Spices, seasonings, condiments, teas)
Theodore H. McLendon,
Managing Director
McCormick & Co.

Memorex
61 Barry St.
Neutral Bay, New South Wales
2089, Australia
(Magnetic recording tapes)
Memorex Corp.

Metro-Goldwyn-Mayer
GPO Box 2576 E
Sydney, New South Wales
2000, Australia
(Motion pictures)
Metro-Goldwyn-Mayer Film Co.

Milton Bradley
Unit 6 Brodie St.
Rydalmere, New South Wales
2116, Australia
(Toys)
Barry Jones, Managing Director
Milton Bradley

Nabisco
424 St. Kilda Rd.
Melbourne, Victoria 3004,
Australia
(Meats, groceries)
I.A. Gittus, Chairman
Nabisco

NCR Australia
8-20 Napier St.
Sydney North, New South
Wales 2060, Australia
(Computers, semiconductors, printing)
NCR Corp.

Parker Pen
159 Cleveland St., P.O. Box 52
Chippendale, New South Wales
2008, Australia
(Writing instruments, temporary help, leisure apparel and equipment)
Parker Pen Co.

Pizza Hut Australia
11 Gibbon Rd.
Baulkham Hills, New South
Wales 2153, Australia
(Franchises and operates restaurants)
Pizza Hut

Rank Xerox
970-980 Pacific Hwy.
Pymble, New South Wales 2060,
Australia
Tel.: 61 02 9225055
(Copiers and duplicators, computers, data processing equipment, computer service)
Xerox Corp.

Richardson-Merrell
9 Help St., P.O. Box 469
Chatswood, New South Wales
2067, Australia
(Consumer health and personal care products)
Richardson-Vicks

Robert Harper & Co.
P.O. Box 177
Dunlop & Pickering Rds.
Mulgrave, Victoria 3170,
Australia
(Poultry and livestock feed, cereals, food products)
Ralston Purina Co.

Rotor Dynamics
1 Millers Rd., P.O. Box 134
Altona, Victoria 3018, Australia
(Electronic monitoring systems)
Bently Nevada Corp.

Sara Lee Corporation
610 Heatherton Rd.
Clayton, 3169, Australia
(Consumer packaged goods, food service distribution)
Sara Lee Corp.

Scholl-Plough Australia
13-15 Kilpa Rd.
Moorabbin, Victoria 3189,
Australia
(Footwear, drugs, sundries)
Scholl

Viacom International
31 Market St.
Sydney North, New South
Wales 2060, Australia
(Television distributor)
Anthony Manton, Managing
Director
Viacom International

Wang Computer
55 Herbert St.
St. Leonards, New South Wales
2065, Australia
(Rent/lease data processing
equipment)
Wang Labs.

Warner Bros.
49 Market St., Suite 3, 7th Floor
Sydney, New South Wales
2000, Australia
(Motion picture films,
television, music recording,
publishing)
Warner Bros.

SERVICE INDUSTRIES

Air Express International
Eleventh St., 292 Coward St.
Mascot, New South Wales
2020, Australia
Tel.: 61 02 6695191
(Air freight forwarder)
Air Express International Corp.

American Airlines
GPO Box 3261
Sydney, New South Wales
2001, Australia
(Air transportation)
American Airlines

Associated Press
364 Sussex St., Box K35
Haymarket
Sydney, New South Wales
2001, Australia
(News gathering agency)
Associated Press

AT&T Australia
CBA Centre, 21st Level
60 Margaret St.
Sydney, New South Wales
2000, Australia
Tel.: 61 02 2213055
(Telecommunications)
Rodney T. Halstead, Director
AT&T International

Australian Airborne
P.O. Box 486
Mascot, New South Wales 2020,
Australia
(Total air transportation
services)
Airborne Express

Avis Rent A Car System
212 Dryurgh St.
North Melbourne, Victoria
3000, Australia
(Car rentals)
Avis

Bechtel Pacific Corp.
303 Collins St.
Melbourne, Victoria 3001,
Australia
(Engineering, construction)
Bechtel Group

Brown & Root
5 Neil St.
Osborne Park, Western Australia
6016, Australia
(Construction, consulting)
Brown & Root

Budget Car Services
14 Queens Rd.
Melbourne, Victoria 3000,
Australia
(Car rentals)
Citicorp

Burlington Air Express
13 Rosebery Ave.
Sydney, New South Wales 2018, Australia
(Air express service)
Burlington Air Express

Leo Burnett
464 St. Kilda Rd.
Melbourne, Victoria 3004 , Australia
(Advertising agency)
Leo Burnett Co.

Burson-Marsteller
11 Queens Rd.
Melbourne, Victoria 3004, Australia
(Advertising, marketing research, sales promotion)
Marsteller International

Christian Science Monitor
57A Lucinda Ave.
Wahroonga, New South Wales 2076, Australia
(Publishing)
Christian Science Publishing Society

Collier Macmillan Australia
P.O. Box 52, Camperdown
North Ryde, New South Wales 2050, Australia
(Publishing, printing, textbooks)
Macmillan

Compton Advertising
41 McLaren St.
North Sydney, New South Wales 2060, Australia
(Advertising)
Compton International

Coudrey Dailey
213-219 Miller St.
North Sydney, New South Wales 2060, Australia
(Advertising agency, public relations)
Dailey & Associates

Deloitte Haskins & Sells International
GPO Box 243
Sydney, New South Wales 2001, Australia
(Accountants and auditing, tax and management advisory services)
Deloitte Haskins & Sells International

Diner's Club
394 Latrobe St.
Melbourne, Victoria 3000, Australia
(Credit card service)
Diner's Club International

Dun & Bradstreet
24 Albert Rd.
Melbourne South, Victoria 3205, Australia
Tel.: 61 03 6989400
(Business information services)
Marc Olsen, Managing Director
Dun & Bradstreet International

Grey Advertising Australia
420 Pacific Hwy.
Crows Nest, New South Wales 2065, Australia
Tel.: 61 02 4376300
(Advertising)
Garry R. Murphie, Managing Director
Grey Advertising

Greyhound International
Riley & Oxford Sts.
Darlinhurst, New South Wales 2010, Australia
(Bus lines)
Greyhound Corp.

H & R Block Australia
P.O. Box 147
Thorneigh, New South Wales 2120, Australia
(Income tax preparation and general public business service)
H & R Block

Harper & Row Australia
P.O. Box 226
Artarmon, New South Wales 2064, Australia
(Book publishers)
Harper & Row Publishers

Hertz Asia Pacific
390 St. Kilda Rd.
Melbourne, Victoria 3004,
Austrialia
(Automobile and truck leasing)
Hertz Corp.

Hilton International Co.
259 Pitt St.
Sydney, New South Wales
2000, Australia
(Hotel operations)
Hilton International Co.

Hyatt
Russell & Collins Sts.
Melbourne, Victoria 3000,
Australia
(International hotel
management)
Hyatt International Corp.

Korn-Ferry International
167 MacQuarie St., Top of Kyle
Sydney, New South Wales
2000, Australia
Tel.: 61 02 277941
(Executive search)
David Benn, Managing Vice
President
Korn-Ferry International

McCann-Erickson Advertising
Northpoint 100 Miller St.
North Sydney, New South
Wales 2060, Australia
Tel.: 61 29 235555
(Advertising)
Stephen Treble, Manager
McCann-Erickson Worldwide

McGraw-Hill Book Co. Australia
4 Baarcoo St.
Roseville East, New South Wales
2026, Australia
Tel.: 61 02 4064288
(Book publishing)
David Fowke, Managing
Director
McGraw-Hill

McKinsey & Co. Inc
50 Bridge St., 11th Floor
Sydney, New South Wales 2000,
Australia
(Management consultant)
McKinsey & Co.

Newsweek
100 Miller St.
North Sydney, New South
Wales 2060, Australia
(Publishing)
Newsweek International

A. C. Nielson
50 Miller St., P.O. Box 457
North Sydney, New South
Wales 2060, Australia
Tel.: 61 02 8872222
(Market research)
A. C. Nielson Co.

Ogilvy & Mather International
132 Arthur St.
North Sydney, New South
Wales 2065, Australia
Tel.: 61 03 5296566
(Advertising agency)
Renny Cunnack, Chairman
Ogilvy & Mather

George Patterson
394 LaTrobe St.
Melbourne, Victoria 3000,
Australia
(Advertising agency)
Ted Bates Worldwide

Peat, Marwick, Mitchell, & Co.
Tower Bldg. Australia Sq.
P.O. Box H67
Sydney, New South Wales 2000,
Australia
(International accountants,
consultants)
Peat, Marwick, Mitchell, & Co.

Prentice-Hall of Australia
7 Grosvenor Pl., P.O. Box 151
Brookvale, New South Wales
2100, Australia
Tel.: 61 02 9391333
(International group)
Simon & Schuster

Price Waterhouse & Co.
GPO Box 4177
Sydney, New South Wales
2001, Australia
(Accountants & auditors)
Price Waterhouse & Co.

Ramada International
c/o Thompson & Co.
47 Waymouth St.
Adelaide, South Australia 5000,
Australia
(Hotel operations)
Ramada

Sheraton Corporation
Nauru House
80 Collins St.
Melbourne, Victoria 3000,
Australia
(Hotel operations)
Sheraton Corp.

Spencer Stuart & Associates
Collins Wales House, 22nd Floor
360 Collins St.
Melbourne, Victoria 3000,
Australia
(Management)
Spencer Stuart & Assocs

SRI Australia
114 Williams St., 21st Floor
Melbourne, Victoria 3000,
Australia
(International consulting and
research)
SRI International

J. Walter Thompson Australia
St. Kilda Rd., P.O. Box 6182,
Central
Melbourne, Victoria 3004,
Australia
(Advertising)
J. Walter Thompson Co.

Time-Life International
Sun Alliance Building, 22-30
Bridge St.
Sydney, New South Wales
2000, Australia
(Magazine and book publishing,
forest products)
Time

TWA
GPO Box 5078
Sydney, New South Wales
2000, Australia
(Air transportation)
Trans World Airlines

United Cargo Corp.
John Fletcher
83 Murphy St., P.O. Box 271
Richmond, Victoria 3121,
Australia
(Air transportation)
United Air Lines

Walshes World
31 Murray St.
Hobart, Tasmania, Australia
(Air transportation)
Pan American World Airways

Warner Electric
2 Mary Parade
Ryde West, New South Wales
2114, Australia
Tel.: 61 02 6380414
(Sales advisors)
Dana Corp.

Westin Hotel Co. of Australia
61-101 Phillip St.
Sydney, New South Wales
2000, Australia
(Hotel management)
Westin Hotel Co.

Eric White Associates
115 Pitt St.
Sydney, New South Wales
2000, Australia
(Public relations, public affairs,
community counseling)
Hill & Knowlton

Young & Rubicam
1 York St.
Sydney, New South Wales
2000, Australia
(Advertising agency)
Young & Rubicam

MAJOR DOMESTIC COMPANIES IN AUSTRALIA

The following is a listing of the major domestic companies of Australia. They are classified by business area: Banking and Finance; Industrial Manufacturing; Retailing and Wholesaling; and Service Industries. Company information includes type of business and contact name. These companies will generally hire their own nationals first but may employ Americans.

BANKING AND FINANCE

Australia and New Zealand Banking Group
55 Collins St.
Melbourne, Victoria 3000, Australia
Tel.: 61 03 6582955
Fax: 61 03 6581769
(International and merchant banking services)
W.J. Bailey, CEO and Group Managing Director

Australian Mutual Provident Society
AMP Building, Alfred St.
Sydney Cove, New South Wales 2000, Australia
Tel.: 61 02 2575000
Fax: 61 02 2577886
(Insurance)
I.F. Stanwell, Managing Director

Bell Resources
R&I Tower
108 St. George's Terrace
Perth, Western Australia 6000, Australia
Tel.: 61 9 3246000
Fax: 61 9 3246081
(Investment)
Alan Bonds, Chairman

Edwards Dunlop & Co.
289 Clarence St.
Sydney, New South Wales 2000, Australia
Tel.: 61 02 2603000
(Holding company)
John Dunlop, Managing Director

Elders IXL
1 Garden St., P.O. Box 128
South Yarra, Victoria 3141, Australia
Tel.: 61 03 2492424
Fax: 61 03 2409310
(Finance and investment)
John Elliott, Chairman

FAI Insurances
FAI Insurance Bldg.
185 Macquarie St., 12th Floor
Sydney, New South Wales 2000, Australia
Tel.: 61 02 2211155
Fax: 61 02 2231144
(Insurance underwriter, investment, financial, and property services)
R.S. Adler, Chief Executive

National Australia Bank
500 Bourke St.
Melbourne, Victoria 3000, Australia
Tel.: 61 03 6413500
Fax: 61 03 6414196
(Banking)
Neil R. Clark, Managing Director

Westpac Banking Corp.
60 Martin Place
Sydney, New South Wales 2000, Australia
Tel.: 61 02 2263311
Fax: 61 02 2312661
(Banking and investment)
Stuart A. Fowler, Managing Director and CEO

INDUSTRIAL MANUFACTURING

Ampol
580 George St.
Sydney, New South Wales
2000, Australia
Tel.: 61 02 3644444
Fax: 61 02 3644700
(Petrochemicals, exploration)
Sir Tristan Antico, Chairman

Australian National Industries
Birnie Ave., P.O. Box 105
Lidcombe, New South Wales
2141, Australia
Tel.: 61 02 6484366
(Iron, steel, engines, machinery)
J.H. Leard, Managing Director

Boral
6-10 O'Cornell St., Norwich House, 10th Floor
Sydney, New South Wales
2001, Australia
Tel.: 61 02 920951
(Concrete, mining, petroleum)
Eric J. Neal, CEO

British Petroleum Company of Australia
1 Albert Rd.
Melbourne, Victoria 3004, Australia
Tel.: 61 03 2684111
Fax: 61 03 2683321
(Petrochemicals, exploration, technology)
Alex Gorrie, Chairman

Broken Hill Proprietary Co.
BHP House, 140 William St.
Melbourne, Victoria 3000, Australia
Tel.: 61 03 6093333
Fax: 61 03 6093015
(Petrochemicals, exploration, steel production)
Sir Arvi Hillar Parbo, Chairman

Comalco
55 Collins St., 38th Floor
Melbourne, Victoria 3000, Australia
Tel.: 61 03 6588300
Fax: 61 03 6583707
(Aluminum products)
J.T. Ralph, Chairman

Elders IXL
1 Garden St., P.O. Box 128
South Yarra, Victoria 3141, Australia
Tel.: 61 03 2492424
Fax: 61 03 2409310
(Brewing, agribusiness)
John Elliot, Chairman and CEO

Ford Motor Company of Australia
1735 Sydney Rd.
Campbellfield, Victoria 3061, Australia
Tel.: 61 03 3598211
Fax: 61 03 3571824
(Manufacturer of automobiles and parts)
John Miller, Manager, Public Affairs

Gibson Chemical Industries
350 Reserve Rd.
Cheltenham, Victoria 3192, Australia
(Disinfectants, deodorants)
John Ashcroft, Managing Director

ICI Australia
ICI House, 1 Nicholson St.
Melbourne, Victoria 3001, Australia
Tel.: 61 03 6657111
Fax: 61 03 6657937
(Industrial chemicals, paints, plastics, explosives, fertilizers)
B.A. Rowe, General Manager, Personnel

Pioneer International
580 George St., Level 20
Sydney, New South Wales
2000, Australia
Tel.: 61 02 3644000
Fax: 61 02 3644009
(Metals, minerals, petroleum, construction supplies)
Desmond John Quirk, Managing Director

RETAILING AND WHOLESALING

Amatil
71 Macquarie St.
Sydney, New South Wales
2000, Australia
Tel.: 61 02 2596666
Fax: 61 02 2596623
(Non-alcoholic beverages, foods, high technology communications)
D.R. Wills, Chairman

Burns Philp & Co.
7 Bridge St.
Sydney, New South Wales
2000, Australia
Tel.: 61 02 2591111
(Freight transport, paints, glass, wallpaper,foods, engineering)
J.D. Burns, Chairman

Coles Myer
800 Toorak Rd.
Tooronga, Victoria 3146, Australia
Tel.: 61 03 8293111
Fax: 61 03 8296860
(Department and food stores and outlets)
Brian Quinn, Chairman

McPhersons
525 Collins St.
Level 43 Rialto
Melbourne, Victoria 3000, Australia
Tel.: 61 03 3620301
(Consumer products, publishing, industrial engineering)
A.D. Lapthorne, Chairman

SERVICE INDUSTRIES

Ansett Transport Industries
501 Swanston St.
Melbourne, Victoria 3001, Australia
Tel.: 61 03 6681211
(Holding company, transportation, carriers, hotels)
V. Catterall, Personnel

Hooker Corp.
GPO Box 2724
Sydney, New South Wales
2001, Australia
Tel.: 61 02 2392222
(Contractors, real estate agents)
J.K. Campbell, Chairman

McConnell Dowell Corp.
65 Berry St., Level 6, The Denison
Sydney, New South Wales, Australia
(Construction)
A. Malcolm, Director

News Corporation
2 Holt Street
Sydney, New South Wales
2010, Australia
Tel.: 61 02 2883000
Fax: 61 02 9225908
(Newspaper, book, and magazine publisher)
Richard Henry Searby, Chairman

TNT
TNT Plaza, Tower One, Lawson Square
Redfern, New South Wales 2016, Australia
Tel.: 61 02 6992222
Fax: 61 02 6999238
(Freight transportation)
Fredrick Millar, Executive Chairman

MAJOR NON-PROFIT ORGANIZATIONS IN AUSTRALIA

Anzus Council
Department of Foreign Affairs
Canberra, Australian Capital Territory 2600, Australia

Commonwealth Council for Education Administration
c/o Basil W. Kings
University of New England, Faculty of Education
Armidale, New South Wales 2351, Australia
Tel.: 61 67 732543

Indo-Pacific Prehistory Association
Department of Prehistory and Anthropology
Australian National University
P.O. Box 4
Canberra, Australian Capital Territory 2601, Australia

International Association of Botanic Gardens
Botanic Gardens of Adelaide
North Terrace
Adelaide, South Australia 5000, Australia
Tel.: 61 08 2282320

International Association for Plant Physiology
c/o Plant Physiology Group
CSIRO Division of Food Research
North Ryde, New South Wales 2113, Australia
Tel.: 61 02 8878333

International Rural Sociology Association
University of Queensland, Department of Agriculture
St. Lucia, Queensland 4069, Australia
Tel.: 61 07 3773620

International Solar Energy Society
National Science Foundation
P.O. Box 52
Parkville, Victoria 3052, Australia
Tel.: 61 03 5562242

Law Association for Asia and the Western Pacific
170 Phillip St., 10th Floor
Sydney, New South Wales 2000, Australia
Tel.: 61 2 2212970

OMEGA Society
P.O. Box 5271
Rockhampton Mail Centre
Rockhampton, Queensland 4069, Australia

South Pacific Association for Teacher Education
c/o Faculty of Education
WAIT
South Bentley 6102, Australia
Tel.: 61 09 3507929

World's Women's Christian Temperance Union
c/o Olive E. Edwards
Cloverlea
Branxholm, Tasmania 7254,
Australia
Tel.: 61 03 546172

MAJOR HOTEL EMPLOYERS IN AUSTRALIA

Adelaide Travelodge
208 South Terrace
Adelaide, New South Wales
5000, Australia
Tel.: 61 08 2232744

Airport Travelodge
Melbourne Airport
Melbourne, New South Wales
3045, Australia
Tel.: 61 03 3382322

Cairns Parkroyal
17 Abbott St.
Cairns, Queensland 4870,
Australia
Tel.: 61 70 211300

Canberra City Travelodge
74 Northbourne Ave.
Canberra, New South Wales
2600, Australia
Tel.: 61 062 496911

Canberra Parkroyal
102 Northbourne Ave.
Canberra, New South Wales
2600, Australia
Tel.: 61 062 491411

Darwin Travelodge
122 The Esplanade
Darwin, Northern Territory,
Australia
Tel.: 61 89 815388

Gazebo Ramada Hotel
2 Elizabeth Bay Rd.
Sydney, New South Wales 2011,
Australia
Tel.: 61 02 3581999

Gazebo Ramada Hotel, Brisbane
345 Wickham Terrace
Brisbane, Queensland 4000,
Australia
Tel.: 61 07 2313131

Hilton International, Adelaide
233 Victoria Square
Adelaide, New South Wales
5000, Australia
Tel.: 61 08 2170711

Hilton International, Brisbane
190 Elizabeth St.
Brisbane, Queensland 4000,
Australia
Tel.: 61 07 2313131

Hilton International, Cairns
Wharf St.
Cairns, Queensland 4870,
Australia
Tel.: 61 70 521599

Hilton International on the Park
Cnr Wellington Parade &
Clarendon
Melbourne, New South Wales
3002, Australia
Tel.: 61 03 4193311

Hilton International Perth, Parmelia
Mill St.
Perth, Western Australia 6000,
Australia
Tel.: 61 09 3223622

Hilton International, Sydney
359 Pitt St.
Sydney, New South Wales 2000, Australia
Tel.: 61 02 2660610

Hilton International, Sydney Airport
20 Levey St.
Arncliffe, New South Wales 2205, Australia
Tel.: 61 02 5970122

Holiday Inn, Menzies
14 Carrington St.
Sydney, New South Wales 2000, Australia
Tel.: 61 02 20232

Hotel Intercontinental, Sydney
117 Mac Quairie St.
Sydney, New South Wales 2000, Australia
Tel.: 61 02 300200

Hyatt Canberra
Commonwealth Ave.
Canberra, New South Wales, Australia
Tel.: 61 062 701234

Hyatt on Collins
123 Collins St.
Melbourne, Victoria 3000, Australia
Tel.: 61 03 6571234

Hyatt Darwin
Commonwealth Ave.
Darwin, Northern Territory, Australia
Tel.: 61 89 3272622

Hyatt Regency
North Terrace
Adelaide, New South Wales 5000, Australia
Tel.: 61 08 3272622

Mayfair-Crest International Hotel
Cnr. Ann & Roma Sts.
Brisbane, Queensland 4000, Australia
Tel.: 61 07 2299111

Parkroyal Adelaide
226 South Terrace
Adelaide, New South Wales 5000, Australia
Tel.: 61 08 2234355

Parkroyal Brisbane
Cnr. Alice & Albert Sts.
Brisbane, Queensland 4000, Australia
Tel.: 61 07 2213411

Parkroyal Capital
1 Binara St.
Canberra, New South Wales, Australia
Tel.: 61 062 478999

Ramada Gazebo
345 Wickham Terr.
Brisbane, Queensland 4000, Australia
Tel.: 61 07 8316177

Ramada Reef Resort
Cnr. Veivers Rd. & William Esplanade
Cairns, Queensland 4879, Australia
Tel.: 61 70 553999

Regent of Melbourne
25 Collins St.
Melbourne, New South Wales 3000, Australia
Tel.: 61 03 6530000

Regent of Sydney
199 George St.
Sydney, New South Wales 2000, Australia
Tel.: 61 02 2380000

Sheraton Alice Spring Hotel
Barret Dr.
Alice Springs, Northern Territory 5750, Australia
Tel.: 61 08 9528000

Sheraton Ayers Rock Hotel
Yulara Dr.
Ayers Rock, Northern Territory 0872, Australia
Tel.: 61 89 562200

Sheraton Breakwater Casino/Hotel
Sir Leslie Thiess Dr.
Townsville, Queensland 4810, Australia
Tel.: 61 77 222333

Sheraton Brisbane Hotel & Towers
249 Turbot St.
Brisbane, Queensland 4000, Australia
Tel.: 61 07 8353535

Sheraton Darwin Hotel
32 Mitchel
Darwin, Northern Territory 5790, Australia
Tel.: 61 89 820000

Sheraton Hobart Hotel
1 Davey St.
Tasmania 7000, Australia
Tel.: 61 02 354535

Sheraton Mirage, Gold Coast
Sea World Dr., Main Beach
Gold Coast, Queensland 4217, Australia
Tel.: 61 75 911488

Sheraton Mirage, Port Douglas
Queensland 4871, Australia
Tel.: 61 70 985888

Sheraton Perth Hotel
207 Adelaide Terr.
Perth, Western Australia 6000, Australia
Tel.: 61 09 3250501

Sheraton Wentworth, Sydney
61-101 Phillip St.
Sydney, New South Wales 2000, Australia
Tel.: 61 02 2300700

Travelodge, Albury
Cnr Dean & Elizabeth St.
Albury, New South Wales 2640, Australia
Tel.: 61 60 215366

Travelodge Brisbane City
Roma St.
Brisbane, Queensland 4000, Australia
Tel.: 61 07 2382222

NEW ZEALAND

New Zealand is located in the South Pacific about 1,200 miles southeast of Australia. With slightly over 100,000 square miles, it is roughly the size of Colorado. The two major islands are North Island, approximately 44,000 square miles, and South Island, over 58,000 square miles. In addition, New Zealand controls Stewart Island, the Chatham Islands, the self-governing Cook Islands, the Tokelau Islands, and Ross Dependency in Antarctica (no jobs here).

Most New Zealanders (about 87%) are of European descent, primarily British. The Maoris, who arrived during the fourteenth century, comprise another 10% of the population, nearly 250,000 people. English is the official language, although Maori is also spoken. In Maori, the islands are called "Aoteara," the long white cloud.

In 1642, the Dutch navigator Abel Janszoon Tasman was the first European to reach the islands, but he was defeated by the Maoris. James Cook arrived in 1769 and explored the area for Britain. By 1840, the British had established control of

New Zealand by signing a treaty with the major Maori leaders. Large numbers of British settlers began arriving soon afterward. From 1860 to 1881, the Land Wars were fought in the central part of North Island between the Maori and the successfully encroaching European farmers and herders.

New Zealand became a British dominion in 1907 and is now a member of the Commonwealth. The country was aligned with the Allies in both world wars and maintained a defense treaty with Australia and the U.S. until 1986 when New Zealand's refusal to allow ships with nuclear weapons to use port facilities terminated the alliance. New Zealand has also begun pursuing closer economic and diplomatic relations with other Pacific Rim states.

New Zealand's political structure features a unicameral parliamentary system. The Labour Party government of David Lange was defeated in a massive landslide election in October, 1990, by the National Party, led by Jim Bolger. From 1984 to 1990, Labour attempted a radical free-market policy that failed to promote economic growth, leading instead to large-scale unemployment.

Current Economic Climate

New Zealand's gross national product of $37 billion and per capita income of over $11,000 provide fairly high living standards. Nonetheless, the economy has faced poor growth patterns in recent years. In 1984, the government attempted a dramatic free-market economic reform program in order to stimulate the country's slow economy. New Zealand consequently succeeded in lowering inflation from 18% in 1985 to 5% in 1990, but today the economy is in a severe recession. Unemployment has increased from 3.5% to 8% during the same time period.

The largest industries in New Zealand are food processing, textiles, lumber and related products, and industrial machinery. Agricultural products provide 70% of the country's exports. Wool is an especially important sector of the economy. There are actually more sheep than people in New Zealand. Normal business hours in New Zealand are from 8:30 am to 5:00 pm, Monday through Friday. Some retail stores open on Saturday. Banking hours are from 9:30 am to 4:30 pm, Monday through Friday. Fletcher Challenge, a lumber and pulp company, is the largest domestic firm.

Nearly 84% of New Zealand's 3.5 million people live in urban areas. Auckland, with 800,000 inhabitants, is the largest city. Other major cities include Christchurch (300,000) and Dunedin (100,000) on South Island; and Wellington (325,000), Napier (100,000), and Hamilton (100,000) on North Island. Over 70% of the people live on North Island.

NEW ZEALAND'S EXPORTS AND IMPORTS

Export Partners:	European Community	20%
	Australia	18%
	Southeast Asia	17%
	Japan	16%
	United States	15%
Major Exports:	Agricultural Products	48%
	Manufactured Goods	30%
Import Partners:	Japan	22%
	United States	18%
	Australia	17%
	Southeast Asia	12%
	European Community	11%
Major Imports:	Industrial Machinery	20%
	Fuel Products	18%
	Chemical Products	16%

Newspapers and Periodicals in New Zealand

Akora Mail
Akora Mail and Banks Peninsula Advertiser
Box 9, Akora, New Zealand
Tel.: 64 32 77622

Dominion Sunday Times
Wellington Newspapers
Box 1297,Wellington, North Island
New Zealand
Tel.: 64 740222
Fax: 64 740350

New Zealand Monthly Review
New Zealand Monthly Review Society
P.O. Box 13-483
Armagh, Christchurch, New Zealand

Getting Around in New Zealand

Air transportation between the major cities is provided by Air New Zealand and Ansett New Zealand. Another domestic carrier, Mt. Cooke Airlines, operates routes to major tourist areas. A variety of airpasses is available from each airline, but they must be purchased before arriving in the country.

New Zealand Railways operates a rail network linking the major cities, supplemented by a bus and ferry system. Passes for the entire system can be purchased at any railway station in New Zealand. The road system is also quite good and various rental car agencies can be found in the major cities.

Employment Regulations for Americans

Americans staying for 90 days or less do not need a visa. You can then apply to extend your visit for up to 12 months. If you already have a tourist visa, you can legally apply for a work permit with proof of employment and if you can prove that a New Zealander is not being denied the job.

Work permits, which can be acquired once in the country, should not be confused with work visas, which must be prearranged before entering. In general, obtaining a work visa is quite difficult because of the country's high unemployment rate.

Many employers in New Zealand are somewhat relaxed about the regulations and may only ask for a tax number rather than a work permit. The Immigration Service, however, has begun enforcing the regulations more tightly in recent years in response to the climbing unemployment rate. Large fruit farms that hire many foreigners have been particularly targeted.

Fruit picking dates in New Zealand

Marlborough region: apples (Feb.-Apr.), grapes (Dec.), berries (Dec.), tobacco (Jan.-Mar.)

Northland Peninsula and area around Auckland: kiwi fruit (May), strawberries (Oct.), peaches (Dec.).

Canterbury region and area around Christchurch: apples (Jan.-May), potatoes (Jan.-Feb.), peaches (Mar.).

Otago region and area around Dunedin: apples (Mar.-Apr.), peaches (Mar.), pears (Apr.)■

Organizations for Further Information

The following organizations, both in the U.S. and New Zealand, may be helpful in the job search. American embassies and consulates have commercial and/or economic sections that can provide you with business information and explain aspects of the local economy. Foreign government missions in the U.S. such as National Tourist Offices and embassies and consulates can furnish visas and information on work permits and other important regulations. They may also offer economic and business information about the country.

CHAMBERS OF COMMERCE

American Chamber of Commerce in New Zealand
Agriculture House, Featherston St.
P.O. Box 3408,Wellington
Wellington, New Zealand
Tel.: 64 4727519

Auckland Chamber of Commerce
1st Floor, C/C Bldg., 2 Courthouse Lane
P.O. Box 47, Auckland
Auckland, New Zealand
Tel.: 64 09 31969

Canterbury Chamber of Commerce
159 Oxford Terr.
P.O. Box 187, Christchurch
Canterbury, New Zealand
Tel.: 64 03 992

Hamilton Chamber of Commerce
Gallagher Group of Companies
Private Bag, Hamilton
Auckland, New Zealand
Tel.: 64 071 437189

Hutt Valley Chamber of Commerce & Industry
228 Jackson St., Petone
P.O. Box 30-653
Lower Hutt, Wellington, New Zealand
Tel.: 64 04 694821
Fax.: 64 04 683054

New Zealand Chambers of Commerce
Enterprise House, Church St.
P.O. Box 11-043, Wellington
Wellington, New Zealand
Tel.: 64 04 723376
Fax.: 64 04 711767

North Shore Chamber of Commerce, Auckland Area
P.O. Box 33-059
Takapuna, New Zealand
Tel.: 64 09 497772

Otago Chamber of Commerce
P.O. Box 7021, Dunedin
Dunedin, New Zealand
Tel.: 64 024 30689

Rotorua Chamber of Commerce
P.O. Box 385
Rotorua, New Zealand
Tel.: 64 073 476901

Wellington Chamber of Commerce
Enterprise House, 5th Floor, 309 Church St.
P.O. Box 1590, Wellington
Wellington, New Zealand
Tel.: 64 04 722725
Fax.: 64 04 711767

CONSULAR OFFICES

American Consulate General, Auckland
4th Floor, Yorkshire General Bldg.
Private Bag, Auckland
Aukland, New Zealand
Tel.: 64 9 3660870
Bobette K. Orr, Commercial Officer

American Embassy, Wellington
29 Fitzherbert Ter.
Throndon, Wellington
Wellington, New Zealand
Tel.: 64 4 722068
Robert A Callard, Consular Officer

Embassy of New Zealand
37 Observatory Cir. N.W.
Washington, DC 20008
Tel.: (202) 328-4800

OTHER INFORMATIONAL ORGANIZATIONS

New Zealand Tourist & Publicity
P.O. Box 95, Wellington
Wellington, New Zealand
Tel.: 64 4 728860
Fax.: 64 4 781736

New Zealand Tourist & Publicity
10960 Wilshire Blvd. #1530
Los Angeles, CA 90024
Tel.: (213) 477-8241
Fax.: (213) 473-5621

New Zealand Tourist & Publicity
630 Fifth Ave. #530, Rockefeller Center
New York, NY 10111

Business Directories

Although not always easy to find, business directories can prove invaluable in the international job search. Most directories list company names, addresses, products, and phone numbers. Some directories include executive names and titles and financial information about the company. These sources provide you with the names of the people to contact for employment information as well as financial data.

American Chamber of Commerce in New Zealand Directory. Published annually by the American Chamber of Commerce, Box 3408, Wellington, New Zealand. Provides basic information on over 300 companies engaged in bilateral trade and investment.

New Zealand Business Who's Who. Annual publication of FEP Productions, Box 9344, Wellington, New Zealand. Includes basic information on about 12,000 firms.

New Zealand Company Register. Published annually by Mercantile Gazette of New Zealand, 8 Sheffield Crescent, Christchurch, New Zealand. Contains detailed financial data on companies listed on the stock exchange.

New Zealand Export Yearbook. Annual publication of Cranwell Publishing Co., 46 Lake Rd., Northcote, Auckland 1, New Zealand. Lists companies engaged in export, with brief financial data.

MAJOR AMERICAN COMPANIES IN NEW ZEALAND

Some American firms operate in New Zealand. The following companies are classified by business area: Banking and Finance; Industrial Manufacturing; Retailing and Wholesaling;

and Service Industries. The company information includes type of business, American parent company, and contact name where possible. Your chances of achieving employment are substantially greater if you contact the subsidiary company in New Zealand rather than the parent comany in the U.S.

BANKING AND FINANCE

Alexander Stenhouse
Quay Tower, 16th Floor
29 Customs St. W., Auckland
Auckland, New Zealand
Tel.: 64 9793161
(Insurance)
Alexander Stenhouse Holdings

Chase Corp.
Chase House, Level 50
50 Anzac Ave., Auckland
Auckland, New Zealand
Tel.: 64 09 686969
(Holding company)
Colin Reynolds, Executive Chairman
Chase Corp.

Cigna Insurance New Zealand
Cigna House
345 Queen St., Auckland
Auckland, New Zealand
Tel.: 64 9771459
(Insurance)
Bruce Gee, Secretary
Cigna Corp.

INDUSTRIAL MANUFACTURING

Abbot Laboratories
227 Cambridge Terr.
Lower Hutt, Wellington, New Zealand
Tel.: 64 4670039
(Pharmaceuticals)
Abbot Labs

Amdahl International Corp. New Zealand
1st Floor, Natwest House
132 The Terrace, Wellington
Wellington, New Zealand
Tel.: 64 4730525
(Mainframe computers)
Amdahl Corp.

Diamond Shamrock Oil Co.
c/o Ennis Callander & Git
140-150 Lambton Quay, Wellington
Wellington, New Zealand
(Oil and gas exploration)
Maxus International Energy Co.

Ford Motor Co. of New Zealand
Seaview Rd.
Lower Hutt, Wellington, New Zealand
(Aluminum wheels)
William Hartigan, Managing Director
Ford Motor Co.

General Motors New Zealand
Alexander Rd.
Upper Hutt, Wellington, New Zealand
(Automobiles)
Raymond Halliday, President
General Motors Acceptance Corp.

Goodyear Tire & Rubber Co. of New Zealand
Port Rd.
Lower Hutt, Wellington, New Zealand
(Tires)
Goodyear Tire & Rubber Co.

W. R. Grace (NZ)
Prosser St., Elsdon
Wellington, New Zealand
Tel.: 63 25218328
(Chemicals)
W. R. Grace & Co.

Johnson & Johnson
710-712 Great South Rd.
Penrose, Auckland, New Zealand
Tel.: 64 92677660
(Hospital products)
Barry Fitzgibbon, Managing Director
Johnson & Johnson

Kodak New Zealand
54-58 Cook St., Auckland
Auckland, New Zealand
(Photographic equipment)
R. J. Keegan, Manager
Kodak (Australasia)

Eli Lilly & Co.
Norman Spencer Dr., Auckland
Auckland, New Zealand
(Pharamceuticals)
Lilly Industries

Mattel Toys
13-15 Beth St.
Auckland, Auckland, New Zealand
(Toys)
Mattel

Merck Sharp & Dohme
Plunkett Ave., Wire Station Rd.
Wiri, Auckland, New Zealand
(Pharmaceuticals)
B. J. O'Grady, Managing Director
Merck & Co.

New Zealand Petroleum Co.
BP Bldg., 3rd Floor
20-30 Customhouse Quay
Wellington, New Zealand
(Oil and gas exploration)
Triton Energy Corp.

Plough
111 Apirana Ave., Glen Innes
Auckland, New Zealand
(Pharmaceuticals)
Schering International

Polaroid New Zealand
Augustus House
15 Augustus Terr., Parnell
Auckland, New Zealand
(Photographic products)
Polaroid Corp.

Richardson-Vicks
47 St. Paul St., Auckland
Auckland, New Zealand
Tel.: 64 933829
(Pharmaceuticals)
G.C. Leonard, Managing Director
Richardson-Vicks

Rohm & Haas New Zealand
16 Beach Rd., Auckland
Auckland, New Zealand
(Industrial chemicals)
B.W. O'Neill, Managing Director
Rohm & Haas Co.

E. R. Squibb & Sons
25-27 Virginia Ave.
Eden Terr., Auckland
Auckland, New Zealand
(Pharmaceuticals)
Squibb-Matheson International Corp.

Wrigley Co.
393 Ellerslie-Panmure Hwy.
Auckland, New Zealand
(Chewing gum)
Robert Andrew, Managing Director

RETAILING AND WHOLESALING

Avon Cosmetics
P.O. Box 1828
Auckland, New Zealand
(Cosmetics)
John Mellers, Manager
Avon International Operation

Rank Xerox New Zealand
Heagraves St.
New Market, Auckland, New Zealand
(Copiers)
Rank Xerox

Wang Computer
Eden House
44 Khyber Pass Rd.
Auckland, New Zealand
(Processing equipment)
Wang Labs

Warner-Lambert
37 Banks Rd.
Auckland, New Zealand
(Pharmaceuticals)
Warner-Lambert Co.

WEA Records
14-18 Federal St.
Auckland, New Zealand
(Records and tapes)
WEA International

SERVICE INDUSTRIES

Ogilvy & Mather
Burton St. Grafton
Auckland, New Zealand
Tel.: 64 9795313
(Advertising agency)
Michael Meredith, Managing Director
Ogilvy & Mather Worldwide

Time-Life International
Guardian Assurance Bldg.
Queen St., Auckland
Auckland, New Zealand
(Publishing)
Time-Warner

Whitehall Books
53 Jackson St.
Petone, Wellington, New Zealand
Tel.: 64 4684146
(Business services)
Norman Fletcher, Managing Director
Simon & Schuster

MAJOR DOMESTIC COMPANIES IN NEW ZEALAND

The following is a listing of the major domestic companies of New Zealand. They are classified by business area: Industrial Manufacturing; Retailing and Wholesaling; and Service Industries. Company information includes type of business and contact name. These companies will generally hire their own nationals first but may employ Americans.

INDUSTRIAL MANUFACTURING

Tait Electronics
558 Wairakel Rd.
Christchurch, Canterbury
New Zealand
Tel.: 64 3583399
(Radio products)
Angus Tait, Managing Director

RETAILING AND WHOLESALING

New Zealand Dairy Board
25 The Terrace
Wellington, New Zealand
(Dairy products)

New Zealand Lamb Co.
Woolhouse 5th Floor
Jurvis Quay, Wellington
Wellington, New Zealand
Tel.: 64 4724271
(Frozen foods)
A. R. Hutton, Chairman

SERVICE INDUSTRIES

Air New Zealand
1 Queen St., Auckland
Auckland, New Zealand
Tel.: 64 09 797515
Fax.: 64 09 394134
(Air transportation)
R.J. Scott, Chief Executive

Brierley Investment
Level 9 CML Bldg.
22-24 Victoria St., Wellington
Wellington, New Zealand
Tel.: 64 04 738199
(Holding company)
Ronald Brierley, Chairman

Fletcher Challenge
Fletcher Challenge House
810 Great South Rd.
Penrose, Auckland, New Zealand
Tel.: 64 09 590000
Fax.: 64 09 5250559
(Construction, energy, fishing, agriculture)
Sir Ronald Trotter, Chairman

MAJOR NON-PROFIT EMPLOYERS IN NEW ZEALAND

Commonwealth Heraldry Board
P.O. Box 23-056
Papatoetoe, New Zealand
Tel.: 64 2787415

International Federation of Health Records Organizations
Masterton Hospital
Private Bag, Masterton
Wellington, New Zealand
Tel.: 64 233 832036

IUMS Bacteriology Division
University of Otago,
Microbiology Department
P.O. Box 56, Dunedin
Dunedin, New Zealand
Tel.: 64 24 771640

Postal History Society of New Zealand
P.O. Box 38-503
Howick, Auckland
Auckland, New Zealand

MAJOR HOTEL EMPLOYERS IN NEW ZEALAND

Alexandra Court
960 Colombo St.
Christchurch, Canterbury
New Zealand
Tel.: 64 361855

Allenby Park Motor Lodge
477 9T South Rd.
Auckland, New Zealand
Tel.: 64 09 2777320

Alpine Village
Lakeside Frankton Rd.
Queenstown, Dunedin
New Zealand
Tel.: 64 27795

Auckland Airport Travelodge
Cnr. Kirbride & Ascot Rds.
Auckland, New Zealand
Tel.: 64 09 2751059

Auckland City Travelodge
96-100 Quay St., Auckland
Auckland, New Zealand
Tel.: 64 09 770349

Bay Plaza Hotel
40-44 Oriental Parade, Wellington
Wellington, New Zealand
Tel.: 64 04 857799

Beach Lodge
38 Victoria Rd., Dunedin
Dunedin, New Zealand
Tel.: 64 24 55043

Belmont Luxury
168-172 Bealey Ave., Christchurch
Canterbury, New Zealand
Tel.: 64 794037

Courtesy Court
30 Golf Road, Nelson
Wellington, New Zealand
Tel.: 64 54 85114

Holiday Inn, Queenstown
Sainbury Rd., Fernhill
Queenstown, Dunedin
New Zealand
Tel.: 64 0294 26600

Hyatt Kingstate
Princess St., Auckland
Auckland, New Zealand
Tel.: 64 79 97220

Parkroyal
Queen & Customs Sts., Auckland
Auckland, New Zealand
Tel.: 64 09 778920

Penrose Lodge
167 Penrose Rd., Auckland
Auckland, New Zealand
Tel.: 64 09 595923

Plaza International Hotel
148-176 Wakefield St., Wellington
Wellington, New Zealand
Tel.: 64 04 733900

Quality Inn
150 Anzac Ave., Auckland
Auckland, New Zealand
Tel.: 64 09 798509

Quality Inn, Nelson
Nile & Church Sts., Nelson
Wellington, New Zealand
Tel.: 64 54 82229

Quality Inn, Palmerston
110 Fitzherbert Ave.
Palmerston North, Wellington
New Zealand
Tel.: 64 63 68059

Quality Inn, Rose Park
100 Gladstone Rd., Auckland
Auckland, New Zealand
Tel.: 64 09 773619

Ranfurly Court
285 Manukau Rd., Auckland
Auckland, New Zealand
Tel.: 64 09 689059

Regent of Auckland
Albert St., Auckland
Auckland, New Zealand
Tel.: 64 09 398882

Sheraton Auckland Hotel and Towers
83 Symonds St., Auckland
Auckland, New Zealand
Tel.: 64 09 49795132

Sheraton Rotorua Hotel
Fenton St., P.O. Box 983
Rotorua, Auckland
New Zealand
Tel.: 64 09 387139

Tourist Court
842 George St., Dunedin
Dunedin, New Zealand
Tel.: 64 24 774270

Singapore

The Republic of Singapore is located off the southern tip of the Malayan Peninsula in Southeast Asia. Its closest neighbors are Malaysia to the north and Indonesia to the south. The entire country measures 224 square miles, consisting of the main island and about 50 smaller islets. Most of the terriotry is flat, low-lying land. The city is on the southern shore of the main island.

Chinese comprise about 76% of the population, an additional 15% are Malays, and 7% are Indians. Mandarin Chinese, Malay, Tamil, and English are all official. Buddhists, Christians, Taoists, Hindus, and Muslims are all very prominent in the country's religious composition. Nearly 2.8 million people live in Singapore, resulting in the fourth highest population density of any city in the world.

Singapore was founded in 1819 by Sir Thomas Stamford Raffles as an East India Company trading post. It became a colony in 1867 and gained autonomy within the British Commonwealth in 1959. Singapore joined the Federation of

Malaysia in 1963. Ethnic tensions between Malays, the majority in Malaysia, and Chinese, the majority in Singapore, led to a separation in 1965.

Lee Kuan Yew served as prime minister from 1959 to 1990. His People's Action Party won every parliamentary seat contested between 1968 and 1980. In recent elections, the party has won all but one or two seats. Singapore has a moderately democratic system, but the opposition is usually initimidated by government persecution. The Singapore Democratic Party is the leading opposition party. The next general election is due in 1993. Singapore is a member of ASEAN, the Association of Southeast Asian Nations.

Lee Kuan Yew resigned as prime minister in 1990 and now serves as senior minister without portfolio. He governed Singapore in a very authoritarian but extremely efficient and effective manner. During his tenure, Singapore was transformed from an undeveloped island into one of the world's leading financial centers and fastest growing economies. Lee also enforced a strict Confucian paternalism at almost every level of society.

Lee's successor is Goh Chok Tong, who has promised to pursue a policy of greater consultation with all sectors affected by government decisions. Prime Minister Goh has sought to enhance the intangible aspects of social and cultural life in Singapore. He has therefore relaxed much of the country's censorship restrictions. Dow Jones quit selling its Asian Wall Street Journal in Singapore in 1990 because of government restrictions. Young Singaporeans, mostly educated in the U.S. and Britain, are eager for greater openness in society.

SINGAPORE'S 3 LARGEST COMPANIES
(figures represent 1990 market value in billions of U.S. dollars)

1. Singapore Airlines	$4.6
2. Development Bank of Singapore	$3.5
3. Overseas Chinese Bank	$2.8

Current Economic Climate

Singapore's gross national product is over $24 billion and grew by 8% in 1990 and 9% in 1989. GNP is expected to grow by 5 to 6% in 1991. The economy has grown at an annual average of 9% from 1965 to 1990. With a per capita income over $12,000, Singapore enjoys one of the highest standards of living in Asia. The overall quality of life is higher than in many European countries and second only to Japan in Asia. Inflation has averaged about 1.5% in recent years but reached 3% in 1990 and is likely to climb to 5% in 1991.

Singapore's government has guided the country's economic development by targeting specific industries for investment and assistance. Currently the Economic Development Board is focusing upon the petroleum and petrochemical industries.

The largest industries include shipbuilding, banking, electronics, textiles, oil refining, and tourism.

The international container port has recently overtaken Hong Kong's as the world's busiest. Singapore's banking and finance sector, one of the country's principal sources of economic development, grew by 17% in 1990. The construction industry grew by 7% in 1990 and should expand by 5% in 1991. Industrial manufacturing in 1990 grew by about 8%. The tourist industry is also experiencing strong growth, expanding by 10% in 1990.

Singapore is encouraging the emergence of a growth triangle in cooperation with Malaysia's Johor state and Indonesia's Riau Islands. The plans would facilitate Singaporean capital investment in Johor and the Riaus. Singapore has already invested $120 million on the island of Batam in the Riau Islands. Other industrial parks are now under construction. Singaporean companies are seeking lower land and labor costs than those available at home. Indonesia has been receptive to the proposals, but Malaysia is weary of only benefiting Singapore.

Business hours are generally from 8:00 or 9:00 am to 5:00 or 6:00 pm, Monday through Friday. Many businesses also operate for a half-day, usually until 1:00 pm, on Saturday. Banking hours are from 10:00 am to 3:00 pm, Monday through Friday, and from 11:00 am to 4:30 pm on Saturday. Post offices are open from 8:00 am to 5:00 pm, Monday through Friday, and from 8:00 am to 1:00 pm on Saturday. Stores usually open from 9:00 am to 6:00 pm during the week.

SINGAPORE'S LARGEST TRADING PARTNERS

Imports:	Japan	20%
	United States	16%
	Malaysia	14%
	Hong Kong	9%
	Indonesia	4%
Exports:	United States	22%
	European Community	17%
	Malaysia	16%
	Japan	11%
	Hong Kong	7%

Getting Around in Singapore

Changi Airport in Singapore is considered to be the world's best in terms of efficiency and cleanliness. Singapore's bus system is extremely convenient, cheap, and efficient. Singapore Airlines flies into the country from North America. It takes about half an hour to get from the airport to the city center.

The Singapore Mass Rapid Transit (MRT) rail system is cheap and extremely comprehensive, operating from 6:00 am to midnight. The MRT is currently the world's newest subway system and certainly the fastest way to get around.

Bus passes are available, allowing unlimited travel for specified periods of time. Singapore's 10,000 taxis can also get you around the island at all hours and are very cheap. Rental cars are available, and road signs are in English. Be careful not to litter on your way around the city. Littering is punished by a harsh fine of $600, making Singapore the world's cleanest big city.

Employment Regulations for Americans

Americans do not need a visa to enter the country for stays of less than 90 days although a work permit must be obtained from an employer before securing a job. Singapore has few restrictions on the employment of foreigners and maintains very liberal foreign investment and profit repatriation rules.

Consequently, foreigners who can market themselves effectively have no legal barriers to finding employment in Singapore. The country is much like Hong Kong in that respect. Qualified, skilled Americans should find themselves on a relatively equal footing with nationals of other countries in applying for employment. Most of the Singapore language schools, however, recruit qualified English teachers abroad rather than hire casual teachers.

Singapore is facing a labor shortage due to its great economic growth, which has outpaced expansion in the workforce. The government plans to allow in 100,000 Hong Kong immigrants in order to alleviate the situation. Meanwhile, the lack of sufficient qualified personnel means that companies filling job vacancies will seriously consider foreigners. The lack of sufficient workers makes it easier for companies to show that a foreigner is not taking a job from a qualified local resident.

Making a good first impression

It is a good idea to carry business cards in Singapore. The cards should contain one's name, full title or position, employer or organization, phone number, and address. You should have this information in Chinese on one side and in English on the other. This is primarily for the Chinese business people, but you will find it convenient also to print cards in Malay and Tamil. Even though most people in Singapore speak English, presenting business cards is a common custom in East Asia and will help potential employers, customers, clients, or anyone else you may meet remember you.■

Organizations for Further Information

The following organizations, both in the U.S. and Singapore, may be helpful in the job search. American embassies and consulates have commercial and/or economic sections that can provide you with business information and explain aspects of the local economy. World Trade Centers usually include many foreign companies operating in the country. Foreign government missions in the U.S. such as National Tourist Offices and embassies and consulates can furnish visas and information on work permits and other important regulations. They may also offer economic and business information about the country.

CHAMBERS OF COMMERCE

American Business Council of Singapore
354 Orchard Rd., #10-12 Shaw House
Singapore 0923, Singapore
Tel.: 65 2350077

Economic Development Board, Atlanta
234 Peachtree Hollow Ct.
Atlanta, GA 30328
Tel.: (404) 392-9392
Fax.: (404) 668-1084

Economic Development Board, Boston
55 Wheeler St.
Cambridge, MA 02138
Tel.: (617) 497-9392
Fax.: (617) 491-6150

Economic Development Board, Chicago
Illinois Center Two, Suite 2307
233 N. Michigan Ave.
Chicago, IL 60601
Tel.: (312) 644-3730
Fax.: (312) 644-4481

Economic Development Board, Dallas
Park Central VII, Suite 1424
LB38
12750 Merit Dr.
Dallas, TX 75251
Tel.: (214) 450-4540
Fax.: (214) 450-4543

Economic Development Board, Headquarters
Raffles City Tower
250 North Bridge Rd., No. 24-00
Singapore 0617, Singapore
Tel.: 65 3362288
Fax.: 65 3396077

Economic Development Board, Los Angeles
911 Wilshire Blvd., Suite 950
Los Angeles, CA 90017
Tel.: (213) 624-7647
Fax.: (213) 624-4412

Economic Development Board, New York
55 E. 59th St.
New York, NY 10022
Tel.: (212) 421-2200
Fax.: (212) 421-2206

Country-by-Country Listings

Economic Development Board, San Francisco
210 Twin Dolphin Dr.
Redwood City, CA 94065
Tel.: (415) 591-9102
Fax.: (415) 591-1328

Singapore Chinese Chamber of Commerce
Chinese Chamber of Commerce Bldg.
47 Hill St., No. 07-02
Singapore 0617, Singapore

Singapore Federation of Chambers of Commerce
Chinese Chamber of Commerce Bldg., No. 03-01
47 Hill St.
Singapore 0617, Singapore

Singapore Indian Chamber of Commerce
101 Cecil St., No. 23-01
Singapore 0106, Singapore

Singapore International Chamber of Commerce
Denmark House
6 Raffles Quay, No. 05-00
Singapore 0104, Singapore

Singapore Manufacturers Association
World Trade Center, No. 2-18
Singapore 409, Singapore

Singapore Trade Development Board, Headquarters
World Trade Center, 1 Maritime Sq., No. 10-40
Telok Blangah Rd.
Singapore 0409, Singapore
Tel.: 65 2719388
Fax.: 65 2740770

Singapore Trade Development Board, Los Angeles
Los Angeles World Trade Center
350 S. Figueroa St., Suite 272
Los Angeles, CA 90071
Tel.: (213) 617-7358

Singapore Trade Development Board, New York
745 5th Ave., Suite 1601
New York, NY 10022
Tel.: (212) 421-2207
Fax.: (212) 888-2897

CONSULAR OFFICES

American Embassy
30 Hill St.
Singapore, Singapore
Tel.: 65 3380251

Embassy of the Republic of Singapore
1824 R St. N.W.
Washington, DC 20009
Tel.: (202) 667-7555
Fax.: (202) 265-7915

WORLD TRADE CENTER IN SINGAPORE

World Trade Center Singapore
1 Maritime Square, No. 02-11
World Trade Centre
Singapore 0490, Singapore
Tel.: 65 271221, ext. 2791

OTHER INFORMATIONAL ORGANIZATIONS

Singapore Tourist Promotion Board, Chicago
333 N. Michigan Ave., Suite 818
Chicago, IL 60601

Tel.: (312) 220-0099
Fax.: (312) 220-0020

Singapore Tourist Promotion Board, Headquarters
Raffles City Tower, No. 36-04
250 N. Bridge Rd.
Singapore 0617, Singapore
Tel.: 65 3396622
Fax.: 65 3399423

Singapore Tourist Promotion Board, Los Angeles
8484 Wilshire Blvd., Suite 510
Beverly Hills, CA 90211
Tel.: (213) 852-1901
Fax.: (213) 852-0129

Singapore Tourist Promotion Board, New York
520 5th Ave., 12th Floor
New York, NY 10036
Tel.: (212) 302-4861
Fax.: (212) 302-4801

Singapore Tourist Promotion Board, San Francisco
251 Post St., Suite 308
San Francisco, CA 94108-5068
Tel.: (415) 391-8476

Cost of staying in East Asia

If you are already in the Asia Pacific region looking for employment or just visiting, Singapore is a good place to use as a base. According to the Japan National Tourist Office (JTNO), Singapore is the cheapest city to stay in for three days while Tokyo is the most expensive. The survey was based on hotel, dining, and transportation costs for three days for one person, calculated in U.S. dollars. The following are the 10 cities in the region surveyed by JTNO:

Tokyo, Japan	$1,442
Sapporo, Japan	$823
Taipei, Taiwan	$808
Sydney, Australia	$797
Seoul, South Korea	$763
Hong Kong	$744
Kyoto, Japan	$739
Fukuoka, Japan	$721
Bangkok, Thailand	$716
Singapore	$682.■

Business Directories

Although not always easy to find, business directories can prove invaluable in the international job search. Most directories list company names, addresses, products, and phone numbers. Some directories include executive names and titles and financial information about the company. These sources provide you with the names of people to contact for employment information as well as financial data.

Kompass Singapore. Annual publication of Kompass South East Asia, 326 C, King George Ave., Singapore 820, Singapore. Provides detailed information on over 15,000 companies in various fields.

Singapore Indian Chamber of Commerce Directory. Published annually by the Singapore Indian Chamber of Commerce, 55 A, Robinson Rd., Box 1038, Singapore, Singapore. Provides basic information on several hundred member firms.

Singapore Manufacturers Association Directory. Annual publication of the Singapore Manufacturers Association, World Trade Center, No. 2-18, Singapore 409, Singapore. Provides detailed financial information on over 1,000 member companies.

Stock Exchange of Singapore Companies Handbook. Published annually by the Stock Exchange of Singapore, Hong Leong Bldg., Rm. 16-03, 16 Raffles Quay, Singapore 104, Singapore. Contains very detailed information on several hundred companies traded on the stock exchange.

Times Business Directory of Singapore. Annual publication of Times Periodicals, 1 New Rd., Singapore 1953, Singapore. Provides basic information on large companies and government agencies involved with business and trade.

MAJOR AMERICAN COMPANIES IN SINGAPORE

The following is a listing of the major American companies of Singapore. They are classified by business area: Banking and Finance; Industrial Manufacturing; Retailing and Wholesaling; and Service Industries. Company information includes type of business, American parent company, and contact name where possible. Your chances of achieving employment are substantially greater if you contact the subsidiary company in Singapore rather than the parent company.

BANKING AND FINANCE

AIU (Singapore)
78 Shenton Way, #07-01/03
Singapore 0207, Singapore
Tel.: 65 3225000
Fax.: 65 2253076
(Insurance)
Gary L. Buckingham, President
American International Group

American Express Bank
Shing Kwan House, 4 Shenton Way
Singapore 0106, Singapore
Tel.: 65 2203211
Fax.: 65 2255341
(Banking and credit service)
Werner Langenbach, General Manager
American Express Corp.

Bank of America
78 Shenton Way
Singapore 0207, Singapore
Tel.: 65 2236688
Fax.: 65 3203068
(Banking)
Richard C. Wortley, Country General Manager
BankAmerica Corp.

Bankers Trust International (Asia)
Shell Tower, 50 Raffles Place 2601-2606
Singapore 0104, Singapore
Tel.: 65 2229191
(Banking)
David J. Ryan, General Manager
Bankers Trust New York Corp.

Chase Manhattan Bank
50 Raffles Place, #01-01 Shell Tower
Singapore 0104, Singapore
Tel.: 65 5304111
Fax.: 65 2247950
(Banking)
R. D. Freed, Country Manager
Chase Manhattan Bank, New York

Citibank
UIC Bldg., 5 Shenton Way
Singapore 0106, Singapore
Tel.: 65 2242611
Fax.: 65 2249844
(Banking and finance)
David J. Browning, Vice President
Citicorp

First Chicago Asia Merchant Bank
76 Shenton Way, #01-02 Ong Bldg.
Singapore 0207, Singapore
Tel.: 65 2254982
(Banking)
Bharat Parashar, Managing Director

Merrill Lynch Pierce Fenner & Smith (Singapore)
Shell Tower, 50 Raffles Place
Singapore 0104, Singapore
(Securities)
Merrill Lynch & Co.

Morgan Guaranty Pacific
6 Shenton Way #31-01
Singapore 0106, Singapore
Tel.: 65 2208144
(Banking)
Sum Soon Lim, Vice President
J. P. Morgan & Co.

Prudential-Bache Securities Asia Pacific
UIC Bldg., 5 Shenton Way
Singapore 0109, Singapore
Tel.: 65 2208721
(Securities broker)
William L. Custard, President
Prudential Insurance Co. of America

Republic National Bank of NY (Singapore)
143 Cecil St., #01-00 GB Bldg.
Singapore 0106, Singapore
(Banking)
Republic NY Corp.

INDUSTRIAL MANUFACTURING

Abbott Laboratories (Singapore)
456 Alexandra Rd., Nol Bldg. #19-03
Singapore, Singapore
(Pharmaceuticals)
Abbott Laboratories

Armstrong (Singapore)
No. 1 Queensway, #03-03
Queensway Shopping Centre
Singapore 0314, Singapore
Tel.: 65 4754315
(Furniture, building products)
Armstrong World Industries

Bristol-Meyers (Singapore)
50 Genting Ln.
Singapore 1334, Singapore
(Pharmaceuticals)
Bristol-Meyers Squibb Co.

Colgate-Palmolive
29 First Lok Yang Rd. off
International Rd.
Jurong, Singapore 2262,
Singapore
Tel.: 65 2650433
Fax.: 65 2610745
(Toiletries, detergents)
Y. K. Yap, General Manager
Colgate Palmolive Co.

Compaq Asia
50 Tagore Lane #03-07
Singapore 2678, Singapore
Tel.: 65 4599977
(Computers)
Steve Hamblin, Manager
Compaq Computer Corp.

ConAgra International
#27-04 Raffles City Tower
Singapore, Singapore
Tel.: 65 3392200
(Beef products)
ConAgra

Dow Chemical (Singapore)
806 Cathay Bldg.
Singapore 9, Singapore
(Plastic products)
Dow Chemical Co.

Du Pont (Singapore) Electronic
6 Gul Circle, 5 Jurong Industrial
Estate
Singapore 2262, Singapore
(Electronic connectors)
E. I. Du Pont De Nemours & Co

Eastman Christensen
No. 11 Gul Lane
Jurong, Singapore 2262,
Singapore
Tel.: 65 2659855
(Diamond tools)
Norton Co.

Ethyl Asia Pacific Co.
06-05 Unity House,1 Science
Center Rd.
Singapore 2260, Singapore
Tel.: 65 5610433
(Petroleum chemicals)
B. C. Gottwald, President
Ethyl Corp.

Exxon Chemical Simco
1 Raffles Place, #27-00 OUB
Centre
Singapore 0104, Singapore
Tel.: 65 5355533
(Petrochemicals)
C. W. Emerson, Chairman
Exxon Chemical Co.

Ford Motor Co.
137 Bukit Timan Rd.
Singapore
Ford Motor Co.

Goodyear Orient Co.
1211 Up Boon Keng Rd.
Singapore 1438, Singapore
Tel.: 65 7475361
Fax.: 65 7440340
(Tires)
Peter Tan Weng Chye,
Managing Director
Goodyear Tire & Rubber Co.

W. R. Grace (Singapore)
25 Tanjong Perjuru
Singapore 2260, Singapore
Tel.: 65 2653033
(Chemicals)
W. R. Grace & Co.

Johnson & Johnson
18/20 Third Lokyang Rd.
Jurong, Singapore 2262,
Singapore
Tel.: 65 2658922
(Hospital products)
Tay Peng Kok, Managing
Director
Johnson & Johnson

Kimberly Clark Far East
34 Boon Leat Terrace, Off Pasir
Panjang Rd.
Singapore 0511, Singapore
Tel.: 65 4711466
(Facial tissue and feminine
products)
Harry Thong, Managing Director
Kimberly-Clark Corp.

Kodak (Singapore)
305 Alexandra Rd.
Singapore 0315, Singapore
Tel.: 65 4736611
Fax.: 65 4798397
(Cameras)
J. G. Fenimore, General Manager
Eastman Kodak Co.

Lockheed Aircraft Asia
230 Orchard Rd., #06-230/2
Faber House
Singapore 0923, Singapore
Tel.: 65 2350474
Fax.: 65 7326487
(Aerospace equipment)
D. J. Neese, Managing Director
Lockheed Corp.

Martin Marietta International
250 N. Bridge Rd. #30-10
Raffles City Tower
Singapore 0617, Singapore
Tel.: 65 3383722
Fax.: 65 3380007
(Aerospace and electrical technology)
Richard Idtensohn, Vice President
Martin Marietta Corp.

Mobil Oil Singapore
18 Pioneer Rd.
Jurong, Singapore 2262, Singapore
Tel.: 65 6606000
Fax.: 65 2656570
(Petroleum products)
A. V. Liventals, Managing Director
Mobil Oil Corp.

Monsanto Singapore Co.
101 Thomson Rd., #19-00 and #20-03/05 Goldhill Square
Singapore 1130, Singapore
Tel.: 65 2502000
Fax.: 65 2533723
(Plastics, resins, chemicals)
D. S. Ellis, Personnel Director
Monsanto Co.

Motorola Electronics
10 Ang Mo Kio St. 64
New 410 Chu Kang Rd.
Singapore 2056, Singapore
Tel.: 65 4550100
Fax.: 65 4573879
(Electronic parts)
Motorola Inc.

Pfizer Private
Block 3 1009-1017 PSA Multi St.
Complex, Pasir Panjang Rd.
Singapore 0511, Singapore
Tel.: 65 2723677
(Pharmaceuticals)
L. M. Y. Woo, Manager
Pfizer Inc.

Proctor & Gamble (Singapore)
1 Maritime Square, #12-01/02
World Trade Centre
Singapore 0409, Singapore
Tel.: 65 2719155
(Personal consumer products)
W. Kastner, Manager
Proctor & Gamble Co.

Scott Paper (Singapore)
3450/452 Alexandra Rd.,
Inchcape House #08-03
Singapore 0511, Singapore
Tel.: 65 4751655
Fax.: 65 4747705
(Paper products)
Scott Paper Co.

Texas Instruments (Singapore)
101 Thomson Rd., 23-01 United Square
Singapore 1130, Singapore
Tel.: 65 3508100
Fax.: 65 2536655
(Semi-conductor materials)
David Smith, Managing Director
Texas Instruments

Union Carbide Singapore
9 Hill View Rd.
Singapore 2366, Singapore
Tel.: 65 666777
(Chemicals, plastics, carbon products)
Union Carbide Corp.

RETAILING AND WHOLESALING

3M Singapore
9 Tagore Ln.
Singapore 2678, Singapore
Tel.: 65 4548611
Fax.: 65 4568953
(Copiers, electrical equipment)
W. D. Perkins, Managing Director

Bausch & Lomb (Singapore)
10 Anson Rd. Ste. 33-10, International Plaza
Singapore 0207, Singapore
Tel.: 65 2254222
(Opthalmic goods and research)
Victor Lee, General Manager
Bausch & Lomb

Beatrice Foods Singapore
32 Quality Rd.
Jurong, Singapore 22, Singapore
Tel.: 65 650088
(Food products)
J. C. M. Shaw, Manager
Beatrice Co.

Ciba-Geigy South East Asia
4 Fourth Lok Yang Rd.
Singapore 2262, Singapore
Tel.: 65 2653622
Fax.: 65 2685670
(Pharmaceuticals, chemicals)
D. R. C. Free, Managing Director
Ciba-Geigy Group of Companies

Esso Singapore
1 Raffles Place, OUB Centre
Singapore 0104, Singapore
Tel.: 65 5355533
Fax.: 65 5353473
(Petroleum product refining and marketing)
T. J. Bolam, Managing Director
Exxon Company International
New Jersey

Getz Corp. (Singapore)
100-F Pasir Panjang Rd.
Singapore 0511, Singapore
Tel.: 65 4759777
Fax.: 65 4731028
(Consumer products, pharmaceuticals, building materials)
John H. Bordwell, Managing Director
Getz International

Hewlett-Packard Singapore
(Sales)
1150 Depot Rd.
Singapore 0410, Singapore
Tel.: 65 2737388
Fax.: 65 2788990
(Computers, medical equipment)
Victor Ang, Managing Director
Hewlett-Packard Co.

Kodak (Singapore)
305 Alexandra Rd.
Singapore 0315
Tel.: 65 4736611
Fax.: 65 4798397
(Photography equipment)
J. G. Fenimore, General Manager
Eastman Kodak Co.

Rank Xerox (Singapore)
18th Fl., 190 Middle Rd., #18-00 Fortune Centre
Singapore 0718, Singapore
Tel.: 65 3362266
Fax.: 65 3364490
(Office equipment)
John Drinkwater, Director
Xerox Corp., USA, Joint Venture with Rank Organization, U.K.

Readers Digest Asia
#3-04 Union Bldg., 37 Jalan Pemimpin
Singapore 2057, Singapore
Tel.: 65 2581411
(Publishing)
Robert W. Adam, Managing Director
Readers Digest Assn.

Tandem Computers International
24 Raffles Place #19-03 Clifford Centre
Singapore 0104, Singapore
Tel.: 65 5337611
(Computers)
Tandem Computers

Wang Computer
Tong Bldg. Suite 1204, 12th Floor, 302 Orchard Rd.
Singapore 0923, Singapore
(Data processing equipment)
Wang Labs

SERVICE INDUSTRIES

AT&T International (Singapore)
Shell Tower, 50 Raffles Place
Singapore 0104, Singapore
(Telecommunications)
AT&T International

McCann-Erickson (Singapore)
206-208 Thong Tack Bldg., Scotts Rd.
Singapore, Singapore
Tel.: 65 2357523
(Advertising)
Brian A. Watson, Managing Director
McCann-Erickson

Ogilvy & Mather (Singapore)
1 Maritime Square, #11-01
World Trade Centre
Singapore 0409, Singapore
Tel.: 65 2738011
Fax.: 65 2742156
(Advertising)
John Seifert, Managing Director
Ogilvy Group

MAJOR DOMESTIC COMPANIES IN SINGAPORE

The following is a listing of the major domestic companies of Singapore. They are classified by business area: Banking and Finance; Industrial Manufacturing; Retailing and Wholesaling; and Service Industries. Company information includes type of business and contact name. These companies will generally hire their own nationals first but may employ Americans.

BANKING AND FINANCE

Asia Commercial Bank
60 Robinson Rd.
Singapore 0106, Singapore
Tel.: 65 2228222
Fax.: 65 2253493
(Banking)
Lee Hee Seng, Chairman

Associated Merchant Bank
Straits Trading Bldg., #08-03
9 Battery Rd.
Singapore 0104, Singapore
Tel.: 65 5359833
Fax.: 65 5331580
(Banking)
Gerald Mah Kah On, General Manager

Country-by-Country Listings

Bank of Singapore
101 Cecil St. #01-02
Singapore 0106, Singapore
Tel.: 65 2239266
Fax.: 65 2247407
(Banking)
Tan Tock San, Chairman

Chung Khiaw Bank
1 Bonham St., #01-00 UOB Bldg.
Singapore 0104, Singapore
Tel.: 65 2228622
Fax.: 65 2254404
(Commercial banking)
Wee Cho Yaw, Chairman

Credit Corp. Singapore
1 Scotts Rd., #18-07 Shaw Centre
Singapore 0922, Singapore
Tel.: 65 7376466
Fax.: 65 7343523
(Credit co.)
M. R. Taylor, Chairman

Far Eastern Bank
1 Bonham St., #01-11 UOB Bldg.
Singapore 0104, Singapore
Tel.: 65 2216024
Fax.: 65 2235620
(Banking)
Wee Cho Yaw, Chairman

Great Eastern Life Assurance Co.
65 Chulia St., #18-01 OCBC Centre
Singapore 0104, Singapore
Tel.: 65 5324331
Fax.: 65 5323478
(Life insurance)
Tan Sri Tan Chin Tuan, Chairman

Industrial and Commercial Bank
#01-01 Industrial & Commercial Bank Bldg., 2 Shenton Way
Singapore 0106, Singapore
Tel.: 65 2211711
Fax.: 65 2259777
(Banking)
Wee Cho Yaw, Chairman

Insurance Corp. of Singapore
ICS Bldg., 137 Cecil St.
Singapore 0106, Singapore
Tel.: 65 2218686
Fax.: 65 2247242
(Insurance)
Chong Kie Cheong, Director

International Bank of Singapore
50 Collyer Quay, #02-01
Overseas Union House
Singapore 0104, Singapore
Tel.: 65 2234488
Fax.: 65 2240236
(Banking)
Lien Ying Chow, Chairman

Overseas-Chinese Banking Corp.
65 Chulia St., #08-00, OCBC Centre
Singapore 0104, Singapore
Tel.: 65 5357222
Fax.: 65 5337955
(Banking, investments)
Teo Cheng Guan, Chief Executive Officer

Tat Lee Bank
Tat Lee Bank Bldg., 63 Market St.
Singapore 0104, Singapore
Tel.: 65 5339292
Fax.: 65 5331043
(Banking)
Goh Tjoei Kok, Chairman

United Malayan Banking Corp.
150 Cecil St., #01-00 Wing On Life Bldg.
Singapore 0106, Singapore
Tel.: 65 2253111
Fax.: 65 2247871
(Banking)
Kong Sik Hung, Executive Vice President

United Overseas Bank
1 Bonham St., #01-00 United Overseas Bank Bldg.
Singapore 0104, Singapore
Tel.: 65 5339898
Fax.: 65 5342334
(Banking)
Wee Cho Yaw, Chairman

United Industrial Corp.
13th Fl. ULC Bldg., 5 Shenton Way
Singapore 0106, Singapore
Tel.: 65 2201352
(Real estate investment)
Peter Chong, Manager

INDUSTRIAL MANUFACTURING

ABB Regional Product Centre
2 Ayer Rajah Crescent
Singapore 0513, Singapore
Tel.: 65 7753777, 7765711
Fax.: 65 7780222
(Electrical equipment)
Paul Ziegler, President

Far East Motors
45 Leng Kee Rd.
Singapore 0315, Singapore
Tel.: 65 4791111
(Automobile parts)
Ong Han Lee, Senior Executive

Fluid Power
1189, Block 12, Lorong 8, Toa Payoh Industrial Park
Singapore 1231, Singapore
Tel.: 65 2547777/80
Fax.: 65 2530319
(Hydraulic components)
Ang Sin Nee, Chairman

FMC Corp.
#23-01/02 Shaw Centre, 1 Scotts Rd.
Singapore 0922, Singapore
Tel.: 65 7346522
Fax.: 65 7320940
(Chemicals)
S. L. Stetson, Senior Executive

Hwa Hong Corp.
29 Jurong Port Rd.
Jurong, Singapore 2261, Singapore
Tel.: 65 2659711
Fax.: 65 2658876
(Food products, engineering, investments)
Ong Chay Tong, Chairman

Jurong Cement
15 Pioneer Crescent
Singapore 2262, Singapore
Tel.: 65 2618016
Fax.: 65 2659187
(Cement)
Whang Tar Liang, Chairman

Keppel Corp.
325 Telok Blangah Rd.
Singapore 0409, Singapore
Tel.: 65 2706666
Fax.: 65 2742176
(Shipbuilding and offshore construction)
Sim Kee Boon, Executive Chairman

Singapore Petroleum Co.
6 Shenton Way, #42-01 DBS Bldg.
Singapore 0106, Singapore
Tel.: 65 2213166
Fax.: 65 2213691
(Petroleum products)
Cheng Hong Kok, President

Singatronics Ltd.
512 Chai Chee Ln. #06-01/06, Bedok Industrial Estate
Singapore 1646, Singapore
Tel.: 65 65 01311
(Electronic products)
Eddie C. K. Foo, Managing Director

RETAILING AND WHOLESALING

Asia Motor Co.
1 Kampong Ampat, off MacPherson Rd.
Singapore 1336, Singapore
Tel.: 65 2804666
Fax.: 65 2823396
(Motor vehicles)
Mrs. Catherine Ng-Phng, Managing Director

Asia Radio (Singapore)
41 Benccolen St.
Singapore 0718, Singapore
Tel.: 65 336-3477/82
Fax.: 65 339-6339
(Electronics)
C. C. Chong, Managing Director

Bousteadco Singapore
15 Hoe Chiang Rd., #12-01
Sanford Bldg.
Singapore 0208, Singapore
Tel.: 65 2255177
Fax.: 65 2248920
(Marketing and distribution)
K. A. Wallen, Managing Director

Champion Motors
2 Pandan Crescent
Singapore 0512, Singapore
Tel.: 65 7776677
Fax.: 65 7784412
(Motor vehicles)
K. P. Chandran Nair, Managing Director

General Diesel Supplies (Singapore)
7 Jurong Pier Rd.
Singapore 2261, Singapore
Tel.: 65 2655222
(Diesel engines)
Cheang Wai Yew, General Manager

General Engineering and Trading (Singapore)
16 Kalling Way, 4 Kallang Basin Industrial Estate
Singapore 1334, Singapore
Tel.: 65 7488880
Fax.: 65 7465315
(Electrical and air-conditioning equipment)
Dennis Lee Kim Yew, Chairman

Haw Par Brothers International
154 Clemenceau Ave., #04-01
Haw Par Centre
Singapore 0923, Singapore
Tel.: 65 3379102
Fax.: 65 3382573
(Consumer products, international trading)
Mohd Ismail bin Shariff, Group Personnel Manager

Intercontinental Engineering & Trading
803 King George's Avenue, #01-182
Singapore 0820, Singapore
Tel.: 65 2968890
Fax.: 65 2965006
(Electronic parts)
Lee Kok Keong, Director

Malayan Motors
45 Leng Kee Rd.
Singapore 0315, Singapore
Tel.: 65 4737755
Fax.: 65 4740853
(Motor vehicles)
Royston Tan, Senior Executive
Wearne Bros. Group, Singapore

Singapura United Tobacco
SUTL House, 100-J Pasir Panjang Rd.
Singapore 0511, Singpore
Tel.: 65 4798833
Fax.: 65 4744760
(Cigarettes, alcohol)
Tay Choon Hye, Chairman

SERVICE INDUSTRIES

Apollo Enterprises
405 Havelock Rd.
Singapore 0316, Singapore
Tel.: 65 7332081
(Property development, hotels)
Sheng Hwai Nak, Managing Director

Cathay Organization
11 Dhoby Ghaut #05-00, Cathay Bldg.
Singapore 0922, Singapore
Tel.: 65 3378181
Fax.: 65 3395609
(Theater and property management)
Meileen Choo, Chairman

Central Properties
1 Goldhill Plaza, #03-45, Podium Block
Singapore 1130, Singapore
Tel.: 65 2500510
Fax.: 65 4711201
(Investments)
Khoo Ban Tian, Chairman

City Developments
36 Robinson Rd., #20-01 City House
Singapore 0106, Singapore
Tel.: 65 2212266
Fax.: 65 2232746
(Property development)
Kwek Hong Png, Chairman

Intraco
456 Alexandra Rd., #14-00 NOL Bldg.
Singapore 0511, Singapore
Tel.: 65 2780011
Fax.: 65 2789938
(Trading)
Hwang Peng Yuan, Chairman

Jurong Engineering
25 Tanjong Kling Rd.
Jurong, Singapore 2262, Singapore
Tel.: 65 2653222
Fax.: 65 2684211
(Engineering)
Lau Chan Sin, Chairman

Singapore Airlines
Airline House, Singapore Changi Airport
Singapore 1781, Singapore
Tel.: 65 5423333
Fax.: 65 5455034
(Airline)
Yap Kim Wah, Director of Personnel

Singapore Telecom
Comcentre, 31 Exeter Rd.
Singapore 0923, Singapore
Tel.: 65 7343344
Fax.: 65 7328428
(Telecommunications and postal service)
Wong Hung Khim, President

United Engineers
UE Bldg., 187-209 River Valley Rd.
Singapore 0923, Singapore
Tel.: 65 3374161
Fax.: 65 3393160
(Engineering)
Paul Chen Pao Sun, Group Managing Director

United Overseas Land
7500A Beach Rd., #04-301 The Plaza
Singapore 0719, Singapore
Tel.: 65 2922833
Fax.: 65 2960208
(Development)
Wee Cho Yaw, Chairman

MAJOR INTERNATIONAL COMPANIES IN SINGAPORE

The following is a listing of the major international companies of Singapore. These companies will be classified by business area: Banking and Finance; Industrial Manufacturing; Retailing and Wholesaling; and Service Industries. The company information includes type of business, international parent company, and contact name where possible. Your chances of achieving employment are substantially greater if you contact the subsidiary company in Singapore rather than the parent company in the home country.

BANKING AND FINANCE

Algemene Bank Nederland
18 Church St., P.O. Box 493
Singapore 0104, Singapore
Tel.: 65 5355511
Fax.: 65 5323108
(Banking)
J. Slotema, General Manager
Algemene Bank Nederland, Netherlands

Allianz Insurance (Singapore)
156 Cecil St., 09-01 Far Eastern Bank Bldg.
Singapore 0106, Singapore
Tel.: 65 2227733
Fax.: 65 2242718
(Insurance)
Hwang Soo Jin, Managing Director
Allianz Holding, Germany

Allied Irish Banks
11th Fl., Hong Kong Banking Bldg.
21 Colliver Quay, Singapore 0104
Tel.: 65 2558666
(Banking)
Allied Irish Banks, Ireland

Banco Nacional de Mexico
50 Raffles Place, No. 10-06
Singapore 0104, Singapore
Tel.: 65 2241355
(International banking)
Banco Nacional de Mexico (Banamex), Mexico

Bangkok Bank
Bangkok Bank Bldg., 180 Cecil St.
Singapore 0106, Singapore
Tel.: 65 2219400/20
Fax.: 65 2255852
(Banking)
Athit Wasantachat, General Manager
Bangkok Bank, Thailand

Bank Brussels Lambert
Singapore Branch
1 Raffles Place, 42-00 OUB Centre
Singapore 0104, Singapore
Tel.: 65 5324088
(Banking)
Luc Delva, General Manager
Bank Brussels Lambert, Belgium

Bank of Nova Scotia
#15-01/05 Ocean Bldg., 10 Collyer Quay
Singapore 0104, Singapore
Tel.: 65 5358688
Fax.: 65 5322440
(Banking)
Anatol von Hahn, Manager
Bank of Nova Scotia, Canada

Banque Indosuez
Shenton House, 3 Shenton Way
Singapore 0106, Singapore
Tel.: 65 2207111
Fax.: 65 2242140
(Banking)
Renaud de la Geniere, Chairman
Banque Indosuez, France

Barclays Bank
50 Raffles Place, #23-01 Shell Tower
Singapore 0104, Singapore
Tel.: 65 2248555
Fax.: 65 22404717
(Banking)
Patrick A. Perry, Senior Executive
Barclays Bank Group, U.K.

Commercial Union Assurance Co.
Commercial Union Bldg., 4 Robinson Rd. #11-00
Singapore 0104, Singapore
Tel.: 65 2246677
Fax.: 65 2250938
(Insurance)
N. H. Baring, Chairman
Commercial Union Assurance Co. , U.K.

Commerzbank (South East Asia)
8 Shenton Way #32-00
Singapore, Singapore
Tel.: 65 2234855
(Banking)
Commerzbank, Germany

Credit Agricole (CNCA) Representative Office
Standard Chartered Bank Bldg.
6 Battery Rd. Hex 11-08
Singapore 0104, Singapore
Tel.: 65 2253266
Fax.: 65 2242469
(Banking)
Jean-Michel Severyns, Manager
Caisse Nationale de Credit Agricole, France

Deutsche Bank
#01-01 Treasury Bldg., 8 Shenton Way
Singapore 0106, Singapore
(Banking)
Frederick J. A. Brown, General Manager
Deutsche Bank, Germany

Development Bank of Singapore
DBS Bldg., 6 Shenton Way
Singapore 0106, Singapore
Tel.: 65 2201111
Fax.: 65 2211306
(Banking)
Howe Yoon Chong, Chairman
Commerzbank, Germany

Dresdner (South East Asia)
20 Collyer Quay, #22-00 Tung Centre
Singapore 0104, Singapore
Tel.: 65 2228080
Fax.: 65 2244008
(Banking)
Dr. Christopher von der Decken, Chairman
Dresdner Bank AG, Germany

Fuji Bank
1 Raffles Place, #20-00 OUB Centre
Singapore 0104, Singapore
Tel.: 65 5343500
Fax.: 65 5327310
(Banking)
Kuniharu Ichikawa, General Manager
Fuji Bank, Japan

Lloyds Bank
4 Shenton Way, #18-01 Shing Kwang House
Singapore 0106, Singapore
Tel.: 65 2203222
Fax.: 65 2253169
(Banking)
A. E. R. Garai, General Manager
Lloyds Bank , UK

Mitsui Trust Futures (Singapore)
6 Shenton Way, #35-01 DBS Bldg.
Singapore 0106, Singapore
Tel.: 65 2208553
Fax.: 65 2241669
(Investments)
Keisuke Akeboshi, Managing Director
Mitsui Trust and Banking Co., Japan

Morgan Grenfell (Asia)
36 Robinson Rd., #13-01 City House
Singapore 0106, Singapore
Tel.: 65 2258080
Fax.: 65 2252869
(Securities)
Lim Ah Doo, Managing Director
Deutsche Bank, Germany

National Australia Bank
10 Collyer Quay, 26-02/07 Ocean Bldg.
Singapore 0104, Singapore
Tel.: 65 5357655
Fax.: 65 5344264
(Banking)
A. P. Kavanagh, Managing Director
National Australia Bank, Australia

National Westminster Bank
#05-01/06 Shell Tower, 50 Raffles Place
Singapore 0104, Singapore
Tel.: 65 2204144
Fax.: 65 2259827
(Banking)
T. R. Buddell, Chief Manager
National Westminster Bank, U.K.

NMB Postbank Groep
Standard Chartered Bank Bldg., 6 Battery Rd. #30-01/02
Singapore 0104, Singapore
Tel.: 65 2204644
Fax.: 65 2256880
(Investments and finance)
Gerrit J. Tammes, Chairman
NMB Postbank Group , Amsterdam

Nomura Singapore
Standard Chartered Bank Bldg., 6 Battery Rd. 39-01
Singapore 0104, Singapore
Tel.: 65 2208766
(Investment banking)
Nomura Securities Co., Japan

Overseas Union Bank
OUB Centre, 1 Raffles Place
Singapore 0104, Singapore
Tel.: 65 5338686
Fax.: 65 5332293
(Banking)
Lien Ying Chow, Chairman
Overseas Union Bank

Paribas South East Asia
16, Raffles Quay 39, 02 Hong Leong Bldg.
Singapore 0104, Singapore
Tel.: 65 2227222
(Financial services)
Compagnie Financiere de Paribas, France

Royal Trust Merchant Bank
#19-01 Shell Tower, 50 Raffles Place
Singapore 0104, Singapore
Tel.: 65 2249111
Fax.: 65 2253809
(Banking)
Fock Siew Tong, Managing Director
Royal Trustco, Canada

Sanwa Bank
50 Raffles Place, No. 25-01, Shell Tower
Singapore 0104, Singapore
Tel.: 65 2249822
(Banking)
Takehiko Okubo, General Manager
Sanwa Bank, Japan

Standard Chartered Merchant Bank Asia
6 Battery Rd., #22-01
Singapore 0104, Singapore
Tel.: 65 2252000
Fax.: 65 2252022
(Banking)
D. G. Moir, Chairman
SCMB Overseas, England

Sumitomo Trust & Banking Co.
#02-16, 1st UIC Bldg.
5 Shenton Way
Singapore 0106, Singapore
Tel.: 65 2249055
(Banking)
Takashi Yamaguchi, General Manager
Sumitomo Trust & Banking Co., Japan

Westpac Banking Corp.
4301 OCBC Centre, 65 Chulia St.
Singapore 0104, Singapore
Tel.: 65 5338673
Fax.: 65 5326781
(Banking)
David Burrill, Chief Manager
Westpac Banking Corp., Australia

INDUSTRIAL MANUFACTURING

Bayer (Singapore)
4 Penjuru Lane
Singapore 2260, Singapore
Tel.: 65 2654855
(Agricultural chemicals)
Rolf Rebstock, Managing Director
Bayer, Germany

BP Singapore
P.O. Box 2814, BP House
1 Pasir Panjang Rd.
Singapore 0511, Singapore
Tel.: 65 4756633
Fax.: 65 4759273
(Petroleum products)
D. H. W. Payne, Chairman
British Petroleum Co., England

British-American Tobacco Co.
57 Senoko Dr.
Singapore 2775, Singapore
Tel.: 65 7588555
Fax.: 65 7557798
(Tobacco products)
M. Y. Y. Kan, Director
British American Tobacco Co., England

Castrol (Far East)
6 Hillview Rd., Princess Elizabeth Ext., Km 15, Bukit Timah Rd.
Singapore 2366, Singapore
Tel.: 65 7607711
Fax.: 65 7608055
(Lubricating oils and greases)
Larry Smith, Managing Director
Castrol Ltd., England

Chemical Industries (Far East)
52 Jln Buroh, Jurong Town
Singapore 2261, Singapore
Tel.: 65 2650411
Fax.: 65 2656690
(Chemical manufacturing)
Lim Soo Peng, Managing Director

Elf Petroleum Sea
2 Gul Crescent
Singapore 2262, Singapore
Tel.: 65 8622900
Fax.: 65 8613059
(Lubricants)
Eric Painvin, Chairman
Societe des Lubrifiants Elf Aquitaine, France

EMI (Singapore)
Unit 13-04 Manhattan House
151 Chin Swee Rd.
Singapore 0316, Singapore
Tel.: 65 7320808
(Music products and publications)
T. W. Wee, Managing Director
Thorn EMI, England

Expandite
61 Gul Drive
Jurong, Singapore 2262, Singapore
Tel.: 65 8611266
Fax.: 65 8610308
(Adhesives, compounds)
Ronald N. Smith, Director
Burmah Oil, U.K.

Hitachi Consumer Products Singapore
206 Bedok South Ave. 1
Singapore 1646, Singapore
Tel.: 65 2419444
Fax.: 65 4444572
(Electrical goods)
S. Osaki, Chairman
Hitachi Ltd., Japan

Hume Industries (Singapore)
13.7 Km, Bukit Timah Rd.
Singapore 2158, Singapore
Tel.: 65 663288
(Concrete, steel, plastic)
Michael Yue-Onn Fam, Chairman
Hume Industries (Far East), New Zealand

ICI (Singapore)
4 Raffles Quay, #09-00
Finlayson House
Singapore 0104, Singapore
Tel.: 65 2243811
Fax.: 65 2254095
(Chemicals, fertilizers)
J. D. Rushton, Chairman
Imperial Chemical Industries, U.K.

John Lysaght (South East Asia)
18 Benoi Sector
Jurong, Singapore 2262, Singapore
Tel.: 65 2641577
Fax.: 65 2650951
(Construction materials)
John Gourlay, General Manager
John Lysaght Ltd., Australia; BHP Steel International, Australia

Matsushita Refrigeration Industries
1 Bedok S. Rd.
Singapore 1646, Singapore
Tel.: 65 2410022
(Home appliances)
Matsushita Electric Industrial Co., Japan

Philips Singapore
Lorong 1, Toa Payoh
Singapore 1231, Singapore
Tel.: 65 3502000
Fax.: 65 2533395
(Electronics, appliances)
B. H. Hylkema, Managing Director
NV Philips, Holland

Sanyo Industries (Singapore)
117/119 Neythal Rd.
Jurong, Singapore 2262, Singapore
Tel.: 65 2650077
Fax.: 65 2653015
(Electrical products)
Ng Ghit Cheon, Managing Director
Sanyo, Japan

Shell Companies in Singapore
Shell Tower, 50 Raffles Place
Singapore 0104, Singapore
Tel.: 65 2247777
Fax.: 65 2241935
(Petrochemical products)
D. Van Hilten, Chairman
Royal Dutch/Shell Group of Companies, Netherlands

Toshiba Singapore
1906, Orchard Towers, 400 Orchard Rd.
Singapore 9, Singapore
Tel.: 65 373911
Fax.: 65 34765
(Television components)
Toshiba Corp., Japan

RETAILING AND WHOLESALING

Australian American Engineering Corp.
203 Henderson Rd. #12-06
Henderson Industrial Park
Singapore 0315, Singapore
Tel.: 65 2717822
Fax.: 65 2733214
(Engineering supplies)
John Mackenzie, Chairman
Australian American Engineering Corp., Australia

Borneo Motors (Singapore)
31-33 Leng Kee Rd.
Singapore 0315, Singapore
Tel.: 65 4751288
Fax.: 65 4794562
(Motor vehicles)
Alan Tan Tatt Huat, Managing Director
Inchcape Berhad, U.K.

Caldbeck, MacGregor (Singapore)
Inchcape House, 3rd Floor, 450/452 Alexandra Rd.
Singapore 0511, Singapore
Tel.: 65 4740621/8
Fax.: 65 4728580
(Alcoholic beverages)
Gerald Foo, Director
Guiness, England

Chubb Singapore
207 Kallang Bahru
Singapore, Singapore
Tel.: 65 2928421
Fax.: 65 2987310
(Security equipment)
Sime Darby, Malaysia

CIBA-Geigy South East Asia
4 Fourth Lok Yang Rd.
Singapore 2262, Singapore
Tel.: 65 2653622
Fax.: 65 2685670
(Pharmaceuticals and chemicals)
D. R. C. Free, Managing Director
CIBA-Geigy Group of Companies, U.K.

Firestone Singapore
101 Cecil St., #13-11/12 Tong Eng Bldg.
Singapore 0106, Singapore
Tel.: 65 2242836
(Tires)
C. B. Pettit, Managing Director
Firestone Tyre & Rubber Co., U.K.

General Electric Co. of Singapore
Magnet House, 985 Bukit Timah Rd.
Singapore 2158, Singapore
Tel.: 65 4663011
Fax.: 65 4698258
(Electronics)
Lim Kee Ming, Chairman
General Electric Co., U.K.

George Cohen (Far East)
600 House, 257 Jalan Ahmad Ibrahim
Singapore 2262, Singapore
Tel.: 65 2654233/8
Fax.: 65 2658347
(Machine tools and mechanical equipment)
John Parker, Chairman
600 Group, U.K.

Jardine Matheson (Singapore)
#17-00, Shing Kwan House, 4 Shenton Way
Singapore 0106, Singapore
Tel.: 65 2205111
Fax.: 65 2246370
(Marketing, shipping, engineering)
Boon Yoon Chiang, Chairman
Jardine Pacific Holdings, Hong Kong

Mitsubishi Corp.
#08-09-10 Hong Leong Centre, 138 Robinson Rd.
Singapore 0106, Singapore
Tel.: 65 2209111
Fax.: 65 2256047
(Importing and exporting)
E. Yoshizaki, General Manager
Mitsubishi Corp., Japan

Nestle Singapore
200 Cantonment Rd., Unit 03-01, South Point
Singapore 0208, Singapore
Tel.: 65 2215522
Fax.: 65 2240402
(Food and dairy products)
J. T. Watson, Managing Director
Nestle S.A., Switzerland

Roche Singapore
Roche Bldg., 30 Shaw Rd.
Singapore 1336, Singapore
Tel.: 65 2830033
Fax.: 65 2878100
(Pharmaceuticals, chemicals)
Koh Choon Hui, Managing Director
F. Hoffmann-La Roche & Co., Switzerland

Rolex Singapore
302 Orchard Rd., #01-01 Tong Bldg.
Singapore 0923, Singapore
Tel.: 65 7379033
Fax.: 65 7342094
(Watches)
J. C. G. Ramsey, Managing Director
Rolex Holding, Switzerland

Wellcome (Singapore)
33 Quality Rd.
Singapore 2261, Singapore
Tel.: 65 2654922
Fax.: 65 2656579
(Pharmaceuticals)
C. R. Rennie, Managing Director
Wellcome Foundation, U.K.

SERVICE INDUSTRIES

ASEA Singapore
2 Sixth Lok Yang Rd.
Singapore 2262, Singapore
Tel.: 65 2652677
Fax.: 65 2652004
(Engineering)
Jorgen Centerman, Managing Director
ASEA Sweden, Sweden

Ben Line Agencies
200 Cantonment Rd. #13-05, Southpoint
Singapore 0208, Singapore
Tel.: 65 2253522
Fax.: 65 2240163
(Shipping)
W.R.E. Thomson, Chairman
Ben Line Group, England

Harrisons & Crosfield (Singapore)
10-12 Third Lok Yang Rd.
Singapore 2262, Singapore
Tel.: 65 2653677
Fax.: 65 2640422
(Trading, commodities)
R. N. H. Jago, Chairman
Harrisons & Crosfield, U.K.

ICL Singapore
World Trade Centre, 1 Maritime Square #11-22
Singapore 0409, Singapore
Tel.: 65 2733322
Fax.: 65 2731993
(Computer programming and equipment)
Dennis J. Haines, Chairman
ICL, England

Jacks International
29 Joo Koon Rd.
Singapore 2262, Singapore
Tel.: 65 8623306
Fax.: 65 8621159
(Trading)
Tan Kay Hock,Chairman
Johan Holdings

John Manners & Co.
51 Anson Rd., #11-51 Anson Centre
Singapore 0207, Singapore
Tel.: 65 2208622
Fax.: 65 2257870
(Trading)
E. F. de Lasala, Chairman
John Manners & Co. , Hong Kong

Macmillan Southeast Asia
41 Jalan Pemimpin 03-04
Singapore 2057
Tel.: 65 2521337
(Book publishing)
Joseph Kang, Executive Director
Macmillan Publishers, England

Ogilvy & Mather (Singapore)
Ste., 11-01, World Trade Center,
1 Maritime Sq.
Singapore 0409, Singapore
Tel.: 65 2738011
Fax.: 65 2742156
(Advertising)
John Seifert, Managing Director
WPP Group, England

Reuters Singapore
50 Raffles Place #17-01, Shell Tower
Singapore 0104, Singapore
Tel.: 65 2253848
(News service)
Reuters Holdings, England

MAJOR NON-PROFIT ORGANIZATIONS IN SINGAPORE

Asian Association of Occupational Health
Department of Social Medicine and Public Health
National University of Singapore
Outram Hill
Singapore 0316, Singapore
Tel.: 65 2226444

Asian Mass Communication Research and Information Centre
39 Newton Rd.
Singapore 1130, Singapore
Tel.: 65 2515106

Asian-Pacific Tax and Investment Research Centre
2 Nassim Rd.
Singapore 1025, Singapore
Tel.: 65 235954

South-East Asia Mathematical Society
Math Department
National University of Singapore
Singapore 0511, Singapore
Tel.: 65 7722764

South East Asia Regional Computer Confederation
c/o National Computer Board
5 Portsdown Rd., off Ayer Rajah
Singapore 0513, Singapore
Tel.: 65 3362344

Technonet Asia
1 Goldhill Plaza
Podium Block 03-35/37
Singapore 1130, Singapore
Tel.: 65 2508161

MAJOR HOTEL EMPLOYERS IN SINGAPORE

Boulevard Hotel Singapore
200 Orchard Blvd.
Singapore 1024, Singapore
Tel.: 65 7372911

Century Park Sheraton
16 Nassim Hill
Singapore, Singapore
Tel.: 65 7321222

Goodwood Park Hotel
22 Scotts Rd.
Singapore 0922, Singapore
Tel.: 65 7377411

Hilton International Singapore
581 Orchard Rd.
Singapore, Singapore
Tel.: 65 7372233

Holiday Inn Park View
11 Cavenagh Rd.
Singapore 0922, Singapore
Tel.: 65 7338333

Hotel Meridian Singapore
100 Orchard Rd.
Singapore 0923, Singapore
Tel.: 65 7327886

Hyatt Regency Singapore
10-12 Scotts Rd.
Singapore 0922, Singapore
Tel.: 65 7331188

Le Meridien Singapore Changi
1 Netheravon Rd.
Singapore 1750, Singapore
Tel.: 65 5427700

Mandarin Singapore
333 Orchard Rd.
Singapore 0923, Singapore
Tel.: 65 7322361

Marina Mandarin Singapore
6 Raffles Blvd.
Marina Square
Singapore 0103, Singapore
Tel.: 65 3383388

New Park Hotel
181 Kitchener Rd.
Singapore 0820, Singapore
Tel.: 65 2915533

Novotel Orchid Inn
214 Dunearn Rd.
Singapore 1129, Singapore
Tel.: 65 2503322

Omni Marco Polo Hotel
247 Tanglin Rd.
Singapore 1024, Singapore
Tel.: 65 4747141

Pan Pacific Singapore
Marina Square, 7 Raffles Blvd.
Singapore 0130, Singapore
Tel.: 65 3368111

Regent of Singapore
1 Cuscaden Rd.
Singapore 1024, Singapore
Tel.: 65 7338888

Royal Holiday Inn Singapore
25 Scotts Rd.
Singapore 0922, Singapore
Tel.: 65 7377966

Shangri-La Hotel
22 Orange Grove Rd.
Singapore 1025, Singapore
Tel.: 65 7373644

Sheraton Towers Singapore
39 Scotts Rd.
Singapore 0922, Singapore
Tel.: 65 7376888

Tai Pan Ramada Hotel Singapore
101 Victoria St.
Singapore 9718, Singapore
Tel.: 65 3360811

Westin Plaza
2 Stamford Rd.
Singapore 0617, Singapore
Tel.: 65 3388585

Westin Stamford
2 Stamford Rd.
Singapore 0617, Singapore
Tel.: 65 3388585

York Hotel
21 Mount Elizabeth
Singapore 0922, Singapore
Tel.: 65 7370511

INTERNATIONAL SCHOOLS IN SINGAPORE

International Schools Services
P.O. Box 5910
Princeton, NJ 08543
American teachers seeking employment abroad may contact this recruitment service.

International School of Singapore
Preston Road,
Singapore 0410, Singapore
Tel.: 65 4754188
(U.S.-U.K. school, K-12 and Junior College Divsion)

Singapore American School
60 King's Rd.
Singapore 1026, Singapore
Tel.: 65 4665611
(U.S. school, pre-K-12)

Tanglin Trust Schools
Portsdown Rd.
Singapore 0513, Singapore
Tel.: 65 7780771
(U.K. school, K-6)

United World College of South East Asia
Dover Rd.
Singapore 0513, Singapore
Tel.: 65 7755344
(U.K., International Baccalaureate school, grades 7-13)

The Pacific Islands: Fiji, Papua New Guinea, Vanuatu, Nauru, Tonga, Kiribati, Tuvalu, Western Samoa, Solomon Islands, Hawaii

FIJI

The Republic of Fiji is located in the southern Pacific Ocean, 1,300 miles north of New Zealand and near the Solomon Islands and Tonga. The country measures approximately 7,000 square miles, about the size of Massachusetts. Fiji consists of over 800 islands, of which 100 are inhabited. The largest island, Viti Levu, has nearly half of the total territory. Other large islands include Vanua Levu, Taveuni, and Ovalau. Most of the country is mountainous.

Indians are the largest ethnic group in Fiji, with about 48% of the population. During the nineteenth century, Indians were brought to Fiji to work on sugar plantations. Today, Indians are dominant in business and the professions. Indigenous Fijians, descendants of Melanesian and Polynesian peoples, provide another 46% of the population. Europeans and Chinese comprise most of the remainder. English is the official language, but Hindustani and Fijian are also spoken. Over 50% of the population is Christian, about 40% Hindu, and almost 10% Muslim.

Fiji was inhabited by Melanesians and Polynesians for hundreds of years before the first Europeans arrived. The Dutch explorer Abel Tasman reached Fiji in 1643. British explorer James Cook arrived in 1774. In 1874, the islands became a British colony. Independence as a parliamentary democracy within the British Commonwealth occurred in 1970.

Cultural tensions between the economically dominant Indians and ethnic Fijians result in instablitiy in Fijian politics. In 1977, a largely Indian government was overthrown in a military coup led by Sitiveni Rabuka. In a second coup that same year, Rabuka proclaimed Fiji a republic. The new constitution is designed to guarantee that ethnic Fijians receive economic and political power. Indians are effectively barred from governing. The current civilian government was placed in power by Rabuka.

Current Economic Climate

Fiji's gross national product is slightly over $1 billion, higher than most of the other southern Pacific states. The country's per capita income of $1,000 is also high for the region. Major industries include sugar and sugar refining, tourism, and some light manufacturing. Fiji has a population of 770,000 people, about 70,000 of whom live in the capital, Suva.

Regular business hours are from 8:00 am to 4:30 pm, Monday through Friday. Stores close at 5:00 pm and open on Saturday. Businesses often close for an hour for lunch. Banking hours are from 9:30 am to 3:00 pm, Monday through Thursday, with a 4:00 pm closing time on Friday.

FIJI'S MAJOR TRADING PARTNERS

Export Partners:	Great Britian	32%
	Australia	25%
	New Zealand	10%
Import Partners:	Australia	29%
	New Zealand	20%
	Japan	15%

Getting around in Fiji

Air Pacific, Air New Zealand, and Quantas provide service into Nadi International Airport from Los Angeles, Vancouver, and

Honolulu. Domestic service is provided by Fiji Air, Air Pacific, and Turtle Island Airways. Helicopter service to anywhere in Fiji is provided by Pacific Crown Aviation.

Buses are the easiest way to get around. Open-air buses are very cheap and convenient on the major islands. Air-conditioned buses are available for longer trips. Taxis and several rental car companies are also available. Ferries can be used to travel among the major islands.

Employment Regulations for Americans

Americans do not need a visa to visit Fiji for a period of 30 days or less. Visitor permits can also be acquired in Fiji. Work permits can be issued as well. The country's use of English means that Americans can easily communicate, but so can the major competitiors for skilled jobs: Australians, New Zealanders, and Britons.

Fiji has a small economy, so you shouldn't expect to find many job opportunities. The country has more jobs than other Pacific nations but still fewer than East Asian countries. Tourism is the most promising industry. Over 200,000 tourists visited Fiji before the coups in 1987. Visits dropped off afterward, but the industry is picking up again.

Organizations for Further Information

The following organizations may be helpful in the job search. American embassies and consulates have commercial and/or economic sections that can provide you with business information and explain aspects of the local economy. Foreign government missions in the U.S. such as embassies and consulates can furnish visas and information on work permits and other important regulations. They may also offer economic and business information about the country.

CHAMBERS OF COMMERCE

Ba Chamber of Commerce
P.O. Box 103
Ba, Fiji

Ba Maunfacturers Association
P.O. Box 42
Ba, Fiji

Federated Chambers of Commerce
P.O. Box 337
Suva, Fiji

Fiji Manufacturers Association
P.O. Box 1308
Suva, Fiji

Labasa Chamber of Commerce
P.O. Box 303
Labasa, Fiji

Lautoka Chamber of Commerce
P.O. Box 336
Lautoka, Fiji

Levuka Chamber of Commerce
Levuka
Ovalau, Fiji

Nadi Chamber of Commerce
P.O. Box 113
Nadi, Fiji

Sigatoka Chamber of Commerce
P.O. Box 117
Sigatoka, Fiji

Suva Chamber of Commerce
P.O. Box 347
Suva, Fiji

Suva Retailers Association
P.O. Box 1117
Suva, Fiji

Vatuwaqa Industrialists Association
P.O. Box 5224
Raiwaqa
Suva, Fiji

CONSULAR OFFICES

American Embassy
31 Loftus St., P.O. Box 218
Suva, Fiji
Tel.: 679 314466

Embassy of Fiji
2233 Wisconson Ave. N.W.
Washington, DC 20007
Tel.: (202) 337-8320

Fiji Mission to the United Nations
One U.N. Plaza, 26th Floor
New York, NY 10017
Tel.: (212) 355-7316

OTHER INFORMATIONAL ORGANIZATIONS

Fiji Visitors Bureau, Headquarters
Thomson St.
GPO Box 92
Suva, Fiji
Tel.: 679 300970

Fiji Visitors Bureau, Los Angeles
5777 W. Century Blvd., Suite 220
Los Angeles, CA 90045
Tel.: (213) 568-1616
Fax: (213) 670-2318

MAJOR AMERICAN COMPANIES IN FIJI

The following companies are classified by business area: Banking and Finance; Industrial Manufacturing; and Service Industries. Company information includes type of business, contact name, and American parent company. Your chances of achieving employment are substantially greater if you contact the subsidiary company in Fiji rather than the parent company in the home country.

BANKING AND FINANCE

Alexander Stenhouse
Ratu Sakuna House, 2nd Floor
Victoria Parade,
Suva, Fiji
Tel.: 679 315355
(Insurance)
Alexander & Alexander Services

INDUSTRIAL MANUFACTURING

Colgate-Palmolive (Fiji)
C.P.O. Box 1195
Suva, Fiji
(Personal care products)
Colgate-Palmolive Co.

Johnson & Johnson (Fiji)
Bulei Rd., Laucala Beach Estate
Suva, Fiji
Tel.: 679 391155
(Pharmaceuticals and personal products)
Nitin Singh, General Manager
Johnson & Johnson

SERVICE INDUSTRIES

Price Waterhouse
Dominion House, 6th House
Thomson St.
Suva, Fiji
Tel.: 679 313955
Fax: 679 300981
(Accounting and management services)
Price Waterhouse

MAJOR DOMESTIC COMPANIES IN FIJI

The following company information includes type of business and contact name. Some of these companies are largely state-controlled and thus unlikely to hire foreigners. Americans with high-demand business skills may nonetheless be able to find a position.

Fiji Development Bank
360 Victoria Parade, P.O. Box 104
Suva, Fiji
Tel.: 679 314866
Fax: 679 314886
(Banking)
Laisenia Qarase, Managing Director

National Bank of Fiji
107 Victoria Parade, P.O. Box 1166
Suva, Fiji
Tel.: 679 311999
Fax: 679 303217
(Banking)
V. P. Makrava, Chief Manager

Reserve Bank of Fiji
Pratt St., G.P.O. Box 1220
Suva, Fiji
Tel.: 679 313611
Fax: 679 301688
(Banking)
E. B. Mavoa, Chief Manager

MAJOR INTERNATIONAL COMPANIES IN FIJI

The following companies are classified by business area: Banking and Finance or Industrial Manufacturing. Company information includes type of business, contact name, and parent company. Your chances of achieving employment are substantially greater if you contact the subsidiary company in Fiji rather than the parent company in the home country.

BANKING AND FINANCE

Australia and New Zealand Banking Group
Dominion House, 2nd Floor
Suva, Fiji
Tel.: 679 302144
Fax: 679 301938
(Banking)
ANZ Banking Group, Australia

Barclays Bank
Dominion House, Thompson St.
Suva, Fiji
Tel.: 679 312333
(Banking)
R. W. White, Manager
Barclays Bank, England

Hongkong and Shanghai Banking Corp.
Civic House, G/F, Townhall Rd.
Suva, Fiji
Tel.: 679 314133
(Banking)
Hongkong and Shanghai Banking Corp., Hong Kong

Westpac Banking Corp.
Civic House, 6th Fl., Town Hall Rd.
Suva, Fiji
Tel.: 679 311666
Fax: 679 300718
(Banking)
John H. Stone, General Manager
Westpac Banking Corp., Australia

INDUSTRIAL MANUFACTURING

Wormald International Fiji
Hume St., Lami Suva, Fiji
Tel.: 679 361455
(Security and fire protection equipment)
R. P. Hay, Manager
Wormald International, Australia

MAJOR NON-PROFIT ORGANIZATIONS IN FIJI

Asian Association of Insurance Commissioners
c/o S. Siwatibau
G.P.O Box 1220
Suva, Fiji
Tel.: 679 313611

Committee for Coordination of Joint Prospecting for Mineral Resources in South Pacific Offshore Areas
c/o Mineral Resources Department
P.M.B., G.P.O.
Suva, Fiji
Tel.: 679 381377

MAJOR HOTEL EMPLOYERS IN FIJI

Hyatt Regency
Korolev, Fiji
Tel.: 679 50555

Nadi Airport Travelodge
Nadi Airport 9203
Nadi, Fiji
Tel.: 679 72277

Regent
Nadi Bay
Nadi, Fiji
Tel.: 679 70700

Sheraton Resort
Denarau Beach
Nadi, Fiji
Tel.: 679 72668

Suva Travelodge
Victoria Parade
Suva, Fiji
Tel.: 679 314600

INTERNATIONAL SCHOOL IN FIJI

International Schools Services
P.O. Box 5910
Princeton, NJ 08543
American teachers seeking employement abroad may contact this recruitment service.

International School (Fiji)
Vere Rd., Laucala Beach Estates
Suva, Fiji
Tel.: 679 393300
(U.S.-U.K.-Fiji-Australia-New Zealand school, K-12)

PAPUA NEW GUINEA

Papua New Guinea measures nearly 180,000 square miles, roughly the size of California, on the island of New Guinea. Indonesia forms the western border and Australia lies to the south. Thickly forested mountains cover most of the country, with upland valleys and lower coastal plains. The country also includes several island groups: New Britain, New Ireland, Bouganville, and Buka.

The population consists of a variety of ethnic groups such as Papuans, Melanesians, Polynesians, and minorities of Chinese and Europeans. Many of the groups are almost completely isolated in the forests. English is the official language, but at least 700 local languages and dialects are spoken throughout the country. Pidgin is the language understood by most people. Protestants and Roman Catholics are the largest religious groupings, along with numerous indigenous faiths.

Human remains as old as 10,000 years have been found in Papua New Guinea. Melanesian and Polynesian peoples began migrating to the island several thousand years ago. Europeans made no land claims until the nineteenth century, as the Dutch began controlling the western part of the island, Irian Jaya, which became a part of Indonesia.

On the eastern half of New Guinea, the British claimed the southern part and the Germans took the northern section. The British region became known as Papua New Guinea. In 1905 Australia assumed sovereignty over the British region and then occupied the German area during World War I. Australia administered the eastern half of New Guinea until 1973, when the territory was given self-administration. Papua New Guinea was granted independence in 1975. The country is a parliamentary democracy.

The government of Papua New Guinea has been fighting an armed insurgence on the Bouganville island group. The area was annexed to the German administrative territory before World War I but has traditionally been dissatisfied with belonging to Papua New Guinea. Bouganville's copper deposits accounted for 35% of Papua New Guinea's exports in 1990.

Current Economic Climate

Papua New Guinea has a gross national product of $2.5 billion and a per capita income of $700. The economy is predominantly agricultural, with over 80% of the workforce engaged in agriculture. Coffee, coconuts, palm oil, cocoa, copper, and timber are the leading products. One of the world's largest copper deposits is located in Papua New Guinea.

The country's population is over 3.5 million, with only 15% of the population in urban areas. Port Moresby, the capital, has 125,000 inhabitants. The next largest town and port is Lae with 65,000 people. Other major cities are Rabaul with a population of 15,000; Madang with 21,000; and Wewak, Goroka, and Mt. Hagen with 20,000 each.

Regular business hours are from 8:00 am to 4:30 pm, Monday through Friday. Banking hours are from 9:00 am to 2:00 pm, Monday through Thursday, with a 5:00 pm closing time on Friday. Some stores open on Saturday but not most government and business offices.

PAPUA NEW GUINEA'S MAJOR TRADING PARTNERS

Export Partners:	Japan	26%
	Australia	20%
	European Community	10%
Import Partners:	Australia	40%
	Japan	18%
	United States	10%

Employment Regulations for Americans

Foreigners seeking employment in Papua New Guinea need a work permit, which requires demonstration that no local workers are available to fill the position. Granting of the work permit may also require that local workers be trained.

Papua New Guinea's economy is small and does not grow very fast, meaning that foreigners seeking jobs have very few options. Even the tourist industry is very small and undeveloped. Some companies, such as British Petroleum (BP), are considering extracting mineral and gas deposits, but little opportunity exists at this time.

Organizations for Further Information

The following organizations may be helpful in the job search. American embassies and consulates have commercial and/or economic sections that can provide you with business information and explain aspects of the local economy. Foreign government missions in the U.S. such as embassies and consulates can furnish visas and information on work permits and other important regulations. They may also offer economic and business information about the country.

CONSULAR OFFICES

American Embassy
Armit St. P.O. Box 1492
Port Moresby, Papua New Guinea
Tel.: 675 211455/594/654
Lawrence G. Richter, Consular Officer

Embassy of Papua New Guinea
1330 Connecticut Ave. N.W., No. 350

Washington, DC 20036
Tel.: (202) 659-0856

OTHER INFORMATIONAL ORGANIZATION

Department of Culture and Tourism
P.O. Box 7144
Boroko, Papua New Guinea

MAJOR AMERICAN COMPANIES IN PAPUA NEW GUINEA

The following companies are classified by business area: Banking and Finance; Industrial Manufacturing; and Service Industries. Company information includes type of business, contact name, and American parent company. Your chances of achieving employment are substantially greater if you contact the subsidiary company rather than the parent company in the home country.

BANKING AND FINANCE

Price Waterhouse
Invesmen Haus, 7th Floor,
Douglas St.
P.O. Box 921
Port Moresby, Papua New Guinea
Tel.: 67 22233
(Financial services)
Price Waterhouse

INDUSTRIAL MANUFACTURING

Crown Cork & Seal
Lai, Papua New Guinea
(Packaging products)
Cliff Yarde, Directing Manager
Crown Cork & Seal Co.

Wrigley Co.
Port Moresby, Papua New Guinea
(Food products)
Wm. Wrigley Jr. Co.

SERVICE INDUSTRIES

Air Express International
Dogura PI
Dogura Rd. 6 Mile
Port Moresby, Papua New Guinea
Tel.: 67 5254447
(Air freight forwarder)
Air Express International Corp.

MAJOR INTERNATIONAL COMPANIES IN PAPUA NEW GUINEA

The following companies are classified by business area: Banking and Finance; Industrial Manufacturing; Retailing and Wholesaling; and Service Industries. Company information includes type of business, contact name, and parent company. Your chances of achieving employment are substantially greater if you contact the subsidiary company rather than the parent company in the home country.

BANKING AND FINANCE

Westpac Bank-PNG
Mogoru Moto Bldg., 5th Floor
P.O. Box 706
Port Moresby, Papua New Guinea
Tel.: 67 220800
Fax: 67 213367
(Banking)
Neil Kinney, Managing Director
Westpac Banking Corp., Australia

INDUSTRIAL MANUFACTURING

BP Papua New Guinea
Ela Beach Tower, Level 2
Musgrave St.
Port Moresby, Papua New Guinea
(Petrochemicals)
Fred Haynes, Corporate Affairs Manager
BP Petroleum Development

M.I.M. Ltd.
c/o Blake Dawson Waldron
Mogoru Moto Bldg., 4th Floor
Port Moresby, Papua New Guinea
(Mining)
M.I.M. Holding, Australia

Misima Mines
Loose Bampton St., 2nd Floor
P.O. Box 851
Port Moresby, Papua New Guinea
Tel.: 67 5 213599
Fax: 67 5 213612
(Mining)
Lawrence C. Reinertson, Managing Director
Placer Dome, Canada

Stettin Bay Lumber Co.
Bluma, West New Britain
Papua New Guinea
Tel.: 67 935266
(Timber)
Nissho Iwai Corp., Japan

RETAILING AND WHOLESALING

North Solomons Plantation Development Corp.
Port Moresby, Papua New Guinea
(Commodities)
Berisford International, England

Shell Papua New Guinea
Port Moresby, Papua New Guinea
(Petrochemicals)
Royal Dutch/Shell Group, Netherlands

SERVICE INDUSTRIES

Mitsui & Co.
A.N.G. House, 8th Floor, Hunter St.
Port Moresby, Papua New Guinea
Tel.: 67 5 211900
(Trading)
Mitsui & Co., Japan

MAJOR HOTEL EMPLOYERS IN PAPUA NEW GUINEA

Port Moresby Travelodge
Cnr. Hunter & Douglas Sts.
Port Moresby, Papua New Guinea
Tel.: 67 212266

Rabaul Travelodge
Mango Ave.
Rabaul, Papua New Guinea
Tel.: 67 922111

INTERNATIONAL SCHOOLS IN PAPUA NEW GUINEA

International Schools Services
P.O. Box 5910
Princeton, NJ 08543
American teachers seeking employment abroad may contact this recruitment service.

Aiyura International Primary School
Ukarumpa
Papua New Guinea
Tel.: 675 771059
(U.S.-Australia-New Zealand)

Goroka International Primary School
Griffiths St.
Goroka, E.H.P.
Papua New Guinea
Tel.: 675 721466/721452
(U.S.-U.K. school, K-6)

Highland Lutheran International School
Wabag, Enga Province
Papua New Guinea
Tel.: 675 574043
(U.S. school, K-6)

Port Moresby International High School
Bava St.
Boroko, Port Moresby
Papua New Guinea
Tel.: 675 253166
(U.K.-Australian-New Zealand, IB schools, grades 7-12)

Ukarumpa High School
Ukarumpa
Papua New Guinea
Tel.: 675 771059
(U.S.-Australia-U.K. school, 7-12)

Foreign aid as a percentage of GNP in the South Pacific

Most countries in the South Pacific are extremely poor, largely due to a lack of natural resources and foreign investment. Consequently, most of these states receive significant amounts of foreign development aid. For some of these countries, foreign aid represents most of their economic livelihood. In general, finding employment will be easier in the countries that receive less foreign aid as a percentage of GNP because that indicates a stronger economy.

Tuvalu	98%
Vanuatu	60%
Kiribati	42%
New Caledonia	40%
Tonga	38%
Solomon Islands	31%
Western Samoa	24%
Papua New Guinea	22%
French Polynesia	20%
Fiji	6% ■

VANUATU

Vanuatu is located in the southwestern Pacific Ocean between Fiji and New Caledonia, measuring 5,700 square miles. Most of the islands are densely forested. The people are mainly Melanesian, with some Polynesians, Micronesians, and Europeans. English and French are both official, but Bislama is the most commonly spoken language. Protestants form 55% of the population and Catholics another 17%.

The islands were formerly known as the New Hebrides. Britain and France jointly administered the New Hebrides from 1906 to 1980, when the territory became the independent republic of Vanuatu. The country is heavily dependent upon foreign aid.

Current Economic Climate

Major industries include fishing and fish canning, copra, coffee, and tourism. The Vanuatu franc is the official currency, but the Australian dollar is widely accepted. Australia, Britain, France, and Japan are the country's principal trading partners. About 15,000 of Vanuatu's 150,000 people live in the capital, Vila.

MAJOR COMPANIES IN VANUATU

Company information includes type of business, contact name, and parent company. Your chances of achieving employment are substantially greater if you contact the subsidiary company rather than the parent company in the home country.

ANZ Bank
ANZ House, Kumul Highway
Vila, Vanuatu
Tel.: 2814
(Banking)
R. G. Jones, Managing Director
Australia and New Zealand
Banking Group, Australia

Barclays Bank
P.O. Box 123
Vila, Vanuatu
Tel.: 2536
(Banking)
J. J. O. Wilson, Manager
Barclays Bank, England

Caisse Centrale de Cooperation Economique
Immeuble Oceania, Rue de Paris
P.O. Box 296
Vila, Vanuatu
Tel.: 2171
(Banking)
Mr. de Lamberterie, Manager
Caisse Centrale de Cooperation
Economique, France

Hongkong and Shanghai Banking Corp.
Hong Kong and New Zealand
House
Rue Emile Mercet, P.O. Box 169
Vila, Vanuatu
Tel.: 2714
(Banking)
C. S. Dargie, Manager
Hongkong and Shanghai
Banking Corp., Hong Kong

Maitland-Smith International
31F LO LAM House
Port Vila, Vanuatu
(Building materials and
hardware)
Masco Corp., United States

Melanesia International Trust Co.
P.O. Box 213
Vila, Vanuatu
Tel.: 2551
Fax: 2884
(Finance)
Cliff W. Burmister, Managing
Director
Austalia and New Zealand
Banking Group, Australia

Westpac Banking Corp.
Kumul Hwy., Port Vila
Vanuatu
Tel.: 2084
Fax: 2357
(Banking)
Ian Smith, Manager
Westpac Banking Corp.,
Australia

NAURU

The Republic of Nauru measures only 8 square miles and is located directly south of the equator, near Kiribati. The island is a plateau with a coral reef. Most of the people are Melanesian, Micronesian, and Polynesian, with Chinese and European minorities. Nauruan is the official language, but English is widely spoken. Various Christian denominations are represented.

The British arrived in 1798, but the Germans annexed the territory in 1886. Australia occupied the island during World War I. The Japanese then captured Nauru during World War II and shipped away over 1,000 Nauruans as laborers. Australia resumed administrative control in 1947. In 1968, Nauru became an independent republic.

Current Economic Climate

Nauru has a gross national product of $160 million, almost all of which results from phosphate mining. The currency is the Australian dollar. Thanks to plentiful and easily accessed deposits of high grade phosphates, Nauru's 8,000 people enjoy one of the world's highest per capita revenues. Yaren is the capital.

MAJOR COMPANIES IN NAURU

The following company information includes type of business, contact name, and parent company if applicable. Your chances of achieving employment are substantially greater if you contact the subsidiary company rather than the parent company in the home country.

Bank of Nauru
Civic Ctr., P.O. Box 289
Nauru
Tel.: 674 5239674
(Banking)
M. R. Sethuraman, General Manager

Barclays Bank
Nauru
(Banking)
Barclays Bank, United Kingdom

Westpac Banking Corp.
Nauru
(Banking)
Westpac Banking, Australia

The Peace Corps in the Pacific

If you're interested in doing volunteer work in the Pacific, then don't forget to examine opportunities offered by the the United States Peace Corps. It maintains operations in virtually all of the countries in the South Pacific. The Corps is involved with agricultural work and other development and education projects.

Peace Corps
Recruitment Office
806 Connecticut Ave. N.W.
Washington, DC 20526
Tel.: 1-800-424-8580, ext. 93■

TONGA

The Kingdom of Tonga, measuring 270 square miles, is located north of New Zealand, east of Fiji, and south of Samoa. The country consists of 169 islands, 45 of which are inhabited. About 98% of the population is Polynesian. Tongan and English are the major languages. A large variety of Christian denominations are found in Tonga.

The Dutch were the first Europeans to arrive in the seventeenth century. The islands were characterized by warfare among various groups until the Tupou dynasty was established in 1845. Britain eventually established a protectorate in 1900. Tonga became an independent constitutional monarchy and a member of the British Commonwealth in 1970.

Current Economic Climate

Tonga's gross national product is $65 million. The country's major economic activities involve coconuts, bananas, and tourism. Australia and New Zealand are the primary trade partners. Tonga has a population of 100,000, with over 30,000 in Nuku'alofa, the capital.

MAJOR COMPANIES IN TONGA

Company information includes type of business, contact name, and parent company if applicable. Your chances of achieving employment are substantially greater if you contact the subsidiary company rather than the parent company in the home country.

Bank of Tonga
P.O. Box 924
Nuku'alofa, Tonga
Tel.: 23933
Fax: 23634
(Banking)
Peter B. Jones, General Manager
Bancorp Hawaii Inc., United States

Westpac Banking Corp.
c/o Bank of Tonga, Taufa'ahau Rd.
Vaiku, Nuku'alofa, Tonga
Tel.: 676 23933
Fax: 676 23634
(Banking)
Bryn Harris, General Manager
Westpac Banking Corp., Australia

Tonga Development Bank
Fatafehi Rd., P.O. Box 126
Nuku'alofa, Tonga
Tel.: 676 21333
(Banking)
Lisiate 'A 'Akolo, Managing Director

KIRIBATI

Kiribati is pronounced "kiribass." The country measures 266 square miles and is located in the middle of the Pacific Ocean, north of Tuvalu. Almost all of the islands are low-lying. The equator runs across the archipelago. Most people are Micronesian, with some Polynesian. English and Gilbertese are both official languages. About half of the population is Protestant and half Roman Catholic.

The Gilbert and Ellice Islands became a British protectorate in 1892. The colony was granted self-rule in 1971. The Ellice Islands separated in 1975 and eventually became Tuvalu. The Gilbert Islands became independent in 1979 as the Republic of Kiribati. The country includes Christmas Island, which the British used for nuclear testing.

Current Economic Climate

Kiribati has a gross national product of $24 million, much of which is foreign aid. The currency is the Australian dollar and virtually all trade occurs with Australia. The main economic products are fish, copra, coconuts, and bananas. Kiribati has a population of 65,000, with 22,000 people in the capital, Tarawa.

MAJOR COMPANIES IN KIRIBATI

The following company information includes type of business, contact name, and parent company if applicable. Your chances of achieving employment are substantially greater if you contact the subsidiary company rather than the parent company in the home country.

Bank of Kiribati
Bairiki, Kiribati
Tel.: 686 21095
Fax: 686 21200
(Banking)
P. J. Jackson, General Manager

Westpac Banking Corp.
c/o Bank of Kiribati, Bairiki
Tarawa, Kiribati
Tel.: 686 21095
Fax: 686 21200
(Banking)
Stephen Baker, General Manager
Westpac Banking Corp., Australia

TUVALU

Tuvalu consists of 9 islands totaling 10 square miles in the southwestern part of the Pacific Ocean. Fiji to the south and Samoa to the east are the nearest neighbors. All of the islands are low-lying atolls comprised of coral reefs. Almost all of the people are Polynesians. Tuvaluan and English are both spoken. Most people are Protestants.

Tuvalu was formerly known as the Ellice Islands in the British colony of the Gilbert and Ellice Islands, which were granted self-rule in 1971. The territory separated from the rest of the colony in 1975 and became independent Tuvalu in 1978.

Current Economic Climate

The only measurable economic products are copra and coconuts. The Australian dollar is the currency used in Tuvalu. About 9,000 people live in the country. The capital, Funafuti, has a population near 3,000. No significant economic activity takes place in Tuvalu, so nearly 1,500 Tuvaluans work abroad. Almost all of Tuvalu's economy is dependent upon foreign aid.

MAJOR COMPANY IN TUVALU

Westpac Banking Corp.
c/o Bantional Bank of Tuvalu
Vaiaku, Funafuti, Tuvalu
Tel.: 802/3
(Banking)
M. G. Tanner, General Manager
Westpac Banking Corp.,
Australia

WESTERN SAMOA

The Independent State of Western Samoa is roughly the size of Rhode Island, measuring over 1,100 square miles. The country is located near Fiji and Tonga. American Samoa lies directly to the east. The country contains four major islands: Savai'i, Upolu, Manono, Apolima. Nearly 90% of the population is Polynesian and approximately 10% European and others. Samoan and English are both official languages. About 70% of the people are Protestants and 20% Catholics.

Germany controlled Samoa from 1899 to 1914, when New Zealand took control of the islands during World War I. New Zealand then administered the territory until 1959, when an elected government assumed homerule. Western Samoa became an independent constitutional monarchy in 1962.

Current Economic Climate

Western Samoa has a gross national product of $110 million. Major economic products are cocoa, bananas, copra, and fish. New Zealand, Australia, Germany, and the United States are the principal trading partners. The country has a population of 169,000, of which 35,000 live in the capital city of Apia.

MAJOR COMPANY IN SAMOA

Westpac Banking Corp.
c/o Pacific Commercial Bank
Beach Rd., Apia, Western Samoa
Tel.: 20000
Fax: 22848
(Banking)
Michael Halloran, General Manager
Westpac Banking Corp., Australia

SOLOMON ISLANDS

The Solomon Islands are located in the southwestern part of the Pacific Ocean, near Papua New Guinea. The country measures over 300,000 square miles, nearly the size of Maryland, with 10 large islands and numerous smaller islets. Guadacanal is the largest island.

About 95% of the people are Melanesian, with a Polynesian minority. English is the official language, but Pidgin is most commonly understood, and over 40 other languages are spoken throughout the islands. About 35% of the people are Anglicans, 20% are Roman Catholic, and 25% are Evangelical Protestant.

The Spanish were the first Europeans to sight the islands in 1568, although human remnants as old as 3,500 years have been found. Britain established a protectorate over most of the islands in the 1890s. Several important World War II battles were fought on and around the islands. Self-government was granted in 1976 and independence in 1978. The Solomon Islands is a parliamentary democracy and a member of the British Commonwealth.

Current Economic Climate

The Solomon Islands has a gross national product of $140 million and a per capita income of $300. Major economic products include fishing and fish canning, coconuts, bananas, and forest products. The country's largest trading partners include Australia, Japan, Britain, and Singapore. About 15% of the country's 250,000 people live in urban areas, the largest of which is the capital, Honiara, with 28,000 inhabitants.

HAWAII

The State of Hawaii measures nearly 6,500 square miles, about 2,400 miles west of California. Hawaii joined the union in 1959 as the 50th state. Over 1 million people live in Hawaii, with about 400,000 in Honolulu. Approximately 87% of Hawaiians live in urban areas. Europeans comprise 25% of the population, Japanese 24%, Hawaiians 20%, and Filipinos 12%.

Current Economic Climate

Per capita income in the state is over $18,000. Unemployment in Hawaii is typically low, around 3%. The largest industries are tourism, defense, and agriculture. Sugar and pineapples are the most significant agricultural products. Tourists spend an average of $9 billion annually in Hawaii. Employment is almost always available in the tourist industry.

Country-by-Country Listings

Numerous Japanese and other international companies are located in Honolulu, but foreign investment also focuses significantly in real estate. Japanese investment in the state has financed projects in various industries, particularly tourism. Firms based in Hong Kong and Taiwan also utilize Hawaii as a base of operations for North America.

Organizations for Further Information

Hawaii Chamber of Commerce
Dillingham Bldg.
735 Bishop St.
Honolulu, HI 96813
Tel.: (808) 522-8800

Honolulu Visitors Bureau
2270 Kalalkaua Ave.
Honolulu, HI 96815
Tel.: (808) 923-1811

MAJOR INTERNATIONAL COMPANIES IN HAWAII

Company information includes type of business, contact name, and parent company. Your chances of achieving employment are substantially greater if you contact the subsidiary company rather than the parent company in the home country.

BANKING AND FINANCE

Liberty Bank
99 North King St.
Honolulu, HI 96817
Tel.: (808) 548-5000
(Banking)
Hajime Wada, Senior Vice-President
Sanwa Bank, Japan

Nomura Securities International
Pacific Trade Center, Ste. 2760
Honolulu, HI 96813
Tel.: (808) 538-3837
(Financial services)
Masanori Honda, Senior Officer
Nomura Securities Co., Japan

INDUSTRIAL MANUFACTURING

Hawaiian Independent Refinery
733 Bishop St.
P.O. Box 3379
Honolulu, HI 96842
Tel.: (808) 547-3222
(Petrochemicals)
Broken Hill Co., Australia

Toshiba Hawaii
327 Kamakee St.
Honolulu, HI 96814
Tel.: (808) 521-5377
Fax: (808) 531-3285
(Radios)
Shinji Tamura, President
Toshiba Corp., Japan

RETAILING AND WHOLESALING

Canon U.S.A.
Bldg. B2, 1050 Ala Mona Blvd.
Honolulu, HI 96814
Tel.: (808) 521-0361
(Photographic equipment, office machines)
Canon, Japan

Daiei
801 Kaheki St.
Honolulu, HI 96714
Tel.: (808) 949-6155
(Supermarket)
Tetsu Aiko, President
Daiei , Japan

NEC America
Central Pacific Plaza No. 255
220 South King St.
Honolulu, HI 96813
Tel.: (808) 599-3833
Fax: (808) 599-1772
(Communications systems, computers, electronics)
NEC Corp., Japan

SERVICE INDUSTRIES

China Airlines
Pacific Tower, Ste. 1414
1001 Bishop St.
Honolulu, HI 96813
Tel.: (808) 536-6951
Fax: (808) 536-0369
(Air transportation)
China Airlines, Taiwan

KG Corp.
1585 Kapiolani Blvd., Ste. 1404
Honolulu, HI 96814
Tel.: (808) 942-7743
(Real estate)
Katsuya Kakuri, Chairman
Kumagai Gumi Co., Japan

Ohbayashi HI Corp.
1001 Bishop St.
Honolulu, HI 96813
(Construction)
Ohbayashi Corp., Japan

North American Pacific Rim

The Pacific Rim areas in North America discussed in this chapter include California, Washington, British Columbia, Alaska, and Oregon. Hawaii is discussed in Chapter 15, while Mexico and Central America are found in the next chapter.

Pacific Rim companies now find that investing in the United States and Canada may be their best option. In the past, many firms would open manufacturing facilities or business offices in East Asia to capitalize on the region's comparatively lower production costs. While wages are still lower in Indonesia than in California and property is still cheaper in Kuala Lumpur than in San Francisco, the differences have begun to shrink.

It may be cheaper to produce goods in East Asia, but transportation costs to North America and the possibility of trade barriers in the near future are making Asian investors reconsider their long-term interests. Products assembled in California or services based in Vancouver may initially raise operating costs, but the access to the U.S. and Canadian market can outweigh these considerations. Hong Kong companies are especially eager to relocate many of their assets and operations to North America before the colony returns to China in 1997.

Americans seeking employment in Asia or the Pacific may find working for a Japanese, Taiwanese, or Korean firm in Los Angeles, for example, to be the first step. Once you are established with the company in the U.S., you may be able to transfer abroad. But you should be aware that most of these firms, especially the Japanese, are highly unlikely to place an American or any other foreigner in a management position back home. These companies may, however, place foreigners in positions in other countries.

As usual, the best way to find work abroad is to take a position with an American company that has international operations and then transfer overseas with that firm. American companies involved in the Pacific Rim are listed in the preceding country-by-country chapters.

The company listings in this chapter are not intended to be fully comprehensive. The focus is on large East Asian companies that operate in North America. These are the firms most likely to hire skilled foreigners. Finding a position with one of these companies and then transferring abroad later is a very good option for gaining work in the Pacific Rim. The regions listed in this chapter are those with the most activity by East Asian firms.

ALASKA

Alaska's geograpahy means that its integration into the Pacific Rim is more limited than California's, the Pacific Northwest, and British Columbia. Natural resources, especially petroleum, are Alaska's leading industries. Alaska may eventually benefit if the Soviet Union opens access to its Pacifc Rim, the Soviet Far East. If so, Anchorage may serve as a convenient base of operations between the Soviet Far East and the North American Pacific Rim. Alaska Airlines already flies to several cities in the Soviet Far East.

MAJOR INTERNATIONAL COMPANIES IN ALASKA

The following are the major Asian Pacific companies in Alaska.

China Airlines Ltd.
Anchorage International Airport
P.O. Box 191013
Anchorage, AK 99502
Tel.: (907) 243-5727
(Air transportation)
David Chu, General Manager
China Airlines, Taiwan

Cominco Alaska Inc.
5660 8th St.
Anchorage, AK 99518
Tel.: (907) 563-3686
Fax: (907) 561-1401
(Mining)
Cominco, Canada

CALIFORNIA

Asian companies have a long record of investment in the North American Pacific Rim. Japanese firms, in particular, have been very active in California. Real estate and finance are probably the two fastest growing economic sectors in Southern California in which Asian companies are involved. Sony's purchase of Columbia's movie studios captured headlines across the world, but Japanese investment in California is actually more significant outside of Hollywood.

In the **real estate** market, some estimates classify up to two-thirds of downtown Los Angeles property as Japanese-owned. Estimates vary depending upon the extent of ownership and the definition of downtown property. Nevertheless, Japanese investors are extremely important in the Southern California real estate sector. Japanese investment is taking place in Los Angeles real estate because its a good deal. Property prices in California may be higher on average than in the rest of the U.S., but they are still cheaper than in Tokyo or some other large Asian cities.

Japanese **banking** is also a prominent force in California. Major Japanese banks find that the local markets in Los Angeles and in the state are quite lucrative, but an operational base in Southern California also allows access to the rest of the U.S. while still remaining in relatively easy reach of Tokyo. Mitsui Trust, Dai-Ichi Kangyo, and Daiwa are all highly involved in the California banking industry. A large number of Japanese banks also operate in San Fransisco.

Other Asian companies, in addition to the Japanese, operate in California as well. Firms from Hong Kong, Taiwan, and South Korea have significant interests in the state. Korean companies are most evident in Los Angeles and Southern California while many Chinese firms, from Taiwan and Hong Kong, are found in the San Francisco Bay Area as well as in Southern California.

MAJOR INTERNATIONAL COMPANIES IN CALIFORNIA

The following are the major Asian Pacific companies in California. These firms are probably willing to hire Americans to staff their local offices, but some may be reluctant to promote foreigners to management positions in their home countries. The Japanese companies, for example, are unlikely to place foreigners in management positions abroad. Australian and Hong Kong firms, however, are much more likely to promote foreigners at all levels. The following listings include type of business, a contact name, and the parent company.

BANKING AND FINANCE

Bank of China
444 Flower St., Suite 3900
Los Angeles, CA 90071
Tel.: (213) 688-8700
(Banking)
Jia-Ling Zhang, Manager
Bank of China, China

Commonwealth of Australia
600 Wilshire Blvd.
Los Angeles, CA 90017
Tel.: (213) 689-4702
Fax: (213) 489-3045
(Banking)
John Fitzpatrick, Senior Vice President
Commonwealth Bank Group, Australia

Dai-Ichi Life Insurance Agency
611 West 6th St., Suite 1520
Los Angeles, CA 90017
Tel.: (213) 624-7759
Fax: (213) 624-1659
(Life insurance)
Takahiko Hondo, Senior Vice President
Dai-Ichi Mutual Life Insurance, Japan

Dai-Ichi Kangyo Bank
770 Wilshire Blvd.
Los Angeles, CA 90017
Tel.: (213) 612-6400
Fax: (213) 624-5258
(Banking)
Masahiro Shimizu, General Manager
Dai-Ichi Kangyo Bank, Japan

Daiwa Securities America
333 South Grand Ave., Suite 3636
Los Angeles, CA 60602
Tel.: (213) 628-0201
Fax: (213) 626-5461
Y. Nakati, Vice President
Daiwa Securities Co., Japan

Fuji Bank International
601 California St., Suite 400
San Francisco, CA 94108
Tel.: (415) 362-4740
(Banking)
Hideyuki Shimanuki, President
Fuji Bank, Japan

Hokkaido Takushoku Bank
333 South Grande Ave., Suite 3522
Los Angeles, CA 90071
Tel.: (213) 620-9100
Fax: (213) 620-9321
(Banking)
Yoshinori Kato, General Manager
Hokkaido Takushoku Bank, Japan

International Commercial Bank of China
445 S. Figueroa St., Suite 3200
Los Angeles, CA 90017
Tel.: (213) 489-3000
Fax: (213) 489-1183
(Banking)
Hsien-Jen Tang, Senior Vice President
International Commercial Bank of China, Taiwan

Kyowa Bank of California
635 W. Seventh St.
Los Angeles, CA 90017
Tel.: (213) 626-6266
(Banking)
Tsutomu Itoh, President
Kyowa Bank, Japan

Mitsubishi Bank of California
800 Wilshire Blvd.
Los Angeles, CA 90017
Tel.: (213) 621-1200
(Banking)
Yutaka Hasegawa, President
Mitsubishi Bank, Japan

Mitsui Bank
515 S. Figueroa St., Suite 400
Los Angeles, CA 90071
Tel.: (213) 680-2900
(Banking)
Naruo Otsubo, General Manager
Mitsui & Co., Japan

Mitsui Trust & Banking Co.
611 West 6th St., Suite 3800
Los Angeles, CA 90017
Tel.: (213) 654-5201
Fax: (213) 622-0378
(Banking)
Kazuoki Sone, General Manager
Mitsui Trust & Banking Co., Japan

Nikko Securities Co.
800 Wilshire Blvd., Suite 1050
Los Angeles, CA 90017
Tel.: (213) 626-7163
(Financial services)
K. Susuki, Executive Vice President
Nikko Securities Co., Japan

Nomura Securities International
333 S. Hope St., 41st Floor
Los Angeles, CA 90014
Tel.: (213) 620-7400
(Banking)
Nomura Securities Co., Japan

Sanwa Bank
444 Market St. 18th Floor
San Francisco, CA 94111-9981
Tel.: (415) 597-5200
(Banking)
Masahiko Takeuchi, General Manager
Sanwa Bank, Japan

Sumitomo Bank of California
320 California
San Francisco, CA 94104
Tel.: (415) 445-8000
(Banking)
Keizo Yoshida, President
Sumitomo Bank, Japan

Westpac Banking Corp.
300 S. Grande Ave., Suite 3800
Los Angeles, CA 90017
Tel.: (213) 621-2333
Fax: (213) 627-2809
(Banking)
Sam Mills, Jr., Senior Vice President
Westpac Banking Corp., Australia

INDUSTRIAL MANUFACTURING

Hyundai Steel Industries
6505 Paramount Blvd.
Long Beach, CA 90805
Tel.: (213) 423-6889
(Steel products)
B.H. Ahm, President
Hyundai Corp., South Korea

Kobe Steel USA
300 S. Grande Ave., Suite 2620
Los Angeles, CA 90017
Tel.: (213) 628-8480
Fax: (213) 624-0026
(Steel products)
Shinji Yano, Vice President
Kobe Steel, Japan

Nippondenso of Los Angeles
3900 Via Oro Ave.
Long Beach, CA 90810
Tel.: (213) 834-6352
Fax: (213) 513-7319
(Automotive parts)
K. Amano, President
Toyota Motor Corp., Japan

RETAILING AND WHOLESALING

Broken Hill Co.
550 California St.
San Francisco, CA 94104
Tel.: (415) 774-2288
(Minerals)
Broken Hill Co., Australia

Burns Philp & Co.
750 Bryant St.
San Francisco, CA 94107
Tel.: (415) 777-1850
(Foods)
M.L. Tripathi, President
Burns Philp & Co., Australia

Daihatsu America
4422 Corporate Center Dr.
Los Alamitos, CA 90720
Tel.: (714) 761-7000
Fax: (714) 952-3197
(Automobiles)
John Fujunaka, President
Daihatsu Motor Co., Japan

Hanwa American Corp.
624 S. Grand Ave., Suite 2304
Los Angeles, CA 90017
Tel.: (213) 627-9931
Fax: (213) 687-0559
(Petrochemicals, foods, timber, machinery)
Hanwa Co., Japan

Hyundai Motor America
10550 Talbert Ave.
Fountain Valley, CA 92728
Tel.: (714) 965-3000
Fax: (714) 965-3816
(Automobiles)
H.W. Baik, President
Hyundai Corp., South Korea

Ishihara Corp.
Transamerica Pyramid, 42nd Floor
600 Montgomery St.
San Francisco, CA 94111
Tel.: (415) 421-8207
(Chemicals)
E. Aoki, Vice President
Ishihara Sangyo Kaisha, Japan

Mitsui & Co.
One California St., Suite 3000
San Francisco, CA 94111
Tel.: (415) 765-1195
(Trading)
M. Ejima, General Manager
Mitsui & Co., Japan

NEC America
1411 W. 190th St.
Gardena, CA 90248
Tel.: (213) 719-2400
Fax: (213) 719-2401
(Business communications)
NEC Corp., Japan

Nichimen America
235 Montgomery St.
San Francisco, CA 94104
Tel.: (415) 981-0650
(Trading)
Tadashi Kamej, Vice President
Nichimen Corp., Japan

Sumitomo Corp. of America
Wells Fargo Bank Bldg., Suite 1600
444 S. Flower St.
Los Angeles, CA 90071
Tel.: (213) 627-4783
Fax: (213) 489-0300
(Machinery, steel products)
Koichi Narikawa, Senior Vice President
Sumitomo Corp., Japan

SERVICE INDUSTRIES

China Airlines
6053 W. Century Blvd., Suite 800
Los Angeles, CA 90045
Tel.: (213) 641-8888
Fax: (213) 641-8864
(Air transportation)
C.Y. Lee, Director, Marketing
China Airlines, Taiwan

Korean Air Lines
6101 W. Imperial Hwy.
Los Angeles, CA 90045
Tel.: (213) 417-5200
Fax: (213) 417-3051
(Air transportation)
I.J. Kim, Vice President, Americas
Korean Airlines Co., South Korea

North America Taisei
301 E. Ocean Blvd.
Long Beach, CA 10022
Tel.: (213) 432-5020
(Contracting, engineering)
Yasuo Sento, Manager
Taisei Corp., Japan

Ohbayashi America Corp.
2975 Wilshire Blvd.
Los Angeles, CA 90010
Tel.: (213) 385-8361
(Construction)
Yoshiro Ohbayashi, Chairman
Ohbayashi Corp., Japan

Philippine Airlines
447 Sutter St.
San Francisco, CA 94108
Tel.: (415) 391-0270
Fax: (415) 433-6733
(Air transportation)
Philippine Airlines, The Philippines

Quantas Airways
360 Post St.
San Francisco, CA 94108
Tel.: (415) 445-1400
Fax: (415) 981-1152
(Air transportation)
W.L. Dix, Chairman
Quantas Airways, Australia

Thai Airways International
88 Kearny St., Suite 810
San Francisco, CA 94108
Tel.: (415) 397-8300
(Air transportation)
Gary Jones, District Manager
Thai Airways International, Thailand

MAJOR NON-PROFIT PACIFIC RIM ORGANIZATIONS IN CALIFORNIA

American-Australian Association
P.O. Box 4096
Glendale, CA 91202
Tel.: (213) 243-7770

Chinese Culture Association
P.O. Box 1272
Palo Alto, CA 94304
Tel.: (415) 948-2251

Far East Society
1555 Lake Dr., Rm. 111
Oakland, CA 94612
Tel.: (415) 451-3062

Foundation for the Peoples of the South Pacific
Pacific House, 2-12 W. Park Ave.
P.O. Box 727
Long Beach, NY 11561
Tel.: (516) 432-3563
This organization is actually in New York, not California, but is highly involved with the island nations in the southern Pacific.

Indonesian-American Society of the U.S.
c/o John R. Jeffries
2252 Hedding St.
San Jose, CA 95121

Japan America Society of Southern California
355 E. 1st St.
Los Angeles, CA
Tel.: (213) 629-3400

Japan Business Association of Southern California
350 S. Figueroa St.
Los Angeles, CA 90071
Tel.: (213) 628-1263

Japan Society of San Francisco
312 Sutter St., Rm. 406
San Francisco, CA 94108
Tel.: (415) 986-4383

Japanese American Association
1759 Sutter St.
San Francisco, CA 04115
Tel.: (415) 921-1782

New Zealand-American Association of San Francisco
530 Howard St.
San Francisco, CA 04105
Tel.: (415) 543-0760

Pacific-Indonesian Chamber of Commerce
303 World Trade Center
San Francisco, CA 94111
Tel.: (415) 433-2491

South East Asia Resource Center
P.O. Box 4000-D
Berkeley, CA 94704
Tel.: (415) 548-2546

CANADA

Canada's Pacific Coast is enjoying economic growth while the rest of the country is currently in a recession. Vancouver, the largest city in the province of British Columbia, is responsible for the boom. Most of the same factors that lead Asian companies to invest in L.A., San Francisco, and Seattle also apply to Vancouver.

In addition, free trade between the U.S. and Canada now allows investors to operate in Vancouver and still have access to the U.S. market. Vancouver is located near Seattle, providing for a greater metropolitan area that should soon approximate the Los Angeles-San Diego or San Fransisco Bay Area metropolitan areas. Many business people and companies from Hong Kong are focusing on Vancouver as well. They find that moving to Canada, another member of the British Commonwealth, is more comfortable than even the U.S.

MAJOR INTERNATIONAL COMPANIES IN CANADA

The following are the major Asian Pacific companies in Vancouver. These firms are probably willing to hire Americans to staff their local offices, but some may be reluctant to promote foreigners to management positions in their home countries. The Japanese companies, for example, are unlikely to place foreigners in management positions abroad. Australian and Hong Kong firms, however, are much more likely to promote foreigners at all levels. The following listings classify companies by business area and provide type of business, a contact name, and the parent company.

BANKING AND FINANCE

Bank of Tokyo Canada
One Bentell Centre 505, Suite 1830
Burrard St.
Vancouver, BC V7X 1G1, Canada
Tel.: (604) 689-8661
(Banking)
Bank of Tokyo, Japan

Dai-Ichi Kangyo Bank
Park Place, Suite 1190
Burrard St.
Vancouver, BC V7X 1L4, Canada
Tel.: (604) 684-4954
Fax: (604) 684-4954
(Banking)
Kunio Kotani, Senior Vice-President and General Manager
Dai-Ichi Kangyo Bank, Japan

Hongkong Bank of Canada
885 W. Georgia, Suite 300
Vancouver, BC V6C 3E9, Canada
Tel.: (604) 685-1000
Fax: (604) 641-1849
(Banking)
Jill Calhan, Corporate Secretary
Hongkong & Shanghai Banking Corp., Hong Kong

Sanwa Bank Canada
650 W. Georgia St., Suite 2040
Vancouver, BC V6B 4N8, Canada
Tel.: (604) 683-8344
(Banking)
Sanwa Bank, Japan

INDUSTRIAL MANUFACTURING

Sanyo Kokusaku Pulp Co.
2525 Willow St., No. 509
Vancouver, BC V5Z 3N8, Canada
Tel.: (604) 873-5358
(Lumber and wood products)
Sanyo Kokusaku Co., Japan

RETAILING AND WHOLESALING

Mitsui & Co.
Four Bentall Centre, 33rd Floor
1055 Dunsmuir St.
Vancouver, BC V7X 1E6,
Canada
Tel.: (604) 668-3100
(Trading)
A. Doy, Vice-President &
General Manager
Mitsui & Co., Japan

Nissho Iwai Canada
1055 Dunsmuir St., Suite 2624
Vancouver, BC V7X 1L3,
Canada
Tel.: (604) 684-8351
(Trading)
Nisshi Iwai Corp., Japan

Ssanngyong Corp.
1112 W. Pender St.
Vancouver, BC V6E 2S1, Canada
Tel.: (604) 669-2882
Fax: (604) 689-0494
(Trading)
Ssangyong Group, South Korea

Sumitomo Canada
IBM Tower 1690, 701 W.
Gerogia St.
P.O. Box 10141, Pacific Center
Vancouver, BC, Canada
Tel.: (604) 682-2256
(Trading)
T. Uchiyama, President
Sumitomo Corp., Japan

SERVICE INDUSTRIES

Quantas Airways
Four Bentall Centre, Suite 1714
P.O. Box 49288
Vancouver, BC V7X 1L3,
Canada
Tel.: (604) 684-8231
(Airline)
R. Nuyen, Sales Manager,
Western Canada
Quantas Airways, Australia

Thai Airways International
726 Richards St.
Vancouver, BC V6B 3L2, Canada
Tel.: (604) 687-1412
(Airline)
Jim Lim, District
Representative, Sales
Thai Airways International,
Thailand

OREGON

Oregon is benefiting from Asian investment too, although at a slower rate and to a smaller extent than Washington. Many of the same cost-driven motivations that led Japanese firms to move to Seattle instead of Los Angeles or San Francisco are now leading them to Portland.

MAJOR INTERNATIONAL COMPANIES IN OREGON

The following are the major Asian Pacific companies in Oregon. These firms are probably willing to hire Americans to staff their local offices, but some may be reluctant to promote foreigners to management positions in their home countries. The Japanese companies, for example, are unlikely to place foreigners in management positions abroad. Australian and Hong Kong firms, however, are much more likely to promote foreigners at all levels. The following listings provide type of business, a contact name, and the parent company.

Bank of Tokyo
411 S.W. 6th St.
Portland, OR 97204
Tel.: (503) 222-3661
(Banking)
M. Shichijo, General Manager
Bank of Tokyo, Japan

Suburu Northwest Inc.
8040 N.E. 33rd Dr.
Portland, OR 97211
Tel.: (503) 287-4171
(Automobiles)
Joe Dylag, Vice President
Fuji Heavy Industries, Japan

Mitsui & Co.
First Interstate Tower
1300 S.W. 5th
Portland, OR 97201
Tel.: (503) 226-3546
(Trading)
Mitsui & Co., Japan

WASHINGTON

The State of Washington is currently the second leading area for Asian investment in the North American Pacific Rim. Seattle is beginning to assume much of the same international character that Los Angeles enjoys. Japanese companies are leading the investment drive in Washington as well. Many Hong Kong investors are also safeguarding their money by moving it to the U.S. and find that investing in Seattle is cheaper than in Southern California and almost as convenient.

These firms find that property and labor costs are lower in Washington than in California. While they sacrifice the business environment found in L.A. or San Francisco, the savings often make the move to Washington worth the trade-off. The increased investment, however, is now driving up prices in Seattle. Additionally, many Southern Californians are moving to the Pacific Northwest to escape L.A.'s congestion and high cost of living.

MAJOR INTERNATIONAL COMPANIES IN WASHINGTON

The following are the major Asian Pacific companies in Washington. These firms are probably willing to hire Americans to staff their local offices, but some may be reluctant to promote foreigners to management positions in their home countries. The Japanese companies, for example, are unlikely to place foreigners in management positions abroad.

Australian and Hong Kong firms, however, are much more likely to promote foreigners at all levels. The following listings classify companies by business area and provide type of business, a contact name, and the parent company.

BANKING AND FINANCE

Hokkaido Takushoku Bank
1001 4th Ave., Suite 3920
Seattle, WA 98104
Tel.: (206) 624-0920
Fax: (206) 345-0393
(Banking)
Noriyasu Komata, Vice President
Hokkaido Taakushoku Bank, Japan

Mitsui Bank
900 4th Ave., Suite 1610
Seattle, WA 98164
Tel.: (206) 622-0330
(Banking)
Hisao Oshima, Chief Representative
Mitsui & Co., Japan

Taiyo Kobe Bank
900 4th St.
Seattle, WA 98164
Tel.: (206) 682-2312
K. Kuwabura, General Manager
Taiyo Kobe Bank, Japan

INDUSTRIAL MANUFACTURING

Sanyo Kokusaku Pulp
Norton Bldg., 801 2nd Ave.
Seattle, WA 98104
Tel.: (206) 682-4698
(Pulp manufacturing)
H. Shugano, Manager
Sanyo Kokusaku Pulp Co., Japan

Westward Seafoods
1111 3rd Ave., Suite 1450
Seattle, WA 98101
Tel.: (206) 682-5949
Fax: (206) 682-1825
(Seafood processing)
Hugh Reilly, President
Taiyo Fishery Co., Japan

Yokohama Rubber Co.
701 5th Ave., Suite 7100
Seattle, WA 98104
Tel.: (206) 622-4810
Fax: (206) 621-9448
(Tires, rubber goods)
Tsuyoshi Sugimoto, General Manager
Yokohama Rubber Co., Japan

RETAILING AND WHOLESALING

Daiei International
Queen Anne Sq., Suite 507
220 W. Mercer St.
Seattle, WA 98119
Tel.: (206) 282-5573
Fax: (206) 282-7009
(Purchasing)
Yuzuru Shingai, Chief Operations Officer
Daiei, Japan

Hanwa American Corp.
Bank of California Center, Suite 1640
900 4th Ave.
Seattle, WA 98164
Tel.: (206) 622-2102
(Seafood, timber)
Hisatake Nakano, General Manager
Hanwa Co., Japan

Honshu Paper Co.
One Union Sq., Suite 2300
600 University St.
Seattle, WA 98101
Tel: (206) 625-5145
Fax: (206) 625-1362
(Wood materials)
S. Takeyama, Vice President
Honshu Paper Co., Japan

Kyokuyo U.S.A.
100 West Harrison Plaza South Tower
Seattle, WA 98119
Tel.: (206) 281-1262
Fax: (206) 281-1255
(Food products)
Hiroshi Arai, President
Kyokuyo Co., Japan

Sumitomo Corp. of America
Two Union Sq., Suite 4500
601 Union Sq.
Seattle, WA 98101
Tel.: (206) 623-5270
Fax: (206) 447-1879
(Foods, steel products, lumber)
T. Yuge, Senior Vice President
Sumitomo Corp., Japan

SERVICE INDUSTRIES

Thai Airways International
720 Olive Way, Suite 1400
Seattle, WA 98101
Tel.: (206) 467-9898
Fax: (206) 467-8461
(Air transportation)
Prasert Lipiwathana, General Manager
Thai Airways International, Thailand

17 Latin American Pacific Rim

The Pacific Rim in Latin America currently focuses primarily upon Mexico and Panama. Although some Japanese banks and other firms invest there, other Latin American Pacific Rim players such as Chile, Colombia, Peru, and Ecuador are engaged to a lesser extent. In the future, Japanese companies are expected to increase their involvement in Latin America to extract natural resources. This chapter centers upon Mexico, Panama, and a few South American countries.

Asian companies are beginning to invest significantly in Mexico and Panama for several reasons. Labor costs in Latin America are now competitive with those in East Asia. Whereas companies sought Malaysian or Indonesian bases for manufacturing, for example, economic growth in those countries has narrowed the gap with wages in Latin America. In many cases, production costs can actually be lower in Latin America.

Country-by-Country Listings

Americans seeking employment in the Pacific Rim may find working for an Asian firm in Latin America to be the first step. Once you are established with the company in Latin America, you may be able to transfer to Asia. But you should be aware that most of these firms, especially the Japanese, are highly unlikely to place an American or any other foreigner in a management position back home. These companies may, however, place foreigners in positions in other countries, including Latin America.

As usual, the best way to find work abroad is to locate a position with an American company that has international operations and then transfer overseas with that firm. American companies involved in the Pacific Rim are listed in the preceding country-by-country chapters.

The company listings in this chapter are not intended to be fully comprehensive. The focus is on large East Asian companies that operate in Latin America. These are the firms most likely to hire skilled foreigners. Finding a position with one of these companies and then transferring abroad later is a very good option for gaining work in the Pacific Rim. The countries listed in this chapter are those with the most activity by East Asian firms.

CHILE

Chile has one of the most prosperous economies in Latin America and has long maintained a favorable foreign investment climate. Japanese banks are very active in Santiago. Other Asian Pacific companies, especially from South Korea and Hong Kong, are also present in Chile. The mineral extraction industry is one of the leading economic sectors, but manufacturing is also increasing.

Organizations for Further Information

The following organizations may be helpful in the job search. American embassies and consulates have commercial and/or economic sections that can provide you with business information and explain aspects of the local economy. Foreign government missions in the U.S. such as National Tourist Offices and embassies and consulates can furnish visas and information on work permits and other important regulations. They may also offer economic and business information about the country.

CHAMBERS OF COMMERCE

Chamber of Commerce of the U.S. in Chile
Av. Americo Vespucio Sur 80, 9 Piso

P.O. Box 4131
Santiago, Chile
Tel.: 56 2 484140

Chile-North American Chamber of Commerce
220 E. 81st St.,
New York, NY 10028
Tel.: (212) 288-5691

San Antonio Chamber of Commerce
Casilla 30, Angamos 1662
San Antonio, Chile
Tel.: 56 035 31045

CONSULAR OFFICES

American Embassy
Codina Bldg., 1343 Agustinas
Santiago, Chile
Tel.: 56 2 710133/90

Embassy of Chile
1732 Massachusetts Ave. N.W.
Washington, DC 20036
Tel.: (202) 785-1746

OTHER INFORMATIONAL ORGANIZATION

Chilean National Tourist Board (Sernatur)
P.O. Box 14082,
Santiago, Chile
Tel.: 56 2 696474

MAJOR PACIFIC RIM COMPANIES IN CHILE

Company information includes type of business, contact name, and parent company. Your chances of achieving employment are substantially greater if you contact the subsidiary company in Chile rather than the parent company in the home country. These firms are probably willing to hire Americans to staff their local offices, but some may be reluctant to promote foreigners to management positions in their home countries.

Bank of Tokyo
Moneda 772
Santiago, Chile
Tel.: 56 2 332031
(Banking)
Bank of Tokyo, Japan

Export-Import Bank of Korea
Providencia 2653, Forum Bldg., Rm. 512
P.O. Box 124
Santiago, Chile
Tel.: 56 2 2515787
(Banking)
Kum-Jae Oh, Chief Representative
Export-Import Bank of Korea, South Korea

Hongkong and Shanghai
Banking Corp.
Agustinas 604, Casilla 67-D
Santiago, Chile
Tel.: 56 2 397535
(Banking)
A. Wilkinson, Manager
Hongkong and Shanghai
Banking Corp., Hong Kong

Mitsui Chilena Commercial
Calle Agustinas 1235, 7 Piso
Santiago, Chile
Tel.: 56 2 6981974
(Trading)
Mitsui & Co. , Japan

NEC Chile
San Crescente 81, Pisos 2-3
Los Condes, Santiago, Chile
(Communications equipment)
NEC Corp., Japan

COLOMBIA

Colombia's economy has traditionally been based upon coffee and still depends upon the commodity for much of its export earnings. Other economic sectors, especially manufacturing and banking, have begun to grow in recent years. The drug-related violence in Colombia has not deterred many foreign investors. The country has a large and diversified economy, drawing investment from Japan and other Asian Pacific countries.

Organizations for Further Information

The following organizations may be helpful in the job search. American embassies and consulates have commercial and/or economic sections that can provide you with business information and explain aspects of the local economy. Foreign government missions in the U.S. such as National Tourist Offices and embassies and consulates can furnish visas and information on work permits and other important regulations. They may also offer economic and business information about the country.

CHAMBERS OF COMMERCE

Colombian-American Association
111 Broadway, Rm. 1408
New York, NY 10006
Tel.: (212) 233-7776

Colombian-American Chamber of Commerce, Bogota
Apto. Aereo 8008, Calle 35 No. 616
Bogota, Colombia
Tel.: 57 2 857800

Colombian-American Chamber of Commerce, Cali
Av. In #3N97, P.O. Box 5943

Cali, Colombia
Tel.: 57 610162/672992

San Andres Chamber of Commerce
Avenida 20 de Julio, No. 1A-85, Edifico Balul, Of. 202
San Andres, Colombia
Tel.: 57 6287

CONSULAR OFFICES

American Embassy
Calle 38, No. 8-61
Bogota, Colombia
Tel.: 57 1 2851300/1688

Embassy of Colombia
2118 Leroy Pl. N.W.
Washington, DC 20008
Tel.: (202) 387-8338

WORLD TRADE CENTER

World Trade Center Bogota
P.O. Box 6005
Bogota, Colombia
Tel.: 57 2 184411

MAJOR PACIFIC RIM COMPANIES IN COLOMBIA

Company information includes type of business, contact name, and parent company. Your chances of achieving employment are substantially greater if you contact the subsidiary company in Colombia rather than the parent company in the home country.

Bank of Tokyo
Cra 8, No. 15-42
Edif Banco Frances e Italiano de Bogota
Bogota, Colombia
Tel.: 57 1 2817347
(Banking)
Bank of Tokyo, Japan

Mitsui de Colombia
Cra 7, No. 24-89 Piso 15
Edificio Col.pa
Bogota, Colombia
Tel.: 57 1 2824136
(Trading)
Mitsui & Co., Japan

NEC de Colombia
Carrera 9, No. 80-32
Bogota D.E., Colombia
Tel.: 57 2 2101023
Fax: 57 2 2101054
(Communications equipment)
A. Takao, General Manager
NEC Corp., Japan

Overseas Union Bank
Calle 19, No. 3-50, Ofca 2004
Bogota, Colombia
Tel.: 57 2 817979
(Banking)
Aurelio Correa, Manager
Overseas Union Bank, Singapore

ECUADOR

Although Ecuador is one of the smaller economies in South America, it offers significant natural resources, including petroleum. The country also has a good port facility and has experienced more political stability than its neighbors, Peru and Colombia. Coffee, fishing, and light manufacturing are important economic sectors.

Organizations for Further Information

The following organizations may be helpful in the job search. American embassies and consulates have commercial and/or economic sections that can provide you with business information and explain aspects of the local economy. Foreign government missions in the U.S. such as National Tourist Offices and embassies and consulates can furnish visas and information on work permits and other important regulations. They may also offer economic and business information about the country.

CHAMBERS OF COMMERCE

Ambato Chamber of Commerce
Montavlo 630 y Bolivar, P.O. Box 89
Ambato, Ecuador
Tel.: 593 820003

Ecuadorean-American Association
115 Broadway, Rm. 1408
New York, NY
Tel.: (212) 233-7776

Ecuadorian-American Chambers of Commerce
Imbabura 214 y Panama, Piso 2
P.O. Box 11305
Guayaquil, Ecuador
Tel.: 593 312760

Ecuadorian-American Chamber of Commerce
Edif. Multcentro, La Nina y 6 de Diciembre
Quito, Ecuador
Tel.: 593 543512

CONSULAR OFFICES

American Embassy
Avenida 12 de Octubre y Avenida Patria
P.O. Box 538
Quito, Ecuador
Tel.: 593 2 562890

Embassy of Ecuador
2535 15th St. N.W.

Washington, DC 20009
Tel.: (202) 234-7200

MAJOR PACIFIC RIM COMPANY IN ECUADOR

Mitsui del Ecuador SA
Edificio Seguros Condor
P. Ycasa 302,
Guayaquil 4, Ecuador
Tel.: 593 304760
(Trading)
Mitsui & Co., Japan

MEXICO

American companies have taken advantage of Mexico's low production costs for years. Maquiladora plants in Tijuana and across the Rio Grande provide extremely low wages and immediate proximity to the U.S. Over 500,000 Mexicans work in Maquiladoras. Some companies, however, found even lower production costs in Asia. Today, many of these firms are relocating again, but this time from Asia to Mexico.

Mexico offers companies numerous advantages. A large scale economic reform program is now underway, making it easier for foreigners to invest and repatriate profits. Privitization is also proceeding at a rapid pace. Moreover, wages in Mexico are lower than in the industrialized countries of East Asia and not much higher than in the less developed countries. Mexican workers, however, have a higher literacy rate than most workers in Asia and often possess more desirable skills.

Even with a slightly higher wage, Mexico is still economically preferable because of its relationship with the United States. Transportation costs into the U.S. are certainly lower from Mexico than from East Asia, and the upcoming Free Trade Agreement will give Mexican goods free access to U.S. and Canadian markets. Companies fear that Asia may be excluded from the emerging North American trade bloc that will include the U.S., Canada, and Mexico. Investing in Mexico will allow access to the new economic bloc.

Banking is another important aspect of foreign investment in Mexico. As in California, most of the foreign banks in Mexico are Japanese, primarily located in Mexico City. Banking regulations have recently been liberalized by the government, which should lead to more activity in this economic sector as well.

Average hourly wages, 1990

United States	$14
Taiwan	$4.0
South Korea	$3.0
Singapore	$2.3
Mexico	$1.6■

Organizations for Further Information

The following organizations may be helpful in the job search. American embassies and consulates have commercial and/or economic sections that can provide you with business information and explain aspects of the local economy. Foreign government missions in the U.S. such as National Tourist Offices and embassies and consulates can furnish visas and information on work permits and other important regulations. They may also offer economic and business information about the country.

CHAMBERS OF COMMERCE

American Chamber of Commerce, Guadalajara
Avenida 16 de Septiembre 730-1209
Guadalajara, Jalisco, Mexico
Tel.: 52 146300
Fax.: 52 502231

American Chamber of Commerce, Mexico City
P.O. Box 82, Lucerna 78-4
Mexico, D.F. 06600, Mexico
Tel.: 52 7050995
Fax.: 52 5353166

American Chamber of Commerce, Monterrey
Picachos 760, Despachos 4 y 6, Col.onia Obispado
Monterrey, Nuevo Leon, Mexico
Tel.: 52 484749

American-Mexican Chamber of Commerce
P.O. Box 626
Phoenix, AZ 85001
Tel.: (602) 252-6448

Center of Economic Development
Margarita Escobedo Rodriguez, Santa Margarita 526
Mexico, D.F. 03100, Mexico
Tel.: 52 5751593

Center of Economical Studies of the Private Sector
Lic. Jose Luis Vaxquez Samano, Homero 527, pisos 4-6
Mexico 11570, D.F., Mexico
Tel.: 2 50 69 77

Mexican Chamber of Commerce, Los Angeles
125 Paseo de La Plaza, Rm. 404
Los Angeles, CA 90012
Tel.: (213) 668-7330

Mexican Chamber of Commerce, New York
655 Madison Ave., Woolworth Bldg., 16th Floor
New York, NY 10021
Tel.: (212) 759-9505

Mexican Institute for Foreign Trade
9 E. 53rd St., 25th Floor
New York, NY 10022
Tel.: (212) 759-9505

U.S.-Mexico Chamber of Commerce
1900 L St. N.W., No. 612
Washington, DC 20036
Tel.: (202) 296-5198

U.S.-Mexico Quadripartite Commission
Center for Inter-American Relations
680 Park Ave.
New York, NY 10021
Tel.: (212) 249-8950

CONSULAR OFFICES

American Embassy
Paseo de la Reforma 305
Mexico City, D.F. 5, Mexico
Tel.: 52 52110042

Embassy of Mexico
2829 16th St. N.W.
Washington, DC 20009
Tel.: (202) 234-6000

OTHER INFORMATIONAL ORGANIZATION

Mexico Government Tourism Office
405 Park Ave., No. 1002
New York, NY 10022
Tel.: (212) 755-7261

MAJOR JAPANESE COMPANIES IN MEXICO

The following company information includes type of business, contact name, and parent company. Your chances of achieving employment are substantially greater if you contact the subsidiary company in Mexico rather than the parent company in Japan.

BANKING AND FINANCE

Bank of Tokyo
Avda Paseo de la Reforma 359
6 Piso, Col. Cuauhtemoc
Mexico City, D.F. 06500, Mexico
Tel.: 52 5 5285504
(Banking)
Bank of Tokyo, Japan

Bank of Yokohama
Paseo de la Reforma 382-302
Col.. Juarez, Deleg. Cuauhtemoc
Mexico City, D.F. 06600, Mexico
Tel.: 52 5 5149104
Fax: 52 5 5255240
(Banking)
Kazuo Hiratsuka, Chief Representative
Bank of Yokohama, Japan

Dai-Ichi Kangyo Bank
Campos Eliseos, 345-12, 9 Piso
Col.. Chapultepec Polanco
Mexico City, D.F. 11560, Mexico
Tel.: 52 5 2022100
Fax: 52 5 2022069
(Banking)
Yoshihiro Kikuchi, Chief Representative
Dai-Ichi Kangyo Bank, Japan

Daiwa Bank
Rio Nilo 90, 4 Piso
Col.. Cuauhtemoc
Mexico City, D.F., Mexico
Tel.: 52 5 5119503
(Banking)
Shin Hatta, Manager
Daiwa Bank, Japan

Export-Import Bank of Japan
Paseo de la Reforma 390-1502
Col.. Juarez
Mexico City, D.F. 06600, Mexico
Tel.: 52 5 5286480
Fax: 52 5 5253473
(Banking)
Hideo Tokuda, Chief Representative
Export-Import Bank of Japan, Japan

Fuji Bank Ltd.
Paseo de la Reforma 390-1401
Col. Juarez
Mexico City, D.F. 06600, Mexico
Tel.: 52 5 5334443
(Banking)
Koichi Hirokawa, Chief Representative
Fuji Bank, Japan

Hokkaido Takaushoku Bank
Paseo de la Reforma 300, 8 Piso
Col. Juarez
Mexico City, D.F. 06600, Mexico
Tel.: 52 5 5110347
Fax: 52 5 5110227
(Banking)
Toshiyuki Oba, Chief Representative
Hokkaido Takushoku Bank, Japan

Long-Term Credit Bank of Japan
Paseo de la Reforma 390, Desp 901
Col. Juarez, Deleg Cuauhtemoc
Mexico City, D.F. 06600, Mexico
Tel.: 52 5 5331800
(Banking)
Yoshikazu Kameyama, Representative
Long-Term Credit Bank of Japan, Japan

Mitsubishi Bank
Paseo de la Reforma 390-1101
Col. Juarez, Deleg Cuauhtemoc
Mexico City, D.F. 6695, Mexico
Tel.: 52 5 5334878
(Banking)
Kenichi Makino, Representative
Mitsubishi Bank, Japan

Mitsui de Mexico
Campos Liseos 400, piso 14
Col. Lomas
Mexico 11000 Mexico, Mexico
Tel.: 52 5 5405583
(Trading)
Mitsui & Co., Japan

Mitsui Taiyo Kobe Bank
Paseo de la Reforma 390
Mexico City, D.F. 06695, Mexico
Tel.: 52 5 5334860
Fax: 52 5 8125949
(Banking)
Yutaka Demura, Chief Representative
Mitsui Taiyo Kobe Bank, Japan

Nissho Iwai Mexicana
Ave. Jose Vasconcelos No. 208
Desp. 701 Col., Condesa Mexico
D.F., Mexico
Tel.: 52 5 5531066
(Trading)
Nissho Iwai Corp., Japan

Sumitomo Bank
Campos Eliseos 345, 11 Piso
Col. Chalpultepec Polanco
Mexico City, D.F. 11560,
Mexico
Tel.: 52 5 5206030
Fax: 52 5 2021714
(Banking)
Yasuhiko Okunishi, Chief
Representative
Sumitomo Bank, Japan

Tokai Bank
Campos Eliseos No. 345-8
Col. Polanco
Mexico City, D.F. 11560,
Mexico
Tel.: 52 5 5200214
Fax: 52 5 5200074
(Banking)
Tokai Bank, Japan

INDUSTRIAL MANUFACTURING

Hitachi Consumer Products de Mexico
Ave. Industrial No. 105
Cuidad Industrial Mesa de Otay
Tijuana, Mexico, Mexico
Tel.: 52 66 233055
(Televisions, cabinets)
Shigemasa Ito, Plant Manager
Hitachi, Japan

Industria Mexicana Toshiba
Calzada de Guadalupe No. 303
Cuautla, Edo de Mexico, Mexico
Tel.: 52 5650088
Fax: 52 1772560
(Electronic components)
Lic. Eugenio Erana G., CEO
Toshiba Corp., Japan

Kobe Steel
Rio Danubio No. 69, 9 Piso
Col. Cauauhtemoc
Mexico City, D.F.16500, Mexico
Tel.: 52 5 5114003
Fax: 52 5 5113630
(Steel)
Kobe Steel, Japan

Kyowa Hakko Kogyo
Homero No. 148, Piso 11
Col. Polanco, Delegacion Miguel
Hidalgo
C.P. 011570, Mexico City, D.F.,
Mexico
Tel.: 52 5 2505851
Fax: 52 5 2547413
(Pharmaceuticals)
Kyowa Hakko Kogyo Co., Japan

Matsushita Industrial de Baja California
Blvd. Alivio No. 5 NTE S/N
Cuidad Industrial Mesa de Otay
Tijuana, Mexico, Mexico
Tel.: 55 66 533350
(Televisions)
Akira Miyazu, President
Matsushita Electric Industrial
Co., Japan

NEC de Mexico
Aven. de Los 50 Metros No. 6
Civac, Jiutepec, Mexico, Mexico
Tel.: 52 91 73153520
Fax: 52 91 5462851
(Radio and transmission
equipment)
O. Tauchi, Director General
NEC Corp., Japan

Nissan Mexicana
Ave. Insurgentes Sur No. 1457
Mexico City, D.F., Mexico
(Manufactures and distributes automobiles)
Issei Yoshino, President
Nissan Motor Co., Japan

PANAMA

After Mexico, Panama is enjoying the strongest growth in foreign investment. Many of the factors regarding costs of production that motivate businesses to locate in Mexico also operate in Panama. The country does, however, possess some assets that others lack.

Panama's infrastructure and international connections are excellent. The Panama Canal has obvious advantages, and the large U.S. military presence has also led to an extensive transportation and communication network. The U.S. dollar is the currency utilized in Panama, facilitating international banking and financial transactions. Likewise, the country enjoys a special trade relationship with the United States, so products manufactured in Panama have intrinsic trade advantages over goods from Asia.

Many Asian investors also appreciate the security of investing in Panama. They believe that the U.S. will guarantee Panama's internal stability and external security. This perception is particularly important for Hong Kong investors. They are apprehensive about Hong Kong's reversion to China in 1997 and would like to relocate their assets in a country that they consider safe. The U.S. invasion of Panama in 1989 confirmed this view.

Investors from Hong Kong and Taiwan also like Panama because of the large Chinese community present in the country. This allows Chinese investors from Hong Kong and Taiwan to find suppliers and distributors who speak their language and understand the local business practices and regulations already in place.

MAJOR PACIFIC RIM COMPANIES IN PANAMA

The following company information includes type of business, contact name, and parent company. Your chances of achieving employment are substantially greater if you contact the subsidiary company in Panama rather than the parent company in the home country.

BANKING AND FINANCE

Bank of China
Balboa Ancon, Apartado Postal 871056
Panama City, Panama
Tel.: 507 239114
(Banking)
Bank of China, China

Bank of Tokyo
Via Espana y Calle, Aquilino de la Guardia
Apartado Postal 1313
Panama City, Panama
Tel.: 507 636777
(Banking)
Bank of Tokyo, Japan

Central Trust of China
Trade Center, P.O. Box
Apartado Postal 2052
Col.on-Col.on Free Zone, Panama
Tel.: 507 452277
Fax: 507 414106
(Banking)
Frank C. H. Feng, Representative
Central Trust of China, Taiwan

Daiwa Bank
Edif Interseco, Calle Elvira-Mendez No. 10
Panama City, Panama
Tel.: 507 696648
(Banking)
Nobuhiro Kawamura, Representative
Daiwa Bank, Japan

Industrial Bank of Japan
Edif Vallarino, Piso 6
Calles Elvira Mendez y 52
Apartado Postal 3239 Balboa, Ancon
Panama City, Panama
Tel.: 507 638233
Fax: 507 638614
(Banking)
Fumio Koshida, Chief Representative
Industrial Bank of Japan, Japan

International Commercial Bank of China
Calle 16, Local No. 4, Edif. No. 49
Apartado Postal 555
Col.on-Col.on Free Zone, Panama
Tel.: 507 450560
Fax: 507 471600
(Banking)
San-Shine Huang, General Manager
International Commercial Bank of China, Taiwan

Korea Exchange Bank
Edif Apede (Cesa) Esq. de Avda Calle Balboa y Calle 42
Apartado Postal 8358
Panama City, Panama
Tel.: 507 638108
Fax: 507 638392
(Banking)
Tae-Kyung Yang, Representative
Korea Exchange Bank, South Korea

Long-Term Credit Bank of Japan
Torre Bancosur, Piso 14
Calle 53 Este, Apartado Postal 506
Panama City, Panama
Tel.: 507 643451
(Banking)
Yoshikazu Kameyama, Representative
Long-Term Credit Bank of Japan, Japan

Mitsubishi Trust and Banking Corp.
Edif Torre Bancosur, Piso 13
Calle 53, Urbanizacion Obarrio
Aportado Postal 3651 Balboa, Ancon
Panama City, Panama
Tel.: 507 641400
(Banking)
Takahiko Suzuki, Manager
Mitsubishi Trust and Banking Corp., Japan

Mitsui & Co. Panama
Edificio Banco de Boston
Via Espana y C. Panama 9A
Panama City, Panama
Tel.: 507 235125
(Trading)
Mitsui & Co., Japan

Mitsui Taiyo Kobe Bank
Edif Torre Banco Sur, Piso 13
Apartado Postal 8018
Panama City, Panama
Mitsui Taiyo Kobe Bank, Japan

INDUSTRIAL MANUFACTURING

Toshiba de Panama
Via Tespana No. 58 Bella Vista
Edificio Fatima Planta
Panama City, Panama
Tel.: 507 692066
(Industrial equipment)
Toshiba Corp., Japan

Sumitomo Bank
Plaza International, Via Espana
Apartado Postal 8-029
Panama City, Panama
Tel.: 507 693344
Fax: 507 693858
(Banking)
Eichi Motoshige, General Manager
Sumitomo Bank, Japan

PERU

Partly hoping for Japanese investment, voters in Peru recently elected Alberto Fujimori, an ethnic Japanese, as President. Japanese companies have offered to finance and build a new road to facilitate Peruvian transportation in the Amazon region. The country's economic promise is limited by the guerilla movement, which is currently assassinating Japanese business people and aid officals.

Organizations for Further Information

The following organizations may be helpful in the job search. American embassies and consulates have commercial and/or economic sections that can provide you with business information and explain aspects of the local economy. Foreign government missions in the U.S. such as embassies and consulates can furnish visas and information on work permits and other important regulations. They may also offer economic and business information about the country.

CHAMBERS OF COMMERCE

American Chamber of Commerce of Peru
Av. Ricardo Palma 836
Lima 18, Peru
Tel.: 51 479349

Lima Chamber of Commerce
Gregorio Escobedo 398
Lima 11, Peru
Tel.: 51 257

Peruvian-American Association
50 W. 34th St., 6th Floor, No. C2
New York, NY 10001
Tel.: (212) 564-3855

CONSULAR OFFICE

Embassy of Peru
1700 Massachusetts Ave. N.W.
Washigton, DC 20036
Tel.: (202) 833-9860

Index